MANAGING YOUR PERSONAL FOOD SUPPLY

MANAGING YOUR PERSONAL FOOD SUPPLY

Edited by Ray Wolf
Organic Living Editor, Organic Gardening and Farming®

 Rodale Press, Inc., Emmaus, Pa. 18049

Printed in the United States of America on recycled paper

Illustrations by Joe Charnoski and Pat Traub

Library of Congress Cataloging in Publication Data

Main entry under title:

Managing your personal food supply.

    Bibliography: p.
    Includes index.
    1. Food. 2. Nutrition. 3. Organic gardening.
4. Stock and stock-breeding. 5. Cookery. I. Wolf,
Ray.
TX353.M27   641   76-50569
ISBN 0-87857-121-3

2 4 6 8 10 9 7 5 3 1

Contents

Acknowledgements

Although this book is a product of the editors at Rodale Press, we sought out experts in several areas to do chapters for us. Chapter 1 was written by Catherine Lerza. Cathy worked for the Center for Science in the Public Interest and was instrumental in getting the first Food Day started. She coedited *Food For People, Not For Profit,* and currently is working with the Institute for Policy Studies concerning the problems with America's food distribution system. Chapter 5 was written by Jerome Belanger, who many feel is the foremost authority on the selection and care of small livestock in this country. He has authored *The Homesteader's Handbook to Raising Small Livestock,* and is Publisher and Editor of the monthly magazine *Countryside and Small Stock Journal.* Chapter 6 was done by the team of Nikki and David Goldbeck. The Goldbecks have long worked on ways to help consumers find the best foods in today's supermarket. They've written several books on whole foods, including *The Supermarket Handbook.* Nancy Bubel wrote chapter 7. She is a regular contributor to several magazines, including *Organic Gardening and Farming.* Her many years experience in home processing of foods makes her a particularly unique source of practical information. Much of the recipe work was researched by *Organic Gardening and Farming* Food Editor Nancy Albright, and tested at the Rodale Press experimental kitchen, Fitness House, with the help of Home Economist Anita Hirsch. The writing of those sections was done by Carol Hupping Stoner, Executive Editor of our Book Division.

Introduction

Managing Your Personal Food Supply—I can think of no topic more important to anyone in America today. For a country with the agricultural richness we have, our daily diet is abominable. Every day people are dying, suffering, or not enjoying life to the fullest because of the food they eat. It is sometimes hard to believe we have done some of the things we have to our food, and yet the daily adulterating of our foodstuffs continues.

As the melting pot of the world, you would hope the culinary richness of the many lands that contributed to that title would give us a truly unique diet, based on many cultures, making full use of all types of foods and cooking practices, but nothing could be further from the truth. Instead of taking the best from all countries, instead it seems as if we knocked off the edges and only used what would fit in our mold: a mold of bland, fattening, expensive, unhealthy foods with no character to speak of, and few redeeming social qualities.

But enough of that. What we have undertaken in this book is a revolution of food and your involvement with it. We had experts in their fields contribute to help us assemble the best and most practical information possible to help you regain control of your food supply from a national food chain that appears to be completely out of control.

It would be presumptuous of us, or any other publisher, to think that in one book we could tell you everything you need to know about anything, much less something as complicated as your food supply. What we have sought to do is talk about food, how it is used, grown, prepared, and consumed, from a management perspective.

We have sought to give you those guidelines you will need to know to make decisions about how you will be changing your food supply and your eating habits in the future. For instance, in the section on gardening we talk about how to plan a garden, get more vegetables into the space you have, make your seasons longer, decide what to raise, and how to decide what methods of storage you will use. Actual information on how to grow a carrot is not presented. Our hope is that once you are armed with specific information on how to make decisions critical to your food supply, you will go to the list of books at the end of this book to find a more specific book on the area you are going to become involved in.

By taking this approach, we hope to let you see that there is a completely different alternative to the food and the food supply system people are currently using. Perhaps you are already doing some of the things we talk about in this book, but almost surely no one is doing all that we discuss, nor will you be able to do it all. But you certainly will be able to improve the quality of the food you are eating by applying some of the things in this book.

Changing food habits is not easy, but it is not impossible either. We hope this book will be a guide for you, as you begin what is, admittedly, no small chore. As you read it, we hope you will keep in mind that what you do is important, not just to your own personal health and pocketbook, but as part of a growing nationwide movement toward better eating.

First we will examine the typical American diet, find its good points, its bad points, and some of the effects this diet has had on our health. After understanding the average diet and its problems, we look at the basic nutritional facts everyone should know to be a good cook and food manager. We then use that information to propose a new approach to meal planning and food use, a more efficient, healthy, and cheaper way to eat.

Once you are equipped with the information on planning meals, we will look at ways to acquire the needed ingredients. First we will show you how to grow much of the food your family needs, with surprisingly little space and time. Livestock production is covered for those with more room and the desire to become truly food-self-sufficient. If you don't have the room, time, or desire to grow and raise your own food, we'll show you how to buy it and still get the best quality for your money. Then we show you how to process food at home. Whether you grow it or buy it, you can still save money and improve the nutritional benefits of your food by doing much of the processing and preserving in your home.

Lastly, we will show you how to use all this information to put the best meals possible, for the least amount of money, on your table. We show you how to save time, nutrients, and money by slightly changing your cooking and eating habits. In short, from the time you pick up your first seed catalog until you are enjoying meals of your own food, we'll show you how to do it.

As Organic Living Editor for *Organic Gardening and Farming* magazine, I have been in a unique position to see both how terribly badly our national food supply is handled and how easy it is to take control of your food supply and manage it yourself for improved nutrition, health, and much less money. The one thing to remember, the type of food revolution we need all starts with you, so let's get going!

Ray Wolf

Chapter 1

The U.S.—Healthiest and Best-Fed Nation?

We've all grown to believe that the United States is the healthiest and wealthiest nation in the world, and that Americans are the best-fed people on the face of the earth. But this is wrong, unfortunately for most of us. We may be the most fed people in the world, but statistics strongly indicate we are not the best fed people. In fact, diet appears to be a major contributing factor to our national epidemic of degenerative diseases. The reason for our poor diet is not, in most cases, inadequate amounts of money to spend on food, but rather a lack of basic nutritional information combined with an abundance of nutritional misinformation in food company advertisements and the proliferation of overly refined, processed, "junk" foods.

America has long been proud of the near-eradication of infectious diseases within its borders. What we have failed to see is that communicable diseases have been replaced by degenerative diseases as leading causes of death. These diseases — cancer, heart disease, diabetes, stroke — are all at least partially related to diet and are not more prevalent among the poor than among the more affluent in this country.

It appears that, in the U.S. at least, higher income is no guarantee of improved diet or improved health. Those with in-

1

comes sufficient to provide an adequate diet may simply be trading deficiency diseases for degenerative diseases. In fact, several studies bear out the idea that rising income does not necessarily result in better eating habits. A 1968 U.S. Department of Agriculture study indicated that an increase in income does not insure an improvement in diet, while a 1974 USDA Economic Research Service survey demonstrated that low income families tend to get better nutrition for their food dollar than affluent families. (This is because the poor must buy basic foods and cannot afford the more expensive convenience foods available to most Americans.)

A Canadian nutrition study (conducted 1970–72) concluded that nutrition education and the increased availability of healthy foods were more important to insuring good nutrition than was increased income. The important factor in good nutrition, the study found, was not the number of food dollars but the way in which they were spent. Another study — this one a comparison of garbage content — conducted by three members of the American Public Health Association in 1974 showed that the poor waste less food than the affluent. For the poor in the U.S., as it is for the poor around the world, the problem is not so much what they eat, but how little they can afford to eat. For the middle class it isn't a question of how much to spend on food, but what to spend it on.

What Has Happened To Our Food — And To Our Health?

What has created this paradoxical situation in which both rich and poor suffer from diet-related illnesses? Food has become big business in America; the object of our food production system is not to make available the healthful foods necessary to maintain human life, but rather the creation of a highly profitable industry. And, unfortunately for most of us, big profits lie not in the production and distribution of whole, unadulterated foods, but in highly processed, precooked, and over-packaged convenience foods. Gradually what the food industry marketing experts term "fun foods" have replaced whole, natural foods as the most readily accessible items in the marketplace. Think about it. How often do you find fresh fruit or milk in a convenient vending machine? Not very often — more likely, you'll only find candy, soft drinks, pastries, and crispy, crunchy fried foods to satisfy your hunger.

This change in eating habits or, more realistically, in the kinds of food most available to us has been documented by the U.S. Department of Agriculture. Since World War II, the consumption of dairy products has gone down 21 percent, of vegetables 23 percent, and of fruits 25 percent. Accordingly, soft drink consumption is up almost 300 percent, consumption of dessert-type baked goods up 70 percent, and "munchie" consumption (potato chips, crackers, etc.) up 85 percent. Another USDA study contrasted "typical" diets of 1965 against those of 1955 and found the number of households with "good" diets (those in which per person daily vitamin intake was equal to or above the Recommended Daily Allowance [RDA] for seven different nutrients) declined from 60 percent to 50 percent. The percentage of "poor" diets (those in which per person daily intake was less than two-thirds of the RDA for one or more nutrients) increased from 15 percent to 20 percent.

According to the U.S. Food and Drug Administration (FDA), consumption of vitamins A, C, and B complex peaked in the mid-1940s, due to the large number of wartime victory gardens in the nation at the time. Consumption of vitamin A-laden dark green and yellow vegetables has dropped considerably since that time.

The diet of "convenience" Americans have been encouraged to eat for the past 30 years has cost us dearly — cost us in terms of declining health and higher food bills, not to mention the environmental damage related to the "new food chain" forged by big food processors and corporate farmers.

University of California nutritionist Dr. George Briggs has termed the American diet "a nutritional disaster." Briggs and colleague Helen Ulrich have estimated that the annual cost to the nation of "hunger and . . . mismanagement of food to the detriment of one's health is approximately $40 billion." We pay this price in medical bills, poor health, lost work and leisure time, and sometimes in death.

Increased consumption of sugar, fats, salt, and refined grains have been the major reasons behind the national nutritional decline of the past three decades.

Dr. Michael Jacobson, of the Center for Science in the Public Interest, has estimated that half of annual American deaths, or one million deaths, are related in part to diet. Diet-related causes of death include stroke, heart disease, bowel cancer, and diabetes. Other illnesses don't necessarily cause death, but do cause discomfort and can aggravate other illnesses: obesity, tooth decay, gum disease, anemia, and constipation.

The consequences of our diet of affluence have been studied and contrasted to the diets of other cultures. For example, Dr. Denis Burkitt, a British medical researcher, found that Japanese emigrants to the U.S. demonstrate a marked rise in their rate of bowel cancer and other such diseases when they switch from a traditional Japanese diet to a typical American diet. And two "special" groups within the American population who eschew the standard dietary bill of fare have demonstrably lower cancer, heart disease, and hypertension rates than the general populace. They are Seventh Day Adventists, who are vegetarians, and Mormons, who do not ingest any form of stimulant, including coffee, tea, or cola-type drinks.

Dr. K. W. Heaton, a British gastroenterologist, believes that our "civilized" diet has two main defects: it provides "too much energy" and "too little residue." As he explains, "Both these defects can be explained by the fact that in our diet the carbohydrate is mainly in refined form. As a result, we get 'too much' out of our food. . . . Overnutrition is not normally due to overeating, but to eating food with an artificially high energy/satiety ratio, namely refined carbohydrates." In other words, we must eat more refined foods to feel "full" than is necessary with whole grains and unprocessed foods.

What's Wrong With Refined Carbohydrates?

Despite the fact that refined foods tend to overload our bodies with empty, nonnutritious calories, the average American consumed in 1970 (according to USDA statistics) 264 pounds of these nutritionally valueless foods, including white sugar, flour, and rice. In fact, the British journal *New Scientist* recently reported that over 70 percent of the food consumed in North America has been processed. And the processing itself is only the beginning of this unhealthy story — most processed and refined foods have been dosed with chemical additives which enhance, thicken, soften, flavor, or color our food.

Wheat That Makes Better Glue Than Bread

The processing of food often removes many of the good things naturally found in whole foods. This is especially true of grains — wheat, oats, corn, rice. The USDA says that people who eat white bread made from refined flour get 87.5 percent less fiber than do people who eat whole wheat bread. And that's not the only thing white bread eaters miss out on.

While cereal and flour manufacturers claim that nutrients lost during processing are replaced through "fortification," the flaking, shredding, toasting, and crisping of grains necessary to transform them into breakfast cereals reduces vitamin content by 90 percent. The processing of whole wheat into white flour reduces the amount of 14 essential vitamins and minerals by half and replaces only seven of them in the enrichment process. Nutrients lost via processing include biotin, inositol, panothenic acid, zinc, magnesium, and chromium. Jim Hightower of the Agribusiness Accountability Project, in his book *Eat Your Heart Out,* reports that a nutritionist appearing before a Senate Committee hearing in 1970 said, "The milling process removes 40 percent of the chromium, 86 percent of the manganese, 89 percent of the cobalt, 68 percent of the copper, 78 percent of the zinc and 48 percent of the molybdenum — all elements essential for life and health." None of these items are restored in enriching. Noted nutritionist Adelle Davis once summed up the process of enrichment with her analogy that if people were likewise financially enriched, it would be like someone stealing $25 from you and returning 99¢.

Once It's Gone, It's Gone

French scientists have long contended that adding synthetic vitamins and inorganic iron to processed foods cannot make up the deficiencies in an inadequate diet. A recent study of nutritional status conducted by the Canadian government appears to bear out this hypothesis. The study, called Nutrition Canada, showed that three-quarters of the women sampled did not obtain enough iron from their diets, one-quarter of all adults suffered from a folic acid deficiency, one-half the population had inadequate thiamine, and, among the women surveyed, there was a widespread calcium deficiency. Canadian flour, like American, is "enriched" with synthetic vitamins and minerals — including iron and thiamine — which should preclude these large-scale dietary problems. But, as French nutritionists who have fought for years against the addition of all enriching substances and shelf-life lengthening preservatives now note, the addition of these chemicals appears to have made no positive contribution to the Canadian diet.

In 1970, Dr. Roger Williams, a biochemist and nutritionist at the University of Texas, performed the most damning of all experiments concerning "enriching." Dr. Williams fed 64 rats an all-enriched bread diet for 90 days. At the end of the test, two-thirds of the rats had died. When Williams performed the experiment feeding the rats bread fortified with all the nutrients removed from flour by commercial milling, all of them survived.

Thinking about the kind of diet food advertisements and grocery store displays encourage us to eat and about the rats in Dr. Williams's experiment should give all of us an uneasy feeling. Barry Commoner, the noted ecologist, said a nutritious mouthful when he remarked, "Mother Nature knows best." That's a statement all of us would do well to remember as we make decisions about the food we eat.

Sweet but Deadly

But refined grains are only the beginning. Their comrade in nutritional disaster is white sugar, the most ubiquitous and insidious agent of the American diet. Sugar out of the bowl or cannister is not the big problem, since it accounts for only about 25 percent of our average sugar intake. White sugar is in virtually every processed food we eat.

The greater portion of the 125 pounds of sugar Americans consume every year comes from soft drinks, baked goods, canned fruits, canned soups, peanut butter, and even baby food. Prepared foods such as dinner rolls and some cheese spreads contain sugar, even though their homemade counterparts do not. In 1700 the average refined sugar consumption was only about four pounds per year, in 1821 it climbed to 10 pounds per year, but by 1931 it had reached 108 pounds per year, and it has continued to increase to our current 120+ pounds a year level. About 20 percent of the average American's caloric intake today comes from sugar.

The development of sugar refining as a big business has made what once was a hard-to-obtain substance a major component of our diet. Although most people have a psychological weakness for the sweet taste of sugar, it is a substance which does not occur in concentrated form in nature. Eight pounds of apples contain about the same amount of sugar (sucrose) as only one 12-ounce bottle of sugary soft drinks.

Let's compare how the body uses two carbohydrates, sugar and starch, to see why this food substance that tastes so good is so bad for your health. Starch is a chain of glucose molecules known as a polysaccharide. In products like wheat, rice, and other cereals, starches are linked with vitamins, minerals, proteins, and enzymes. When cooked and digested the starches are slowly broken down into their component parts and used by the body at an even rate. Thus the intake of glucose from starches is gradual and is regulated by the accompanying intake of other nutrients.

However, when you ingest sugar, there are no accompanying nutrients, since sugar is 99.9 percent pure sucrose. This requires extra effort by the digestive system because there are no accompanying vitamins, minerals, or fiber to aid the digestive process, so the body must use supplies of those nutrients it has stored away to help digest the sugar. It is for this reason that sugar is referred to as "empty calories." When you eat it, all you get is sucrose and nothing else; your body has to deplete its stores of other nutrients to digest sugar.

What has sugar consumption done to our health? Sugar has been linked with the rising incidence of diabetes, tooth decay, obesity, heart disease, and hypoglycemia (low blood sugar). Eating refined sugar creates a dangerous cycle in the body: we begin to "need" those doses of concentrated energy in order to maintain safe blood sugar levels. However, as Harvard nutritionist Jean Mayer has said, "You need glucose sugar for your brain to function, but you do not need sugar in the diet. The body makes its own sugar out of starch and protein." The presence of excess sugar in our diets has yet another deleterious effect: by eating so much sugar, we limit our ability to eat other, more nutritious foods. This can aggravate vitamin, mineral, and protein deficiencies — or lead to obesity.

And The Problems Don't Stop There

Today's food is not only hyped up with sugar and robbed of nutrients, another factor is sorely missing from processed foods. Dietary fiber is just recently being "discovered," and its discovery is bringing relief to millions of people who for many years suffered the pain of diseases caused by eating processed foods.

When millers began removing the germ and the bran from flour, no one worried. Soon people noticed an increased incidence of disease. Knowing the nutritional power of wheat germ, flour was "enriched" in hopes of replacing nutrients, but no one seemed to care about the bran, for it contained few nutrients and was virtually indigestible for humans. It's this very quality that makes bran or dietary fiber worth the most to your health; it is nearly indigestible in the human system. The body can do nothing with bran, so it is voided.

Fibrous foods add bulk to the diet. In the intestinal tract, fiber absorbs water, acids, and bacteria. That makes stools larger and softer than stools of people eating refined diets. A large, soft stool prevents constipation and shortens transit time, the time it takes food to pass through the body. The average American eating a refined diet has a transit time of about 90 hours, but African villagers eating a diet high in roughage average only 35 hours transit time. And, as we'll explain in a minute, increased transit time has been linked to at least one serious health problem.

The relationship of fiber in the diet to disease is just recently becoming clear. For example, appendicitis became common only in this century, hiatus hernia (a condition caused by excessive intestinal straining) became common only 30 years ago, and coronary heart disease was considered a rarity 50 years ago. Cancer of the colon is the second most common cause of cancer death today, yet in most parts of rural Africa the rate is one-fifteenth that of the U.S.'s 90,000 deaths a year. Remember, it is estimated that the current U.S. annual intake of cereal fiber is currently only one-tenth what it was at the turn of the century.

Cancer of the colon is believed to result from carcinogenic (cancer-causing) chemicals produced by bacteria in the bowels. With hard, small, slow-moving stools bacteria have more time to act — and the carcinogens they produce are concentrated in the small stools and can act for longer periods on the lining of the colon.

Coronary heart disease may be related at least in part to lack of fiber in the diet. Many studies indicate that people on high-fiber diets have lower blood cholesterol levels and less cholesterol deposits in the coronary arteries feeding the heart.

To better understand how fiber helps your insides, let's take a quick look at how things should work. Following chewing and swallowing of your food, your stomach breaks the food into elements your body can utilize. Those items not used are shifted to the lower gut to be eliminated. Through waves of muscular contraction, waste is moved through the intestines. When the bowels are relatively full of waste matter, as they are in people who eat a diet high in roughage, such as vegetarians or people living in more primitive cultures, the muscles surrounding the intestines need only contract slightly to move things along. However, when waste matter is scanty and compacted, as it is in persons eating a soft or highly refined diet, the muscles have to contract with much greater force to create the pressure required to move things along. It is these powerful contractions that are the source of much misery. When this tremendous pressure builds up to move along waste, the unfortunate result often is that the bowel lining bursts through the surrounding muscles and forms a balloon or diverticulum. Diverticulosis was not even mentioned in medical textbooks in 1920; today it is the most common colon disorder in western countries.

Studies of what dietary fiber can do for other problems are under way. Already there is evidence of fiber's value in combating obesity. Providing no calories, it displaces other nutrients that do. Fiber also requires added chewing, which not only slows intake but limits it by increasing the secretion of both saliva and gastric juice that produces satiety in the stomach. Fiber also cuts down on the body's absorption of other foods. Investigators have found that a total of 97 percent of dietary energy is absorbed on a low-fiber diet, but only 92.5 percent is absorbed on a high-fiber diet.

Other Changes In Our Food Supply

Unlike refined sugar, fat is a necessary component of the diet, but, like sugar, it has become too large a portion of most American diets. Fat consumption has risen from 114 pounds a year in 1961 to 125 pounds a year in 1971. Nutritionists recommend that fat provide less than one-third of our caloric intake, but it now provides, on the average, over 40 percent of our daily calorie consumption.

Fast foods and snack foods are laden with fat. The USDA noted in 1974 that snack foods had risen sharply in popularity and that "similar growth had occurred in the fast food enterprise, including hamburger and french fry franchises and the chicken and fish carry-outs." Increasingly popular "munchie" foods, quick-fix desserts, fabricated foods (Breakfast Squares, for instance) and even some breakfast cereals have high fat contents. As evidence of this trend to high fat foods, we now eat 30 pounds of french fries every year, an increase of 460 percent since 1960.

Dr. Michael Jacobson reports in *Nutrition Scoreboard* that if saturated fat is not the only cause of heart disease, it is surely one of the causes. In one recent study, hundreds of patients in two hospitals in Finland were kept on special diets for six-year periods. For the first six-year period, patients in one hospital had a diet low in saturated fat and cholesterol and high in polyunsaturated fat; patients in the other hospital had a diet that was relatively high in saturated fat and cholesterol and low in polyunsaturated fat. After six years, the diets were switched. During both six-year periods blood cholesterol levels and the rate of deaths due to heart disease reflected the amount of saturated fat (and cholesterol) in the diets. The more saturated fat, the higher the rate of fatal heart attacks.

Meat Adds to the Problem

Processed foods are not the only cause of our greater consumption of saturated fats; modern methods of raising beef also add to our increased saturated fat intake. The American way of raising beef is a double problem in that it not only provides us with meat of lesser quality, but it is extremely wasteful of grain that could be used to alleviate starvation in many parts of the world.

Now that may be a hard idea for you to accept, that we are raising harmful meat in a wasteful way, but it's true. Steers are confined to small lots, their movement is reduced as much as possible, and they are forced to eat protein-rich grain to gain as much weight as possible as fast as man can make them. This removes beef animals from their traditional role of converting unusable grasses to edible meat, and puts the animal in a new role of converting edible grain into edible meat.

When placed in this new role, the animals fail miserably from an efficiency standpoint. Just how inefficient cows are at converting grain into meat has been best documented by Frances Moore Lappé in her million-copy bestseller *Diet for a Small Planet.* Lappé points out that an average feedlot steer requires 16 pounds of grain and soy to put one pound of meat on our plates. The other 15 pounds are used by the animal to produce energy, build up inedible body parts, or go into manure. But twenty years ago no one cared how inefficient cows were at turning grain into hamburgers, as long as surplus grain supplies were used and meat was produced. Thus an abundance of cheap meat became commonplace in American supermarkets. With the chance to buy meat at low prices American shoppers rose to the challenge, raising per capita meat consumption from 58 pounds per person in 1940 to 116 pounds per person by 1972.

The beef fattening syndrome is a good example of how parts of our food supply have gotten out of hand. Once we were faced with grain surpluses, and new chemicals promised even greater yields the next year, and people desired meat, so the answer was feeding grain to cattle. American consumers in 20 years of eating cheap meat developed a taste for grain-fattened beef. Now that there are no grain surpluses and in fact there are shortages, farmers continue to feed grain to cattle to satisfy consumer tastes.

Massive feedlots have now perfected the forced feeding of thousands of animals at a time. Under these highly unnatural conditions, the animals create mostly fat poundage that is either trimmed away as waste or is marbled into the muscle meat for human consumption. Feedlots place emphasis on producing fat, not usable protein, for the economics of the beef marketing system reward cattle with a high fat content. For instance, a choice grade beef carcass has about 60 percent more fat, and therefore substantially more calories and cholesterol, but less protein than standard grade animals, and the choice carcass is worth almost seven cents a pound more to the feedlot at slaughter-time.

Beef Grades and Composition

GRADE	PROTEIN	FAT
Choice	17.4%	25.1%
Good	18.5%	20.4%
Standard	19.4%	15.8%

To sum up beef raising in America: The product produced is bad for your health, and an incredible amount of potential human food is wasted in the production of this detrimental meat. According to Lappé, we now get rid of the production from about one-half of our agricultural land by feeding it to animals. We feed about 90 percent of our corn, oats, barley, and sorghum and over 90 percent of our unexported soybean crop to animals. In 1973, American livestock consumed the protein equivalent of six times the recommended protein allowance of our human population.

Lappé has arrived at some very startling statistics. If we exclude dairy cows, the average conversion ratio for U.S. livestock, including relatively high (chicken) and low (steer) efficiency converters, is seven pounds of grain and soy fed to produce one pound of edible meat. According to this estimate, of the 140 million tons of grain and soy fed to cattle, poultry, and hogs in 1971, one-seventh, or only 20 million tons, was returned to us in meat. The rest, almost 118 million tons of grain and soy, became inaccessible for human consumption. Although we lead the world in exports of grain and soy, this incredible volume "lost" through livestock was twice the level of our current exports.

While the case against saturated fat is not complete, it is clear that cutting down on the amount of fat in our diet would be beneficial to our health. However, the nature of most easily obtainable foods in the supermarket — and along the highways in vending machines and restaurants — makes such a reduction difficult.

Salt . . . When it Pours, We Suffer

Most foods which contain a lot of fat also contain lots of salt, creating a two-pronged attack on health. Salt — really the sodium in salt — can aggravate hypertension by helping the body retain water, thus placing more pressure on blood vessels. Salt, like sugar, is a taste human beings are especially fond of.

Our national taste for salt has been encouraged even in infancy. Until 1970, baby food manufacturers added salt to their products to improve flavor. However, it was not clear exactly for whom the flavor was improved. According to the Center for Science in the Public Interest's study of infant feeding, a 1970 experiment proved that infants cannot differentiate between salted and unsalted foods. As study author Patricia Hausman notes, "The salt serves only to please the taste buds of parents." Manufacturers have reduced salt content in baby foods to one-quarter of one percent in response to a 1970 National Academy of Sciences recommendation, but some pediatric nutritionists feel even this is too much, since the addition of salt is totally unnecessary.

Other foods with high salt content include canned and dehydrated soups, canned vegetables, convenience "one-dish" dinner products, and most snack items. As with sugar, it's not the salt we add to our food that creates the health problem, but the salt already present in processed foods that does the damage.

Organic Gardening and Farming editor Robert Rodale points out that while peas in their natural state contain two milligrams of sodium chloride per serving, canned peas contain 236 milligrams. He also explains that the addition of salt to food during processing decreases the amount of potassium, an element necessary for maintaining proper pressure in blood vessels. This high-sodium, low-potassium state leads to hypertension, kidney disease, and urinary problems. According to Rodale, medical researchers say that most people need only 1 gram of salt per day. "Since close to one percent of an edible portion (100 grams) of any kind of processed food is salt," writes Rodale, "we can guess that most people consume far more salt than their bodies need."

Out of the Laboratory and Into Your Food

As if an overabundance of refined sugar and grains, saturated fats, and salt weren't enough, the myriad of chemical additives in processed foods make yet another assault on our health. In order to fabricate "new" foods or promote long shelf lives, food manufacturers rely heavily on various chemical additives to add color, flavor, texture, and "freshness" to their products. Some 1,800 chemicals are routinely added to our food, the British magazine *New Scientist* reports,

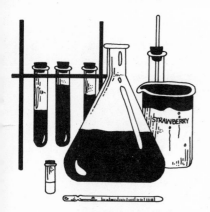

while several thousand more are used for "special purposes."

Food additives — preservatives, flavorings, colorings, stabilizers, thickeners, emulsifiers, etc., etc. — are the mainstay of the food industry. They allow food manufacturers to make popular products which, without artificial coloring, flavoring, and texturizing, would be totally unacceptable to consumers; these fabricated foods are profitable and, more importantly, highly marketable via high pressure advertising. Food additives also allow manufacturers to create foods that retain acceptable taste and consistency over long periods of time. The increasing use of food additives coincides with the processed food boom. The use of food colorings has increased 20-fold since 1940 to the point where the average person eats more than five pounds of chemical ingredients a year.

However, it is in the area of colorings, flavorings, thickeners, and stabilizers that the food industry is receiving the most flak. The use of preservatives can to some extent be slightly justified, but the use of exotic chemical concoctions simply to reduce manufacturing cost or to turn an unacceptable foodstuff into a desired food cannot be justified when it is a question of the safety of these chemicals.

For the longest time, only a few lonely voices were speaking out in alarm about food additives. People like Adelle Davis and Beatrice Trum Hunter were saddled with the title "food faddists" because they did not believe people should be ingesting strange chemicals without knowing it. So proficient are food chemists that it is hard to tell the artificial from the real thing in many products. In fact, in some cases by using chemicals food technologists have been able to concentrate a desired taste to an extreme; for instance, they can make an artificial chocolate that tastes more chocolatey than the real thing.

However, the government has recently begun to crack down on labeling requirements, forcing manufacturers to list ingredients. Ingredient disclosures, combined with newspaper headlines linking many chemicals to illness and cancer, has more and more consumers reading labels and refusing to buy certain products.

What someday may prove to be the fatal blow to the chemicals and the artificial foods they produce may result from the work of Benjamin Feingold, the former director of the Kaiser Research Institute's Laboratory of Medical Entomology. Feingold found a direct link between the intake of food processing chemicals and the epidemic of hyperkinesis in school-age children. At least one independent major test has already concluded that Feingold's theory is valid, and chemicals in our food supply are partly to blame for increased rates of hyperkinesis. In his book *Why Your Child is Hyperactive,* Feingold proposes that an identifying logo be put on all food products certified free of flavoring and coloring chemicals. If the concept of a nationwide seal of pureness were accepted by the government, food manufacturers would either have to disclose what they put in their food or do without the emblem that signifies good health.

The most important reason why manufacturers insist on using so many chemicals is that these relatively cheap substances permit greater centralization of food production and the replacement of expensive natural ingredients. Many additives, even those on the FDA's Generally Recognized as Safe list, are untested, some are thought to be unsafe, and others have been banned in the recent past. Some of these now-illegal additives include the low calorie sweetener cyclamate, DEPC (a preservative), red No. 2, and violet No. 1 dye (ironically once used to stamp the USDA seal on meats signifying the product was inspected and found to be safe). Sodium nitrite, used to preserve and color processed meats such as bacon, bologna, and other luncheon meats, hot dogs, and canned ham, is a proven carcinogen (cancer-causing agent) in laboratory experiments, yet its use continues to be permitted. Food activist Dr. Michael Jacobson terms bacon "the most dangerous food in the supermarket" because of its high nitrite content.

Other dangerous chemicals find their way into our food supply inadvertently. These "unintentional" additives include traces of pesticides, herbicides, growth-inducing hormones, and antibiotics. Although the presence of these chemicals in food may be a health hazard, they are permitted to remain in food, in small amounts, because their use is profitable for food producers. The most notorious of the unintentional additives is diethystilbesterol (DES), a growth-promoting hormone added to cattle feed. Known to cause cancer in laboratory animals, traces of DES are sometimes found — despite regulations against it — in beef liver. The additive was banned by the FDA in 1973, but the ban was overturned in 1974 on a procedural technicality. The Canadian government has banned the use of DES and refuses to allow the import of beef which has been given the hormone.

Why Don't We Have Quality Food?

It is clear that for consumers, the food production system has few benefits: we get nonnutritious foods at ever-increasing prices and squander resources in the process. But someone must be benefitting from this system or it could not continue.

It is certainly not farmers who are reaping profits from food. As retail food prices have risen, farm prices have remained relatively stable. According to the U.S. Senate Select Committee on Nutrition's 1975 *Report on Nutrition,* the difference between farm prices and retail prices increased by more than 21 percent during 1974. As food prices rose some 10 percent during 1974, the farmer received only 41 cents of every food dollar — down from 46 cents in 1973. The same Senate *Report on Nutrition* quotes former Federal Trade Commission Bureau of Economics director Russel Parker's testimony on food prices: "During the first half of 1974, three out of four of the largest product firms had greater profits than during the same period last year. Between January and July, 1974, farm prices dropped 10.8 percent . . . and consumer food prices rose by 4.4 percent." What this all means is that a small sector of the country — 35 food manufacturers and processors — are getting rich as the rest of us pay high prices or, in the case of the family farmer, face continually sagging incomes.

The reason that farmers and consumers alike are being squeezed by high prices is the domination of the food economy by a few large food processors, marketers, and retailers. The FTC study showed that consumers were overcharged about $2.1 billion in only 13 food lines in 1972. Of 32,500 food processors in the U.S., 100 account for 71 percent of all profits. Four companies control 90 percent of the U.S. breakfast cereal market. Campbell's soup controls 90 percent of the canned soup market. Agribusiness interests control 70 percent of the vegetable production in California. Multinational corporations and corporate conglomerates also control 70 percent of

American potato production, 100 percent of sugar cane and beet production, and 98 percent of fluid-grade milk production. Corporate control also dominates the poultry industry: 40 percent of egg production, 54 percent of turkey production, and 97 percent of broiler chicken production.

In most American cities, four or fewer grocery chains control 50 to 60 percent of all retail food sales. Since economists term the control of more than 50 percent of a given product market by four or fewer concerns an "oligopoly" (a shared monopoly), it is clear that the consumer protection afforded by competition has all but disappeared for today's shoppers.

If the big food companies exploit consumers and farmers alike, why don't most people *do* something about it? Many of us have fallen victim to the food industry's $4-billion-a-year advertising effort. Our changing eating habits may be a direct result of the fact that the biggest profits lie not in the sale of farm-fresh whole foods, but in the sale of frozen or dehydrated or in any way transformed food products. You can get an idea how expensive processing is from Table 1-1, which traces marketing of potatoes.

As evidence of our changing eating habits, let's look at the lowly potato and its changing role in the American diet. In 1960, the average American consumed 108 pounds of potatoes a year, and 85 percent of the spuds were bought fresh. By 1973, we were still eating the same amount of potatoes, but 57 percent of them were processed, be it frozen, fried, chipped, dehydrated, mashed, or reconstituted.

All of the changes in our eating habits are not necessarily by choice. The food industry is constantly looking for new ways to sell its products, and nutrition is not necessarily always their main concern. The question they must first answer is not "is it healthy," but "will it sell?" As an example of this philosophy let's look at one recent introduction to the marketplace: Pringles potato chips.

What Are They Doing to Potatoes?

In *Eat Your Heart Out,* Jim Hightower does a masterful job of analyzing how Procter & Gamble has exploited the potato to its outer limits in constructing Pringles, a potato chip made from reconstituted potatoes.

Standard chips are simply sliced potatoes fried in oil. To make a Pringle, the potatoes are peeled, cooked, and mashed,

TABLE 1–1

The High Cost of Food Processing

	package size	price	price per pound
fresh potatoes	20 lb.	$1.99	$ .10
fresh potatoes	5 lb.	.79	.16
sliced, canned potatoes	1 lb.	.25	.25
frozen French fries	1 lb.	.35	.35
frozen potato puffs	1 lb.	.35	.35
frozen French fries (extra crisp)	10 oz.	.35	.56
instant mashed potatoes	1 lb.	.71	.71
potato sticks	7 oz.	.47	1.07
potato chips	10 oz.	.69	1.10
Tuna Helper (potatoes and artificial mushroom flavor sauce)	7.5 oz.	.59	1.26
Crisp-i-Taters (potato snack)	6 oz.	.55	1.47
Hamburger Helper (sliced potatoes with a sour cream and beef-flavored sauce)	7 oz.	.63	1.53
instant potato soup mix	5 oz.	.49	1.57
Munchies (potato crisp snack)	5 oz.	.53	1.70
Chipsters (potato snack)	4.75 oz.	.51	1.72

Compiled by John Feltman for Organic Gardening and Farming

and then the water is removed. Later, water is added to the dehydrated mash along with a helping of chemicals (mono- and diglycerides, sodium phosphates, sodium bisulfite, and BHA preservative), sugar, vitamin C, and some salt. The mixture is then poured into molds and passed through hot oil to solidify it into what are advertised as perfectly shaped chips. For all of this, Pringles cost 50 percent more than standard chips.

Why, you might ask, would a company go to all the trouble to make what appears to be an inferior product? Because Pringles have greatly increased marketability, that's why. As

Hightower notes, traditionally, thè potato chip market is highly competitive with many local producers fighting for customers. Because of the fragility of chips and the absence of preservatives, most chips are sold within 200 miles of where they are made. However, with Pringles all of a uniform size and contour, they can be neatly stacked and sealed in a fancy container. This allows Pringles to be shipped anywhere in the country. By having a nationwide market, the parent company can easily afford to cut their price in one locale to establish the product and drive off competition, while relying on profits in other regions to sustain the effort. Pringles can also be advertised nationally, and there is no problem with shelf life. The coup de grace for Pringles is that they now allow P&G to wield extreme pressure on potato farmers. With a product like Pringles, P&G can hold off on their buying of potatoes until prices drop when the market is flooded, or they can buy field grade potatoes for processing, or they can simply hold the size of their order over a farmer's head until the poor soul is forced to drop his price. Hightower concludes that no matter how you look at it, Pringles are bad for consumers and farmers, but great for the producer. They have absolutely no nutritional points superior to traditional chips, but they have a much higher profit potential, and that's what counts in the food production business.

When food corporations advertise their processed products, they obviously do not tell us the unpleasant truth about their wares. What could they say? "Pringles cost more, have fewer vitamins and minerals, and are more fattening than fresh potatoes?" Obviously not. Instead, we read or see on television that these chips "don't break," "stay crisp longer," and "stack neatly."

Most of us are victims of a malady called the "pineapple juice bias," an illness induced and nurtured by high-powered, nonstop food industry advertising. "Pineapple juice bias" is the food industry's term for the fact that most people are so used to canned pineapple juice and its tinny taste that they think fresh juice "tastes funny." After all, doesn't one food manufacturer make an orange juice product that "tastes better than fresh squeezed?" The nation has become so totally addicted to artificial flavoring and convenience foods that the taste of "real" foods has been forgotten. Says a vice-president for a food advertising firm, "There has been a definite shift in food preference to the taste of processed foods. If you give someone strawberry ice cream made with fresh strawberries, you'd have a totally unacceptable product. People would say, 'I wouldn't eat that artificial stuff.' "

Advertisers Should Not Plan Meals

Advertising also plays an important role in the food corporations' development of "new" products. The "product differentiation" game is played enthusiastically by all foodmakers. *Fortune* magazine, in an article on Proctor & Gamble, reported that, "once a brand is established, Procter and Gamble changes it in some major or minor way twice a year." In 1969 alone, *Washington Post* columnist Colman McCarthy discovered that 9,450 new items were introduced into supermarkets, but only 20 percent of them were successful.

It is a never-ending parade of new gimmicks that allows foodmakers to launch continuous new advertising campaigns designed to keep consumers reaching for products that essentially are "the same old stuff." As an example, Jim Hightower in *Eat Your Heart Out* described the fate of what ought to be a healthy product: Kretchmer's Wheat Germ. "Once an independent company, Kretchmer was bought out by a large food conglomerate, International Multifoods, when the larger firm realized that 'healthy' breakfast foods were becoming good business. Right off, International bolstered the advertising budget for Kretchmer's," Hightower writes, "and moved quickly from the basic product to offer four different varieties: regular, sugar and honey, cinnamon-raisin, and carmel-apple. 'Kretchmer's announces two new wheat germ flavors that don't taste much like wheat germ,' ran a 1974 ad."

Food companies spend anywhere from 1.6 percent to 18.6 percent of total sales on advertising, according to figures compiled in 1974 by *Advertising Age*. Advertising helps food companies counter claims that their products are not nutritious. Despite its proud boasts about fortification and enrichment, the unvarnished truth is that processing and manufacturing destroy more vitamins, minerals, and trace elements than are ever replaced. Besides, the products themselves, as we have seen, are full of sugar and fat and contribute to poor health in a myriad of ways. Spray-on synthetic vitamins do little to mitigate these effects.

The foodmakers' other major claim is that their new foods are "convenient." "Women get their kicks from things other than standing over a stove, and that means processed foods are here to stay," rationalizes Aaron Strauss, marketing research director of Best Foods. Advertising has convinced us that "old-fashioned" food preparation takes too long and takes time away from "more important" things. Frozen dinners, for instance, are marketed on the premise that fixing a meal is a bother that must be avoided at all costs. The same premise motivates the sale of everything from instant pudding to Hamburger Helper. But the cooks of generations past didn't suffer from an inconvenience phobia and you don't have to either. As you'll see in chapters 8 and 9, making from scratch doesn't take as much time as advertising campaigns would have us believe.

When you start thinking about changing the way you eat and acquire your food, don't feel like some sort of revolutionary — it's a trend beginning to sweep the nation.

A survey conducted by *Better Homes and Gardens* in 1974 found that 63 percent of all respondents felt they were making "important and lasting changes" in the way they shop and eat. As evidence of this, a May 1975 *Wall Street Journal* article cited statistics from a Chicago-based supermarket chain which indicated that in 1974, purchases of baking ingredients such as flour in large-sized containers were up 10 percent (reversing a 20-year decline), baking soda purchases were up 28 percent, and dry yeast sales 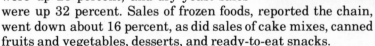 were up 32 percent. Sales of frozen foods, reported the chain, went down about 16 percent, as did sales of cake mixes, canned fruits and vegetables, desserts, and ready-to-eat snacks.

As even further evidence of the awareness more and more people are showing towards food, the prestigious business publication, *Forbes,* ran an early 1976 article on America's emerging awareness of food. They concluded their lengthy article by saying, "It's impossible to say where the public's heightened food-consciousness will lead the food companies or other businesses — but something big is unquestionably happening and any businessman ignores it at his peril." How right they were.

The fight for good food is mainly being fought on two fronts, by those old enough to remember what good food was all about, and by those young enough to be willing to buck society and look for something different. Regardless of the motivations, food is being rediscovered. Now we have reached the point where it is fashionable to prepare six and seven course gourmet dinners from scratch as opposed to going out to eat. Food and cooking are becoming fashionable for three reasons: it gives people a say in their lives, it is healthier, and it is cheaper. Or to put it in one word, it's sensible.

And the exciting thing about becoming involved in your food supply is that you are not alone. Every month more than 7.5 million people read *Organic Gardening and Farming* and *Prevention* magazines. Millions more read *Countryside, Maine Times, Mother Earth News, Country Journal,* and other books and magazines, while additional millions are busily going about the job of planning gardens, ordering seeds, harvesting, raising livestock, and in general becoming involved in their future, and they're enjoying every minute of it.

The entire movement adds up to what OGF editor Robert Rodale has termed "food power." The goal is to shorten the food chain, that expensive and often detrimental route foods take from producer to consumer. That's the goal of this book, to shorten your food chain. The more of your food you produce and/or process, the shorter your food chain, and the better your food.

Let's start your personal food revolution by learning a few things about what foods your body needs and how your body uses food.

Chapter 2

A Look at the Basics of Nutrition

Nutrition is a hard concept to define. Webster's dictionary tells us it's "the sum of the processes by which an animal or plant takes in and utilizes food substances," but that isn't the whole story. Nutrition is menu planning, it's fresh chopped vegetables quickly stir fried, it's combining beans and rice for a meal with the protein impact of a T-bone, and it's dieting. In short, nutrition is the relationship of foods to the health of your body.

Food is the fuel that powers the human machine. Like an engine, when the human body is functioning, it is expending energy; energy is required to breathe, to walk, to stand, to move a finger, even to think and sleep. People obtain energy from the foods they eat: we burn food, much as an automobile burns gasoline or a steam engine burns coal.

The energy that food provides determines the quantity of food that is required by the body. In making this calculation, the total potential energy is measured in a heat unit called a food calorie. The calorie rating given to food — 63 calories for a slice of white bread, for example — simply indicates the amount of heat energy theoretically contained in that food. A total of about 2,900 calories of food is needed every day by an average American man.

While the quantity of food is measured by its energy content, quality of food is determined by its chemical ingredients. Specific compounds and elements are needed to nourish the uncountable number of individual cells — blood cells, nerve cells, muscle cells — that make up the human body. Each kind of cell has a job to do, and each cell must "eat" to do its job.

At least 45 chemical compounds and elements are believed to be needed by human cells. Each of these 45 substances, called essential nutrients, must be present in adequate diets, either directly, when the nutrient itself is in the food, or indirectly, as a raw material in food that can readily be converted to bodily use.

Thus, food is the subject of the study of nutrition. However, people around the world have vastly different ways of "studying" nutrition. Let's look at two cases.

Two Ways to Use Soybeans

In the United States a simple diet of homegrown foodstuffs 70 years ago has given way to a multitude of processed convenience foods. In the conquest of nature, foods and their nutrients were systematically analyzed and characterized. The resulting facts were cataloged and organized into distinctive branches of scientific and technological knowledge. This all resulted in the creation of a scientific discipline of nutrition: a relatively young interdisciplinary science based on empirical knowledge gained through quantitative measurements, systematic analyses, and controlled feeding experiments.

The Chinese, on the other hand, never sought to tame nature on a large scale, nor in any systematic fashion. Through trial and error and untiring experimentation at a utilitarian and nonscientific level over the course of some 4,000 years, they have evolved a body of nutritional knowledge. This information is of an artistic nature, aimed at securing the greatest food value and personal enjoyment from limited natural resources.

With these two distinct nutritional philosophies in mind, let's look at how these two cultures approach the problem of a protein shortage.

By striving to bring out the natural qualities of foodstuffs, the Chinese have worked out various means of diversifying, enriching, and balancing their diet with foods and food mixtures. The soybean has long played an important role in these mixtures.

Unprocessed, the soybean has an unpleasant bitter taste and contains several natural inhibitors that interfere with the biological utilization of its protein. To counter these negative aspects the Chinese process it by natural methods, including soaking, grinding, and fermentation with microorganisms, into such products as curd, milk, and sauce. In so doing, they introduce a safe source of protein into their diet and diversify their diet with three additional soybean foods, each with distinctive flavors, textures, and usages. The curd is cooked with vegetables and sometimes small amounts of meat or eaten with rice for lunch or dinner, the milk is served with wheat pancakes for breakfast, and soybean sauce is the most commonly used condiment in Chinese cooking.

Quite in contrast, in the United States the soybean is chemically softened and mechanically pressed to separate the oil from the protein-rich meal. The meal is then converted into flour and protein concentrates. Oil, meal, and the concentrates are each further processed to inactivate inhibitors and improve taste. Nevertheless, it still remains lacking in popular appeal, and soybean derivatives must be incorporated into such products as margarine, bread, and imitation meat. The object is to hide the taste of the soybean, or to artificially make it resemble a popular food, while making use of its protein.

The differences in the use of the soybean are a result of the two countries' backgrounds. America attempts to overcome the drawbacks of soybeans through technology, while the Chinese work with nature to form the soybean into useful products. However, both approaches have one common nutritional principle in that they seek a balance to its use. Neither tries to rely solely on the soybean for nourishment.

Balance is the key word to remember whenever talking about nutrition. If you are to remain healthy your food must contain a balance of a wide variety of foodstuffs to insure adequate nutritional intake.

In the United States, variety and balance are represented by the basic four food groupings. The basic four food groups —

meats, dairy, vegetable and fruit, and bread and cereal — were conceived by the U.S. Department of Agriculture and adopted by home economists as a method of ensuring that everyone eats a balanced meal. The message is simple: "Eat a food from each food group at every meal and you'll do OK."

However, there are some problems with this approach. Foremost, we don't know enough about nutrition to design and recommend the perfect diet. Like other scientists dealing with the human body, nutritionists are constantly frustrated by how little we know about the way our bodies work. Scientists are baffled about why an animal fed a diet consisting of all the recommended nutrients in refined or artificial form dies, yet animals allowed to forage for themselves in the wild seemingly eat a diet deficient in nutrients, and live full lives. There are many factors about diets that are mysteries. As one nutrition researcher responded, "We don't even know what questions to ask, no less the answers." The only definitive fact science can tell us about nutrition is that we don't know all there is to know.

The idea behind the basic four food groups is sound. Find a simple guide to help busy meal planners produce good meals. However, where this falls apart is the type and quality of foods available to select from.

Americans have access to one of the most dependable, abundant, and efficient food supply systems mankind has ever known. But modern methods of production, processing, transportation, and marketing take a heavy toll on the nutrient content of these foods. As a result of this, Americans now have access to more foods than our forefathers ever dreamed possible, but unfortunately these foods are of marginal quality. Consequently, we are eating more additives, more white flour and sugar, and less roughage and nutrients, principally trace minerals which are lost in the refining process. It is these trace minerals that the American diet is robbed of, that science knows the least about in the field of nutrition.

The main problem with refined foods being introduced into the diet is that it completely upsets the natural selection process nature equipped us with. The process of feeding oneself is the most primitive and universal common denominator of all men, animals, and plants. Humans have survived millions of years, not because of a formal body of intellectually gathered nutrition information, but through the process of natural selection.

Natural Selection Is Best

As you will see in the next chapter, a look around the world at the many varied and differing dietary patterns should discourage any idea that there is an ideal diet. People around the world, most of them illiterate for the greater part of human history, have evolved varied dietary patterns, each distinctive in its own right and each healthy. The common denominator of all these diets is their harmonizing with the features, resources, and cultural norms of their locality. People eat almost anything that grows on  this planet, and their enormously diverse diets — whether based on beef and potatoes, rice and fish, seal meat and blubber, or tortillas and beans — are all capable of meeting the basic human need for food.

The most conclusive scientific test of the natural selection process was done in 1939 by C. M. Davis. In her test, 15 infants were weaned to a diet consisting of commonly used, but unprocessed and unpurified foods. Each infant selected what he wanted from a tray on which several foods were individually placed in separate dishes. Amounts eaten were recorded for each child over feeding periods ranging from six months to four years. In all cases excellent health was maintained. Davis noted that self selection worked because "the subjects were presented only with wholesome natural foods." Adding processed foods to the choices would change the results, as the children would actually be choosing from fractions of foods, not whole foods.

An additional obstacle to the natural selection process was documented in 1973 by S. Lepkowsky in the *American Journal of Clinical Nutrition*. He noted that in the Davis study young children were used, and that it would not work with American adults. He concluded that food selection based on body needs under the control of the body is obscured in adults by information from higher brain centers in the form of habits, customs, prejudices, social pressures, and advertising messages.

Quite the opposite, the Chinese diet is still governed by the natural selection process, but it deals with whole foods and is not subjected to food marketing advertisements. Their folk customs call for full enjoyment of the sensual feelings of food and consider it a birthright to enjoy a good meal. This out- look has given the Chinese a vast amount of culinary experience and nutritional information that is more custom and social norm than scientific information. By trial and error, nutritional concepts and dietary practices based on natural se- lection have evolved over the centuries. Those concepts and practices which were found to enhance the well-being of the greatest number consistently were the ones which endured and were passed on from one generation to the next. Those concepts that resulted in illness were bypassed.

Today's Chinese cuisine reflects these years of testing and perfecting. Regardless of how exotic or plain a dish may be, if properly perpared it must be gratifying from the standpoint of taste, color, texture, and fragrance. It is this blending of artistic values with time-tested nutritional concepts that allows the Chinese to so fully enjoy their meals and maintain health despite seeming repetition and a lack of abundant sup- plies of meat and dairy products.

Hopefully, someday our rather boring and limited basic four food groups will become a thing of the past, as nutrition information places emphasis on making meals appealing and satisfying as well as nutritionally sound.

In the remainder of this chapter we will look at how our bodies turn food into energy and what food elements science currently knows we must have to maintain proper health. However, first a word of caution: The science of nutrition is young, and there are many more questions than answers — the information presented is by no means complete. It represents the state of the art at this time. Consider the information presented as the tip of an iceberg; there is a lot more to be dis- covered.

In chapter 3 we will use the information covered in this chapter and show you a new way to look at nutrition planning. Our emphasis will be on meeting the body's needs through a wide variety of foods. We will strive to present as diverse a diet as possible, leaving you, the cook, as many choices as you wish. We will show you what needs must be met, and what foodstuffs meet these needs. The choice is then up to you. For regardless of how much scientific information you have, in the end it is the individual cook who is responsible for meals that not only fill the stomach, but satisfy the head and heart as well.

How Your Body Uses Food

Food is the conveyor of nutrients, substances which are necessary for energy production and body building. The foods we eat are incredibly complex and must be broken down into their individual chemical components before the body can absorb them. The broad outlines of how the body uses food are now clear. Like a chemical factory, the body converts raw materials supplied by food into usable substances; in this case the 45 essential nutrients that build cells and fuel activity. Food is first digested in the alimentary canal, which extends from the mouth to the anus. That is, meat, fish, grains, and vegetables are physically and chemically changed from their original forms into simple, more soluble substances. The nutrients in these substances are absorbed by the tissues that surround part of the canal. They are then transported to the 100 trillion cells that need them. Finally, the nutrients are assimilated to build body tissue or generate energy.

Food nourishes our bodies in three major ways: by supplying heat and energy; by providing the materials required for building and repairing body tissue; and by supplying certain substances to regulate and coordinate body processes. A single food item may contribute nourishment in one, two, or all three ways. Too little or too much of a nutrient can injure the body. Thus, your diet must supply the body with all the needed nutrients in a relatively close balance.

The concept that illness might be caused by the absence of something that belonged in the diet was a long time gaining credence. It was easy enough to understand how a person could be poisoned by a toxic substances in the food she or he ate, but to accept that she or he could be as seriously harmed by a substance *not* in the food, by a deficiency, seemed alien to common sense and experience. Not until the twentieth century, when refined methods of research revealed the crucial role in human nutrition of such complex and elusive food compounds as vitamins and minerals, were deficiency diseases recognized for what they were. Only then could the missing substances, which are needed in extremely small amounts, be identified and established as causes of illnesses.

In the mouth, food undergoes repeated maceration through the grinding and crushing action of the teeth and is moistened and softened by saliva. Saliva aids in swallowing and also serves a chemical function since it contains a starch-splitting enzyme which chemically breaks carbohydrates into dextrins and maltose.

The process of chewing brings moistened and ground-up food into intimate contact with nerve ends located in the tongue and palate for the sense of taste. If agreeable, the taste sensation (really the result of the combined action of taste and smell) serves as a stimulus for continued food intake. It also serves the important purpose of stimulating the flow of gastric digestive juices. Thus, a well-prepared meal really can be "mouth-watering good."

Swallowing begins the trip down the esophagus into the stomach. Normally, an adult's stomach will hold from three to five pints of liquid and is responsible for liquefying food and chemically breaking down protein. In the stomach food is mixed with gastric juices, produced in millions of glands lining the stomach wall, containing three important elements, hydrochloric acid, rennin, and pepsin.

Hydrochloric acid and the enzyme pepsin break protein down into a jellylike substance of simple chemical compounds. There are an estimated 20,000 to 30,000 enzymes in the human body. Only about 1,000 enzymes have been identified, but their great importance in nutrition and other living processes has been established beyond any doubt. They are all incredibly complex proteins that act as catalysts to speed up chemical reactions. The action of an enzyme is vital, powerful, and more efficient than that of any reagent concocted by man. The element iron, for example, will break down hydrogen peroxide, a poisonous by-product of the human body. But an iron-containing enzyme called catalase will break down as much hydrogen peroxide in one second as a similar quantity of iron could handle by itself in 300 years. Chemists can separate proteins into their component amino acids by boiling them at 330° F. for 18 to 24 hours in a strong solution of hydrochloric acid; the enzymes of the small intestine perform the same operation in under three hours at body temperature and in a neutral or even slightly alkaline medium.

Liquids begin to leave the stomach in 15 to 30 minutes.

Starches and sugars when eaten alone leave the stomach more rapidly than proteins. Fats remain longer than other foods. Mixtures of these three foods remain in the stomach longest, which is why a meal balanced in fats, carbohydrates, and proteins "sticks to your ribs" longer than a quick snack of equal calories. A normal stomach empties itself in from four to six hours.

Food then moves into the small intestine where the most important digestive processes take place and the end products of digestion are absorbed into the bloodstream. After passing into the intestine, the liquefied food is subject to a variety of muscular movements and digestive juices. The digestive secretions in the small intestine come from three sources: the pancreas, the glands of the intestine, and the liver.

The pancreas furnishes enzymes to change starches into their simple form, glucose, ready for absorption. Proteins enter the small intestine already partially digested, and the pancreas furnishes enzymes which complete the breakdown of protein into amino acids and peptides, ready for absorption. The pancreas also secretes a substance that neutralizes digestive acids.

The small intestine contributes intestinal juices containing an enzyme that acts upon sugars, breaking them down into glucose, fructose, and galactose. In these simple forms they also are ready for absorption.

Normally, the liver converts significant amounts of cholesterol to bile salts, and this bile constitutes a major route of disposal for cholesterol. Bile does not contain digestive enzymes of importance, but is of extreme significance for proper digestion and absorption of fat by virtue of its efficient emulsifying action. The bile salts lower the surface tension of large fat globules and particles in the semiliquid intestinal contents and facilitate their subdivision into progressively smaller globules under the constant mechanical churning action of the small intestine.

Practically all the absorption of nutrients takes place in the small intestine. Preliminary gastrointestinal digestion has broken down proteins, carbohydrates, and fats into more soluble, simple compounds of smaller molecular size. Absorption is thus concerned with amino acids, fatty acids, glycerol, monosaccharides, minerals, and vitamins, and their transportation into the circulatory system.

Food, in a liquid state and broken into simple chemical

components, is absorbed by four to five million hairlike projections called villi, which line the small intestine. Nutrients pass through the villi into capillaries, lacteals, and blood vessels. The artery in each villi transports nutrients, except fat, to the portal vein and from there to the liver.

Fats move through a series of ducts called lymphatics that run from the villi to the bloodstream, and through the blood to the cells. Only fats and fat-soluble vitamins take this route. The other nutrients follow a different route. They are carried away from the villi by tiny blood vessels called capillaries, which funnel them into the portal vein leading to the liver. If we considered the body as a complex chemical factory, the liver is its main processing and storage plant. Here, many kinds of enzymes help change the nutrient molecules into new forms for new purposes. Unlike earlier changes, which prepared nutrients for absorption and transport, the reactions in the liver produce the end products needed by individual cells. Some of the products are used by the liver itself. Part of the rest is held in storage by the liver, to be released into the body as needed. The remainder goes into the bloodstream, from which it is picked up by the cells of the body and put to work.

The process and rate by which cells convert digested nutrients into energy and building materials for living tissues is called metabolism. At the individual cells an osmotic exchange takes place between the capillary blood and the cell requiring nutrients. Through a medium of an extracellular fluid, fresh nutrients are passed to the cell, and spent nutrients are sent to the bloodstream. This process both nourishes the cell and disposes of its waste.

The spent nutrients mainly are then carried to the excretory organs by the bloodstream. Carbon dioxide is eliminated by the lungs, and any excess of water in the extracellular fluids is eliminated by the kidney.

The large intestine serves as the terminal reservoir of the gastrointestinal tract. It absorbs the last remaining digested food and actively reabsorbs any excess fluid from the semiliquid digested mass. Waste material gathers in the colon and gradually solidifies as water and salts are absorbed into the bloodstream. The solid matter forms the feces, which consists of cellulose, bacteria, and other nondigestible materials.

The Body-Building Nutrients

Food consists of five different classes of nutrients: 1) carbohydrates, 2) proteins, 3) fats, 4) vitamins, and 5) minerals. Carbohydrates, proteins, and fats are known as energy nutrients because they supply fuel for body heat and work. Their fuel potential is expressed in calories. (A calorie is the amount of heat necessary to raise the temperature of 1 gram of water 1° centigrade.)

Body weight is an excellent barometer for gauging your intake of the energy nutrients. Underweight is an indication that the energy supply is not sufficient to meet energy needs, while overweight indicates a more than adequate intake of calories. If more calories are consumed than are burned, the excess will be stored as body fat. The maintenance of ideal weight is an indication that energy intake is balanced with energy output.

The dangers of overeating were known more than half a century ago, when actuarial studies by life insurance companies showed that fat policyholders were poor risks. By now there are mountains of statistics that establish beyond any question that overweight people do not live as long, on the average, as slimmer ones. A table prepared by the Metropolitan Life Insurance Company, showing the mortality rate among men, notes that 10 percent in excess poundage increases the likelihood of death by 13 percent. And the risk increases with every additional pound of weight. Men who are 20 percent overweight have a 25 percent greater chance of dying prematurely than do those of normal weight; those who are 30 percent overweight have a 42 percent greater chance.

In the United States, the risk of premature death from overweight is especially widespread because so many Americans weigh more than they should — that is, more than a so-called "normal weight" determined by age, height, and body build. A person who weighs from 10 to 19 percent more than the norm is considered overweight; one whose weight exceeds the norm by 20 percent or more is considered obese. About one-third of all Americans are obese, and many more are overweight.

Foods that are high in energy value are high in calories, and foods that are low in energy value are low in calories. Fats are king of the calorie race, yielding approximately nine calories per gram of food, while carbohydrates and proteins yield approximately four calories per gram of food.

Looking around the world we find vast differences in the proportions of the three energy nutrients in healthy diets. In the tropics carbohydrates are likely to contribute up to 80 percent of daily caloric needs, yet herdsmen and Eskimos exist on an animal diet which is high in protein and fat and includes only 20 percent or less carbohydrates.

Barring ecological considerations, as in the Eskimo's case, economic status and agricultural practices greatly influence the proportion of carbohydrates in the diet. Rice, potatoes, cereals, flour products, and vegetables, all predominantly carbohydrate foods, are considerably cheaper to grow and store than meat, eggs, poultry, and dairy products, which are primarily sources of proteins and fats.

In the United States and Canada, roughly 50 percent of calories are supplied by carbohydrates, well below the world-wide average of close to 70 percent. Remember, the American level of 50 percent should not be considered a standard of good nutrition. Recent research indicates that indeed it is too low, and that carbohydrates should comprise approximately two-thirds of the diet. With a higher proportion of carbohydrates, your diet will still provide optimal nutritional value, provided it assures an adequate vitamin and mineral intake, contains sufficient fat to supply essential fatty acids and soluble vitamins, and contributes a level of protein sufficient to fulfill the needs for growth, defense mechanisms, tissue repair, and maintenance. As you will see in the discussion of protein in this chapter and later in chapters 3 and 9, a carbohydrate-based diet can easily meet all of these nutritional goals. First let's look at carbohydrates and fats separately to see what they are made of and how they affect our bodies.

Carbohydrates

Carbohydrates have been labeled the "body's most preferred foods," since they are the easiest nutrients for the body to digest and use. The chief functions of carbohydrates are to provide energy for body functions and muscular exertion, and to assist in the digestion and assimilation of other foods. Carbohydrates provide us with immediate calories for energy, so our bodies can save protein for the building and repairing of body tissues.

Carbohydrates are important in nu- trition for many reasons other than their main job of providing energy. Some of them make our food sweet. Some of them cling to our teeth and serve as food for bacteria. Some determine what types of bacteria will grow in our intestines. Car- bohydrates help regulate protein and fat metabolism; fats require carbohydrates for their breakdown within the liver. The bulk in our food, which helps to prevent constipation, consists mostly of car- bohydrates.

To understand how carbohydrates perform these functions and how they are used in our bodies, we need to know some- thing about their chemistry. This requires a little technical discussion.

Carbohydrates are divided into three major types accord- ing to the complexity and size of their molecules. These divi- sions are important since complex carbohydrates must be broken down by digestion into the simple sugar groups before they can be absorbed and used by the body. The three types are known as simple sugars or monosaccharides (one sugar group per molecule), disaccharides or double sugars (two sugar groups per molecule), and polysaccharides (many sugar groups per molecule). The sweet taste of fresh vegetables like green peas and just-ripe corn is due to the presence of these sugars.

Simple sugars, such as those in honey and fruits, are very easily digested. Double sugars, such as table sugar, require some digestive action, but they are not nearly as complex as the polysaccharides, starch and cellulose. Polysaccharides are literally hundreds of simple sugars bound together. To be digested, starch must be broken down into the simple sugar groups of which it is composed.

Cellulose is a polysaccharide of glucose, but it is harder to digest than starches. Cellulose must be cooked if it is to be digested by humans. Even then most of the cellulose remains undigested. However, it is extremely important as it provides bulk to the food residues in the large intestine to promote their evacuation and good health.

These simple sugars are absorbed by the blood and carried to the liver. Once in the liver a series of complicated chemical changes occurs. Glucose remains glucose and is dumped into the blood stream for energy or is converted to fat or glycogen and stored for later use. As the tissues use glucose, the glycogen is then turned back to glucose for use. Fructose, on the other hand, is converted to glycogen or glucose. When converted to either, it follows the same pattern as the glucose outlined above. Galactose is simply converted to glycogen and stored in the liver for future energy. Glycogen is sometimes referred to as animal starch since it is a polysaccharide stored in animal tissue. Since only limited amounts of glycogen can be stored in the liver, it is rapidly used up during fasting or muscular work.

However, the body has a limited capacity for storing glycogen, while its ability to store fats is not limited. When carbohydrates are consumed in excess of the capacity of the body to use them or store glycogen, they are chemically converted into fats and stored. Thus, overconsumption leads to weight gain. Conversely, when carbohydrate is no longer available for energy production, the body begins to draw on its reserve of fat to provide energy.

Today we eat far fewer raw or complex carbohydrates than our forefathers did. They often ate heaping plates of vegetables and grains, with meat and dairy products totalling plenty of calories, but you have to remember their carbohydrates were not refined. One of today's fancy pieces of pastry after dinner can include as much sugar, and hence refined carbohydrate for the body to process as an entire dinner of vegetables and grains included a few years ago.

To sum up the role of carbohydrates in the American diet: Carbohydrates do not account for a high enough percentage of our diet, and those carbohydrates we do eat are too refined, presenting our bodies with too high a percentage of glucose and not enough starches and cellulose.

Fats

Ounce for ounce, fats provide twice as much usable fuel to the body as do carbohydrates and proteins. One gram of fat yields approximately nine calories to the body. In addition to being such a concentrated source of energy, fats have three other roles: 1) they contribute to our enjoyment of food by adding flavor, 2) because they slow digestion, they delay the onset of hunger, and 3) fats contain fat-soluble vitamins and essential fatty acids.

Even though fats play an important role in keeping your body in good health, many people view them as a culprit of bad health. Perhaps this stems from what the word fat has come to signify around the American waistline. There is nothing evil about fats in moderation, but too many of them can cause you real problems. When dealing with carbohydrates or proteins, four extra grams of food would mean only about 16 extra calories, but four extra grams of fat gives you 36 extra calories, and if you eat these extra grams for long, you're going to be gaining weight.

We noted when discussing carbohydrates that the proportion of carbohydrate in the human diet is greatly influenced by the standard of living: The less money people have to spend on food, the more carbohydrates they consume. We can find a similar relationship for fats: The more money people have to spend for food, the more fats they consume. If carbohydrates are to be known as poor people's food, then fats should be listed as rich people's food. In underdeveloped, overpopulated parts of the world, fats may contribute only six to ten percent of the total calories, while in some western countries fats account for almost half the total caloric intake.

Historically, fats have never played more of a role in the American diet than they currently do. Before 1900, fats accounted for about 30 to 33 percent of the calories consumed in an American home. That level rose to 35 to 38 percent in the mid-1930s and reached 42 to 44 percent in the mid-1950s. Luckily, it has held at about that level since then. The proportion of calories from protein sources has remained steady over this period at about 11 to 12 percent. Thus, increased fat intake has come at the expense of carbohydrates. Authorities estimate that fat levels for optimum health should be held between 20 and 30 percent of total calories, far below the level consumed in the U.S. today.

Fats come in several forms, known as saturated, unsaturated, and polyunsaturated. These terms refer to the chemical construction of the fat unit. Each fatty acid is made up of carbon atoms joined like links of a chain. The carbon chains vary in length, with most edible fats containing four to 20 carbons. Each carbon atom has hydrogen atoms attached to it, much as charms might be on a bracelet. When each carbon atom in the chain has attached two hydrogen atoms, as many as it can hold, it is called a saturated fatty acid; when a hydrogen atom is missing from two neighboring carbon atoms, a double bond forms between the two carbon atoms, and the fatty acid is called unsaturated. A fatty acid which contains more than one such double bond in the chain is called polyunsaturated. Looking back to the chain analogy, some of the links are open on the chains forming unsaturated and polyunsaturated fatty acids. Other chains are solidly closed, or saturated.

When open links, unsaturated or polyunsaturated fats, enter the body, the openings allow some body substance to enter and combine with them. This combination allows for a new use of the fat in the body and easy absorption. But a saturated fat can combine with nothing in the body and must be absorbed or eliminated as is. This is where the problem occurs. When the body is not ready or able to absorb a saturated fat, the fat wanders aimlessly in the bloodstream where it can pile up and clog blood passages, a killing condition known as atherosclerosis.

These differences in chemical structure and behavior affect fats' ability to control cholesterol in the bloodstream. Saturates tend to raise the blood-cholesterol level, unsaturates to be neutral, and polyunsaturates to lower it.

Once these facts about fats and cholesterol are understood the heart disease picture becomes clearer. For example, this is one reason why atherosclerosis has always been rarer among Italians than Danes: the Italians eat less fat, and what they eat comes mainly from olive oil, which is largely unsaturated; the Danes eat a lot of butter and hard cheese which are rich in saturated fats. The same explanation partly accounts for the increase in atherosclerosis in twentieth century America: increased consumption of animal products, particularly of butter and beef fat and most particularly of "prime" beef, all loaded with saturated fats. In the past, Americans ate comparatively little beef, and most of that came from range-fed cattle, whose flesh is tough and stringy, with only a little soft fat of low saturation. Today Americans are hearty beefeaters, and they prefer prime beef from corn-fed steers; this meat is tender and tasty because it is "marbled" with hard, saturated fats.

Processing sometimes makes saturated fats out of unsaturated fats. This is called hydrogenation. Hydrogenated fats are those in which hydrogen has been forced to take up the opening in the link of an unsaturated fat chain. Normally, oxygen would take it up, but oxygen can cause rancidity in the fat. Hydrogenated fats don't turn rancid, which is great for food processors interested in a long shelflife, but they are rough on your body.

Most of the unsaturated fatty acids and fatty acids composed of shorter chains have lower melting points and are liquids (oils) at room temperature. All food fats, animal or vegetable, contain a mixture of saturated and unsaturated fatty acids, but generally animal fats are more saturated than liquid vegetable oils and are solid at room temperature. Table 2-1 shows the three fat groupings and their members.

TABLE 2–1

The Three Types of Fats

SATURATED	UNSATURATED	POLY- UNSATURATED
beef	almonds	corn oil
butter	cashews	fish
cheese (whole milk)	chicken	herring oil
chocolate	duck	margarine (special)
coconut	olive oil	safflower oil
cream	peanuts and peanut oil	soybean oil
ice cream	pecans	sunflower oil
lamb	turkey	walnuts
margarines (ordinary)		wheat germ oil
milk (whole)		
pork		
shortenings (hydrogenated)		
veal		

Most of our fat intake comes from the basic fat content of individual foods. Most people only think about visible fats like butter, margarine, lard, and cooking and salad oils when totalling up their fat intake. But much of our fat intake comes from less visible sources: the small fat particles and streaks in meat; the varied amount in nuts, meats, and poultry; the fat added in some cooking; and the fat contained in many processed foods. People are usually aware of only about half their actual fat intake.

Fats incorporated in foods as spreads or cooking oils give both flavor and satiety value. Flavor will vary somewhat with the kind and amount of fat used, and your preference will be based largely on habit and economics. Soy oil is not used much in this country because of its reputation for having a bitter taste, but safflower oil is highly desired for its mild taste and odor, while olive oil has fallen from flavor due to its relatively high price, despite its unquestionable high quality and fine taste.

The satiety value of fats depends on the fact that fats slow the digestion process, and meals containing fat remain longer in the stomach and prevent the early recurrence of hunger sensations. There is a good and bad side to this, depending on the amount of fat in the meal. Small or moderate amounts of fat are a help in preventing hunger, but when too much fat is taken, the meal may stay too long in the stomach, causing discomfort plus a considerable calorie increase.

The most important role of fats in the diet is as a carrier of fat-soluable vitamins and fatty acids. The vitamins will be covered later in this chapter, so we will limit our discussion here to the fatty acids.

There are three essential fatty acids that your body must have for proper health. The term "essential" refers to the fact that our bodies cannot manufacture these substances; they must be present in the foods we eat. The three essential fatty acids are linoleic, arachidonic, and linolenic, and were formerly known as vitamin F.

All three of these essential acids are unsaturated, are needed for normal growth, healthy blood, arteries, and nerves and are only found in fats. There is considerable evidence linking these essential fatty acids with the body's ability to break down cholesterol.

A deficiency of fats in the diet would lead to a deficiency in fat-soluble vitamins and fatty acids. With the amount of fat in most people's diets, we need not worry about a deficiency; our problem concerns an abundance of fats.

Because of the widely varying fat content of diets, the National Academy of Sciences has no Recommended Dietary Allowance (RDA) for fats. We do know that linoleic acid should account for about 2 percent of the calories in the diet, and that fats supply other essential nutrients.

To sum up the role of fats in the American diet, we can safely say that Americans eat far too much fat. Our diets should not derive any more than one-third our total calorie intake from fats, and optimum health is achieved with a fat intake of from 20 to 30 percent. We also know that the American diet contains too many fats from saturated sources, and more of our fats should come from unsaturated and polyunsaturated vegetable oils.

Protein

Of the three calorie providing nutrients, protein must be considered the glamour nutrient. In the past couple of years newspeople have discovered protein. We are exposed every day to news of a world protein shortage, protein supplements, the ever rising cost of protein, and on and on. Because of all this publicity, in many minds protein has become identified as some type of wonder food. It is touted as helping to build strong bodies, improving intelligence, revitalizing sex lives and worn appearances, and any number of other attributes.

Truthfully, protein is important to our diets, but no more so than any other element, although protein is involved in almost endless functions in the body. Next to water, protein is the most abundant substance in the human body and is the major building ingredient of fingernails, blood, hair, skin, and our internal organs.

We can best understand what proteins are and how they work through the use of an analogy. Protein is actually a complex group of food elements known as amino acids; consider these amino acids like letters of an alphabet. There are currently 22 known amino acids, or letters in the protein alphabet, that science has identified. Combinations of these 22 amino acid letters are used to form words or carry out bodily functions. Each cell or body function is its own unique word, to be spelled out with just the right combination of amino acid letters.

Different combinations of amino acids in protein are required by the body for building and maintaining body tissues, and are part of deoxyribonucleic acid (DNA), which controls the genetic code and thus all hereditary characteristics in body cells. However, the greatest amounts of protein are needed when the body is building new tissue rapidly, such as during infancy, pregnancy, or when a mother is nursing a child. Extra protein is also needed when excess destruction or loss of body protein occurs from hemorrhage, burns, surgery, infections, or other causes. Proteins are needed for building the thousands of enzymes which control the speed of chemical reactions in the body and for producing hormones. Proteins also are needed for forming antibodies which combine with foreign proteins that enter the body, producing an immunity response to ward off infections. Suffice it to say protein is essential.

Like carbohydrates and fats, proteins can be burned to supply energy, and when the diet does not supply enough calories from the other two nutrients, proteins are used for energy, even at the expense of body building protein. Some protein is needed regularly in the diet because the body has little protein reserve, but if more protein is eaten than is required for the nitrogen needs of the body, the extra protein is converted to body fat. This excess protein consumption is economically wasteful because foods that provide primarily carbohydrates and fats are cheaper sources of calories. It is also biologically wasteful because only part of the protein molecule can be used for energy; the amino acid groups cannot be used for energy and must be split off and excreted by the kidneys.

Getting back to the alphabet analogy, our bodies have the ability to synthesize most of the amino acid letters from other letters. For example, let's look at the amino acids needed to spell out the word HELP. If your dinner does not provide the amino acid represented by the letter H, your body would be able to take two Ls or an L and an E and make an H. However, there are eight amino acid letters that your body cannot manufacture from other amino acids. If your dinner did not provide a P, your body would not be able to make one, and the bodily function represented by our word HELP would not occur. These eight amino acids are known as essential amino acids because it is essential to good health that they be present in your food intake, because your body cannot produce them.

Here's where things begin to get confusing. In addition to there being essential and nonessential amino acids, our bodies have to use amino acids in just the right proportions for each job. Thus, you need some kinds of protein more than others. Again, going back to the alphabet, the most used letter is the vowel E; you would need more of these letters to write something than you would need X's or Z's. Thus, proteins that contain the right proportion of the amino acids are better for you and have what is known as a higher biological value. Biological value is an arbitrary method of assigning a score to the value of a protein source to your body.

The most perfect protein source is human milk, with a value of nearly 100. Eggs are a close second with a score of about 94, with cow's milk getting an 85 and meats and fish coming in around 76 to 86. Brown rice is the highest ranking vegetable source of protein with a score of 80.

Note that the sources with the best protein for human use are all of animal origin. This should not be surprising, since animals, fish, and birds consist of cells and metabolic systems which are rather similar to humans. It follows that the proteins which are in the cells of cattle, chickens, and fish should be more or less the same proteins we need to form new cells and carry out bodily functions.

Plants, on the other hand, don't look a bit like human beings. They are rooted to the soil and have metabolic functions involved with making food out of sunlight. Their store of essential amino acids should be expected to be somewhat different than ours, and it is. For its own purposes, one plant may need a bit less of amino acid X than we need, so it doesn't contain as much of that amino acid as we need for good health.

As we will see in the next chapter, you can compensate for the amino acid shortcomings of plants by combining them in your diet. This is possible because all protein is broken down by the digestion process into the individual amino acids for absorption and use. Thus, a meal provides a pool of amino acids for your body to select from for its many needs. Going back to the alphabet analogy, a helping of rice may provide say 10 letters, a serving of broccoli six letters, and a glass of milk 12 letters. Your body can then choose from all these letters to spell out the bodily functions needed.

The major problem is that too many people have come to equate the word protein with a big, thick, juicy steak. This just isn't so. Of all the calories in beef, 60 percent come from fats and only about 27 percent of the calories are protein. When you think of meat, think fat as well as protein.

Unlike carbohydrates and fats, there are established RDAs for proteins. By isolating how much nitrogen your body burns, nutritionists have calculated how much protein you need to replace the nitrogen. This method is designed to give us an average per pound of body weight, and does not include the extra needs of pregnant or nursing women, growing children and adolescents, or adults during periods of heavy stress or physical activity.

The established minimum daily intake of protein is .213 grams of protein per pound of body weight. If we allow for a 30 percent deviation to account for extra protein loss due to stresses, minor infections, trauma, pain, and loss of sleep, we get a standard of .277 grams or .28 grams of pure protein per pound of body weight per day. Most nutrition experts agree that this level will provide ample protein for 98 percent of the population. Again, pregnant or nursing mothers and growing children will need slightly more protein. As you will see in the next chapter, you may have to consume slightly more protein than this to get your minimum, for all of it may not be usable to your body.

To sum up the role of protein in the American diet: We eat too much protein, and too much of it comes from meat sources, giving us an elevated intake of calories due to the saturated fat content of meats. Carbohydrates could better supply some of the energy we now derive from excess protein consumption.

Regulating Nutrients

We have already looked at the three nutrients that provide calories to provide our bodies with heat and to build and repair body tissues. Now we will look at two substances that occur in incredibly small amounts in our foods, but are essential for life and growth processes. Vitamins and minerals are needed for transforming foods into energy and body maintenance.

Nutritional science has currently identified anywhere from 15 to 25 substances that may qualify as vitamins and over 20 minerals in the body.

Vitamins

In the early 1900s doctors discovered three ingredients necessary to prevent beriberi, pellagra, and scurvy. The three mystery compounds were felt to be in a class of chemical compounds called amines and were named from the Latin vita, or life, plus amine. Vitamine. Later, the "e" was dropped when it was discovered that not all of the substances were actually amines.

Not knowing what these substances really were, they were identified by letter as they were discovered. In time, what was thought to be one vitamin turned out to be many, and numbers had to be added. Later some vitamins were found unnecessary and were eliminated, which accounts for gaps in the numbering. The vitamin B complex is the best example of this. It now ranges up to B_{12}, but several numbers are missing. Presently, vitamins are not given numbers; the chemical names are being used.

Vitamins are classified in two groups, those dissolved in fats or oils, known as fat-soluble vitamins, and those that can be dissolved in water, called water-soluble vitamins.

The water-soluble vitamins, including the B complex and vitamin C, are usually measured in milligrams (mg) or micrograms (mcg), and the fat-soluble vitamins A, D, E, and K are measured in terms of units of activity known as International Units (IU) or United States Pharmacopeia units (USP units). Each unit represents the amount of the vitamin needed to produce a specific change in the nutritional health of an animal under laboratory tests.

To illustrate the extremely small amounts of vitamins needed by the human body, let's look at the recommended allowance of vitamin B_{12} for adults, 6 micrograms a day. Just 1 ounce of this vitamin would satisfy the daily needs of 4,724,921 people! Another way to look at the size of the substances we are talking about is to think of a level teaspoon of sugar. This would weigh about 4 grams. There are 1,000 milligrams in each gram, or 4,000 milligrams in a teaspoon of sugar. There are 1,000 micrograms in a milligram, or 4,000,000 micrograms in a level teaspoon of sugar.

Excess amounts of the water-soluble vitamins are not retained in the body but are excreted in the urine, so daily intake of these vitamins is needed. However, the fat-soluble vitamins are stored within the body for future use. There is the possibility of persons taking vitamin supplements acquiring too much of a fat-soluble vitamin when taking massive doses of these substances. There is no way you can consume a dangerous amount of fat-soluble vitamins from a balanced diet.

Sooner or later when talking about vitamins, the subject of vitamin supplements comes up. For people buying overly processed convenience foods, vitamin and mineral supplements are just about a must. But for those of us growing most of our own food, do we need to take supplements? The answer is a yes and a no. During the nongrowing season when you're eating from supplies you've canned, smoked, dried, stored, and frozen, chances are you won't be getting the full vitamin content of the foods, for processing takes a toll. During this time of year you should take vitamin and mineral supplements. Be sure to take a supplement made from natural sources, as the vitamins will be in their natural proportions, especially the B complex. During the growing season when you're eating fresh from the garden, you shouldn't really need to take a supplement, but it is cheap insurance to continue taking them.

As you'll see later in this chapter, when we look at minerals, there are a number of trace minerals science knows we need, but they don't know why we need them, or what a deficiency looks like. In a very few cases, your soil may be deficient in some trace minerals. Such a deficiency is more likely to occur on chemically farmed soil, as organic fertilizers and humic acids tend to make trace minerals in the soil more available to plants. You need not worry about such a deficiency, because in all likelihood you will be buying at least some part of your food from other areas. Even if you're just buying your grains from a natural foods store, chances are they were grown hundreds of miles away, and such a trace mineral deficiency did not exist there. If you are one of the very few who absolutely grows everything your family eats, it may be wise to buy a trace mineral-rich supplement like brewer's yeast to be on the safe side. But in most cases you needn't worry. Most deficiency diseases are either a product of overrefining or the body's inability to utilize the nutrient, not a lack of the nutrient in the food.

To sum up the role of vitamins in the American diet: We seem to get an adequate supply of vitamins in the average diet. Elderly persons on reduced diets may have deficiencies, as may poor persons. Processed foods pose the biggest threat to vitamins in this country.

Let's take a quick look at what each vitamin does and what foods it can be found in. For those vitamins and minerals with RDAs, we note the level deemed necessary by the National Academy of Sciences, as listed in the table at the end of this chapter. We'll start by looking at the fat-soluble vitamins.

Vitamin A *(Retinol)*   In general, vitamin A is the most important vitamin for a healthy complexion and good eyesight.

This vitamin is necessary for new cell growth and healthy tissues and is essential for vision in dim light. One of the first symptoms of vitamin A deficiency is an inability of the eyes to adjust to darkness. Deficiency also causes dry, rough skin which may be more susceptible to infection. Too much vitamin A causes headache, nausea, and irritability.

Vitamin A is found in nature in the form of carotene, in green and yellow plants, and as two forms of the vitamin itself in fresh-water fish and land animals.

Vitamin A is found most abundantly in liver, eggs, butter, and whole milk. Green and yellow vegetables and yellow fruits are the best sources of carotene, which the body converts to vitamin A. The RDA of vitamin A is 5,000 I.U. for adults.

Vitamin D *(Calciferol)*   Known as the sunshine vitamin, vitamin D is unique in that it can be formed in the body. The action of ultraviolet rays of the sun activates a form of cholesterol, which is present in the skin, converting it to vitamin D. By improving the absorption and utilization of calcium and phosphorus, vitamin D regulates the amount of these minerals in the blood.

Vitamin D deficiency causes rickets. The earliest obvious signs are skeleton deformation, bowed legs, deformed spine, and sometimes flat feet. Too much vitamin D causes nausea, weight loss, weakness, excessive urination, and the more serious conditions of hypertension and calcification of soft tissues, including the blood vessels and kidneys.

Thanks to the body's ability to manufacture vitamin D, people who spend part of their time in the sun need no other sources of it. Foods which are fortified with vitamin D are intended mainly for infants and the elderly who lack outdoor exposure to sunlight. The RDA for infants and continuing to age 22 is 400 I.U.

Most of the body's need for vitamin D can be met by sufficient exposure to the sun. Good sources of vitamin D are canned fish, egg yolk, and fortified milk.

Vitamin E *(Tocopherol)*   Probably not the most important vitamin, vitamin E may be one of the most talked about. Recent claims and disclaimers have centered around this vitamin's antioxidant properties and its use in treating cancer, heart, and circulatory problems, increasing fertility, and combating aging.

Vitamin E acts as an antioxidant which helps to prevent oxygen from destroying other substances. In other words, vitamin E is a preservative, protecting the efficiency of other compounds such as vitamin A.

The relatively infrequent cases of vitamin E deficiency, and the plentiful supply in all but the worst diets, suggests that if a deficiency does occur, it is probably a result of poor absorption or utilization by the body. Food processing and storage destroy some of the vitamin E in foods, as does cooking, especially under high temperatures for prolonged times.

The RDA is 30 I.U. for adults. The richest sources of vitamin E are cold-pressed vegetable oils, shortening, and margarine. It is also found in fruits, vegetables, eggs, whole grains, and organ meats.

Vitamin K   Actually a group of different substances, the sale of vitamin K is prohibited in the U.S. due to its toxicity. There are several scientific names for vitamin K, which is essential for clotting of the blood. One type of the vitamin is found naturally in food, ample amounts are made in the intestinal tract by bacteria, and a third is made synthetically to treat isolated cases of deficiency.

The body requires only a very small amount of vitamin K, and it can be synthesized by your intestinal bacteria, so there is no RDA for this vitamin. A deficiency of vitamin K is rare, although it can result from a failure of the body to produce bile.

Leafy green vegetables like spinach, lettuce, kale, cabbage, and cauliflower, as well as liver, egg yolk, and fats all have ample amounts of vitamin K.

Water-Soluble Vitamins

The water soluble vitamins, the B-complex and vitamin C, must be present in your food on a daily basis. Because these vitamins are water-soluble they are not stored in the body. Any excess of the vitamin will be excreted by the body in the urine. There is almost no way of ever getting too much of these vitamins through your diet or by taking supplements to cause a toxic reaction. If your diet is not complete, deficiencies of the water-soluble vitamins will result.

Vitamin B Complex Thought originally to be a single vitamin, the B complex is now known to contain at least 11 separate vitamins. The B complex includes vitamins B_1, B_2, B_6, B_{12}, biotin, choline, folic acid, inositol, niacin, pantothenic acid, and para-aminobenzoic acid.

The B complex is destroyed by alkali, such as baking soda added to vegetables during commercial processing to retain their bright color. Oxidation, light, heat, and sulfa drugs also destroy B vitamins. Due to their water solubility, large amounts of these vitamins may be lost during cooking. During the refining of flour and cereal, most naturally-occurring B vitamins, which are present in the outer bran and the inner germ of the grain kernel, are removed.

The B vitamins are active in converting carbohydrates into glucose, which the body burns to produce energy. In addition, the B vitamins are necessary for the normal functioning of the nervous system. They are essential for the maintenance of muscle tone in the gastrointestinal tract and for the health of the skin, hair, eyes, mouth, and liver.

Because the B vitamins occur naturally together, a deficiency in one of them may indicate a deficiency in the others as well. Symptoms of general B complex deficiency may include dry, rough, cracked, scaly skin and dull, dry hair. In addition, fatigue, headache, dizziness, poor appetite, constipation, and other digestive disorders, nervousness, mental depression, and abnormal growth and development may indicate a vitamin B deficiency. One important fact about the B complex to remember is that they should all be taken together. This group of vitamins is so interdependent that sufficient amounts of all of them, with but one ingredient lacking, may prove to be almost valueless. More than with any other vitamin, you have to be sure you're getting the complete B complex to insure good health. Such sources as whole grains, green leafy vegetables, brewer's yeast, or organ meats all have the B vitamins in proper proportions. Many times refined grains will be enriched to replace B vitamins lost in milling, but if the enrichment is not of the same proportions as those vitamins lost, the nutritional benefits will not be the same.

Vitamin B_1 *(Thiamin)* Thiamin is required for normal digestion, proper growth, fertility, and lactation, and the proper functioning of the nervous system. A lack of thiamin will impair the breaking down of carbohydrates into glucose. Since the central nervous system depends on glucose for energy, a B_1 deficiency may result in fatigue, impaired alertness, nerve pain, and numbness.

Thiamin intake should be proportionate to your intake of carbohydrates. The RDA for thiamin is 0.5 milligrams per 1,000 calories. Older persons may need double this amount.

Thiamin is found abundantly in pork, beans, peas, nuts, and in enriched and whole grain breads and cereals.

Vitamin B_2 *(Riboflavin)*   Riboflavin combines with niacin and thiamin to form a group of enzymes involved in the breakdown and utilization of carbohydrates, fats, and proteins. Riboflavin is also necessary for cell respiration, since it works with enzymes to help cells use oxygen.

Symptoms of riboflavin deficiency include inflammation and breakdown of the tissues, particularly those around the nose and mouth. The eyes may burn and itch when the diet does not provide enough riboflavin.

The RDA for riboflavin is .55 milligrams per 1,000 calories. There is an increased need in pregnant or nursing women and infants. B_2 is found abundantly in leafy vegetables, enriched and whole grain bread, liver, cheese, lean meat, milk, and eggs.

Vitamin B_6 *(Pyridoxine)*   Actually, this vitamin is not a single substance, but three related chemical compounds, pyridoxine, pyridoxal, and pyridoxamine. B_6 plays an important role in the breakdown and utilization of energy giving foods. It also aids the utilization of energy in the brain and nervous system.

Deficiency symptoms are muscular weakness, nervousness, irritability, depression, mouth disorders, and dermatitis. The RDA for vitamin B_6 is related to protein intake. Two milligrams of B_6 are needed to help utilize 100 grams of protein per day. Pregnant and nursing women may need as much as 2.5 milligrams. Food sources with ample amounts of B_6 include liver, whole grain cereals, potatoes, red meat, green vegetables, and yellow corn.

Vitamin B_{12} *(Cobalamin)*   This is the only vitamin containing cobalt, an essential trace mineral. Because this vitamin is mainly found only in meats and dairy products, strict vegetarians often have a deficiency and must take supplements.

B_{12} is needed for normal functioning of all body cells, the formation of red blood cells, and is involved in metabolism. A deficiency of B_{12} is usually due to a problem in absorption, not a problem of the diet.

The RDA for B_{12} is 5 micrograms for adults. Abundant sources are organ meats, lean meats, fish, milk, and shellfish.

Biotin   Once known as vitamin H, biotin is now the descriptive term for this member of the B complex. Biotin is a co-enzyme needed for many chemical reactions in the body. Its main roles are in assisting in the making of fatty acids, and the utilization of fatty acids and carbohydrates for body heat and energy.

Biotin is made in considerable amounts by the intestinal bacteria, and is present in organ meats, whole grains, brewer's yeast, eggs, and milk. A biotin deficiency is very rare, but eating a large number of raw egg whites over a long period of time will deplete biotin supplies. Biotin deficiency symptoms include dermatitis, grayish skin color, depression, and muscle pains. There is no RDA for biotin, but intake is estimated at from 150 to 300 micrograms. Added amounts are needed by pregnant and nursing women.

Choline   Choline, usually considered part of the B complex, is made by the body from the amino acid methionine along with folic acid and B_{12}. This vitamin is the basic ingredient of lecithin, which aids the movement of fats from the liver to the cells. There is no RDA for choline, as the body normally produces sufficient amounts. Sources of choline include organ meats, wheat germ, and legumes.

Folic Acid *(Folacin)*   Folic acid, another member of the B complex, helps to manufacture red blood cells and is essential in normal metabolism. Some folic acid is produced by the intestinal bacteria. Thus the chances of developing a deficiency are very rare, except during infancy or pregnancy.

The RDA of folic acid is 0.4 milligram for adults. Many foods contain ample amounts of folic acid. The most abundant sources are liver, navy beans, and dark green leafy vegetables. Other food sources are nuts, fresh oranges, and whole wheat products.

Inositol   One of the lesser known members of the B complex, inositol is concentrated in the brain and other tissues. It is believed necessary for the formation of lecithin when combined with another member of the B complex, choline. Lecithin is needed for proper metabolism of fats.

There is no RDA for inositol, although it is available in a wide variety of foods, specifically whole grains, nuts, organ meats, and vegetables.

Niacin   Part of the B complex, niacin assists an enzyme in the breakdown and utilization of proteins, carbohydrates, and fats. Although rare, symptoms of a niacin deficiency are weakness, diarrhea, dermatitis, and nervous disorders.

Niacin is synthesized by the body from an amino acid, tryptophan. Niacin is present in all foods containing the B complex, such as lean meats, poultry, and milk products. The RDA for niacin is 6.6 milligrams a day.

Para-Aminobenzoic Acid *(PABA)*   PABA is usually considered part of the B complex. It influences the intestinal bacteria, enabling them to produce folic acid. A deficiency of PABA usually results from the use of sulfa drugs. Otherwise, ample amounts are provided in the diet. There is no established RDA for PABA.

Pantothenic Acid   This vitamin, part of the B complex, is needed for the normal functioning of the adrenal gland, which affects growth, and the maintenance of healthy skin and nerves. Pantothenic acid also plays a role in the formation of cholesterol and fatty acids, and in the utilization of other vitamins.

Pantothenic acid is present in all plant and animal foods. There is no established RDA for pantothenic acid, although intake is estimated at 5 to 10 milligrams for children and adults.

Vitamin C *(Ascorbic Acid)*   Surely the most famous of all vitamins, vitamin C is essential for overall body health, especially healthy skin. This is the least stable of all vitamins and is the most easily destroyed. Light, heat, air, prolonged storage, copper and iron utensils, and alkali mediums all cause serious vitamin C destruction. Prolonged cooking, especially if the cooking water is discarded, also results in heavy losses of vitamin C because a great deal of it transfers to the cooking water.

A lack of vitamin C causes scurvy, one of the oldest diseases known to man. The signs of scurvy include weakness, bleeding, loss of weight, and irritability. An early sign is bleeding of the gums. In California during the great 1849 Gold Rush, 10,000 Americans, cut off from a normal supply of fresh vegetables, died of scurvy.

Vitamin C is purported to solve all sorts of nutritional problems. Suffice it to say it is extremely important to your well-being to have a sufficient intake of vitamin C daily. The RDA for vitamin C is 60 milligrams for men and 55 milligrams for women. Abundant sources are citrus and tomato juices, strawberries, currants, and green vegetables such as lettuce, cabbage, broccoli, kale, collards, mustard and turnip greens, and potatoes.

Minerals

If a scientist completely burned a 200-pound body, the only thing left would be about 8 pounds of ashes. These ashes would account for the metallic minerals in the body. Although minerals account for only about 4 percent of body weight, they are just as important to good health as the carbohydrates, fats, proteins, and vitamins we have already covered.

Although needed in small or minute amounts from day to day, every one of the essential minerals is necessary for building tissues and maintaining the life processes of body cells. It is impossible to say that certain minerals are more important than others, despite the fact that some are needed in much larger amounts than others.

For the sake of clarity, nutritionists have placed minerals into two groupings. Those minerals needed in relatively large amounts include calcium, phosphorus, sodium, chloride, potassium, magnesium, and sulfur, and are classified as macrominerals. (To keep things in perspective, remember when dealing with minerals large is considered anything in excess of 100 milligrams a day.) Those minerals needed in even smaller amounts are called trace minerals. This grouping includes iron, manganese, copper, iodine, zinc, cobalt, fluorine, chromium, and many others.

Minerals are present in the bones, teeth, soft tissue, muscles, blood, and nerve cells. They also act as catalysts for many biological reactions within the human body, including muscle response, the actions of the nervous system, digestion, and metabolism. They are also important to the production of hormones.

The efficient use of minerals is possible only when they are present in proper proportion to other minerals and food substances. A good example of this interrelationship is the role of iron and copper.

Iron is one of the elements most vital for the well-being of the body, although only a few thousandths of a gram of it are needed daily. Iron we know is required for making hemoglobin, the pigment in red blood corpuscles that enables them to carry oxygen to, and carbon dioxide away from, cell tissues. Copper is also indispensable in the process of forming hemoglobin, although not present in it. Science does not yet know the exact way copper functions in our bodies, although they do know that animals that get too little copper in their food supply develop iron deficiency anemia despite ample supplies of iron. They theorize that copper probably functions in some enzyme that plays a part in hemoglobin formation, but no one knows for sure.

The biological role of trace minerals has been discovered for only 17 of the more than 100 elements. While all of these and others may someday prove essential to our diets, there are only a few for which present knowledge allows us to discuss their role in human nutrition. The trace minerals we cover should not be considered exclusive, but only a reflection of the present state of our relatively limited knowledge in the field of nutrition.

As you will see in the next chapter, when planning meals strive for diversified selections of foods to guarantee an ample intake of those food elements we know little or nothing about. Highly purified foods such as pure fats, cane sugar, and cornstarch are practically free from mineral elements. Highly milled grains are considerably lower in most minerals than whole grains. In general, foods of high water content, like fruits and vegetables, are diluted sources of minerals. Leafy green vegetables, legumes, whole grains, and some root vegetables all contribute substantial amounts of the minerals we are about to discuss.

Calcium   Calcium is present in the body in greater amounts than any other mineral. Ninety-nine percent of the calcium in the body is deposited in the bones and teeth, and the remainder is in the soft tissues.

The primary role of calcium is to work in cooperation with phosphorus to build and maintain bones and teeth. Calcium also assists in the process of blood clotting, helps prevent the accumulation of too much acid or too much alkali in the blood, plays a part in muscle tone and muscle contractions, heartbeat regulation, and nerve transmission. It aids in the body's utilization of iron, and activates several enzymes.

Throughout our lives we need fresh supplies of calcium to replace that which is constantly called upon to perform necessary bodily functions. The RDA of calcium for ordinary adults is 800 milligrams a day, about the content derived from two glasses of milk. Yogurt, hard cheeses, and milk products are all excellent sources of calcium. Other good sources are green leafy vegetables (except spinach and chard), citrus fruits, and dried peas and beans. Meats, grains, and nuts, which are good sources of many other nutrients, do not provide significant amounts of calcium.

Phosphorus   Phosphorus is the second most abundant mineral in the body. Eighty percent of the phosphorus is present in the bones and teeth, but phosphorus is found in every cell of the body.

With phosphorus present in every cell, it plays a part in almost every chemical reaction within the body. Its key role, besides aiding in bone and teeth formation, is the utilization of carbohydrates, fats, and proteins for the growth, maintenance, and repair of cells. A healthy body maintains a balance of calcium to phosphorus in the bones of about two to one.

Phosphorus absorption is related to the presence of vitamin D and calcium. If there is insufficient supply of either phosphorus, calcium, or vitamin D, stunted growth, poor quality bones and teeth, or other bone disorders may result.

The RDA for phosphorus is 800 milligrams, the same as calcium. The most abundant sources are meat, especially organ meats, fish, legumes, and milk products.

Sodium   Sodium is found mainly in the blood, lymph, and digestive juices, and the fluids which bathe cells. Sodium helps to maintain normal water balance inside and outside the cells.

About a fifth of one percent of your body weight is sodium, a third of that being in the skeleton. Sodium chloride, or salt, is present in most foods, so a deficiency is extremely rare. In fact, Americans eat about ten times more salt than needed. Many processed foods, such as ham, bacon, bread, and crackers have a high sodium content because salt or sodium compounds are added in processing.

Luckily, the amount of sodium absorbed is regulated within the body by a hormone that controls the kidneys. When there is a high intake of sodium, the rate of sodium excretion is high, and if intake is low, the rate of excretion is low.

Because of the abundance of salt in the American diet, there is no RDA for sodium. We can easily meet our sodium needs through a reasonable amount of milk, meat, eggs, carrots, beets, and spinach. The salt shaker should be in the kitchen, not on the dining room table where people tend to salt everything on their plate.

Chloride   Chloride is the other ingredient in table salt, and Americans get more than enough of it in their diets.

Chloride is part of hydrochloric acid, which is found in quite high concentrations in gastric juices. It also helps regulate the balance of acid and alkali in the blood and helps maintain pressure to cause fluids to pass in and out of cell membranes.

Sources of chloride are table salt and sea greens. You can meet all your chloride needs with just the slightest amount of table salt.

Potassium   Potassium is mainly found within the cells, with a small amount of it in the fluids outside the cells. The body has about twice as much potassium as sodium by weight or about two-fifths of one percent of your body weight.

Potassium is vital for maintaining the chemical balance of cellular fluids. Additionally it is required for the work of the muscles, to control amounts of acid and alkali in the blood, and to stimulate nerve impulses.

There is no established RDA for potassium. It is abundant in almost all foods, and the only known deficiencies occur in diets extremely inadequate in protein. The best sources include oranges, bananas, dried fruits, tomatoes, leafy vegetables, peas and beans, meats, and fish.

Magnesium   There is about 1 ounce of magnesium in the body of an average adult. Most of it is united with calcium and phosphorus in the bones. The remainder is in the muscles, red blood cells, and other soft tissues. It is an essential part of many enzyme systems responsible for energy conversion within the body.

Magnesium occurs in many natural foods, particularly nuts, whole grains, dark green vegetables, and seafood. The RDA for magnesium varies depending on body size. Women should have about 300 mg, and men 350 mg. A diet which is high in calcium increases the body's need for magnesium. Conversely, extremely high levels of magnesium may increase the excretion of phosphorus and calcium; however, dietary intake of magnesium is relatively low.

Sulfur   Sulfur is present in all body cells. It is concentrated in the skin, hair, nails, bones, tendons, and the fluids of our joints.

Sulfur is related to protein utilization because it is a component of two amino acids. It is also part of two vitamins of the B complex. The complete role of sulfur in our diets has not yet been established.

Because it plays a role in protein utilization, sulfur is found in protein-containing foods like meats, fish, legumes, and nuts. There is no established RDA for sulfur. Adequate protein intake will insure ample sulfur intake as well.

Trace Minerals

There are any number of trace minerals in our bodies. Some of these minerals are beneficial, others are harmful. For example, cadmium is thought to be beneficial in very small amounts, but harmful in larger amounts. No one knows just what role trace minerals will play in our future, friend or foe, but as industrial pollution increases and heavy metals begin to find their way in ever increasing amounts into our food supplies, trace minerals will receive more and more attention. Some optimists say trace mineral research is at about the same stage vitamin research was in the 1930s, while others claim trace mineral research is only a few years ahead of the period when vitamins were discovered, the early 1900s.

All of the trace minerals in our bodies are thought to weigh less than an ounce combined. In fact, some of these materials are present in such minute amounts that only the most advanced testing procedures designed to search out fractions of a millionth of a gram can find them, no less begin to say what they do.

We will only look at those trace minerals that have been found to have a definite nutritional role. The list is small, not because there are not a great number of trace minerals, but because science simply does not know enough about them at this time.

Iodine   Iodine was the first trace mineral to be found essential to the diet. Iodine deficiency is generally referred to as simple goiter, and until the early 1930s was prevalent in regions of this country. When science found in the early 1920s that goiter was due to the lack of a single trace mineral — iodine — it was almost impossible for people to believe that just a tiny amount of a single substance could produce such ravages.

Iodine is required in extremely small amounts, but the normal functioning of the thyroid gland depends on an adequate supply. Most iodine is converted to iodide in the body and concentrated mainly in the thyroid glands located on either side of the windpipe. Iodide is an essential part of the hormones regulating growth produced by the thyroid.

Iodized salt is the most common source of this mineral. Depending on the iodine content of the soils in which they were grown, vegetables and fruits provide varying amounts of iodine. The best sources are seafoods. Age and sex determine the exact amount of iodine needed. The RDA for adults ranges from 100 to 150 micrograms daily.

Iron   Iron deficiency anemia may be the most prevalent disease in America, excepting overweight. The major job of iron is to act with protein and copper in making hemoglobin, the transporting medium for oxygen in the blood.

Very few foods contain iron, and even fewer contain it in a form the body can use. For that reason it is important to carefully watch your intake of iron. Vitamin C enhances the absorption of iron by changing its composition to a form which is more readily usable by the body. Vitamin C and iron-containing foods should therefore be eaten together.

Luckily, very little iron leaves the body, so our daily needs are rather small. The RDA of iron is 10 milligrams for men and increases to 18 milligrams for women. People deficient in iron will require several months to build up an adequate supply of iron due to the body's limited ability to absorb iron.

Iron is primarily stored in the liver, spleen, bone marrow, and blood. The only way a significant amount of iron can leave the body is through a loss of blood. People who have periodic blood losses or who are forming more blood often have iron needs that cannot be met by diet alone, and should take supplements. Liver is the best general source of iron. Other sources include meat products, egg yolk, fish, green leafy vegetables, peas, beans, dried fruits, and whole grain cereals.

Zinc   The nutritional value of zinc has only very recently been recognized, and may not yet be fully known or appreciated. It was long thought that a zinc deficiency did not exist in the United States, but recent studies on the loss of a sense of taste, delayed wound healing, and lack of sexual maturity all point to a zinc deficiency as the cause.

Zinc is active in many chemical activators or enzymes throughout the body, that among other functions move carbon dioxide via red blood cells from the tissues to the lungs where it can be exhaled. Zinc also plays a part in protein use and cell formation.

In 1974 the RDA was revised to include zinc as an essential mineral. The RDA established for zinc is 15 milligrams a day. Zinc is thought to be widely represented in foods, but research is pointing to increased zinc deficiencies in many of our grains. Good sources of zinc include meats, fish, egg yolks, and milk products.

Fluorine   Fluorine is an essential trace mineral concentrated in the bones and teeth. This mineral is found in the body in compounds known as fluorides.

Some controversy exists over the value or hazards of fluoridated drinking water (water with fluorine added at approximately one part per million). It is known to help prevent tooth decay, and some findings support its bone strengthening properties. However, current research indicates that as little as two parts fluorine per million parts water may cause brittleness in teeth during the forming of tooth enamel. Research continues and is needed as to the benefits of fluoridated drinking water.

There is no RDA for fluorine. Tea and seafoods are both good sources of fluorine, as are both fluoridated drinking water and some natural water supplies. The use of irrigation water containing fluorine may add small amounts of the mineral to vegetables and grains irrigated with it.

Cobalt   By itself, cobalt is not thought to be essential, but it is an integral part of vitamin B_{12} which is essential. Cobalt makes up 4.5 percent of vitamin B_{12} but there is no RDA for cobalt at this time. It mainly occurs along with protein in foods of animal origin. Green leafy vegetables, cereals, and fruits grown in cobalt-rich soil yield only minute amounts of the mineral. Ample intakes of protein will guard against a cobalt and thus a vitamin B_{12} deficiency. Persons on a strict vegetarian diet not eating meat, eggs, or dairy foods should take a B_{12} supplement.

Copper   Traces of copper can be found in all tissues of the body, but it is mainly concentrated in the liver, brain, kidneys, and heart. Copper assists in the formation of hemoglobin and red blood cells by aiding iron absorption. There is no established RDA for copper, but it is known that a copper deficiency will cause an iron deficiency. It is an essential mineral, but in such small amounts that a standard diet provides sufficient amounts of copper. Organ meats, shellfish, nuts, and dried legumes are all good sources of copper.

Chromium   Chromium has a strong influence on our bodies' ability to cope with sugars; thus it has an important role in carbohydrate metabolism. There is no established need for chromium intake, but a deficiency is known to produce a diabetes-like condition. Research continues as to a need for this mineral, but one fact is proven: The American diet does not provide as much chromium as diets based on fewer refined foods. Dr. Henry A. Schroeder, a trace mineral researcher, has noted that when sugar cane is refined to make sugar, 94 percent of the chromium is lost, and when the bran and germ of wheat is removed to make white flour, 50 percent of the chromium is lost. Chromium deficiency appears to be a problem of eating a refined diet.

Manganese   Manganese is an essential element concentrated in bones, liver, pituitary gland, kidney, pancreas, and intestines. It plays a part in carbohydrate and fat production and is needed for skeletal development.

There is no RDA for manganese, although it is known to be needed in the diet. Tea is an excellent source of manganese as are wheat germ, meat, whole grains, green leafy vegetables, beans, nuts, and seeds.

Other trace minerals for which nutritional value is known, but not understood, include molybdenum, selenium, lithium, beryllium, nickel, cadmium, and vanadium. Other minerals are thought to have detrimental effects on health, but whether they have any beneficial effects is not known at this time.

To sum up the role of minerals in the American diet, generally speaking we get sufficient amounts of minerals in our diet. Whether we get these minerals through wise food choices or just from the abundance of food we eat is not known. Refining food takes a heavy toll on minerals.

TABLE 2-2

Food and Nutrition Board, National Academy of Sciences — National Research Council Recommended Daily Dietary Allowances [a]

Revised 1974

| | | | | | | | | | Fat-Soluble Vitamins | | |
| | Age | Weight | | Height | | Energy | Protein | Vita-min A Activity | | Vita-min D | Vita-min E Activity[d] |
	(years)	(kg)	(lbs)	(cm)	(in)	(kcal)[b]	(g)	(RE)[c]	(IU)	(IU)	(IU)
Infants	0.0–0.5	6	14	60	24	kg × 117	kg × 2.2	420	1,400	400	4
	0.5–1.0	9	20	71	28	kg × 108	kg × 2.0	400	2,000	400	5
Children	1–3	13	28	86	34	1,300	23	400	2,000	400	7
	4–6	20	44	110	44	1,800	30	500	2,500	400	9
	7–10	30	66	135	54	2,400	36	700	3,300	400	10
Males	11–14	44	97	158	63	2,800	44	1,000	5,000	400	12
	15–18	61	134	172	69	3,000	54	1,000	5,000	400	15
	19–22	67	147	172	69	3,000	54	1,000	5,000	400	15
	23–50	70	154	172	69	2,700	56	1,000	5,000		15
	51+	70	154	172	69	2,400	56	1,000	5,000		15
Females	11–14	44	97	155	62	2,400	44	800	4,000	400	12
	15–18	54	119	162	65	2,100	48	800	4,000	400	12
	19–22	58	128	162	65	2,100	46	800	4,000	400	12
	23–50	58	128	162	65	2,000	46	800	4,000		12
	51+	58	128	162	65	1,800	46	800	4,000		12
Pregnant						+300	+30	1,000	5,000	400	15
Lactating						+500	+20	1,200	6,000	400	15

[a] The allowances are intended to provide for individual variations among most normal persons as they live in the United States under usual environmental stresses.
[b] Kilojoules (k J) = 4.2 × kcal.
[c] Retinol equivalents.
[d] Total vitamin E activity, estimated to be 80 percent as α-tocopherol and 20 percent other tocopherols.

Water-Soluble Vitamins							Minerals					
Ascorbic Acid (mg)	Folacin[c] (μg)	Niacin[f] (mg)	Riboflavin (mg)	Thiamin (mg)	Vitamin B_6 (mg)	Vitamin B_{12} (μg)	Calcium (mg)	Phosphorus (mg)	Iodine (μg)	Iron (mg)	Magnesium (mg)	Zinc (mg)
35	50	5	0.4	0.3	0.3	0.3	360	240	35	10	60	3
35	50	8	0.6	0.5	0.4	0.3	540	400	45	15	70	5
40	100	9	0.8	0.7	0.6	1.0	800	800	60	15	150	10
40	200	12	1.1	0.9	0.9	1.5	800	800	80	10	200	10
40	300	16	1.2	1.2	1.2	2.0	800	800	110	10	250	10
45	400	18	1.5	1.4	1.6	3.0	1,200	1,200	130	18	350	15
45	400	20	1.8	1.5	2.0	3.0	1,200	1,200	150	18	400	15
45	400	20	1.8	1.5	2.0	3.0	800	800	140	10	350	15
45	400	18	1.6	1.4	2.0	3.0	800	800	130	10	350	15
45	400	16	1.5	1.2	2.0	3.0	800	800	110	10	350	15
45	400	16	1.3	1.2	1.6	3.0	1,200	1,200	115	18	300	15
45	400	14	1.4	1.1	2.0	3.0	1,200	1,200	115	18	300	15
45	400	14	1.4	1.1	2.0	3.0	800	800	100	18	300	15
45	400	13	1.2	1.0	2.0	3.0	800	800	100	18	300	15
45	400	12	1.1	1.0	2.0	3.0	800	800	80	10	300	15
60	800	+2	+0.3	+0.3	2.5	4.0	1,200	1,200	125	18+[g]	450	20
80	600	+4	+0.5	+0.3	2.5	4.0	1,200	1,200	150	18	450	25

[c] The folacin allowances refer to dietary sources as determined by *Lactobacillus casei* assay. Pure forms of folacin may be effective in doses less than one-fourth of the recommended dietary allowance.

[f] Although allowances are expressed as niacin, it is recognized that on the average 1 mg of niacin is derived from each 60 mg of dietary tryptophan.

[g] This increased requirement cannot be met by ordinary diets; therefore, the use of supplemental iron is recommended.

Chapter 3

Improving Your Diet

What can you do to improve your diet? That may well be one of the most important questions of your life, for if you do not improve your diet, and you're eating the average American diet, you're not going to live as long or feel as good as you possibly could.

Jean Mayer, the noted nutritionist, writing on the importance of improving his diet, noted, "I believe the world has rarely been more interesting than it is right now. I suspect that in the approaching future it will be even more interesting, and I want to be around long enough to fnd out how a lot of fascinating things now going on turn out. So I must not include in my diet anything that has even a tiny chance of contributing to my early demise; nor must I leave out of it anything that might help postpone that grim event."

An intimate role in this process is applying proper nutritional guidelines to meal planning. The approach to nutrition we are about to explain depends on only two principles, 1) the simpler the preparation or processing (with a few exceptions), the better the nutrition, and 2) variety and moderation are the keys to a good diet.

The traditional American view towards nutrition and meal planning has been to present the four food groups and allow a choice from each. While designed to provide a varied diet, it leads to sameness of choice, uninteresting meals featuring a main dish of meat with little side dishes from the other three groups. It is possible to eat an item from each of the four food groups at every single meal and still have a perfectly horrible diet. That is particularly true for adults. A meal consisting, for instance, of a "fast food" hamburger with a bit of lettuce and tomato on it, a milkshake, and a piece of cherry pie contains meat, dairy products, fruits and vegetables, and cereal products. But at the same time, the white flour in the hamburger bun and pie is about as useful for building health as sawdust is for building a house. The meat in the hamburger probably weighs less than one ounce. There is barely a trace of roughage. What's more, the meal as a whole is laced with sugar, saturated fats, salt, and additives.

What we suggest is that you look at nutrition as the business of meeting your body's needs. Thus you simply learn what your body must have to function, and choose from the many different foods that fill each need. You could select a combination vegetable-grain main dish to meet your protein need, a vegetable casserole and salad to meet your carbohydrate needs, and depend on salad dressing to provide the fats you need.

Actually, meal planning to meet the body's needs is simpler than working with the basic four food groups, once you begin to learn about food. You already know there are three classes of energy-providing nutrients: carbohydrates, fats, and protein. What you have to do is provide those nutrients in the proper proportions and you've got it made. With this outlook you are not limited to having a meat dish at every meal simply because meat is one of the four groups; likewise, you do not need to have an entry from the bread and cereal group at every meal. What you are concerned with is meeting your needs for protein, carbohydrates, fats, vitamins, and minerals, regardless of source.

A World Of Cuisines That Don't Revolve Around Meat And Potatoes

To see how people around the world meet their body's nutritional needs, let's take a quick tour. Remember, these diets are low cost and usually make do with a limited variety of foodstuffs. They certainly are not the ideal, but they do show the many different ways people meet their nutritional needs.

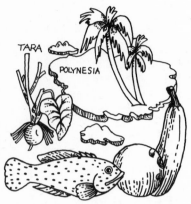

We'll start our tour where it's nice and warm: in Polynesia. These islands are surrounded by the Pacific Ocean, teeming with fish, so naturally fish is a main ingredient of Polynesian diets. However, the mainstay of the Polynesian diet is a root crop called taro. Somewhat like a potato, taro is cultivated in the ground and either baked or boiled and eaten whole or in a paste. The leaves are used as a green vegetable. The average Polynesian diet derives carbohydrates from taro, breadfruit (a tropical fruit that resembles bread when baked), and bananas. Fats come from fish and coconuts. Protein also comes from fish and coconuts. Vitamins are in fish, taro leaves, and fruits. Minerals come from taro leaves and fish bones.

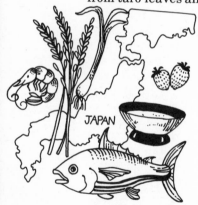

Moving along to Japan, we find another island nation that depends on fish from the sea for much of its food. However, here the staple of the diet is rice; steamed or boiled, it is eaten with almost every meal. (The diet we are about to present should be viewed as a traditional Japanese diet. Since the end of World War II the Japanese have accepted many Western dietary traits, among them the drinking of milk and the craving for beefsteaks. With this change in diet, scientists are noting an increase in many types of disease usually associated with Americans or Europeans.) Carbohydrates are present in rice. Fats are in raw and cooked fish. Protein again comes from raw and cooked fish, rice, and soybean products. Vitamins are in seaweed vegetables, pickled root vegetables, raw and cooked fish, rice, and a few fruit products. Minerals are in raw and cooked fish, seaweed vegetables, pickled root vegetables, and soybean products.

In India, many of the people are strict vegetarians for religious reasons. However, due to the sheer number of people, meat is a rarity for almost the entire population. The staple food is either rice or a flat bread made from wheat known as chapati. This is supplemented with a purée of chick peas known as dahl. For those who do eat meat, lamb is the preferred food. Carbohydrates are in rice, chapati, dahl, and a few fruits. Fats are in lamb and dairy products including a clarified butter called ghee. Protein is in lamb, dahl, chapati, and dairy curds. Vitamins are in green vegetables, rice, lamb, chapati, dahl, ghee, and fruits. Minerals are in dairy curds, green vegetables, dahl, and chapati.

Moving along to South America, let's look at Guatemala. The Guatemalan diet is mainly vegetarian, due to the high cost of meat there. The staple of the typical Guatemalan diet is corn. Despite its widespread use, corn is not a wholly satisfactory staple, as it lacks some essential amino acids. But fortunately, a lot of black beans are eaten, and they contain the amino acids lacking in corn to provide an adequate protein intake. The Guatemalan diet gets carbohydrates from corn products, black beans, papaya, and fruits. 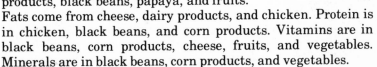 Fats come from cheese, dairy products, and chicken. Protein is in chicken, black beans, and corn products. Vitamins are in black beans, corn products, cheese, fruits, and vegetables. Minerals are in black beans, corn products, and vegetables.

Now for the average U.S. diet. While other countries have a grain as the staple of their diets, in the U.S. the staple of most people is meat, despite an abundance of all types of cereal grains and vegetables. We get carbohydrates from bread, corn, potatoes, vegetables, and fruits. Fats come from meat and dairy products. Protein from meat, dairy products, and bread. Vitamins from bread, vegetables, meat, dairy products, and fruits. Minerals from breads, dairy products, vegetables, meat, and fruits.

At first glance, this may seem to be a good diet, but in most cases it is not. Most of the foods Americans eat have been subjected to some sort of processing, and as we saw in chapter 1, processing and good nutrition do not go hand in hand. Thus many Americans are eating a diet deficient in trace minerals and vitamins, and due to the sheer volume of consumption, most people consume an excessive amount of calories.

In Tables 3-1 and 3-2, compiled from U.N. reports by Ancel

TABLE 3–1

Average Daily Nutrient Intakes

ITEM	GREECE	ITALY	FRANCE[1]	SPAIN	U.S.A.
Calories					
Vegetable sources	2,370	2,300	1,930	2,290	1,890
Animal sources	530	520	1,170	510	1,270
Total	2,900	2,820	3,100	2,800	3,160
Protein					
Vegetable sources, grams	58	50	42	48	27
Animal sources, grams	40	34	56	29	67
Total, grams	98	84	98	77	94
Fat					
Vegetable sources, grams	59	49	64	61	50
Animal sources, grams	36	36	73	37	98
Total, grams	95	85	137	98	148
Percentage of calories from:	13.5	11.9	12.6	11.0	11.9
All proteins					
Animal proteins	5.5	4.8	7.2	4.1	8.5
All fats	29.5	27.1	39.8	31.5	42.2
Animal fats	11.1	11.5	21.2	11.9	27.9

[1]Adjusted to Mediterranean France from data given in *"Études et Conjoncture"* (July 1967), Inst. Nat. Stat. Études Écon., Ministère Écon., Finances, Presses Univ. de France, Paris.

Compiled by Ancel and Margaret Keys from Food Balance sheets, food and agriculture organization of the United Nations, Rome, 1971, for their book "How to Eat Well and Stay Well the Mediterranean Way."

and Margaret Keys for their book *How to Eat Well and Stay Well the Mediterranean Way,* you will see the American diet compared to typical diets from Greece, Italy, France, and Spain. Note that the U.S. and France are the total calorie leaders, and leaders in calories gained from animal sources. Table 3-2 gives you a weekly breakdown of food consumed. By looking over this chart you can begin to get an idea of what types of foods Americans eat as opposed to these countries. As

TABLE 3–2

Average Food Consumed Per Week

FOOD	WEEKLY	GREECE	ITALY	FRANCE[1]	SPAIN	U.S.A.
Cereals, all kinds	oz.	91	89	60	69	44
Potatoes[2]	oz.	32	29	62	72	32
Sugar[3]	oz.	12	17	21	14	32
Pulses (beans, etc.)	oz.	7.4	4.0	3.1	18.0	2.3
Milk[4]	qts.	1.7	1.3	1.7	1.3	3.5
Cheese	oz.	7.9	6.2	8.4	1.2	4.1
Meats	oz.	21	20	45	16	46
Meats	calories	950	1,000	3,100	1,050	3,720
Meats	(Cal/oz.)[5]	(45)	(50)	(69)	(66)	(81)
Poultry	oz.	3.5	4.9	6.4	3.6	12.6
Fish	oz.	12	6	14	20	4
Eggs	eggs	3.4	3.3	3.3	3.7	6.4
Butter	oz.	0.6	0.9	2.6	0.1	1.9
Vegetable oil	fluid oz.	12	10	13	12	4
Wine, table	oz.	27	74	90	49	?

[1]Mediterranean France, Food Balance Sheet data for France adjusted to Mediterranean area using data from *Études et Conjoncture* (July 1967), Inst. Nat. Stat. Études Écon., Presses Univ. de France, Paris.
[2]Including sweet potatoes.
[3]Including syrups and honey, sucrose equivalent.
[4]All kinds, 3.7 per cent butterfat equivalent.
[5]Relative fatness of the meat is indicated by the value for calories per ounce.

Compiled by Ancel and Margaret Keys from Food Balance sheets, food and agriculture organization of the United Nations, Rome, 1971, for their book "How to Eat Well and Stay Well the Mediterranean Way."

you will see later, Americans eat too much meat and not enough vegetables and cereal grains.

Taking A New Approach To Food

To compensate for all the overly processed foods in your diet, you have to take a completely new approach to your food supply. No longer can your health afford to have you just pop something in the oven or throw together a one meal dish. You must start eating (and producing) whole foods, staples that have not had their nutrients processed and refined away.

Looking back to chapters 1 and 2, we found that the average diet in this country is lacking in many respects, and it promotes many types of degenerative diseases. While examining nutrition information and seeing what our bodies need to stay healthy, we discovered four things:

- Carbohydrates do not account for a high enough percentage of our diet, and those carbohydrates we do eat are too refined.
- Americans eat far too much fat. Our diets should not derive any more than one-third our total calorie intake from fats, and optimum health is achieved with a fat intake of from 20 to 30 percent. Plus the American diet contains too many saturated fats from animal sources; more of our fats should come from unsaturated and polyunsaturated vegetable oils.
- We eat too much protein, and too much of it comes from meat sources, giving us an elevated intake of calories due to the saturated fat content of today's meat.
- We appear to get an adequate supply of vitamins and minerals in the average diet. Elderly persons on reduced diets may have deficiencies, as may poor persons. Processing food poses the biggest threat to causing vitamin and mineral deficiencies in this country. Research is finding increasing cases of refined food having trace mineral deficiencies.

Looking at those four points, we see that on the average, U.S. vitamin and mineral intakes are fairly good. The main problems are that we eat too much fat and protein, and not enough carbohydrates. To simplify, actually to oversimplify a bit, Americans should be eating more raw carbohydrates, fewer foods containing saturated fats, less protein, and fewer total calories.

At first that may sound terribly complicated: Eat more carbohydrates, but eat less fat and protein, especially saturated fat, and cut down on your total caloric intake. Actually, it's quite simple to straighten out the average American diet. All you have to do is eat less meat (that will cut your protein and saturated fat intake), and eat more raw carbohydrates (that also cuts your saturated fat content and increases your vitamin and mineral intake). By reducing both your protein and fat intake, and slightly increasing your carbohydrate intake, you'll end up eating a total of fewer calories, which should keep any weight control problems you may have at a minimum.

WHERE WE GET OUR CALORIES FROM vs. AN IDEAL DIET

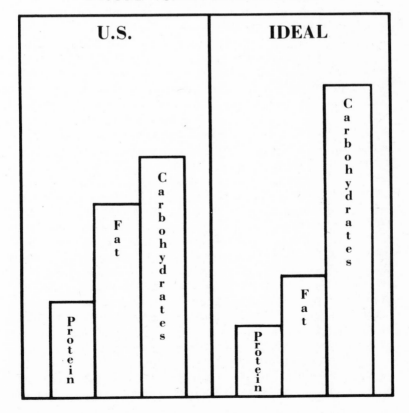

Eating Better
With Less Meat:
Complementary Protein Balancing

Food has lost its glamour and prestige in America. The kind of food revival we are talking about in this book is a type of middle class gourmet cookery. We aren't talking about fancy pastries or thick, fattening creams and sauces with exotic names, but meals based on whole foods that are economical to fix, a joy to eat, and are far better for your health. We're talking about the kind of dinner that accents what nature put into food, and not what modern technology can do to food.

When talking about including less meat in your diet, people always begin to envision a slow form of starvation due to a lack of protein. Many Americans have been led to believe that without that weekend steak, at least four hamburgers a week, and no less than one serving of meat a day, the bones slowly grow brittle, the sex life soon terminates, and intelligence rapidly fades. This just isn't so. Millions of people are perfectly healthy and they live on no meat whatsoever. But we aren't talking about doing away with meat anyway; what we are saying is that you have to reduce your intake of meat — reduce, not forsake (unless of course you choose to).

Good nutrition depends on moderation, but few of today's cooks practice it. Meat and sweets are the two biggest American culinary loves. Neither needs to be completely left out of the diet, but they should each be reserved for special occasions. A great number of people view a roast beef dinner as one mighty fine meal. But do you need, even deserve, such a grand meal every week or even monthly? Foods soon lose their majestic qualities when eaten too often. And that's our problem — we are too dependent on abundance; eating high off the hog has become an expected thing. As one writer put it, "we have forgotten how to be poor." Indeed, today people feel cheated if they don't eat the "best" available, every day.

What we are about to show you is how you can get all the protein you need without basing your every meal on meat, yet maintain that good skeleton, active sex life, and hold the old intelligence right where it is, or maybe even raise it a few points by reading and practicing the next few pages.

The whole thing depends on a concept known today as complementary protein balancing — our great-great-grandparents called it good cooking. Although many people have worked with balancing protein, Frances Moore Lappé put it all together in terms people can understand in her million copy bestseller *Diet for a Small Planet*.

Pay close attention to what follows, for in chapter 9 we will be putting this theory to work, and you will catch on a lot quicker if you understand what it's all about.

Remember our discussion of protein in the last chapter, when we pointed out that protein is made up of amino acids. There are 22 amino acids, and all must be present in order for your body to properly absorb protein. Of the 22 amino acids, your body can produce all but eight of them from other substances. Thus there are eight essential amino acids that your body cannot produce, and they must be present in your daily food supply. The eight essential amino acids are tryptophan, leucine, isoleucine, lysine, valine, threonine, the sulfur-containing amino acids, and the aromatic amino acids, but you need not remember their names.

Not only must these eight essential amino acids all be present, but they must be in the proper ratio for your body to get the most out of the protein you eat. The body can use the essential amino acids in only one pattern or ratio. In most food all of the essential acids are present, but unfortunately one or more of them is usually present in a disproportionately small amount. In such a case the amino acid present in the least amount is known as the limiting amino acid.

To better understand the importance of a proper ratio of essential amino acids, look at these statistics from Table 3-3. Beans consist of about 25 percent protein, beef about 18 percent, and eggs 13 percent. However, the essential amino acids in beans are not in the proper ratio; thus only about half the protein in beans is usable to your body, while almost all the protein in meat is usable. On a theoretical scale of 0 to 100, the amino acid pattern of eggs rates a 100, or almost all of the protein is usable by the human body. Chicken rates an 84 and beef an 81. Rice gets a 70, whole wheat bread 59, beans only 46, and corn 42. The protein in meat and eggs is known as complete protein because all the essential amino acids are there in the proper proportion, while the protein in beans is known as incomplete, because all the essential amino acids are not present in the proper proportion.

For example, if you eat protein containing enough tryptophan to meet 100 percent of your body's utilizable protein pattern, 100 percent of the leucine level and so forth, but only

TABLE 3–3

Protein Quantity and Quality

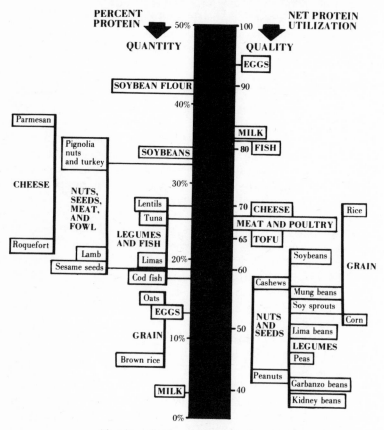

Adapted from *Diet for a Small Planet* by Frances Moore Lappé

50 percent of the needed lysine, your body will be able to absorb only 50 percent of the protein you ate. Your body can only use as much protein as the least amount of any one of the essential amino acids.

Table 3-3 shows the effect limiting amino acids have on our food. Note that milk is at the bottom of the quantity scale, but nearly at the top of the quality scale. Likewise, soybean flour is at the very top of the quantity scale, but in the middle of the quality scale. The actual protein your body uses is a combination of these two scales. One shows how much protein is in

TABLE 3–4

Cost of 20 Grams of Protein From Various Sources

Food	Market unit	Price per market unit[1]	Part of market unit to give 20 grams of protein[2]	Cost of 20 grams of protein
Dry beans	lb	$0.36	.24	$0.09
Peanut butter	12 oz	.67	.23	.15
Eggs, large	doz	.74	.25	.19
Beef liver	lb	.88	.24	.21
Hamburger	lb	.93	.24	.23
Milk, whole fluid	half gal	.77	.29	.23
Chicken, whole, ready-to-cook	lb	.69	.37	.25
Bean soup, canned	11.5 oz	.26	.96	.25
Turkey, ready-to-cook	lb	.74	.35	.26
Tuna, canned	6.5 oz	.59	.44	.26
American process cheese	8 oz	.76	.38	.29
Ham, whole	lb	1.26	.29	.36
Chuck roast of beef, bone in ..	lb	1.12	.35	.39
Ocean perch, fillet, frozen	lb	1.12	.36	.41
Round beefsteak	lb	2.02	.22	.44
Frankfurters	lb	1.28	.36	.46
Rump roast of beef, boned	lb	1.97	.26	.50
Pork loin roast.............	lb	1.56	.33	.52
Haddock, fillet, frozen	lb	1.52	.35	.54
Sirloin beefsteak	lb	2.21	.28	.62
Rib roast of beef	lb	2.00	.33	.66
Veal cutlets	lb	3.26	.21	.70
Pork chops, center cut	lb	2.04	.35	.71
Porterhouse beefsteak	lb	2.65	.34	.89
Bacon, sliced	lb	1.92	.52	1.01

[1]Average retail prices in U.S. cities, Bureau of Labor Statistics, U.S. Department of Labor, August, 1975.
[2]One-third of the daily amount recommended for a 20-year-old man. Assumes that all meat, including cooked fat, is eaten.
Compiled by U.S.D.A.

the food, and the other shows how much of the protein your body can use.

One thing to note from the table on protein quantity: Pound for pound, meat has about the same amount of protein (20 to 30 percent) as dried beans, peas, and lentils. Noting that meat costs two or three times what beans, peas, and lentils cost, if you could find a way (which we are about to show you) to enable your body to use all the protein in the peas and beans, you would really be saving yourself a good deal of money. Meat is the most expensive protein source we know of, as shown in Table 3-4.

Through complementary protein balancing, you can compensate for the incomplete protein in beans and other plant sources. This technique takes the amino acids in one food source and theoretically combines them with the amino acids in another food to create a new amino acid pattern for the two foods combined. We say theoretically, because you don't actually alter the amino acid patterns of the foods. You eat the two foods at the same meal, like a meal of beans and rice, and provide your body with a new amino acid pattern based on the entire meal. This is possible because your body breaks protein down to individual amino acids before absorbing them. Thus, once your dinner is broken down, your body has a pool of amino acids to use. All foods have their own individual amino acid patterns that you can combine to create varying total patterns for your meals. It doesn't matter how many foods provide the needed nutrients, so long as when combined they are present in the pattern in which your body needs them.

When combining plant sources of protein this way it is very easy to get your daily required protein intake. For example, combining wheat and beans at the same meal will increase the protein actually utilized by your body by about one-third. If you ate the same amount of beans for breakfast and then ate wheat for dinner, you would not have this increased protein. Figure 3-1 explains how this is done by graphically showing the limiting amino acids in both foods, and how one food source complements the other.

Figure 3-1 compares the four essential amino acids most often deficient in plant protein to the almost perfect amino acid level of eggs. You can see that beans are strong in lysine, but weak in the sulfur-containing amino acids, while wheat is strong in the sulphur-containing amino acids, but weak in lysine. The other two amino acids shown, isoleucine and tryptophan, both are present at somewhat below the levels found in eggs, but are not drastically limiting. When the two foods are combined, there is approximately a 33 percent increase in available protein. It still isn't as high on the usability scale as eggs, but the combination is much higher than either of the separate ingredients.

FIGURE 3-1
THE EFFECT OF COMPLEMENTARY PROTEINS

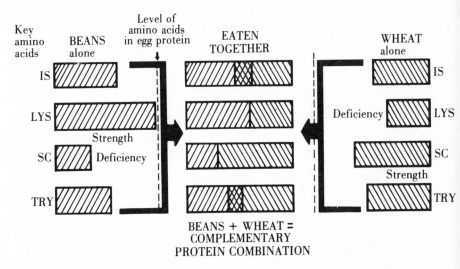

BEANS + WHEAT =
COMPLEMENTARY
PROTEIN COMBINATION

Adapted from *Diet for a Small Planet* by Frances Moore Lappé

Combining plant protein sources can increase a food's protein utilization rating by as much as 50 percent in some cases. Additional increases can be achieved by combining limited plant protein with complete animal protein. The animal sources can be either dairy products, as Lappé suggests, or you can use meat.

In *Diet For A Small Planet,* Lappé recommends people not eat meat, especially beef, at all because of the wasteful way it is raised, and the shortage of grain for human consumption around the world. While we agree with her that current livestock raising practices should certainly not be encouraged, we think the inclusion of meat in your diet doesn't have to be avoided. Remember we said the inclusion of meat, not the dominance of it. Meat and dairy products should be combined with plant sources of protein to form a complete meal. The high protein usability ratings of meat and dairy protein greatly add to the usability of plant protein. An additional point we consider in recommending the eating of meat is that we hope you'll be raising some of your own livestock as shown in chapter 5, in which case the animals will be returned to their original role in our ecosystem, not force-fed in feedlots.

Hopefully, you now have an idea of the concepts of complementary protein balancing. While at first glance it sounds terribly confusing, when you get used to it you'll be surprised at how simple it really is. Table 3-5 was compiled by Anna Gordon, dietition at Columbia-Presbyterian Medical Center in New York. It is an amazing piece of work. The items in the first two columns provide balanced protein intake through comple-

TABLE 3–5

Low-Cost, High-Protein Meals

1	2	3	4	5
2 cups cooked	1 cup cooked	Sauce: 1 can soup & $^3/_4$ c. water	Vegetables to make 1$^1/_2$ c.	3–5 tbsp. topping
Brown Rice	Soybeans	Cream of tomato	Browned celery & green onions	Wheat germ
Macaroni, whole wheat	Lima beans	Cream of potato	Mushrooms & bamboo shoots	Slivered almonds
Corn	Peas	Cream of mushroom	Browned green pepper & garlic	Fresh whole wheat bread crumbs
Spaghetti, whole wheat	Kidney beans	Cream of celery	Cooked green beans	Sesame seeds
White rice, converted (brown rice is preferable)	Black beans	Cheddar cheese soup	Cooked carrots	Brewers' yeast (debittered)
Noodles, whole wheat	Garbanzos (chickpeas)	Cream of pea	Browned onion & pimiento	Sunflower seeds

(each casserole serves 4 to 6 people)
1. Choose one ingredient from each of the five columns.
2. Mix together ingredients from first 4 columns.
3. Pour into greased casserole dish (1 quart) and bake 30 minutes at 375°F.
4. Top with one choice from column 5 and bake 15 minutes longer at 325°F.
5. Salt to taste at the table. Serve with bread and a salad.

Note: The ingredients in the first two columns form complementary proteins.

menting each other, the other three columns provide differing flavors and textures to the meals. Anyone who says meatless eating is boring should take a look at this chart. Using only 30 ingredients, it has an unbelievable 7,776 possible meals.

Figure 3-2 shows the four food groups you will use most often as sources of nonmeat protein. They are milk products, grains, legumes, and seeds. There are three basic beneficial combinations that result in increased proteins; in most cases combining grains with milk products, or grains with legumes, will give you a complementary protein combination, as will

FIGURE 3-2
**SUMMARY OF COMPLEMENTARY PROTEIN
RELATIONSHIPS**

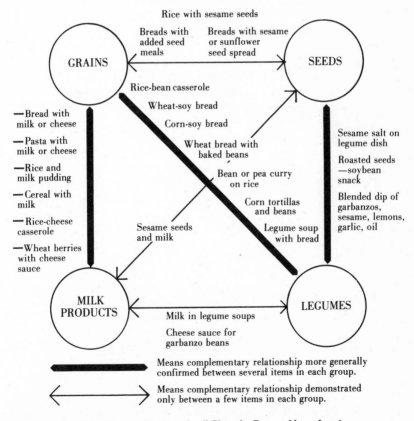

Adapted from *Diet for a Small Planet* by Frances Moore Lappé

legumes with seeds. Those three combinations — grains with milk products, grains with legumes, and legumes with seeds — are the secret to a lifetime of better eating. There are a few beneficial relationships with other combinations of the four foods as noted, but the primary ones are the three listed above.

In chapter 9 you will see these principles of complementary protein balancing put to use. Although science has only recently unlocked the secrets of amino acids, people have been cooking with these beneficial combinations for centuries. They just knew that cooking beans with rice made a better meal than cooking beans with lentils. Scientists by no means discovered complementary protein concepts, they merely explained why they work.

However, in America a meal isn't considered complete unless it features a meat course, and how are you to get around that? Probably the best way to get around such thinking is to gradually change your dining table format. Instead of having a platter of meat with side dishes of other foods around it, begin to combine these foods into one main dish. For starters you may begin slipping a few meat-based casseroles into the menu. From there, once you have the family accepting the concept of seeing a casserole and knowing the entire dinner is in that one dish, it isn't too hard to begin to switch the ingredients to meatless cooking on some nights. Slowly make these changes in your eating regimen. At first shoot for one day a week with a meal having no meat at all, no beef, poultry, or fish, just balanced vegetable proteins. With a meal that depends on beneficial protein combinations, most of your meals will be one main dish, with perhaps a salad, soup, or bread serving and beverage for the entire dinner. Once you begin to learn one dish cooking it becomes very rewarding. You put all your effort into the one item that then dominates the entire meal.

Through complementary protein balancing, you will reduce both the amount of meat you use and your intake of saturated fats and increase your consumption of raw, or complex, carbohydrates. These are two of the goals we set earlier for improving our diet. However, you shouldn't stop there.

Carbohydrates
And Empty Calories

There are many sources of processed carbohydrates and saturated fats in our diets. According to USDA statistics, the average American in 1970 consumed 264 pounds of empty calories — 102 pounds of table sugar, 88 pounds of white flour, 53 pounds of refined fats and oils, 14 pounds of corn sugar, and 7 pounds of white rice. This accounted for a little over 50 percent of the yearly total food intake calculated on a dry-weight basis.

Eating these "empty calories" robs our bodies of badly needed nutrients and an ingredient just recently found to be important, dietary fiber, while adding unneeded calories to our diet. Looking back at the last paragraph and the list of sources for empty calories we consume, think what an improvement in your diet you could make by simply attacking the first two culprits: white flour and sugar.

The average nutrient content of 100 grams of both enriched flour and whole wheat flour are compared in Table 3-6. You can see that enrichment is not all it's cracked up to be. The processing of flour in this country takes a heavy toll of many trace minerals and adds to our calorie intake. Thus, through milling and enriching of flour you get more calories and less nutrients. One final test you may wish to make: take a piece of white bread in one hand and whole wheat bread in the other, and squeeze them into a ball — which would you rather eat, the whole wheat or the ball of white paste?

Luckily, it's very easy to compensate for eating white flour — just use whole wheat flour. For breads and most things, you can either use straight whole wheat flour, or combine it with an unbleached white flour. If you don't have the time to make your own bread, carefully read the labels of whole wheat breads in the store until you find one that does not include artificial coloring and has whole wheat as the major ingredient. Many times bakeries will add a small amount of whole wheat flour and a lot of coloring to white bread to deceive consumers into thinking it's really whole wheat bread.

Many people feel they need some sugar in their diet to provide energy. If you were to completely eliminate all white sugar from your diet and eat a variety of fresh fruits, whole grains, vegetables, eggs, meat, nuts, and milk, you would still

TABLE 3-6

Nutrients Per 100 Grams
(about 3½ ounces) of Bread

	"Enriched" White Flour	Whole Wheat Flour
Calories	364	333
Protein (grams)	10.5	13.3
Fiber (grams)	.3	2.3
Calcium (mg.)	16	41
Iron (mg.)	2.9	3.3
Potassium (mg.)	95	370
Magnesium (mg.)	25	113
Phosphorus (mg.)	87	372
Thiamine (mg.)	.44	.55
Riboflavin (mg.)	.26	.12
Niacin (mg.)	3.5	4.3
Vitamin B_6 (mg.)	.06	.34
Pantothenic Acid (mg.)	.465	1.1

Compiled from the USDA's Handbook No. 8, and Home Economics Research Report No. 36.

get the equivalent of close to two cups of sugar a day from natural sources, more than enough for bodily functions. There is no dietary need for white sugar at all.

Presently Americans eat an average of 120 pounds of refined sweeteners a year, an average of from 5 to 6 ounces of sugar a day. To ingest that much sucrose from its original sources before processing, you would have to eat at least a 2-pound sugar beet every day. Before you shake your head and say there is no way you eat 120 pounds of sugar a year, remember most of the sugar you eat, over 70 percent, is in processed foods and you never see it.

To eliminate sugar from your diet, first try to curtail your intake of sweets from all sources including processed foods. Then replace what sugar you do need with natural sweeteners that provide not only energy but a few vitamins, minerals, and enzymes as well. The most often used natural sweetener is honey. In addition to being 76 percent sugar, honey has seven members of the B complex, vitamin C, and small amounts of many minerals in it. It is extremely versatile, as it can be used as a spread, a syrup, a cooking ingredient, and a topping, plus it comes in a variety of flavors. Darker honeys generally have a stronger taste and a higher mineral content than lighter honeys.

A general rule for substituting honey as a sweetener in a recipe that calls for sugar is this: use honey in one-half the amount of sugar called for; that is, if a cup of sugar is listed, a half-cup of honey will provide the same degree of sweetening. In cooking with honey, remember also that honey is a liquid, and you may have to add more flour or reduce the amount of other liquid in a recipe to get the proper consistency in the final product.

Once you have experienced what honey can bring to your cooking you may want to experiment with some of the less familiar natural sweeteners. Blackstrap molasses is a by-product of the refining process of cane and beet sugars. It's a source of B vitamins and is also high in minerals, particularly calcium, iron, and potassium. Sorghum syrup is similar to molasses in taste, appearance, and nutritional content. This thick liquid comes from the sorghum plant and can be used as you would use molasses.

One final word of caution. Although using honey, sorghum, and blackstrap molasses will slightly improve the nutritional value of your meals as compared to using sugar, don't go overboard. These are all concentrated sources of energy and should only be used when needed.

By cutting down your use of sugar, sugar-containing products, and natural sweeteners, you will reduce your daily calorie intake and make room for more carbohydrate sources that contain not only the energy you need, but vitamins and minerals as well. Remember, the more a food is processed, the less nutrients it has left.

Unprocessed carbohydrates and fibrous foods add bulk to the diet. In the intestinal tract fiber absorbs water, acids, and bacteria. The value of fiber in the diet is just recently becoming known. Dr. Denis Burkitt, an English physician, did the initial studies that compared African diets to Western diets and found dietary fiber to be the missing ingredient. It is estimated that the current U.S. annual intake of cereal fiber is only one-tenth what it was at the turn of the century. As fiber intake went down, the incidence of many degenerative diseases likewise went up.

What you need to know is how do you put more fiber in your diet, and the answer is simple — don't take it out in the first place. Use whole grains for baking, eat the old-fashioned, slow cooking oatmeal instead of the instant kind, use whole grain and wheat cereal, and eat plenty of seeds like sesame and sunflower, and plenty of berries like blackberries, raspberries, and loganberries. And lastly, eat plenty of fresh fruits and vegetables. When cooking high-fiber foods don't overcook them: heat breaks down the dietary fiber or cellulose.

Another possible solution to the problem of a shortage of dietary fiber is the use of miller's bran. This is nothing more than the bran removed during the processing of flour. Bran is 85 percent dry material — just 20 grams of it has the bulking effect in your stomach of 200 to 300 grams of most whole foods. Coarse, unprocessed bran can absorb up to eight times its own weight in your stomach. Bran is almost tasteless, having a somewhat dry flavor, much like you may imagine a little sawdust would taste. To increase your intake of bran yet not change the flavor of your food, simply sprinkle a teaspoon of bran on your breakfast cereal, sandwiches, or your buttered toast. Add it to cookies, bread, and cake recipes. Substitute one-half cup of coarse bran for an equal amount of flour in any recipe.

But using bran is only a stopgap measure. The best long term solution is to change your diet to include more foods that have their original fiber intact.

Most people like and enjoy fresh fruit, but seldom include it in meal plans, saving it for snacks. That's wrong. Lots of people like to munch on nuts and seeds, but few people include them in their dinner — also a mistake. One of the first things to go in processing is fiber, and it is usually replaced by sugar or saturated fats, which means your body is getting extra calories in return for the part of food nature intended not to provide any calories at all. A study to find the best sources of valuable fiber came up with a listing in this order: mangoes, carrots, apples, Brussels sprouts, eggplants, spring cabbages, oranges, pears, green beans, lettuce, winter cabbages, peas, onions, celery, cucumbers, broad beans, tomatoes, cauliflower, bananas, rhubarb, potatoes, and turnips. As much as possible, eat fruit skins for their fiber content, except where you know the fruit has been sprayed. The skins may provide needed fiber, but pesticide residues are also concentrated in skins.

Where Will it All Get You?

If you follow the dietary advice we have offered up to this point of this chapter, you will be eating less meat and eating more vegetables which are loaded in fiber. You will also be eating more complex carbohydrates like whole grains, which are high in fiber, and lastly you will be severely curtailing your intake of sugar, which has nothing good, but plenty of calories.

What we would like to do here is give you a cut-and-dried prescription of what to eat to maintain optimum health — unfortunately no one can give you such a prescription. All we can do is give you some guidelines of what to watch out for, and what to strive for. Luckily, we can give you an excellent barometer of your diet. There is one mechanism that all your food must pass through, and it will very accurately tell you if you are eating too much or too little of anything. That mechanism is your body, and the gauge to watch is your weight.

Your weight represents a balance between the calories you eat and the calories you expend. It is very cut and dried: if you eat more calories than you use, you will gain weight, and if you use more calories than you eat, you will lose weight. One pound of human fat is equal to 3,500 calories. If you use 500 more calories a week than you eat, you will lose a pound a week. Likewise if you eat 500 more calories (a cup of peanuts has 800 calories) a week than you use, you will gain a pound a week.

Refer back to chapter 2 and you'll see that research has found for good health you should garner your calories from the three energy-providing foods at the ratio of: 55 to 65 percent carbohydrates, 20 to 30 percent fats; and about 10 percent protein. However, it would be almost impossible for you to translate this formula into everyday usage. Some foods are both fat and protein, other are fat and carbohydrate, and some are all three. So what are you to do?

The best way to control what you eat is to alter your eating pattern to conform to what we know are acceptable levels. Thus you should make it a point to start off at least one meal a day with a huge salad. Prepare it from the greatest variety of fresh greens and other vegetables you can find or grow: kale, lettuce, green peppers, cucumbers, tomatoes, onions, scallions, radishes, watercress, parsley, garlic, etc. You'll be pleasantly surprised at how much better salads taste when you add lots of the fresh crisp sprouts we show you how to grow in chapter 8. Use a polyunsaturated oil in your dressing and use the smallest amount you can, relying on herbs to add zest to the dressing.

Don't make the mistake of forcing the salad to compete with the rest of the meal. Serve it as a first course, without any other food on the table. Allow plenty of time for everyone to enjoy the salad. Keep the main course warm in the kitchen while enjoying the salad.

After eating a salad, you should feel mildly stuffed. Then you will probably do best to eat about half of what you normally would consume in the way of steak, pork chops, and other meats, which as we have seen are high in saturated fats and calories. For dessert have something that is natural, like fruit. Stay away from sugary concoctions that serve only to add calories and feed tooth decay.

What this all boils down to is the original premise we set up for an improved diet: variety and moderation are the keys to a good diet; and the less processed your foods are, the better they are for you.

To the greatest extent possible, eat foods that are whole and fresh. By eating the widest possible variety of fruits, vegetables, grains, and legumes, you will not only guard against being deficient in any nutrient, but you will add three items the American diet is sorely lacking: interest, appeal, and variety.

Mark Bricklin, editor of *Prevention* magazine, has summed up our approach to better eating in a sentence: "Spend twice as much money as you ordinarily do in the produce section of the supermarket, half as much in the meat department, and not one cent in the canned goods, deli, or dessert sections."

Using what we have just covered and information in upcoming chapters, you will be able to set up a food budget. If you carefully control the amounts and kinds of food you buy and grow, you will likewise be controlling the types of foods you eat. If it isn't in the house, you won't be able to eat it — keep that in mind when you reach for a bag of candy or fried snacks next time you're in the supermarket.

To set up your food budget, use the tables in chapters 4 and 5 to find out how much vegetables and meat a person or family needs per year. Armed with these figures, decide how much you can produce yourself. Then take into account what items you can do without, or what can be replaced by something you can easily produce, like sprouts for example. In chapter 7 you will use charts explaining how much canned goods you will need and how much to freeze to get through the year. By combining all these charts, you will be able to decide how large a garden you need, and what size livestock operation you will need.

Your final food budget will be arrived at by considering changes you wish to make in your diet and arriving at how much food you will need for a year. Once you have this total, decide how much of it you can produce yourself and how much of it you will still have to buy. Then decide how much of your food supply you will be able to process yourself. The final conclusion you reach should tell you how much meat and vegetables you need to produce, how much canning and freezing you will be doing, and how much food you will be buying.

Making Good Foods Even Better

Because you will be eating a great deal more fresh fruit and vegetables, as well as grains, you should know how to handle them in the kitchen, for not only are they the best foods for you, they are also most easily damaged by mishandling.

The simplest way of avoiding processed food, sugared food, and fiberless food is to eat raw food. Raw food is often better for you than cooked food. Good health pioneers going back centuries have followed a raw-food route to improved well-being. They have preached against the "incineration" of food on stoves and in ovens and have lived long and happy lives munching away on raw fruits and vegetables, raw nuts and  grains, and drinking raw milk. Raw meat and eggs may pose some health problems, so they generally should not be eaten raw.

Aside from the health issue, there's also the sheer pleasure of eating unsprayed raw vegetables right in the garden, or plucking and munching ripe fruit from your own trees. Nothing can match the flavor thrills of such alfresco eating. Eating the first asparagus spears that poke their heads through the earth in early spring is a joy too few of us get to enjoy.

The gardening season should be one raw-food snack after another. The tiniest, tenderest peas are eaten quickly to regain the sensation of their incomparable flavor. Early radishes are quickly nibbled, right where they grow. String beans are great raw if eaten young enough, and what better way is there to eat a tomato than right from the vine or an ear of corn as it's plucked from the stalk on a summer afternoon?

Washing And Cooking To Preserve Nutrients

Vegetables that are soaked in hot or cold water instead of quickly rinsed will be drained of the water-soluble vitamins and such minerals as iron, copper, potassium, magnesium, and manganese. Even nutrients that are not soluble in water can drift into the water in which vegetables are soaked if the cell walls are broken by chopping the food into small pieces. Wash vegetables quickly under running water. Spinach, kale, lettuce, and other greens should be whirled dry in a salad basket. Water left on the leaves dissolves vitamin C, natural sugars, and some mineral compounds. Wash peas and lima beans before — not after — shelling them.

Cut vegetables if you wish, but do it after they are rinsed. Remember that the outer parts of leafy vegetables, while coarser, contain higher concentrations of vitamins and minerals than the more tender leaves and buds they protect, and the leafy portions contain higher concentrations than the fibrous stalk and midribs.

Trimming broccoli, head lettuce, and cabbage usually involves discarding the more nutritious parts. Though often discarded, broccoli leaves are edible and have about 20 times as much vitamin A value as the tender stalks and several times as much as the flowers. If broccoli and cauliflower leaves are tender enough to use when the vegetable reaches the kitchen, they should be chilled and kept moist until they can be used. In lettuce, the dark-green outer leaves are as much as 30 times as high in vitamin A as the bleached inner leaves. Since they might amount to as much as 10 percent of the weight of the whole, discarding these dark green portions might mean the loss of three-fourths of the vitamin A value of the whole head.

Cutting or shredding foods exposes more food surface to oxygen, an element that destroys vitamins. Because cut pieces cook more quickly than if left whole, the adverse effects of extra surface exposure may be offset, at least partly, by the shortened cooking period. Fewer nutrients escape if long vegetables, like carrots, are cut up lengthwise instead of crosswise before washing.

In human history, the taming of fire is generally considered to be one of mankind's greatest steps forward. In her fine book *Food in History,* Reay Tannahill points out that people in prefire Neanderthal times lived short lives. "Less than half the population survived to the age of 20, and 9 out of every 10 remaining adults died before 40," she says.

Fire did several important things for the food of primitive people. First, it cut back on the parasite problem. Cave people lived close together and knew nothing of the value of sanitation. They probably washed seldom, and didn't know how easily intestinal parasites and other disease organisms could be passed from person to person on dirty food.

Fire was an almost-perfect sanitizing agent. Even light cooking of food greatly reduces the hazard of transmitting disease. No wonder life became longer and more pleasant after fire was discovered.

Applying heat to some foods did another beneficial thing. Many foods are inedible when raw, but are fine fare when cooked briefly. Cooking removes harmful oxylates from such food as beets and rhubarb. Favism substances in certain beans are removed by cooking. Raw soybeans contain a substance which prevents the absorption of tryptophan, one of the essential amino acids. Cook soybeans and that inhibitor disappears, making the protein in them easily absorbed.

There is one other important advantage of cooking — aside from the fact that it makes some foods taste so good. We are monogastric, meaning that we have but one stomach. Humans simply don't have the gastrointestinal mechanism that will allow us to digest extremely rough and fibrous food like grass, cornstalks, and so forth. Cows need their multiple stomachs to do that, and even then they have to chew their cud thoroughly.

Cooking certain rough foods, like corn and grains in particular, allows our stomachs to absorb some elements easily that would otherwise not pass through. Without the aid of heat, we would cut ourselves off from rice, for example, one of the most widely used of all foods, and bread would be an impossibility.

Cooking in water will certainly do much more to leach out vitamins and minerals than will soaking in water. And the more water used in cooking, the more nutrients lost to this liquid. It follows, then, that the amount of water added to any vegetable when cooking should be as little as possible. If your cooked vegetables come out of the pot waterlogged and soggy, you'd almost do better, from a nutritional standpoint, to throw the vegetables on the compost pile and drink the water in which they were cooked!

There is no reason to cook any vegetable in more than one-half cup of water. Wait until the water is rapidly boiling, and then take the vegetable out of the refrigerator, wash it briefly, and add it to the boiling water. If the vegetable is frozen, don't defrost it before cooking; water-soluble nutrients will be lost during thawing. Cover the pot tightly with a heavy lid so that the steam doesn't raise the lid, and reduce the heat to a simmer.

Rapid boiling doesn't cook vegetables any quicker than slow boiling because the highest temperature attainable under atmospheric pressure is 212°F., the boiling point of water at sea level. Most vegetables will be done in six to eight minutes this way with a minimum loss of vitamins and minerals.

Make use of whatever water is left in the pot. Put it in soups or gravies, use it to cook rice, or feed it to your dog; do anything with it but throw it away.

Vegetables can be cooked more rapidly in a pressure cooker. A pressure greater than atmospheric pressure can be reached inside the cooker. Consequently a cooking temperature higher than 212°F. can be reached, and food will cook faster. Providing you keep an eye on the cooking time, pressure-cooking vegetables is a good way of preserving food value because little water is needed and foods cook much more rapidly.

The Chinese have perhaps the best approach of all to cooking food. The French call it sautéing and use a heavy skillet, and the Chinese call it stir-frying and use a wok. Their method is to cut food into small pieces before cooking, then use high heat for a brief time. The round- bottomed wok is their basic utensil, and almost everything is stir-fried quickly. Chinese food is still crisp and vitamin-rich inside. Boiling vegetables and then throwing away the water is a method they would never even consider.

Vegetables can also be cooked in the top of a double boiler. Put a few tablespoons of water in the top of a double boiler and bring it to a boil over direct heat. Add the vegetables, cover, and steam for about a minute to quickly destroy enzymes. Then place the top section with the vegetables over boiling water to finish cooking.

Vegetables shouldn't be cooked in water that has had baking soda or salt added. Some French cooks add baking soda to the water when cooking green vegetables to prevent them from darkening. Although this procedure might keep vegetables bright in color, it practically doubles the rate of loss of vitamin B. Salting vegetables in cooking draws off extra moisture which carries away vitamins, minerals, sugars, and flavor.

Don't cook more vegetables than you think will be eaten at one time. Cooked vegetables show losses of vitamin C that progress with the length of time they are kept. According to the U.S. Department of Agriculture, in the *Yearbook of Agriculture* (1959), vegetables have about three-fourths as much vitamin C after a day in the refrigerator as when freshly cooked. They have about two-thirds as much after two days.

Reheating takes another toll of vitamin C, so that cooked vegetables reheated after two or three days in the refrigerator contain only one-third to one-half as much of this vitamin as when freshly prepared, says the USDA.

The vitamins and minerals in vegetables — all foods, for that matter — have four enemies: heat, light, oxygen, and water. The good cook who is as concerned about the food value of meals as their taste and appearance will subject food to these four elements only when necessary, and then only for as brief a time as possible.

By taking more care in the preparation of your foods, selecting foods carefully, rethinking your menu planning, and avoiding those foods you now know are bad for you, you will benefit in three ways: you will feel better; you will probably eat for less money; and meals will begin to assume more of a creative air instead of being a chore. Eating can be one of the most rewarding experiences of life, if only we let it be.

Your enjoyment of home cooked meals will double or triple if you grew the vegetable or raised the meat yourself. Nothing is more natural than tending your garden, picking the bounty of your work, and preparing it for your family and friends. So roll up your sleeves and let's get into the business of producing part or all of your food supply.

Chapter 4

Growing
Your Own

Home food production — that's what this part of the book is all about. And it just might be the most important part of the whole book; at least it might be for many people. Why? Because when you have a hand (or two) in the production of the food you eat, you're getting right down to the basics. You're working from the beginning of the production line, helping to create something from basic raw materials. You're planting seeds and multiplying them maybe a thousandfold. Think what this means in terms of savings at the store, the purity and quality of the food you eat, reduced demand on natural resources, and reduced demands on food supplies around the world.

There are really two groups of food you can produce at home: animal products and vegetable products. Each group involves a different kind of planning and level of commitment and a different set of skills and knowledge, so it's best if we deal with them in separate chapters. First we'll look at vegetables.

Growing vegetable products is possible for most everyone with even a little bit of land (or rooftop or sunny porch). The returns from a garden can be terrific. The food you get from it can be worth many times the money, energy, and time that went into preparing, maintaining, and harvesting it. A great many people who've never gardened before are beginning to realize just this. And so are one-time leisure gardeners who now look at gardening as the way to food production. Gardens have become bigger and more productive, and gardeners are now taking their hobby more seriously. Today's vegetable gardens are earning the place that victory gardens enjoyed during World War II; they're at the center of self sufficiency and food security.

In this chapter we will be limiting our discussion to vegetable growing only. While many people raise their own grains and dried beans, that requires additional space and equipment. For those with the space for such an undertaking, there is ample information available; for starters, consult the books listed in the bibliography at the end of the book.

Gardening is a low-input, soft technology in that it requires human labor and cooperation with the land, not massive machines and use of fossil fuels to force the land to do the unnatural. While large-scale agriculture is currently being damned as an energy user instead of being an energy producer, gardening is just about at the top of the efficiency scale. By working with nature and using a minimal amount of inputs, you convert solar energy into an abundance of energy in the form of food for you and your family. Organic gardening doesn't depend on chemical fertilizers and pesticides; instead you produce most of your own fertilizer from the waste your household produces and from animal manures, and you rely on improved methods of planting and good soil health to keep insects under control. Organic gardening is the most natural relationship you can have with the earth. You work with nature to provide food to support life.

Organic Gardening and Farming magazine polled 20 gardeners (Table 4-1) to find their yearly gardening expenses and value of the food they grow, and it discovered that these good gardeners saved on the average about $300 a year. The National Garden Bureau designed an average vegetable garden for a family of four and calculated that it would save a family $350 a year.

And gardens will become increasingly important as money-savers as food prices rise. As Robert Rodale explained in his June 1974 OGF editorial, "Organic Living Helps You Fight Inflation," home-grown food is inflation-proof food. If the price of store-bought vegetables goes up, that only means that the vegetables you grow yourself are worth more. They certainly won't cost you more to grow (except for maybe a slight increase in the cost of seed), especially if you garden organically, because you don't have to buy more fertilizers (which are also becoming more expensive as food costs rise). The wastes that your family and its land produce become the raw materials for your garden, the only cost being your own labor. And an organic garden is easier and less expensive to work than a chemically fertilized one. Humus-rich soil is productive beyond the level of a regular garden, and natural approaches to the control of destructive insect and disease levels can mean less money spent for expensive pest sprays and dusts.

TABLE 4–1

Average Cost-Value of 20 Organic Gardens*

Yearly garden expenses	Value of food grown	No. in family	Percentage of food grown
$54	$538	3–4 people	60 percent

*The gardens ranged from $100-value kitchen gardens to $2,000 whoppers that feed a large family and more. Eliminating the gardens over $1,000 leaves an average food saving of about $300.

The Importance Of Advanced Planning

It's how and when a garden is planted that contributes most to food savings, and the actual quantity and quality of the harvest. Many gardens, especially beginners' gardens, are haphazardly planted. Because of this, the yield is not what it could be, and much of the garden space is wasted. A well-planted and well-cared for small garden will outyield a poorly run, large plot. Since the small plot will require less work, that's what you want to shoot for; to get the most vegetables possible out of the least amount of space.

There are few things as enjoyable as planning a garden. You start off by ordering seed catalogs. Soon you'll be busily flipping through them and finding literally dozens of varieties you "have always wanted to try." Go ahead and do some window shopping; learn what each company offers, and who seems to specialize in what vegetables, disease resistant varieties, short season varieties, and who has the best selection of each vegetable. Since you'll be doing this during the dead of winter, enjoy yourself — take your time.

Before ordering seeds, decide what foods you and your family eat and make a list. At this stage of the game, you are only interested in what foods you want to grow, not how much or where to grow them. Spend a little time to make sure your list is complete. Don't forget to include those foods you like but seldom get to enjoy due to their cost in the store; your garden will provide these treats for next to nothing. Once your list is complete, set it aside.

Next, carefully analyze and determine how much garden you can handle. This requires two measurements: the first is how much space you have that you are willing to put into garden, and the second is how much energy you are willing to put into gardening. Most people end up with about two acres of space and one-quarter acre of ambition. Once you decide how much work you are willing to do and how much space you have, you will probably have to compromise a bit to decide just how large a garden you end up with. Remember, you can start small and always expand. The thing you want to avoid is having more garden than you can take care of. Remember when computing your estimated work load that not only does the garden take work, it makes it. When you decide how many tomato plants you want to weed and stake, don't forget that you will also be canning the tomatoes when they ripen.

Now comes the hard part. You have to combine the decisions you reached above and decide what type of garden you will have. There are three possibilities.

Three Types Of Gardens

1. A garden to produce all your vegetables year-round. This would quite naturally be the largest of the three possibilities. It takes a lot of work to prepare and to maintain, but you should get enough food from it to see you through the year for both fresh foods and foods to store over the winter. Unless you have lots of mulch or all day to work in the garden, you will want to plan your rows wide enough for mechanical cultivation. In planning such a garden don't forget to grow enough fresh foods to get you through the early and late growing seasons. The longer you eat fresh from this garden, the less you will have to store.

2. A garden to produce selected vegetables for storage and the rest for fresh food. Again, keep the fresh garden going as late into fall as possible. You have to be selective with this garden and plant vegetables to store that go along with your storage areas. If you have a freezer, plant items that freeze well; if you have good root storage capabilities, plant those crops. If you don't want to pressure can vegetables, don't plant more than you can eat fresh or frozen. Make some parts of your garden do double duty by removing early maturing crops and quickly replanting the area for fall fresh foods or storing crops.

3. The fresh food garden or salad garden. This garden requires that you plant something every couple of weeks all season long to maintain top-quality fresh vegetables. You should experiment with small plantings of exotic vegetables you have never tried before. Actually, this garden could be incorporated in either of the two above gardens.

Once you have decided what type of garden you will have, it's time to put the whole mess together by deciding how much of what you will be getting from your garden. It's hard to give any exact figures in this area. The yield you get per row, the amount your family eats, the method of storage you use, even the amount of company you have for dinner, all are variables that can't be taken into account.

The best we can hope for here is an estimate. By keeping close records from year to year, you eventually will be able to know pretty well how much food your family uses and what type of garden you have to plant to meet that need. But for now, look at Table 4-2 and you will get an idea of what one Pennsylvania family of four puts away for the winter. You have to realize that the Bubels have an excellent food production system. They have a large garden, they are good gardeners, and they have a complete food storage system. You probably won't be able to match this system for quite a few years, if ever.

With the Bubels' food storage program in mind, consult Table 4-12 at the end of this chapter for estimated vegetable yields and space requirements. When noting the space requirements, remember that there are many ways to cut down on these estimates, and we will show you several space-saving measures later in this chapter. With your list of the vegetables you want to grow, write down from Table 4-12 how much of each item you will need for your family and how much space it will take to grow that much. Don't forget to add a little extra for crop failure, giving away, eating fresh, or insect damage. Add to that list the vegetables you eat fresh, and you should have a final listing of what you have to get from your garden during the year to meet your food production goals.

Armed with a complete list of what and how much of each vegetable you want to grow, your next step is to get some graph paper and draw up your garden. Don't be cheap with the space; go ahead and design your dream garden first. Then slowly begin the process of whittling down your plans till you reach a level you honestly feel you can achieve. All plans should include such things as where to put the garden, what to plant in each row, how much space to allocate, what shape it will be, and the different succession plantings.

The nine points below should be considered while drawing a garden plan, according to Robert Stevens, extension horticulturist at the University of Delaware:

1. Perennial crops such as asparagus, strawberries, and rhubarb should be located at one side of the garden.

2. Tall-growing crops, such as corn, must be kept away from small crops like beets and carrots to avoid shading.

3. Provide for succession crops. In this way, space for spring crops, which will be harvested early, may be used again for later crops. Examples: tomatoes after radishes; cucumbers after spinach.

4. Early planted, fast-growing, quick-maturing crops should be grouped together. Examples: radishes, lettuce, early cabbage, scallions, etc.

5. Provide plenty of vegetables for canning, freezing, and storing.

6. Do not overplant new varieties, vegetables which the family does not like, or too much of any one vegetable at one time.

7. Rows should follow across the slope (on the contour) in hilly areas.

8. Make sure the plan provides the best spacing between rows for the method of cultivation that you intend to use (hand, roto-tiller, tractor, horse).

9. Run rows north and south if possible to prevent plants from shading one another.

Before you reach your final garden plan, read the following sections on ways to increase the efficiency of your garden. These are all simple techniques that for the most part are just commonsense. In most cases they are old-fashioned ideas that

TABLE 4–2

Amounts to Store

For Nancy and Michael Bubel and their two teenagers, plus a good many guests, they stock their cellar with the following approximate amounts of food.

Canned Foods

Tomatoes . . . 100 qts

Fruits . . . 150–200 qts

Kraut . . . 15–20 qts

Beets (pickled) . . . 20–30 qts

Catsup . . . 25 pts

Pickled cabbage . . . 10 qts

Applesauce . . . 30 qts

Dilled beans . . . 40 pts

Green tomato pickles . . . 25 qts.

Relish . . . 20 pts.

Chutney . . . 10 qts.

Miscellaneous pickles . . . 35–50 pts.

Chow chow . . . 20 pts.

Cherry pepper pickles . . . 30 pts.

Zucchini pickles . . . 20 pts.

Apple butter . . . 30 pts.

Root Cellar Vegetables

Onions . . . 2–3 bu.

Carrots . . . ½–1 bu.

Cabbage . . . 2 bu.

Turnips . . . ½–1 bu.

Potatoes . . . 3–4 bu.

Rutabagas . . . ½–1 bu.

Beets . . . 1 bu.

Kraut . . . 20 lbs.

Garlic . . . 3–4 lbs.

Pumpkins and squash . . . about 20

Frozen Foods (1 pound packages)

Peas . . . 25 packages

Sugar peas . . . 55–70 packages

Snap beans . . . 35–50 packages

Patty pan squash . . . 15–25 packages

Corn . . . 35–50 packages

Greens . . . 15–25 packages

Cooked sweet potatoes . . . 15 packages

Green soybeans . . . 35–50 packages

Broccoli . . . 35–70 packages

Cauliflower . . . 15 packages

Peppers, cut up . . . 30–40 half-cup packages

Dried

Seasoning herbs . . . 8–10 pint jars

Mint . . . 2 gallon jars

Dried comfrey . . . 1–2 gallon jars

Celery tops . . . ½–1 gallon jar

Soybeans . . . 10–15 lbs.

Other

Sunflower seeds . . . 1 bu.

Nuts . . . Hickory, 1 bu.

Black walnut . . . 2 bu.

English walnut . . . small amounts, tree is young

Left in the Ground Under Mulch

Carrots . . . 1–2 bu.

Turnips . . . ½ bu.

Salsify . . . ½ bu.

Parsnips . . . 1 bu.

fell from favor when everyone started to believe a home garden should look like the fields of a 300-acre farm. When you take care of plants by hand, you can tolerate much more congestion in the garden. Try to have as many plants growing in the garden space as you can, or weeds will usually be a problem. Nature intended to have things growing on the soil; it's up to you whether you grow things you can eat or not.

Succession Planting

Without a doubt the easiest way to make your garden more productive is to plant twice as much without digging up twice as large a garden. Most people plant their garden on a sunny spring day, water and weed it occasionally, and harvest as the vegetables mature. As many beginning gardeners find out, the spring planting gets rank, tough, and seedy long about midseason and finishes up in the fall just about useless.

That's wrong; you should be planting in the garden almost continuously. There is nothing worse than spending your time preparing good garden soil and then only using it for one crop and having most of your garden either dead, gone to seed, picked, or in heavy weeds by the end of August.

In its simplest sense, succession planting is designing your garden so that as soon as one crop is finished, another goes in the same space. A spring planting should be only the beginning — with succession plantings continuing right through to September for vegetables that will finish the year in cold frames. If you plan right, the garden will be full of fresh, young vegetables at *all* seasons to bring double and triple yields.

If your succession sowings are to be successful, you need top quality, rich garden soil, because two and three crops a year take a lot of nutrients from the soil. To keep the soil working in the latter part of the season, organic gardeners have developed these techniques:

Some enterprising gardeners continuously bury kitchen garbage along the rows throughout the year, maintaining a fresh supply of organic matter for soil bacteria to thrive on. Tests have shown that plant nutrients are released as soil bacteria decompose organic matter into humus, and so a good, thick mulch — à la Ruth Stout — not only helps with the weeds and holds in water, but feeds the soil bacteria and thus the plants at the same time.

Other techniques include watering regularly with manure tea, dipped from a tub or barrel holding a 50–50 mixture of manure and water; side dressing plants about July 10–15 with freshly made compost; and watering with a fish emulsion and seaweed solution.

To plan your garden for succession plantings, you can leave spaces to be planted later in the season, and you can schedule early crops like peas, spinach, lettuce, radishes, and cress to be out of the garden by the third week in June so the space can be used for new, fresh crops.

Here's how Raymond Poincelot of Milford, Connecticut, describes his practices: "I use closer-than-recommended spacing and a fence for the climbing beans, squash, and cukes to conserve space. I never leave any empty spaces for long. For example, I follow radishes by snap beans, then by rutabagas, and I use early, midseason, and late mixtures to extend yields. Some plants, such as cukes, can be babied along to yield throughout the season with several plantings."

Notice that he started with radishes, which are out in a month. Then came beans, a legume that adds nitrogen to the soil and replenishes any nutrient losses to the radishes. With the soil replenished, the space is ready for a root crop or another type of heavy feeder like a rutabaga. The rutabaga also is a good last planting because of its hardiness and keeping qualities during the winter. Remember that the last planting should be done with winter storage in mind — whether freezing, canning, drying, or storing in a root cellar.

Derek Fell, former director of the National Garden Bureau, has devised a visual planning method to help beginners get the most from their garden through succession planting. With the varieties down the left side, and the months of the year across the top, all you have to do is fill in the planting dates and harvesting dates for all the vegetables you want to grow. Wherever one is harvested before or at the same time another is planted, you can combine the two in the same row. For example, the first planting of loose-leaf lettuce is usually out of the garden by mid-June. At this time you can use that same space to plant beans, beets, broccoli, Brussels sprouts, carrots, cauliflower, more lettuce, parsley, peas, radish, spinach, or turnips. Table 4-3 shows Fell's chart.

You can use Tables 4-4 and 4-5 to do the same for your garden. "Days to maturity" are listed, and from them you can figure about when you'll turn that crop under in favor of a

TABLE 4-3

Visual Planning Chart

SOLID LINE ━━━━━━ PLANT / BROKEN LINE ----------- HARVEST

Times are approximate and will vary according to location.

VARIETY	Jan. Feb.	Mar.	Apr.	May	June	July	Aug.	Sept.	Oct.	Nov.	Dec.
Beans, Snap (50-60 days)											
Beets (55-60 days)											
Broccoli (60-80 days)											
Brussels Sprouts (90-100 days)*											
Cabbage (70-80 days)*											
Cantaloupe (80-90 days)											
Carrots (70-80 days)											
Cauliflower (60-80 days)*											
Celery (120-140 days)											
Corn (80-90 days)											
Cucumbers (60-70 days)											
Eggplant (70-80 days)*											
Leeks (130-140 days)											
Lima Beans (75-90 days)											
Looseleaf Lettuce (50-60 days)											
Okra (60-70 days)											
Onions (100-120 days)											
Parsley (80-90 days)											
Parsnips (100-120 days)											
Peas (65-70 days)											
Peppers (70-80 days)*											
Pumpkin (100-120 days)											
Radish (25-30 days)											
Spinach (50-60 days)											
Squash, Summer (55-65 days)											
Squash, Winter (90-110 days)											
Swiss Chard (60-70 days)											
Tomatoes (70-80 days)*											
Turnips (45-60 days)											
Watermelon (75-90 days)											

*Days from transplanting

By Derek Fell, from *How to Plant a Vegetable Garden*

fresher one. Your finished listing should resemble Table 4-6.

It's a good idea to leave a few unplanted places throughout the garden after the first spring planting. A cold spring might delay the maturity of vegetables you had planned to take out.

Tables 4-4 and 4-5 were compiled from the experience of about 50 gardeners *Organic Gardening and Farming* questioned. The dates are the average dates when these gardeners got their vegetables in. Your own garden may vary from these, but the early and late dates shouldn't be exceeded unless you are using coldframes, hotbeds, or other season-extenders.

The dates given are for the area from Virginia north to southern New England, and from the Atlantic west to Nebraska. If your region has colder or warmer temperatures than the average for this section, you can adjust the dates forward or backward accordingly. The last frost date in this area runs from about May 10 to May 25; the first frost from October 1 to October 20. Check your county extension agent or find the frost dates for your locale on Figures 4-1 and 4-2.

The succession game is made more interesting by the fact that different crops use different elements in the soil. Dovetailing the demands of the first crops with the requirements of the second has all the strategic challenge of a good chess game. For example, root crops use up potash, so the most sophisticated succession plan would replace carrots or beets with a leafy top crop, rather than another root crop. Leafy crops, on the other hand, need a lot of nitrogen. For that reason they should not succeed each other. Lettuce or late cabbage planted after peas will thrive on the nitrogen the peas have added to the soil. So will corn.

Try to take early and late frost dates from Figures 4-1 and 4-2 into account when planning your succession plantings. The earliest, hardiest vegetables — peas, radishes, lettuce, scallions — can be planted as soon as the soil can be worked, without much attention to frost. Early cabbage can stand light frost. Even sunflower seedlings are surprisingly hardy, especially before their true leaves appear.

At the end of the season, estimate the date of the first fall frost and count back from there, allowing a few extra days for an early sneak frost and maybe another two or three for the seedman's optimism.

When you plant seeds later in the season, treat them a bit differently than you do in March and April. For one thing, plant just a bit more deeply, raking the sides of the furrow down over the seed rather than just sprinkling seed on top.

Anything sown after mid-June usually needs a bit of watering to help hasten germination. Summer showers can't be counted on, and when short, they may not soak the ground as spring rains do. So sprinkle water down the row directly on the seeds, then pull dry soil over them. This prevents caking of the soil on top, and puts the moisture where it's needed most. It would also help to pull a loose covering of fine dried grass clippings or light straw over the newly seeded row.

Interplanting And
Companion Planting

Two gardening techniques that often are confused are interplanting and companion planting. Both techniques should be included in your garden plans before arriving at your final plan.

In essence, interplanting is planting two or more crops in the same space at the same time. For instance, *squash, corn, and beans*. This is an old-time favorite grouping with some exquisite variations. Any of the cucurbits — squash, cucumbers, pumpkins, melons — will run along the corn rows, shading out weeds. Pole beans planted after the corn has emerged will use the stalks to climb on. If you're using a winter squash in the rows and a pole bean for dried beans, you can let the whole shebang dry out after the frosts, harvesting cured squashes, dried beans, and dried corn, all ready for storage and all from the same piece of land.

A basic fact about intercropping is that any one crop produces less in an intercropped plot than it would if it had the whole plot to itself. This is why "modern" experts are opposed to traditional intercropping. These experts are not interested in publicizing the other basic fact: An intercropped plot of compatible plants produces a greater total yield than the yield for any single crop. For example, in a 1974 test, a plot of kidney beans alone gave 379 pods, a monocropped plot of corn the same size gave 40 cobs of corn, while an intercropped plot the same size gave 213 bean pods plus 28 cobs of corn. If the intercropped plot had been twice as big, and thus equal in area to the two monocropped plots, it would have yielded 426 bean pods plus 56 corn cobs. The same experiment repeated in the summer of 1975 gave even more favorable intercropped yields.

TABLE 4–4

Succession Planting Plan

First Planting Group	Early Spring Planting	Onion sets, onion seed, radishes, lettuce, peas, spinach
Second Planting Group	Mid-Spring Planting	Early potatoes, carrots, beets, parsnips, chard, New Zealand spinach, transplants of early cabbage, broccoli, cauliflower
Third Planting Group	Late Spring Planting	Tomatoes, snap and bush beans, cucumbers, summer squash, winter squash Succession of sweet corn—each variety blocked out in several short rows to insure good pollination
Fourth Planting Group	Early Summer Planting	Main crop of potatoes Late Cabbage, broccoli, Brussels sprouts Late planting of snap beans
Fifth Planting Group	Mid-Summer Planting	Fall crops of carrots, beets, turnips, rutabagas, kohlrabi, lettuce, radishes, spinach, chard

Interplanting can double and triple the yield from your garden plot by saving space. Combine this with succession planting, already described, which can also double and triple yields by using time wisely and you'll get unbelievable production from a small plot.

According to *The Scientific Basis of Companion Planting As A Means of Insect Control* by Helen S. Raisen:

There is a process of coevolution between plants and insects. Plants respond to the pressure of being consumed by insects by producing poisonous compounds. Insects respond to the pressure of being poisoned by developing the ability to distinguish poisonous plants from those that are food, metabolize the poison, or even find a way to keep the poison harmlessly isolated within their bodies — which is a way of making themselves poisonous to predators.

Through this coevolution, plants developed the ability to produce secondary plant substances for defense and insects evolved to find their specific food plants with the aid of chemical cues which repelled or attracted them.

Many insects find their food through chemicals produced by their host plant. If plants of the same species are clustered together, the chemical signal will be much stronger; therefore, more insects will find their host. Also if an insect is moving about from one plant to another, the closer together its hosts are, the easier they will be to find and the less energy will be spent in searching for food. These factors would tend to lead to larger build-ups of insect populations on more homogenous plantings. Companion planting, by making the field or garden more heterogenous and diverse, would tend to obstruct insect host feeding and keep insect populations lower. Furthermore, if the companion plant has some repelling properties toward certain insect pests, the effect of decreasing pest populations will be even larger.

The insect repellent properties of the strong essential oils in herbs and various weeds have been used in gardens for centuries. Over the years, gardeners have learned to plant herbs with their vegetables, discovering specific herbs to repel pests that attack specific vegetables.

When planting a companion garden, it's good to get the companions right in there together. One way is to plant zig-zag rows, with the zigs and zags of the beets and onions tucked into one another. Another method is to use the techniques of intercropping, and plant several companions in the same row. You'll find that your companionate garden breaks down into loosely defined "sections." The corn, squash, cucumbers, pumpkins, etc., might be in one section. The strawberries, spinach, beans, etc., might be in another. Paths are best between these sections, rather than between companions. Plant borders of wormwood, yarrow, and marigolds. Sprinkle these and the other insect-repelling herbs and flowers among the vegetables, checking Tables 4-6 and 4-7 to make sure you're not near a foe.

Make up your own companionate garden by using the tables. Just remember that while your cucumbers like your peas, and your peas like your beans, and your beans like your potatoes, your potatoes just don't like cucumbers.

Even if you think companion planting is for the birds, you would be well advised to consult Tables 4-6 and 4-7 to make sure you do not intercrop vegetables that do not do well together. Although they cannot explain why, most seed companies will tell you on the seed packet or in their catalog that some varieties just don't perform well when planted near other varieties. Companion planting takes this one step further and concentrates on getting beneficial relationships together.

Here are some favorite interplanting combinations:

Beets and kohlrabi. The beets grow low and the kohlrabi grows high, and together they fill a space that would have been used for only one or the other.

Cabbages, tomatoes, and peppers. These are frequently interplanted because gardeners report they don't compete with one another. We'd advise a midsummer feeding, since all feed heavily on soil nutrients. This combination can really save space.

Lettuce, onions, and carrots. Easy on the lettuce seed in this "salad sowing." Just a few plants give quite a bit of lettuce, the onion reaches above the big, loose lettuce leaves, and the wavy carrot tops get plenty of sun and help shade the tender lettuce in midsummer.

Carrots and radishes. The fast-growing radishes break up the soil and mark the rows for the fine, slow-growing carrot seeds. By the time the carrot roots need room, the radishes are up and out of the rows. By planting the two together the radishes are able to help the carrot seeds grow and two crops are grown in the space normally reserved for one.

Climbing cucumbers and sunflowers. Japanese long pickling cucumbers love to climb and dangle their fruits. Sunflowers — and even okra — are good support plants. Make sure the supports have grown up and away from the ground before planting the quick-growing cukes, or the vines could smother the supports.

These are only samples. Keep in mind that most vegetables get big in mid-August and can shade out other, low-growing crops. Figure the path of the sun at midsummer and plant your taller vegetables toward the back where their shade will fall on a path or out of the garden. And last, read the next section on companion planting.

TABLE 4–5

Succession Planting Information

Months in capital letters indicate major sowings

Vegetable	1st sowing	2nd	3rd
Beans (all types) 50–70 days (snap) 65–100 days (shell)	MAY 15	June 1	July 1
Beets 60 days	April 15	JULY 15	
Broccoli 60 days*	April 20	JUNE 20	
Brussels Sprouts 85 days*	April 20	JULY 1	
Cabbage 90 days*	April 20	JUNE 20	
Carrots 70 days	April 15	JULY 15	
Cauliflower 60 days*	May 1	JULY 1	
Celery 115–135 days*	March 1 (in flats)	May 15 (in garden)	
Chinese Cabbage 70 days	Aug. 1		
Corn 70–90 days	May 20	JUNE 10	July 1
Cucumbers 60 days	May 15	JUNE 1	July 15
Eggplant 70 days*	March 10–20 (in flats)	May 15 (in garden)	
Endive 90 days	July 10		
Garlic	APRIL 1	Oct. 1	
Jerusalem Artichokes 100–105 days	April 20		
Kale 60 days	July 20		
Kohlrabi 60 days	April 20	JULY 10	
Lettuce 45 days	APRIL 15– MAY 15	June 1	July 1

Succession Planting Information— Continued

Vegetable	1st sowing	2nd	3rd
Melons 90 days	May 1 (in flats)	June 1 (in garden)	
Okra 55 days	May 25		
Onions 100 days	MARCH 20– APRIL 20	July 1	
Parsley 80 days	April 10		
Parsnips 100 days	April 15	JULY 10	
Peas 70 days	April 1	APRIL 25	May 10
Peppers 75 days*	Feb. 20– April 15 (in flats)	May 15 (in garden)	
Potatoes 80–140 days	May 15		
Radishes 25 days	APRIL 15	May 15	AUG. 15
Rutabaga 90 days	July 15		
Salsify 120 days	April 20		
Spinach 50 days	APRIL 20	Aug. 1	AUG. 15
Summer Squash 50 days	MAY 15	Aug. 1	
Sunflowers 80 days	May 15		
Sweet Potatoes 140–150 days	JUNE 1		
Swiss Chard 60 days	APRIL 20	Aug. 1	
Tomatoes 70 days*	Feb. 20– April 15 (in flats)	May 15– June 10 (in garden)	
Turnips 50 days	April 1–15	AUG. 1	
Winter Squash 80–100 days	June 1	JUNE 15	

*Number of days to maturity from the time plants are set in the garden.

Dates given for the coles — cabbage, broccoli, Brussels sprouts, and cauliflower — are for sowing seed directly in the garden. They can also be started in flats about mid-March for transplanting to the garden in early May. For finding days to maturity from seed, add 30 days.

Companion Planting

Normally interplanting is used to increase the harvest by extending usable gardening space. However, there is another form of interplanting known as companion planting. When you practice companion planting, you are actually interplanting, but your concern is not so much for increased space as it is for improved performance and insect protection.

Very little is actually known about companion planting. Some of the very best gardeners view companion planting as a mixture of witchcraft and wishful thinking. But some equally good gardeners swear by it, and generations of folks close to the earth have noticed that certain plants seem to grow best when planted with certain others.

There is no explanation given for much of the information on companion plants. "Carrots and dill dislike each other," is all the usual treatment says. No one knows why tomatoes, asparagus, and parsley are supposed to make a companionate threesome. But the value of some types of companionate planting can be explained.

Plants with deep root systems enlarge the feeding area of plants with shallow systems by plunging through compacted subsoil and loosening the ground.

Mixtures of plants are more pest resistant than large blocks of a single crop. Richard Root and others, in research done at Cornell in 1972, found that interplanting can reduce insect problems by 50 percent. Seems the bugs can't smell their favorite vegetable as easily when its characteristic odor is lost in a mingle of other species' smells. "Smell" isn't the exact word — insects pick up on chemical signals from the plants with varying types of receptors — but "smell" probably comes closest.

Add to a good program of companionate vegetables a number of aromatic herbs, flowers, and even weeds, and your garden will mimic nature's mixed crops.

"The presence of companion herbs is thought to improve the growth and flavor of the vegetables and also to deter garden pests," says the Herb Society of America.

Catnip, they say, deters flea beetles, mint drives away the white cabbage butterfly, garlic can turn away the Japanese beetle, and so on. Table 4-7 lists herbs and their uses.

A wide variety of herbs belongs in every organic garden. It's only been since the Renaissance that flower, herb, and vegetable gardens have been generally separated. Before that, everything grew together, and we can believe they grew well.

The secret is to use repellent plants generously and have them started early, so they will be large enough to help ward off the first insect invasion of the season. Include these in your garden plan for sure.

MINTS rate high as insect chasers, and they're useful for flavorings and medicines, too. Peppermint and spearmint appear equally good for repelling flea beetles, cabbage butterflies, and others. Catnip is good also, and unlike most mints, it doesn't spread and become as weedy in the garden. Being taller it can extend its bug fighting powers farther. Unfortunately it is likely to attract all the neighborhood cats, who get quite delirious over it. Some gardeners prefer to stick with peppermint and spearmint for this reason, growing them in large pots or sunken tiles to keep them within bounds.

The ONION family discourages aphids. Plant chives, garlic, onions, and leeks among leafy vegetables like lettuce, spinach, and chard.

Most gardeners agree that MARIGOLDS head the list of flowers to scatter through the garden, with NASTURTIUMS running a close second. Neither will become weedy and both are killed by a light frost, so they can and should be used generously. The taller marigolds with real smelly foliage are best. Marigolds are an effective control for root nematodes. Nasturtiums ward off aphids and bugs that bother the cucurbits — pumpkins, squash, cucumbers, and melons.

PETUNIAS are another useful annual. Besides adding color to the bean patch, they help keep it insect-free.

SAGE, that old English herb brought over with the colonists, was an important plant in every garden in early times. They used it for flavoring and might or might not have known that it also kept away carrot flies and cabbage pests.

HORSERADISH, another vigorous growing herb, has been used effectively to repel potato bugs and other flying insects. Care has to be taken, though, that it doesn't spread throughout the garden. Planting on the edges of the garden works fairly well, but some growers prefer to plant it in tubs and set them generously around the potato patch.

TANSY works well as an insect repellent. Because it grows 4 or more feet tall, it is good in orchards. In early times it was often planted around the house to keep out ants, and dried tansy was kept in kitchen cupboards for the same purpose.

FIGURE 4-1

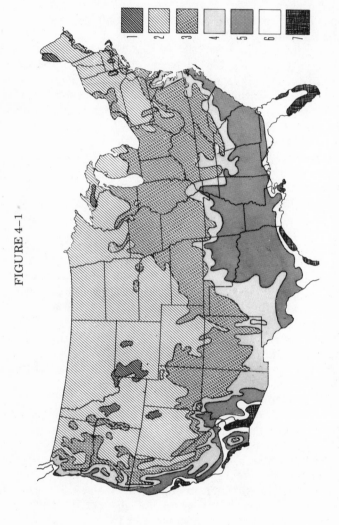

Average date of last expected spring frost: Zone 1, June; Zone 2, May 10-30; Zone 3, Apr. 10 to May 10; Zone 4, March 20 to April 10; Zone 5, Feb. 28 to March 10; Zone 6, Feb. 8-28; Zone 7, Jan. 30 to Feb. 8.

FIGURE 4-2

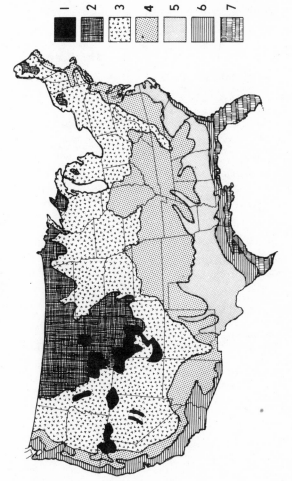

Average date of first hard fall frost: Zone 1, Aug. 30; Zone 2, Sept. 10-20; Zone 3, Sept. 30, Oct. 10; Zone 4, Oct. 20-30; Zone 5, Oct. 30, Nov.; Zone 6, Nov. 20, Dec. 10; Zone 7, Dec. 10-20.

113

TABLE 4–6

Garden Vegetables, Their Companions and Their Antagonists

Vegetable	Likes	Dislikes
Asparagus	Tomatoes, parsley, basil	
Beans	Potatoes, carrots, cucumbers, cauliflower, cabbage, summer savory, most other vegetables and herbs	Onion, garlic, gadiolus
Pole Beans	Corn, summer savory	Onions, beets, kohlrabi, sunflower
Bush Beans	Potatoes, cucumbers, corn, strawberries, celery, summer savory	Onions
Beets	Onions, kohlrabi	Pole beans
Cabbage Family (cabbage, cauliflower, kale, kohlrabi, broccoli, Brussels sprouts)	Aromatic plants, potatoes, celery, dill, camomile, sage, peppermint, rosemary, beets, onions	Strawberries, tomatoes, pole beans
Carrots	Peas, leaf lettuce, chives, onions, leek, rosemary, sage, tomatoes	Dill
Celery	Leek, tomatoes, bush beans, cauliflower, cabbage	
Chives	Carrots	
Corn	Potatoes, peas, beans, cucumbers, pumpkin, squash	Peas, beans
Cucumbers	Beans, corn, peas, radishes, sunflowers	Potatoes, aromatic herbs
Tomato	Chives, onion, parsley, asparagus, marigold, nasturtium, carrot	Kohlrabi, potato, fennel, cabbage
Eggplant	Beans	
Peas	Carrots, turnips, radishes, cucumbers, corn, beans, most vegetables and herbs	Onions, garlic, gladious, potato
Squash	Nasturtium, corn	
Onion (including garlic)	Beets, strawberries, tomato, lettuce, summer savory, camomile (sparsely)	Peas, beans
Leek	Onions, celery, carrots	
Lettuce	Carrots and radishes (lettuce, carrots and radishes make a strong team grown together), strawberries, cucumbers	
Radish	Peas, nasturtium, lettuce, cucumbers	
Parsley	Tomato, asparagus	
Potato	Beans, corn, cabbage, horseradish (should be planted at corners of patch), marigold, eggplant (as a lure for Colorado potato beetle)	Pumpkin, squash, cucumber, sunflower, tomato, raspberry

Vegetable	Likes	Dislikes
Pumpkin	Corn	Potato
Soybeans	Grows with anything, helps everything	
Strawberries	Bush bean, spinach, borage, lettuce (as a border)	Cabbage
Spinach	Strawberries	
Sunflower	Cucumbers	Potato
Turnip	Peas	

More and more horseradish and tansy plants are being planted in orchards each year, for obvious reasons. (Caution: It's toxic to livestock, pets, and children if eaten.)

Many gardeners swear that WORMWOOD, an old-time medicinal plant, is effective in keeping animals away from the garden. Oldtimers used to plant it around the poultry yards, feeling that it discouraged visits from wild animals.

Intensive Gardening

French Intensive Gardening is a system of organic gardening that stresses maximum use of the soil through succession planting, interplanting and, companion planting. The method is very similar to those used in China for centuries to get as much food as possible out of every square foot of soil. Started in the late 1800s, the French method received little notice until it was introduced in the United States in the 1960s by Alan Chadwick at the student gardening project at the University of California's Santa Cruz campus.

Basically the idea behind intensive gardening is to get maximum production with minimum inputs. All soil conditioners are used only in planting beds, not on areas that will be used for paths, thus enabling plants to benefit directly from all the material you put on your garden.

The method relies on raised or rounded planting beds from 3 to 5 feet wide. These beds are prepared by working the soil to a depth of about 2 feet and adding generous amounts of compost and manure. The mounded beds produce a soil that warms quickly, drains well, and takes in air easily. With beds you never walk on or carry equipment across, soil compaction is no problem.

In the mounded beds, plants are spaced as close as possible in hexagonal patterns covering an entire bed. This close spacing encourages improved growth, conserves moisture, and greatly helps to control weeds.

TABLE 4-7

Herbs, Their Companions and Their Uses

Herb	Companions and Effects
Basil	Companion to tomatoes; improves growth and flavor. Repels flies and mosquitoes. DISLIKES rue intensely.
Beebalm	Companion to tomatoes; improves growth and flavor.
Borage	Companion to tomatoes, squash, and strawberries; deters tomato worm; improves growth and flavor.
Caraway	Plant here and there; loosens soil.
Catnip	Plant in borders; deters flea bettle.
Camomile	Companion to cabbages and onions; improves growth and flavor.
Chervil	Companion to radishes; improves growth and flavor.
Chives	Companion to carrots; improves growth and flavor.
Dead nettle	Companion to potatoes; deters potato bug; improves growth and flavor.
Dill	Companion to cabbage; improves growth and health of cabbage. DISLIKES carrots.
Fennel	Plant away from gardens. MOST PLANTS DISLIKE IT.
Flax	Companion to carrots, potatoes; deters potato bug. Improves growth and flavor.
Garlic	Plant near roses and raspberries; deters Japanese bettle; improves growth and health.
Horseradish	Plant at corners of potato patch to deter potato bug.
Henbit	General insect repellent.
Hyssop	Deters cabbage moth; companion to cabbage and grapes. DISLIKES radishes.
Lemon Balm	Sprinkle throughout garden.
Lovage	Improves flavor and health of plants if planted here and there.
Marigolds	The workhorse of the pest deterrents. Plant throughout garden; it discourages Mexican bean beetles, nematodes, and other insects.
Mint	Companion to cabbage and tomatoes; improves health and flavor; deters white cabbage moth.
Marjoram	Here and there in garden; improves flavors.
Mole Plant	Deters moles and mice if planted here and there.

Herb	Companions and Effects
Nasturtium	Companion to radishes, cabbage, and cucurbits; plant under fruit trees. Deters aphids, squash bugs, striped pumpkin beetles. Improves growth and flavor.
Petunia	Protects beans.
Pot Marigold	Companion to tomatoes, but plant elsewhere in garden, too. Deters asparagus beetle, tomato worm, and general garden pests.
Peppermint	Planted among cabbages, it repels the white cabbage butterfly.
Rosemary	Companion to cabbage, beans, carrots, and sage; deters cabbage moth, bean bettles, and carrot fly.
Rue	Plant near roses and raspberries; deters Japanese beetle. DISLIKES sweet basil.
Sage	Plant with rosemary, cabbage, and carrots; Deters cabbage moth, carrot fly. KEEP AWAY from cucumbers.
Southernwood	Plant here and there in garden; companion to cabbage; improves growth and flavor; deters cabbage moth.
Summer Savory	Plant with beans and onions; improves growth and flavor. Deters bean beetles.
Tansy	Plant under fruit trees; companion to roses and raspberries. Deters flying insects, Japanese beetles, striped cucumber beetles, squash bugs, ants.
Tarragon	Good throughout garden.
Thyme	Here and there in garden. It deters cabbage worm.
Valerian	Good anywhere in garden.
Wormwood	As a border, it keeps animals from the garden.
Yarrow	Plant along borders, paths, near aromatic herbs; enhances essential oil production.

This information was collected from many sources, most notably the Bio-Dynamic Association and the Herb Society of America.

Although the intensive system is great for those with limited space, it was not designed with that in mind. All the major gardens in California that use the system have more than enough gardening space. They use the system because of its increased yields, improved quality, and efficiency.

The key to intensive gardening is the construction of a raised bed. With a raised bed, you never walk on the soil your plants are growing in. Once you have prepared the bed, you do your weeding, watering, and harvesting from the sides. For this reason beds should not be made more than 4 to 5 feet wide. For items to be staked such as tomatoes, the bed can be as narrow as a foot and a half. Whenever possible, beds should be laid out for maximum sun exposure. The length of the bed is entirely up to you.

The primary tool for preparing a raised bed is a technique known as double digging. The prescribed method is to dig a trench the width of your bed, removing soil one shovel deep and one shovel wide. Set it aside and use your spade to break up the next level of soil until it is loose and crumbly to a depth of almost 24 inches.

After you have removed one shovel depth of soil and worked the lower layer in your first trench, move the top layer of soil from the next trench into the first trench, filling it and exposing subsoil in the new trench. You continue this digging of a trench and filling it in until the entire bed is dug. Soil removed from the first trench is then used to fill the last trench, as shown in Figure 4–3.

Let the bed set for a few days before working it again. This time, again remove the top layer of soil and loosen the bottom layer. As you return the topsoil to each trench, you add nutrients at different levels. Duane Newcomb, in his book *The Postage Stamp Garden Book,* suggests nutrients be added in this order: bone meal first (4 pounds per 50 square feet), a little topsoil, a 4-inch layer of compost, some more topsoil, about 2 inches of rotted manure, some more topsoil, a small amount of wood ashes (3 pounds per 50 square feet). Cover with soil, and rake the top surface well.

Experienced intensive gardeners estimate it takes as long as six to 12 hours to initially prepare a 5 x 20-foot bed. In successive years, digging the bed can be done in from three to five hours.

Newcomb notes that this is the most exacting method known — but the strict layering of the nutrients promotes tremendous root system development. If this method is too difficult, there are many shortcuts you can take. The main things you should do in preparing a bed is to find a way to work the soil to a depth of 20 to 24 inches, add a generous amount of compost, rotted manure, trace minerals, and sand if your soil is clayey. Because of the number of plants the bed will be supporting, the soil must be almost hand built to insure an ample supply of nutrients. A high organic matter content is a must, and some intensive gardeners lay claim to over 20 percent organic matter in their beds.

The top of the bed should be raised some 4 to 8 inches above ground level when everything has been added. This raised form will allow young roots plenty of air to further stimulate growth. With no one walking on it, the soil will remain light and easy to work throughout the growing season, and the high amount of organic matter will hold moisture.

Add soil conditioners to the upper layers of the bed only, as is done in nature. When leaves fall, they lay on top of the ground, not 15 inches under it. By working manure and compost into the topsoil layers you protect these layers from nutrient leaching, drying, and other ills they are exposed to at the surface.

If you do not have enough compost available to prepare a bed, you can substitute rotted manure. However, manure is richer in nitrogen than compost, and you must compensate for this difference by adding more bone meal and wood ashes.

FIGURE 4-3

Double Digging

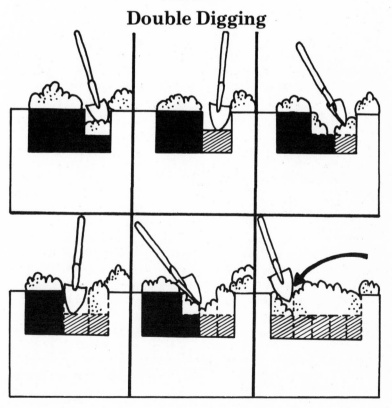

TABLE 4-8

Plant Spacing in Inches for Intensive Planting

beans — bush 4	eggplant 18	radishes 1
beans — pole 8	kale 15	rhubarb 24
beets 3	lettuce — head 10	rutabagas 6
broccoli 12	lettuce — leaf 8	spinach 4
Brussels sprouts ...16	mustard greens 4	squash — bush 18
cabbage 12	onions 3	tomatoes
carrots 2	peas — bush 3	(trained in air) 18
cauliflower 15	peas — pole 6	turnips 4
corn 12	peppers 12	

When planning an intensive garden, remember that plants do not grow in rows in nature, and should not in your garden. Row planting is an invention of man to make it easier to cultivate large areas at one time. In an intensive raised bed, the plants are grown so that their leaves just touch, thus providing a very effective form of living mulch, much like a mature pine forest.

Fortunately, a plant cannot read a seed packet, and thus a carrot does not know that it needs to be only 3 to 4 inches from another carrot in line, but 12 to 14 inches from another row of carrots. Whatever the spacing recommended for between plants, they will do quite well or even better with that same spacing in all directions. (See Table 4-8 for recommended intensive spacings.)

Your plants, or seed, should be planted in diagonally offset patterns, forming a hexagon with all seeds spaced evenly to get maximum production. (See Table 4-9 for an idea of how many plants you can get in one area with this method.) A newly planted area with all the same plants should look like Figure 4-4.

Intensive gardening depends on a "living mulch" to provide plants with optimum growing conditions. Plants are spaced close enough together so their leaves almost touch, providing the base of the plants with a protective layer of green above, trapping moisture between the ground and the leaves, while blocking out sunlight from the soil. Once seeded or set close together, they are thinned out as they grow to keep the leaves almost touching, but not overcrowding each other. (You want them all to touch but not to strangle each other — intensive, not congested.) The shading effect of the growing plants cuts off sunlight to most aspiring weeds, reducing the need for weeding.

Because of the small size of the garden, one thorough weeding is about all it needs. When a weed is pulled from the loose and friable soil, it easily comes out, roots and all. Then, once the vegetables start growing, the protective "living mulch" inhibits any further weed growth.

In experiments on the productivity of intensive gardens, John Jeavons *(How to Grow More Vegetables)* has found that when you put four times the number of plants in a bed that you could if planted in rows, you get up to six times the amount of produce. Jeavons credits this increase to the shading effect that conserves water and keeps soil temperature lower during the peak heat of the day.

Where planning and planting really get fun is when you start interplanting. You may have a fast-growing crop at 6-inch intervals, with a later-maturing crop on 12-inch spacings, using the centers of the hexagons. When you really get good, you may find yourself with a bed having four or more different items growing in it. The ideal for large production is to have one bed for carrots, one for lettuce, maybe one for a combination of peppers and onions, and so on.

The intensive gardens in California all make extensive use of flowers. Not only are flowers pleasing to the eye, but they attract bees for improved pollination and many predatory insects. A balance of flowers and vegetables will lead to a balance of bugs in your garden. This, combined with improved

FIGURE 4–4

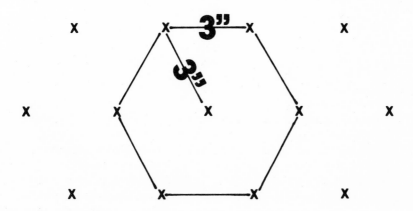

TABLE 4–9

Planting Centers Per 100 Square Feet

Spacing		Centers
1″	—	14,400
2″	—	3,600
4″	—	900
6″	—	400
8″	—	225
10″	—	144
12″	—	100

soil structure and a healthy soil life in a well-prepared raised bed, will give you healthy plants that resist most insect attacks.

The major criticism of the intensive method is that it takes too much work, too much hard work. With a few exceptions, intensive gardeners disdain the use of power tools. The beds are prepared with a spade, spading fork, and a rake. Practitioners of the method are quick to admit that initially this calls for a lot of hard work, but after the first couple of years, the soil is in such great condition that it works quite easily.

The intensive gardening system not only refers to intensive use of land, as in Chinese agriculture, but it is skill-intensive as well. Many hours may go into planning the coming year's garden. Each bed should have regular plantings of legumes for added nitrogen, herbs and flowers for insect protection and beauty, as well as vegetables; in effect, each bed is its own garden.

Broadcast Planting

If the raised bed intensive gardening method sounds a bit too much for you, yet you still want to save as much space as possible, you can broadcast plant some of your crops, and plant the rest in rows.

Broadcasting, briefly, is scattering seed in all directions over a previously prepared soil bed. For most root crops and for many greens, it's an ideal way to make every inch count. Some gardeners even plant nasturtiums, borage, zinnias, and marigolds in beds. It's quick, there's no plotting rows, and it eliminates much cultivation — the vegetables form a blanket that inhibits rampant weed growth. Its main drawbacks are that plants don't have uniform shape and don't mature evenly. But this also can be an advantage.

Consider radishes: Scatter radish seed sparingly in a bed. As they grow, some are further from and some closer to others. The ones with space grow faster and bigger; harvest them first. Next harvest the crowded ones, taking some and leaving others. The leftovers grow quickly, and you can usually harvest them before they get too hot and woody. The result is a whole lot of radishes in a small space, and a naturally staggered harvest.

By now you have a good idea of how this technique works. It's surefire for crops like mustard, cress, and other leafy crops that need to be harvested at a young stage for maximum flavor and tenderness. With leaf lettuce, sow sparingly in a smoothly raked, clod-free bed, and in a month and a half it takes up all the ground space and is so thick you can almost reap it with a lawn mower. With mustard and other greens it's the same way. Often there's even a second crop, as late-germinating plants spring up once the competition is eliminated.

If you're ready to try this method, remember these important considerations:

1. Choose vegetables and flowers that lend themselves to broadcast sowing. For example, bunching onions work fine; tomatoes are a disaster.

2. Use this technique only when you don't intend to do mechanical cultivation and harvesting. Most machinery is designed for row work.

3. Don't expect uniformly shaped produce or uniform maturity. The yield will be staggered and often irregularly shaped.

4. Go heavily on fertilizer high in humus. Broadcasting and such close gardening draws heavily from the soil, and you want to put the ground in better condition than when you started.

Extending The Growing Season

A short growing season needn't be an excuse for not growing long-season crops like celery, tomatoes, and peppers. And it doesn't have to mean you can't get two successive crops out of your garden. There are many ways to gain extra growing time in and out of your garden.

Certainly one of the most common ways of extending the growing season in spring is to start vegetable seedlings indoors, so when it's warm enough to plant outside they're already sturdy little plants, raring to go. Indoor starts are particularly wise for plants that are sensitive to cold and transplant well, like tomatoes, peppers, lettuce, the cole crops, eggplant, and okra.

Most planting directions say to start seeds indoors six to eight weeks before the date when they can safely be planted out. You can stretch that to eight or nine weeks, if you keep the plants under lights to prevent the legginess that otherwise develops if they spend all that time at the windowsill. If you raise seedlings on windowsills, without lights, opt for the shorter six- to seven-week period. Remember that days are longer later in the season — more light for your plants.

There is one vegetable to start very early: peppers, both hot and sweet. If you wait for red peppers in the summer, they seem to stay green almost until frost. Making allowances for differences in climate, plant peppers in late January or early February. Transplant them at least once, keep them under lights, and they should stay in fine shape. They're usually beginning to blossom when it's time to set them out in May. This means picking green bell peppers by the third week in July and red ones by mid-August.

For the other vegetables you start inside (tomatoes, eggplant, broccoli, cabbage, and head lettuce), plant seeds somewhat later, along the lines of the traditional eight weeks before setting-out time.

Setting-out time for the cool-weather crops is sometime in April on this schedule, mid-May for the tomato and eggplant. This timetable corresponds to a middle-Atlantic states' climate.

For care in transplanting, start your seeds in peat pots or pellets so that when the time comes you can set out your plants, container and all, without disturbing the tender root systems. Soil starting mixtures are light, sterile, retain water well, and are free from diseases and weed seeds.

Keep the seeds moist and warm as they're germinating. They won't need light until they form their first leaves, but once they do, give them lots of sun or artificial light.

"Garden" All Winter Long

For example, if after reading over Chapter 7,"Preserving Food," you realize that you don't have all the storage space you'd like (so you can put away a year's supply), make it unnecessary to store a lot from the garden by keeping your garden producing food almost all year 'round. Plan to eat as much fresh as you can even in fall and winter.

Many vegetables are frost-resistant and can be kept in the garden well into fall. Cos lettuce, celery, collards, kale, broccoli, mustard greens, cress, escarole, Chinese cabbage, endive, and chervil all fit into this category and stay in the garden until heavy snows come. Brussels sprouts actually are better after they have been hit with a light frost. If covered with a heavy mulch of straw, dried leaves or such, or with a coldframe, so that they are protected from heavy frosts and snow, they'll stay in good shape right in the garden row all winter. In many parts of the country, even in the North, a hay bale will keep the ground under it unfrozen and relatively warm. Carrots, cabbage, and beets will keep well even in winter with a bale of hay over them.

Don't plant vegetables for winter garden storage until about midsummer so that they'll mature later in the season when the earlier crops have been eaten or packed away. Later planting is also a good idea for the fall crops that can be carried over the winter and spring in a basement, cold cellar, or outbuilding. Such vegetables include cabbage, squash, turnips, and potatoes.

If you want to store carrots this way too, plant both late and early crops and eat the early crop(s) fresh. Most of them, if planted in midsummer (check maturity lengths) will be ready to harvest when the weather is cool enough for "root-cellaring" and when you're finished with most of your canning and freezing.

"Cut and come" vegetables are great for the small garden, or the large one for that matter. Loose-leaf lettuces won't give up growing new leaves after the outer ones are picked until the hot midsummer sun withers them away. You can cut unopened blossom heads from sprouting broccoli and they'll continue to grow new ones throughout much of the summer. Pinch off the growing tips of Brussels sprouts after the sprouts along the base have matured, and although it will be smaller than the first one, you'll get yourself another crop.

Beets and turnips are dual-purpose crops because both their roots and their greens are edible. Sugar or snow peas, while not actually a double-purpose vegetable, produce proportionately more edible tissues than regular peas because both the little embryo peas and the pods are eaten. Sugar peas are incredibly crunchy and sweet (providing you don't let them get too big so that they get tough), and you don't have to spend time shelling them.

Build Your Own Long Season

Two mechanical methods of extending your season are the cold frame and its bigger brother, the hotbed. Either can be easily built, and both will quickly pay for themselves with increased yields. Figures 4-5 and 4-6 show two examples of these garden helpers.

A cold frame (Figure 4-5) basically is a box with soil for the bottom and glass for the top. A frame can be built for small cost, using 1-inch thick boards and a wooden storm window sash, or any glass sash on hand. The box is constructed to exactly fit the sash. The back should be 6 inches higher than the front so the glass slopes to catch the sun and shed the rain. The front can be from 6 to 12 inches high and the back from 12 to 24 inches.

Locate the frame where it will receive maximum sun and protection from cold winds. A site facing south or southeast and backed by a building, hedge, or tight fence would be best. Good drainage is absolutely necessary. The soil is dug out to a depth of at least 6 inches and replaced by a layer of drainage material such as small stones or gravel, and topped with 4 inches of prepared soil. Three parts garden soil, one part sand, and one part compost mixed together and screened is a good mixture.

Seeds may be started in a cold frame weeks earlier than is possible in the open garden. Frame-grown seedlings will be stocky, hardy, and healthy. If sown in rows 6 inches apart and quickly thinned when true leaves appear, no transplanting will be necessary before the plants are transferred to the garden. Such plants as cauliflower, broccoli, cabbage, and lettuce can be started this way.

Fresh salads are possible most of the year if a corner of the frame is devoted to several parsley plants, a clump of chives, a succession of lettuce plants, and small, repeated sowings of radish seed. The frame is a good place to "harden off" seedlings that were started indoors. This simply means to accustom plants gradually to outdoor conditions by exposure to sun and wind for lengthening periods of time.

While operation of the cold frame is simple, it must not be neglected. Early spring care involves ventilation and added protection against freezing. It is a good idea to open the sash a little at midday, weather permitting, to admit fresh air. On warm, sunny days ventilation to avoid excessive heat is important. Too much heat can injure seedlings. Keeping a thermometer in the frame is a good practice. The sash is closed as the outside temperature drops, to hold heat for the night. When freezing nighttime temperatures are predicted, the glass should be covered. Such things as burlap sacks, old quilts, or mats may be used for this purpose. In late spring and summer, the sun's heat may be too much for tender seedlings, particularly if they have not "hardened off" yet. In this situation, substitute window screen, the same size as your storm window sash, to help shade plants.

Basically a hotbed (Figure 4-6) is a cold frame with heat added. The usual way to add warmth is by using a ther-

FIGURE 4–5

Two Sided Cold Frame

mostatically controlled soil-heating cable. Construction is the same as for the cold frame. However, to increase frost resistance, the inside of the box may be lined with roofing paper. Preparation of the seedbed, however, is different. The soil is dug out to a depth of 8 inches or more, and an inch or two of drainage material is put in the bottom of the bed. Place fine screen over the drainage base and 2 inches of sand on top of the screen. Imbed the heating cable in the sand and top with a layer of hardware cloth to prevent injury to the cable when digging. Fill in with prepared soil mix to a depth of at least 4 inches.

The hotbed should be located in a well-drained, sunny place near an electric outlet. Special consideration should be given to wind protection. Daily care is the same as that of the cold frame.

A hotbed is advantageous as it extends the growing season in both spring and fall. This is the place to start tomatoes, peppers, and eggplant.

Extending Your Garden Space, Out Of The Garden

If you've made the most efficient use of all your garden space, you've succession planted, intercropped, started seedlings indoors and everything, what should you do if you still want more production? Move out of the garden. You can create a garden out of the garden by growing edible plants in containers. You can set them anywhere: on a patio, driveway, balcony, even on a rooftop.

One of the nice things about containers is that they are mobile and can be moved around to take advantage of changing season and miniclimates around your house. When chilly autumn weather sets in, you can protect your tomato and pepper plants from frosts by bringing them into the porch or garage and let their fruit ripen there. The south side of your house, because it's protected from winds and receives the most sun, is one of the warmest spots and may be the best place for container squash. In early spring the rest of your yard may not be warm enough to grow anything, but this southern exposure could be 5 or maybe 10°F. warmer than anywhere else, just right for a window box of early lettuce and radishes. Midsummer sun may be too hot for lettuce and spinach, but if these vegetables are container-grown, you can move them under a

FIGURE 4–6

Hotbed

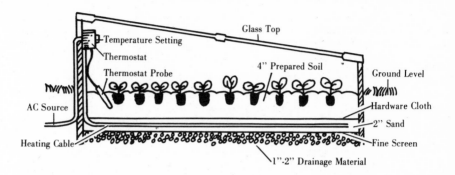

shady tree or to the north side of your house where the sun won't shine on them directly.

The secret to container gardening is to evaluate your resources. You need a container with a minimum area of 2 square feet, which holds about 2 cubic feet of soil, in a space where it can be watered, where it can drain and receive partial sunlight for half the day and full sunlight for the rest of the day. This minimum sunlight requirement is important because leafy vegetables tend to accumulate nitrates when grown in too much shade. Corners of a building are good if they have good-sized windows on both walls, with one receiving morning sun and the other afternoon sun. A full exposure or southern-exposure window, balcony, or rooftop is best for most vegetables.

Tools needed are very simple: a hand shovel (trowel); 2 to 4 square feet of ¼-inch-square mesh screen nailed to a wood frame for sifting; and either a fine-nozzle watering can or a fine-spray nozzle and hose that can be attached to a water supply.

Depending on the urgency and your aesthetics, anything from wooden boxes, tubs, clay pots, 5-gallon square cans, and various styrofoam and plastic containers will work. Five-gallon upright square cans have a little more than ½ square foot of soil surface, which is adequate for most perennial herbs and various flowers; but leafy vegetables like lettuce, brassicas, and spinach produce a much better harvest when they have a minimum of 2 square feet of soil surface. There is less opportunity for companion planting when each container is less than 2 square feet. Radishes, lettuce, and baby carrots can be grown in soil only 6 inches deep, but they do better in 8. Eight inches to a foot is best for most vegetables except tomatoes, squash, broccoli, and cucumbers which will benefit from soil 1 to 2 feet deep. Generally speaking, the larger and deeper the container, the bigger the harvest.

Clay pots of 6 or more inches in diameter may provide homes for a variety of flowers and herbs, such as scented geraniums, calendulas, marigolds, Sweet Williams, parsley, marjoram, sage, salad burnet, thyme, savories, hot peppers, and basil. The hot peppers and basil may prefer a warm, sunny window to the outdoors, depending on your climate.

Drainage grooves, or holes in your containers, should first be covered with a one-half-inch layer of some coarse organic material, gravel, or broken crockery to prevent the soil mix from leaking out.

The next step is to prepare a mix of sifted leaf mold and soil. You are going to have to lug the leaf mold and soil to your residence, so you might as well spend some time selecting the very best in terms of structure and nutrients, and the least polluted. This means staying away from parks and roadside areas where weed-killers are used, as well as from agricultural land under chemical cultivation.

Trees that have the best leaf mold are the deciduous and generally nonaromatic: oak, alder, elm, and maple are good examples. Conifers and eucalyptus leaf molds are unsatisfactory. Under a large tree, remove the top layer of fallen leaves and scoop up the dark, crumbly leaf mold beneath. This mold is nothing but composted leaves, with mother nature doing the composting. The mold can be sifted on the spot and some of the tailings saved for the bottom of the container. One-fourth to one-third of the volume of your mix should be of this sifted leaf mold.

Soil should be somewhere between loam and clay loam. A heavier loam will hold more water and nutrients, which is important when you have only 1 to 2 cubic feet of soil. Any fallow area that supports healthy-looking grasses will probably yield more fertile soil than land that has pioneer weeds growing. Excavation sites are often good areas to acquire a small amount of soil.

The soil should be sifted through the screen to eliminate any unwanted, hard-packed clods. Mix one-third sifted leaf mold with two-thirds sifted soil. If the soil turns out very heavy (sticky and hard to crumble apart into small particles), mix in a little sand. Fill your container to near the top, and water. Allow to settle.

Before planting your seeds, sprinkle bone meal on the surface to create a very thin white covering (about ⅛ to ¼ pound per square yard). On top of this put a ½- to 1-inch layer of sifted compost or well-aged manure, and mix this thoroughly with the top 3 to 4 inches of soil. If you do not have compost, use blood meal or combine equal parts of peat moss and dried cow manure to form a suitable replacement, but check to see that ingredients have not been treated with chemicals.

Grow Vertically

Whether in containers or a regular garden, one sure way to save space and improve performance is to grow your vegetables up, not out. It will not only save gardening space, but training plants upward will expose more vegetables to the sun for quicker ripening and increased yields. Additionally, it will prevent vegetables from rotting on the moist ground, possibly picking up soilborne diseases and being exposed to insect and rodent damage.

A good vertical gardener takes a look at a fence 5 by 20 feet and sees 100 square feet of gardening space. Any plants that vine on the ground can usually be trained, or tied to a vertical growing area.

If you don't have any vertical areas with good sun exposure, vertical growing cages are easily built with standard construction grade reinforcing wire, or any other wire with openings large enough for you to harvest through. To build a simple growing tower, form the wire into a circle with a 30-inch diameter. Staple the wire to 8-foot wooden stakes, leaving about 3 feet of stake at the bottom for hammering into the ground, and to allow you room to reach under the wire cage. The cages can either be permanent, or you can take them down every year. Squash, cucumbers, and small melons all do well in such a tower, as do tomatoes, and, of course, pole beans and peas.

Growing vertically usually requires that you pay a bit more attention to your plants, especially when they start producing. Cucumbers often have to be tied in slings, and branches producing tomatoes have to be better supported to hold the weight of the fruit. One point many people forget is that a vertical garden in a container must be watered more often and usually side-dressed with fertilizer during the season, or watered with a manure tea, to compensate for the reduced root zone and the heavy production of a vertical garden.

By building walls, with wire loosely attached to one side, lined with plastic, and filled with soil, a wall of vegetation can be planted through holes in the retaining plastic. Such a planting wall works especially well for loose-leaf lettuce, tomatoes, cucumbers, and peppers, but not root crops.

Vertical gardening can be anything from a simple stand to set containers on to a suspended platform with plants growing up the suspenders, or hanging over the edge of the platform. But in most cases, it will be staking something to a fence, or erecting a trellis to train crops into the air instead of letting them wander around the garden. One final word of caution: Varieties that produce especially heavy fruit should not be grown vertically, unless special precautions are taken to support the weight.

Soil, Lifeblood
Of The Garden

No matter how well you plan and maintain your garden, if you have poor soil, you'll have a poor garden. Luckily, you can always improve your soil through the addition of organic soil conditioners.

If soil is the heart of your garden, then humus is the heart of your soil. Good garden soil consists of about 5 percent humus. Most soils are from 1 to 2 percent humus, while native prairie soils may be 10 percent humus, and land that has been continuously farmed with chemicals may have as little as ½ or even ¼ of 1 percent humus.

There are two ways you can add humus to your soil. You can either grow it there, or you can put it there. Most gardeners will use both these methods, in that you may actually grow a cover crop or a green manure crop to add humus to the soil (roots of vegetables left in the soil adds humus), and you will also be adding humus to the soil in the form of compost, animal manures, and soil conditioners. The higher your organic matter content, the easier tight clay soils are to work and the better the drainage. In light sandy soils, organic matter holds moisture and nutrients in the root zone. Organic matter holds moisture in all soils and allows air to penetrate and stimulate root growth.

In an organic garden your first concern is soil building; the vegetables will do just fine on their own if you have proper soil. The main tool you will have at your disposal to build soil quality is compost.

To the compost pile comes all your organic leavings: kitchen garbage, pulled weeds, spoiled hay, leaves, and manure. From the pile comes all the major and minor nutrients your garden vegetables need.

A list of compost's major benefits to gardens includes:

- It is food for soil organisms which, during the growing year, feed the plants the nutrients they need.
- Plants thrive in a loose, crumbly, humusy soil, and compost conditions the soil, making it loose and fluffy so that it absorbs water and yet is well drained.
- Soil health requires thriving colonies of bacteria, fungi, and earthworms. Compost feeds these organisms, which in turn aerate and enrich the soil with nitrogen and other elements.
- Trace elements not provided in chemical fertilizers are included in compost. Without these elements imbalance occurs, causing lower yields.
- Weed seeds that often heavily infest all kinds of manure are killed by the high temperatures in compost.
- Soil conditioned by compost allows for stronger root systems. This in turn means healthier, drought-resistant plants.
- A compost pile gives you top-quality potting and seed-flat soil for your house or greenhouse.
- Compost costs very little and often nothing.
- Using waste from around the house means energy saving, in an age when this kind of practice is vital to everyone.

After the condition of your soil, the next limiting factor you have to worry about is soil pH. A correct pH is necessary for plants to absorb nutrients needed for growth.

The letters pH refer to the potential hydrogen and indicate soil alkalinity or acidity. The pH scale ranges from zero to 14, from acid to alkaline. Seven on the scale is neutral. Soils testing 4 to 5 are very acid or sour, and relatively few plants will tolerate them. Similarly, soils of over 7¾ are too alkaline or sweet for most plants to thrive. A large number of commonly grown plants prefer a pH range of 6 to 7½. Testing soil for pH is not a highly technical operation; there are simple, inexpensive kits that are easy to use. By adding various substances to the soil the gardener can adjust the pH to suit a crop. Table 4-10 gives the preferred pH of many commonly grown plants.

Compost, maple leaves, ground oyster shells, marl, and wood ashes all help to increase soil pH. Lime is the most often used as it is inexpensive and fast acting.

Aluminum sulfate is usually recommended to make soil more acid, but organic gardeners prefer generous applications of peat moss, rotted sawdust, cottonseed meal, pine needles, and oak leaves.

A simple soil test will quickly tell you the pH of your soil, and from there it is rather easy to correct. However, if your soil is low in organic matter, it isn't so easily corrected.

Compost is the best way to improve soil organic matter and still maintain a good soil pH. We should offer one word of caution about composting — it is habit forming. Many a gardener has started off with a casual compost pile only to turn into a fanatic about feeding the pile. It doesn't take long to reach the point where you won't throw away anything that could go to the pile, and eventually back to the soil.

These simple steps will help get you started in composting:

1. If possible, shred leaves, cornstalks, and other organic material. Matted clumps of leaves or grass clippings will not allow air to penetrate the pile nor provide the high temperatures needed for quick composting.

2. Scratch the soil where the pile is to be built with a pitchfork. This will expose the bottom of the pile to microorganisms and earthworms.

3. Place a layer of green matter — hay, shredded cornstalks, etc. — on the bare ground. This layer should be a foot thick and 8 feet in diameter for a 5-foot pile.

TABLE 4-10

pH Preferences of Common Plants

Quite Acid (pH of from 4.0 to 6.0)

azalea	heather	pecan
bayberry	huckleberry	pine
blackberry	lupine	potato, Irish
blueberry	lily	radish
chrysanthemum	lily of the valley	raspberry
cranberry	marigold	rhododendron
evergreens	mountain laurel	spruce
ferns	mosses	sweet potato
fescue	oak	watermelon
flax	peanut	yew
heath		

Slightly Acid (pH 6.0 to 6.5)

apple	gooseberry	rape
apricot	grape	rhubarb
barley	kale	rice
beans, lima	lespedeza	rye
bent grass	millet	salsify
bluegrass	mustard	snap bean
buckwheat	oats	soybean
cherry	pansy	squash
collards	parsley	strawberry
corn	parsnip	sudan grass
cotton	pea	timothy
cowpeas	peach	tomato
eggplant	pear	turnip
endive	pepper	vetch
gardenia	pumpkin	wheat
gloxinia		

Neutral to Alkaline (pH 7.0 to 7.5)

alfalfa	cantaloupe	lettuce
alyssum	carrot	okra
asparagus	cauliflower	onion
beet	celery	quince
broccoli	clover	spinach
Brussels sprouts	cucumber	Swiss chard
cabbage	iris	zucchini
carnation	leeks	

4. Cover the green matter with one-fifth as much manure as green matter. What you use depends on what kind of manure is available.

5. Place kitchen garbage on top of manure. This adds trace elements and increases the temperature of the bacterial "fire."

6. Sprinkle on a couple of shovelsful of rock powder and wood ashes. Use rock phosphate, potash, greensand, and crushed limestone. To avoid caking do not overuse these materials.

7. Cover the first layer with an inch or so of good soil providing more bacteria.

8. Water each layer of the pile thoroughly but do not saturate. Neither overly wet nor overly dry compost will work.

9. Lay down a number of small tree branches across the first layer. This provides air channels when removed later, or the pile can be lifted and shaken. Either method provides air, a necessary ingredient for bacterial action.

10. Put down remaining layers in same order as first. Three to five layers will make a 4- or 5-foot pile which is high enough to promote proper temperatures.

11. Top the pile with hay or other green matter and an inch or two of soil. Water the last time.

12. Turn the pile frequently if you want fast action; if you can wait till next year, don't turn at all. Check occasionally to see if it needs moisture.

13. Naturally you need not be as exact as this. The goal is to pile vegetation and manure together in a manner that permits air in the pile, and occasionally turn the pile to subject all parts of it to the high temperatures created within the pile.

If there is no yard where you can make compost, make it in garbage cans; this is the easiest and cleanest way. Here are some guidelines:

1. Use a galvanized garbage can with a good-fitting lid. Punch holes in the bottom and add a layer of gravel and about 3 inches of soil.

2. Add earthworms, preferably some of the red worms or red wigglers. Although they are not necessary, worms will speed up the process.

3. If your lot has good drainage, the can may be sunk in the ground to allow the worms to work through the winter, below the frost line. The can may also be kept in the cellar or

on a balcony if set off the floor on some bricks with a pan underneath to catch any fluids dripping out. These fluids will be odorless and are good for house plant waterings.

4. Throw kitchen wastes into the can. Avoid all but very small amounts of grease or meat scraps. Chicken bones should be added, as they add calcium and can act as a filler in the soil if they don't completely decompose.

5. Odor is usually not a problem if each addition of fresh garbage is covered with a sprinkling of soil or some type of organic matter like leaves, grass clippings, etc. Coffee grounds will act as a natural deodorant and should be included, and a shredded newspaper will take care of any odors almost immediately.

A regular 20-gallon garbage can will just about hold the household waste of a family of four for six months. A good idea, if space permits, is to start one can in the fall, and as it fills up, start another can. This lets you treat your garden before the growing season, and again after the growing season.

Insect Control

More than anything else, insects are thought of as a sign of an unhealthy garden. A healthy garden has insects, but they're in a balance of beneficial insects and problem causers. That's what you want, a healthy balance of insects throughout the garden. That way, no one species ever becomes so populous that it can cause major problems.

By using chemical sprays, you not only destroy the pest you're after, but you kill off the beneficial insects as well. It is one of mother nature's general rules that problem insects have a shorter life span than do predatory insects. Thus, when you kill off all the insects, the problem causers reappear before their enemies do, compounding your insect problems.

The seven steps below will enable you to handle your garden insects in a much more efficient and, we believe, sane method.

1. Encourage soil health — Healthy soil and its dependent life is promoted by adding rich compost, mulch, green manures, animal manures, and natural rock powder fertilizers.

2. Interplant — Insect damage can be cut in half by inter-

planting one crop with another. Intersperse the garden with strong herbs like dill, rosemary, summer savory, garlic, and thyme to confuse insects' senses and make it more difficult for them to find their favorite vegetable.

3. Plant pest-resistant varieties — Search out seed of pest-resistant varieties. Practice crop rotation and stimulate vigorous plant growth by organic soil improvement, watering, and mulching.

4. Practice garden hygiene — Garden hygiene and good cultivation are preferable to poisons as pest control methods. A good tilling of the soil can kill a lot of pests. A healthy mix of good and harmful insects in the garden allows nature to set up her own delicate and effective checks and balances.

5. Biological controls — Biological controls can be the first line of defense against a pest population explosion. Ladybugs, green lacewing, praying mantis, and the trichogramma wasp are all beneficial and can be purchased from many sources. They should be released in late May or early June in order to meet the burgeoning pest populations. Birds are voracious bug-eaters and should be encouraged around the home and garden. Harmless snakes, toads, frogs, and salamanders all have a part in establishing natural control. A spray of *Bacillus thuringiensis*, known as BT (Thuricide, Dipel, Biotrol, and other trade names), is effective against caterpillars that attack members of the cabbage family. BT is also good against gypsy moth, tent caterpillar, and other tree-infesting crawlers. BT doesn't affect beneficial insects, humans, fish, or animals, nor does it build up in the soil. Another insect disease, milky spore disease (trade name Doom), keeps Japanese beetles in check.

6. Physical traps — Plastic jugs painted orange and coated with Tanglefoot or other tree stickum is a trap for flea beetles. The beetles are attracted by the color, jump on and stay on. Strips of plastic, wood, or cardboard painted yellow and coated with stickum controls white fly in the greenhouse.

7. Botanical poisons — As a last resort the gardener can turn to the botanical poisons — pyrethrum, rotenone, and ryania. These are made from plants and are effective, but they are poisons and rotenone is very toxic to fish. Heavy exposure can be mildly toxic to humans and animals, but they can be safely used and they quickly degrade, unlike the long-lasting chemical poisons.

Your garden should easily produce all you ask of it, with a minimal amount of labor. The best advice we can give a gardener is an ancient Chinese proverb, "The best fertilizer is the farmer's shadow." This quite simply means that you have to pay attention to what's going on in the garden. If there is about to be an outbreak of insects, your garden will tell you if you are there to see the signs. This holds true for our next area of coverage, livestock, even more so.

TABLE 4-12

Planting and Planning Guide

Variety	Pounds to Raise Per Person	Pounds Yield Per 10 Foot Row	Feet of Row Needed Per Person	Number of Seeds or Plants Per 10 Foot Row	Inches Between Plants	Inches Between Rows	Storage
Asparagus	6	3–4	20	7–8 crowns	18	36–60	can, freeze
Beans, lima	5–10	4–6	25	1 oz.	B–3–4 P–8	B–18–30 P–24–36	dry, freeze, can
Beans, snap	8	3–5	20–50	1–2 oz.	B–1–2 P–4–12	B–24–30 P–36–48	can, freeze, dry
Beets	5–10	8–10	10	$1/_{16}$ oz.*	2–3	15–24	pickle; moist frost-free storage
Broccoli	8	4–5	20	6 plants	16–18	24–30	freeze
Brussels sprouts	5	4–6	10	7 plants	18–20	24–30	freeze, cold cellar

Plant							Storage / Method
Cabbage	11	8–28	15	7 plants	16–18	24–30	make sauerkraut or store in frost-free place
Cantaloupe	10–15	13	10–20	1/16 oz.*	hills 12	hills 60	freeze
Carrots	11	7–10	15–20	1/16 oz.*	1–2	12–18	cold cellar
Cauliflower	12	8–12	10–15	6 plants	18–20	24–30	freeze
Celery	8	6–13	10	1/16 oz.*	6	24–30	freeze, cold cellar
Collards	14	8–10	15	1/16 oz.*	18–24	24–30	freeze, cold cellar / leave in ground to first hard frost
Corn	30	5–10	50	1/2 oz.	12	24–36	can, freeze, dry
Cucumber	15	8–10	15–25	1/16 oz.*	hills 12	hills 36	pickle
Eggplant	12	20	6	1/16 oz.*	18–24	30–42	cold cellar
Endive	3	3–6	5–10	1/16 oz.*	10–12	18–30	with soil in cool cellar
Kale	5	2–5	10	1/16 oz.*	10–12	18–30	mulch and leave through winter
Kohlrabi	1–2	2–3	5–10	1/16 oz.*	4–5	12–20	moist, frost-free storage
Leek	2–6	5–20	3	1/16 oz.*	2–4	12–24	freeze

TABLE 4–12 (Cont.)

Variety	Pounds to Raise Per Person	Pounds Yield Per 10 Foot Row	Feet of Row Needed Per Person	Number of Seeds or Plants Per 10 Foot Row	Inches Between Plants	Inches Between Rows	Storage
Lettuce	5	5–10	10–25	1/16 oz.*	leaf 6 head 12	12–18 18–30	cool, moist place
Mustard	6	4–8	15	1/16 oz.*	4–6	12–16	cool, moist place
Okra	2–5	5	5–10	1/16 oz.*	12–18	24–48	freeze, can, or dry immediately
Onions	12	7–10	12–25	1/10 lb. sets	3–4	15–24	dry, frost-free storage
Parsley	0–1	1/2–1	1	1/16 oz.*	4–8	12–24	freeze, dry
Parsnip	10	10–12	10	1/16 oz.*	3–4	18–24	leave in ground over winter
Peas	4	2–8	40–60	1 oz.	1–3	12–24	can, freeze
Pepper	10	2–10	6–10	6–7 plants	18–24	30	freeze, pickles, condiments
Potato	100	6–18	150–200	1 lb.	10–12	24–36	moist, frost-free storage

Pumpkin	12	10–20	10	1/16 oz.*	hills 18	hills 60–98	dry, frost-free storage
Radishes	3	1–4	10	1/16 oz.*	1	12–18	frost-free storage
Rhubarb	10	8–12	10	3–4 plants	36–48	36–48	can
Rutabaga	5–10	8–12	10	1/16 oz.*	3–5	18–24	moist, frost-free storage
Spinach	10	4–6	20–40	1/16 oz.*	2–4	12–18	freeze
Squash, summer	7	10–80	6	1/16 oz.*	hills 12	hills 48–60	warm, dry place
Squash, winter	20–50	10–80	15	1/16 oz.*	12	60–84	frost-free storage, freeze
Sweet potato	50–70	8–12	40–100	10 sprouts	12–15	30–42	cool, moderately moist place
Swiss chard	5	8–12	5	8 plants	6–8	18–30	cool, moist place
Tomato	20	10–35	20–25	5 plants	18–30	30–48	cool, moist place, can, freeze
Turnip	10–15	8–12	15	1/16 oz.*	2–4	12–18	moist, frost-free storage

*Such small amounts of seed are needed to plant a 10-foot row of these crops, that we have listed the smallest amount you can buy per ounce. To help you calculate your seed needs further, the below listed amounts of seed are for a 100-foot row. Beets 1/2 oz., Cantaloupe 1/2 oz., Carrot 1/8 oz., Celery 1/16 oz., Collard 1/8 oz., Cucumber 1/2 oz., Eggplant 1/16 oz., Endive 1/8 oz., Kale 1/8 oz., Kohlrabi 1/8 oz., Leeks 1/4 oz., Lettuce 1/8 oz., Mustard 1/16 oz., Okra 1/4 oz., Parsley 1/4 oz., Parsnip 1/4 oz., Pumpkin 1/8 oz., Radishes 1/2 oz., Rutabaga 1/8 oz., Spinach 1/4 oz., Summer Squash 1/2 oz., Winter Squash 1/2 oz., Turnip 1/8 oz.

Chapter 5

Raising
Livestock

Anyone with enough land to support a fair-sized garden can also raise enough rabbits and chickens to supply a good portion of their meat demands. With very little additional space, such livestock as dairy goats, sheep, hogs, geese, and other fowl, or even a beef animal, can be an integral and important part of the homestead. Raising livestock in many ways makes you a homesteader, regardless of the location or size of your place. We look at livestock as the turning point from a productive household gardener into a budding homesteader.

This chapter can't tell you how to raise livestock. Entire books have been written about each specific type of animal, and even those only skim the surface. Instead we're going to discuss managing home-produced livestock products in the broader sense, to see how animals fit into the entire picture of home food production.

What we hope to accomplish in this chapter is give you enough information about the time, space, and money involved in raising livestock to enable you to make an informed decision about whether you wish to try raising livestock. From the charts at the end of the chapter you will be able to calculate roughly how much work and money you'll be putting out for the meat your operation returns to your family.

For the person interested in producing his or her own food, perhaps one of the greatest benefits of homestead meat production is quality. Watery, tasteless chicken has become such a hallmark of modern food production that even people who scoff at organic agriculture readily admit that "chicken doesn't taste like it used to." Home produced chicken, raised organically, does taste like chicken used to, because that's how chickens used to be raised.

It goes without saying that if livestock are part of your home food production, you're in control of your meat supply. The hormones, antibiotics, and other substances increasingly used in the commercial meat supply are used because of the need for profit, with no consideration for quality. And even then, they are very often required only because of the conditions the animals are raised under. A homestead steer is not raised in a bovine concentration camp and therefore is not as subject to the stress and disease encountered by his less fortunate feed-lot located brother. There is less stress on any animal raised in comfortable surroundings, with personal care and attention, than there is on the cow, pig, chicken, or other animal raised in crowded pens, pushed for production by means of medications and high-powered feed additives, subjected to trucking and rough handling and other stress factors.

In addition to all this there can be some very real cost benefits. These vary with the type of enterprise, the management skills of the homesteader, and to some degree the extent of the subsidies farmers are providing consumers at any given time.

Then there is the satisfaction you can get from a livestock enterprise. This can range from the interest and affection a dairy goat can bring to a family, or the charm of a small flock of hens scratching in the yard, to the very real psychological satisfaction of sitting down to a meal you provided — yourself — without the help of big business, unions, or the government. If so many people get a kick out of growing a radish or putting up a jar of pickles — and home economists tell us this is one reason for the surge in interest in home food production — how much more satisfaction is there in a succulent ham that you fed, butchered, cured, and smoked yourself?

The well-managed homestead can compete economically. Consider the savings on feed if the homestead makes use of waste and surplus and weeds and grasses gleaned from fence rows and corners inaccessible to large-scale farmers. There are savings in transportation. (The average chicken travels more than 2,000 miles to reach your table, we're told, and while it doesn't go first class, there still has to be a cost factor and a burning of fossil fuels involved in each bird.) There are savings in the processing, packaging, advertising, wholesaling, and retailing. An 8-ounce glass of milk in a restaurant might cost you 30 cents: 8 ounces of milk on the farm should cost you less than 4 cents.

From the standpoint of world-wide food supplies, home-produced meat represents a tremendous increase in production because it utilizes land, labor, and feedstuffs that in most cases would otherwise be wasted. Take feed as an example. The homestead which is managed to produce as many of the family's needs as possible very often has surpluses of one product or another. It's inevitable. If you plan your home dairy to provide enough milk during the winter when goats are dry and cows slack off in production due to available feeds and climatic conditions, you'll have much more than you can use during the spring and summer when the animals are at the peak of their lactations and when lush pasture is available to even further increase the milk flow. Even if some of the surplus is converted into cheese, butter, and other dairy products, there will be whey, skim milk, and possibly excess buttermilk left over. This makes excellent stock feed. Thus, what would be "waste" is converted into pork or veal or fowl.

Chickens normally lay more eggs during periods when the day is increasing in length than they do when the opposite is true. If you have enough hens to provide all the eggs you'll need during the least productive season, you'll have more than you can use during the most productive season. Like milk, eggs are excellent stock feed.

The garden designed to provide all of a family's requirements will have an overabundance of any crop in one year or another. That surplus can be wasted . . . or it can be turned into nutritious meat.

Even without such surplus there will be waste: sweet corn husks and stalks; thinnings; pea pods and vines; outer leaves of cabbage and similar vegetables; overripe or damaged produce; cull fruit; and trimmings of all kinds. These can all be profitably converted into meat.

You're not losing these materials from the compost heap, either. The manure and bedding from the livestock will have far greater benefit than the original materials. In fact, most organic homesteaders firmly believe you cannot have a viable and self-sufficient homestead without livestock, if only because of the contribution of manure to the health of the soil. In addition to the manure, and bedding which would also be waste material in many cases, the livestock will return to the soil bone, feathers, and entrails via the compost heap.

Some Initial Considerations

The person who decides to grow a garden has a lot to learn in order to become totally self-sufficient in vegetables — and there is even more to learn about livestock! However, once acquired, that knowledge itself is a form of security, a source of pride and personal satisfaction.

Even so, not every backyard is a potential livestock production unit, nor is every homesteader a potential livestock producer. Many factors enter into the picture. These considerations form the basis for good homestead livestock management.

Amount and Availability of Land

In the first place, is your location such that you can even consider raising livestock? The kinds and numbers of animals you can consider will be influenced by the amount of land you have, its productivity, available buildings and fences, and similar factors. (To figure some of these variables see the tables at the end of this chapter.) You might also have to deal with neighbors and zoning regulations.

From the technical standpoint, such meat animals as rabbits and chickens and even goats can be raised on the average city lot. As a practical matter, few *are*. But with proper management such animals will be less bothersome to neighbors and the community at large than many cats and dogs.

But unfortunately, most cities have restrictions on keeping livestock, and what's even more alarming, there are even some predominantly rural areas with such restrictions. These restrictions obviously vary widely, but there are few places where the prospective livestock raiser can be advised to forge ahead without at least discreetly checking into the situation.

It should be noted that since the dramatic increase in food prices in the early 1970s, a number of cities have toned down their restrictions on keeping animals, somewhat. This is as it should be, for properly cared for animals should be neither a health hazard nor a nuisance to the neighbors. This type of zoning restriction is especially hard on elderly people, who not only have a great deal to gain from raising small stock but who are also more likely to live in an urban setting.

Good management is especially important in an area where neighbors might raise cain with your homesteading efforts. Pens must be cleaned regularly and thoroughly to keep down odors, flies, and other nuisances associated with animal manure. Pens must be as presentable as possible: neighbors are much more likely to complain about unsightly, ramshackle, junky rabbit hutches, for example, than they would be to complain about rabbits kept in attractive, freshly painted hutches (perhaps enhanced with plantings of vines, shrubs, or the like). Animals must be adequately penned to keep neighbors happy, and fed and cared for on time so they aren't inclined to cause a disturbance.

What's Your Commitment?

The next most important consideration is your amount of interest. Is it great enough to insure that the animals will receive proper care? The beginning gardener who loses interest after a brief time can simply let the weeds take over and not much damage will be done. But if animals are not fed, watered, and cleaned on a regular basis, a great deal of damage will be done! Not only is this the condition which often instigates the regulations against keeping livestock in urban or suburban locations, but even worse, the animals will suffer. Unlike the garden, which can survive with an occasional cultivating and watering, the raising of livestock requires regular attention several times a day, day in and day out. There are no days off, no vacations. To get an idea of how much work is involved with different animals see the effort index (Table 5-1) later in this chapter.

Most classes of livestock require a great deal more information and skill than gardening. This too requires interest, because without sufficient interest the time and effort required to learn just won't be there.

Financial Investment

Then there is the matter of investment. To again contrast meat production with vegetable production, a very modest garden can be started with a few dollars worth of simple tools and seeds, but the investment in even the smallest livestock enterprise will be considerably more. Meat is more expensive than rice and beans for a very simple reason: it costs more to produce. The purchase of the animals is a very small part of the expense. The investment may also include housing, fencing, feed and watering equipment, bedding, feed, books and magazines on the stock raised, possibly veterinarian fees, and various other requirements depending on the stock raised and the individual's methods.

Since the investment is higher, the risk is greater. A row of green beans can be devoured by wild rabbits or gophers with no great economic loss, but catastrophes can and do confront livestock raisers too. A stray dog can wipe out even a sizeable rabbitry in a matter of minutes; there can be breeding failures and problem pregnancies; and of course disease and accident are ever-present possibilities.

Not only is the time required in terms of man-hours greater to produce meat than to produce vegetables: the time between "planting" and "harvesting" is also greater. You can be eating onions, radishes, and lettuce within a few weeks after you purchase the seeds. But it will take about 12 weeks to harvest a chicken or a rabbit; about five months if you start out with a month-old hog; or a year and a half if you decide to raise a steer.

Dealing with Livestock, Emotionally

Not the least important consideration is whether you or your family would have any qualms about eating your livestock. Very few people (if any) enjoy butchering. But homesteaders with animals consider it more intellectually honest to learn how to butcher, and thus be completely self-sufficient, than to smack their lips over a sizzling steak and pretend that somebody else didn't have to do the dirty work. Butchering becomes easier with practice, both from the standpoint of manual dexterity and the emotional drain involved. Nevertheless, it always remains highly significant: it instills respect for food, and life, that the plastic package eaters will never fully understand.

This is something that you will have to be emotionally prepared for from the beginning.

Start Slowly, Gradually
Working Up To Your Goal

As you study and research in preparation for actually getting into livestock production, you're likely to come across many experts (expert at commercial production, that is) who say homestead stock raising is nothing more than a hobby: it can't be done economically. What's worse, there are many people who have tried homestead-scale farming and quit, because they discovered their eggs cost them several dollars a dozen or their rabbit meat was in the same price range as caviar!

There are several simple reasons for this, which can be summed up in the word "management."

Only a small portion of the price the shopper pays for a cut of meat goes to the farmer. Included in the price may be such items as trucking, brokerage fees, various other selling costs, processing, packaging and handling, more transportation, advertising, and much more. When you buy a slice of bacon you're paying the chemical companies and their salesmen and telephone operators and computer programmers and janitors; people who make paper and those who print on it; meat inspectors and speculators in pork bellies on the commodity market and bag boys at the supermarket, as well as all the plumbers and presidents, secretaries and salesmen it takes to keep all this going. Seems strange to say that this roundabout method of getting meat on the table should be cheaper than buying a pig directly from a farmer, or raising your own! If home-produced is more expensive, it's because you're doing something wrong. The key is management.

Since so many people who decide to provide their own meat know little or nothing about it, the failure rate is high. Or the cost of their output is high enough to make the commercial experts say "I told you so." Commercial farming can't be done without a great deal of knowledge and experience either. The point that livestock raising requires a great deal of knowledge and experience simply can't be overemphasized!

But how do you get experience?

Not too long ago nearly everyone knew the basic skills of animal husbandry because they grew up with it. They learned by watching Dad and Grandpa, listening to dinner table conversation, and by starting to help with the simple and routine tasks at an early age. As capabilities increased, so did responsibilities and proficiency.

Most of us have never lived in that type of environment. But because we're so much more "educated" than our forefathers, most of us assume that if they could do it, it must be child's play for us. It just ain't so.

We have to learn, in most cases, the hard way. We can make up a great deal of lost time by serious study. There are books, magazines, and pamphlets available from many sources on just about every phase of livestock production. Study as many of them as you can, as carefully as you can. Pay special attention to what points the authors agree and disagree on. Blend in your own experience and goals to help evaluate material written for large commercial producers. Much of what applies to them won't apply to you — but much will. Don't listen to the "experts" who say it can't be done. Maybe they're just so tied up in their own way of doing things that they haven't noticed it is being done.

Then, acknowledge your inexperience and start out small. The faster producing, less costly, less demanding livestock provides a good starting point. Chickens are probably ideal in this regard. You can buy day-old chicks and don't have to concern yourself with the intricacies of genetics, management of the breeding flock, incubation, and all of that. Give them plenty of fresh water, clean litter, ample and proper feed, and in about three months you'll get your first butchering experience on what most people consider the easiest livestock to process. You'll sit down to a mouth-watering feast that will have deep psychological significance even aside from the nutritional and gustatory benefits.

And you will have gained that invaluable commodity, experience. Consider yourself fortunate if you encounter a few problems along the way, because if you don't face — and overcome — at least a few setbacks you probably won't learn a great deal. When the chickens fly the coop and scratch in the garden, be glad for the opportunity to learn something about fence building before you get into hogs or goats. When you don't really feel like going out through the rain on a Saturday morning to care for the flock, be glad you're getting the experience of the responsibility of the herdsman with a dozen chickens rather than a hundred, or a goat or a cow who is much more demanding. When you encounter a medical problem, you're gaining veterinary experience that will stand you in good stead with other stock. The same can be said about feeding, record keeping, and other important areas of management.

With some experience under your belt, you'll know whether you're psychologically and physically suited to raising livestock, what particular areas most interest you, and you'll be accustomed to the daily routine of chores.

Don't be discouraged if those first birds cost you more than store-bought chicken. Simply find out why they did, and determine what you can do to change that next time. To do this you need records. Good management is the key to successful livestock raising, and good records are the key to successful management.

Was your expensive chicken dinner the result of waiting too long to butcher? If you weigh a few birds weekly and enter an average on your records, you might be able to see where a pound of extra grain produced less than the desired extra meat. Or maybe you had the wrong breed, or the wrong strain.

Maybe the high cost was due to excessive death losses, in which case you must do some detective work to determine the cause. Maybe you skimped on feed, trying to save money, and ended up with meat that was more expensive. (A good example of this trap would be the homesteader who feeds only corn and kitchen scraps, because protein supplements are so high-priced. But without those high-priced concentrates, it will take longer to produce a bird ready for market, and in that extra time the bird will still be eating.)

Obviously one, two, or even three years isn't enough time to learn a great deal from experience. You'll want to try birds from different sources: there is a difference in strains of birds of the same breed! You'll want to compare one year with the next, experiment with various management systems, apply what you learned the year before. Yes, it will probably cost you more than you reap at first, especially if you don't proceed slowly and carefully. But any education is expensive, in one way or another.

This same type of thinking holds true for eggs, for goat or cow milk, rabbit meat, pork, or anything else. Don't jump into it: grow into it. Each bit of information learned can be applied to other projects. You must learn to walk before trying to run or to perform intricate dance steps.

The intricate dance steps come after you have a good grasp of the basics. You wouldn't, for instance, concoct your own grain mixture for dairy goats before you learn something about goats and about feeds. Formulating a ration requires knowledge of not only the nutritional content of feeds but of the animals' needs for protein, fat, fiber, vitamins, minerals, bulk, and so forth.

The point of all this is, the county agent who says it can't be done or the homesteader who tried and failed are probably right, if they're talking about starting to raise livestock today with the expectation of making a profit a few months from now. It doesn't work that way, and anyone who expects it to simply doesn't have enough respect for the truly fantastic amount of knowledge and skill our "primitive" agrarian ancestors — or today's farmers — had at their command.

On the other hand, it probably isn't as bad as we've made it sound, either! Most people have at least some experience and a little common sense, and with even a little luck, satisfactory results can be had in a short time. Increased experience permits fine-tuning.

The tables on the following pages will hopefully serve to provide some of the most fundamental basic information to help you decide what type of livestock you'd be most interested in raising. You also no doubt have a pretty good idea of what you'd *like* to raise —because of your food preferences, because of animals you've seen at fairs or in farmyards, or because of articles in such magazines as *Organic Gardening and Farming* and *Countryside and Small Stock Journal.*

The next step is to do some serious research. Talk to local feed dealers. They probably have literature from the feed companies that will help you get started. Maybe they can tell you of local people who already raise the animals you're interested in. Ask your county agent and your state agricultural college for help. Check out the library. If possible, attend fairs or shows featuring the animals you're interested in: showmen are almost always good sources of information, and willing to help beginners.

Feed Efficiency

Almost without exception, feed is the outstanding cash expense in livestock production. And for the homesteader this is usually the factor most subject to management or manipulation.

Various authorities have devised different ways of examining the relative efficiencies of different animals. For example, one researcher has estimated that the following average percentages of the gross energy in the feed eaten by different animals are converted into human food:

Food item	Gross energy in feed eaten that is converted into human food
Pork	20%
Cow milk	15%
Eggs	7%
Poultry meat	5%
Beef	4%
Lamb	4%

The major flaw in these figures is that we do not eat animal products primarily as a source of energy. In addition, the figures on pork consider only feed consumed from weaning on, and the others are on a similar basis. In other words, the food consumed by the breeding stock is not counted.

Later research improved on this with a calorie-plus-protein index. This considered that the daily allowance for the average person is 0.15 pounds of protein and 2,600 calories, and these are given equal weight. Then, using 1 pound of corn as the standard feed unit, it takes the following feed units to produce a calorie-plus-protein index of 1:

Milk	6.5
Pork	9.2
Turkey	9.7
Eggs	10.7
Chicken	12.0
Beef	41.3
Lamb	51.7

On this basis, milk comes out ahead of pork, but beef and lamb are still at the bottom of the list. However, this too can be misleading, because beef and lamb make great use of pasture and roughage, usually on land that could not otherwise produce human food. So the ratio on grain and concentrates, without roughage, was also calculated.

Milk	1.6
Lamb	3.2
Pork	8.6
Beef	8.8
Turkey	8.8
Eggs	10.1
Chicken	10.9

Still other authorities have devised more complex (and probably more accurate) relationships based not only on the feed expended on breeding stock and on laying hens and milk cows up to producing age, but also on dress-out percentages and other factors. But even these are not entirely adequate for the person trying to decide what livestock is most economical to produce on the homestead. Not only does the homesteader consider the usual economics of agriculture; the unique management methods found today only in self-sufficient agriculture also play a major role.

As one example, geese and guineas make impressive gains on free range, the geese eating grass and the guineas also eating bugs and weed seeds. In some cases no cultivated grains or other feed products are required. There is no competition with humans for food, and no cash expense. In addition, these birds will reproduce themselves, and while some grain for overwintering will then be required, the homesteader has an ongoing and very economical source of food.

Chickens allowed free range can pick up as much as 20 percent of their nutritional requirements. Milk goats and cows can get a great deal of food value from good pastures during the growing season. Hogs are well-known as scavengers, producing pork on everything from grubs and frogs and worms to garden thinnings and skim milk. Sheep and beef cattle make excellent use of land that is too rocky, too hilly, too dry, or in other ways unsuitable for growing crops.

While feed formulation is a highly complex science involving many important details and interrelationships that cannot possibly be covered here, the homesteader who is willing to spend some thought and energy on feeding can make homestead meat production even more practical and economical.

Based on all the foregoing charts and comments (as well as on personal observation and other information) and without attempting to assign specific numerical values, here is our list of the most efficient livestock for the average homesteader, in order of efficiency:

1. Geese
2. Guineas
3. Rabbits
4. Laying hens
5. Broilers
6. Lambs
7. Dairy goats
8. Hogs
9. Dairy cows
10. Beef cattle

Game, Fish, Honeybees, and Others

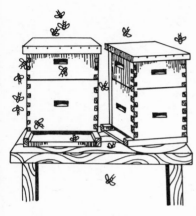

A discussion of homestead meat should include fish and game. In many cases, to be sure, the cost far exceeds the cash value, but not always, and as with homesteading in general there are values that can't be measured in dollars and cents. Tremendous amounts of food are harvested each year by hunters and fishermen, and anyone skilled enough to fill the freezer with fish and game certainly contributes to the overall food production that our land is capable of.

And, while most people won't think of them as livestock, mention should also be made of home-raised fish and honeybees. There is a great deal of interest in both, and both produce large amounts of food. And not only do bees and fish not compete with humans for food as do poultry, dairy animals, and other grain-eaters: they are part of an overall ecological balance that our food-short world is beginning to pay much more attention to. While certain conditions are necessary for fish ponds, almost anyone can keep a hive or two of bees.

Other "exotics" with varying degrees of potential and popularity include quail, frogs, and crawdads . . . and at least one person is convinced that the answer to the protein crisis is domesticated possum!

Which Animals
And How Many?

There is no doubt that well-managed homestead livestock can play a major role in helping you to provide healthful, wholesome food for your family, and economically. There will be side benefits: manure for your compost heap; education for you and other family members, especially children; the pleasure involved in working with living creatures; the satisfaction of providing for yourself; and security. But it has to be done right. You can — you must — study to get started, but in the final analysis, good management is up to you. It's a frame of mind.

The following tables are presented in a sequence to help you decide both if you want to try raising livestock, and secondly, what type of animal you wish to start with.

The tables start with what we call an effort index (5-1). This shows the estimated daily time spent per animal on what is generally considered to be the most common number of animals in a family production unit. Thus, times listed are for one cow, three goats, three rabbits, etc. The estimated time spent per unit of finished product is also given. This information will help you evaluate how much time a livestock production system will require.

We then cover the absolute minimum space requirements for animals (5-2), not including storage of feed and equipment. The figures for pounds of meat produced per year (5-3) will give you an idea of how much return you will get for your invested space, time, and money. Most of this information is summed up in Table 5-4, anticipated harvest per square foot.

The information on feeds (Tables 5-5 and 5-6) may not weigh too heavily in your decision as to what type of animals to

TABLE 5–1

Effort Index

Which animals can be expected to produce the most with the least amount of labor? (Not counting cleaning, butchering, feed growing, or grooming)

Animal	Est. daily chore time	per	Homestead unit (no. of animals)	Estimated time spent per unit produced (meat on dressed basis)
Cow	1 hr.		1	4 minutes/qt. milk
Goat	¹/₂ hr.		3	4 minutes/qt. milk
Pig	¹/₂ hr.		1	1.8 hrs./lb. meat
Rabbit	¹/₂ hr.		3	1.2 hrs./lb. meat
Chicken	¹/₂ hr.		50 broilers	0.3 hrs./lb. meat
			12 layers	0.5 hrs./doz. eggs
Sheep	¹/₂ hr.		3	1.5 hrs./lb. meat

get, unless you will be growing most of your own feed. The remaining information should answer many general questions you may have concerning the different breeds of livestock. The summary is conclusions we have drawn from this information. You, of course, may reach a different conclusion.

TABLE 5–2

Minimum Space Requirements for Housing (Square Feet)

Beef yearling	confinement	25
	unpaved lot	200
Dairy cow	paved lot	100
	dirt lot	200
Penned calf		24
Dairy goat		20
Sheep	dry ewe	35
	ewe with lambs	50
	feeder lamb	35
Swine	sow with litter	128
	feeder pig	20
Chicken	day old	0.5
	layer	3
Rabbit	hutch	9

Like all tables dealing with averages and assumptions, this one is nothing more than a rough guide. However, it does bring up several significant points.

1. Half an hour is a nominal minimum no matter how small your flock or herd. Nonproductive effort can be a major factor in time spent on small units. Things like putting on your boots and coat in the winter can, quite seriously, take more time than actually doing the chores.

2. Partly because of the above there are certain economies of scale. It does not take twice as long, for example, to feed twice as many chickens. In some cases surplus production is easily sold; in others, disposing of the surplus will require a great deal of time and effort, thus cancelling out the benefits of the economies of scale.

3. Also in connection with the above, a diversified operation can be more efficient under homestead management. It's

just the opposite for commercial farming.

4. Consider psychological effort: 12-hour milking intervals, seven days a week, 365 days a year, get some people down. Homesteaders who raise broilers need to work at meat production for only about 12 weeks out of the year. Even with laying hens or rabbits kept year-round, it's possible to give them extra feed and water for occasions when you must miss a feeding.

5. Little efficiencies can make a tremendous difference in your individual effort index. If you must haul water, feed, or bedding long distances, have balky or cumbersome gates or doors, or face any other conditions that take extra time, your effort index increases. One single minute a day is six hours a year — and most people waste many minutes each day.

6. This chart clearly shows that most homesteaders cannot expect to make minimum wage at today's low food prices. (Yes, LOW: in spite of the price of milk, to take one example, farmers have been selling below the cost of production.) In spite of that, home livestock production can be extremely

TABLE 5-3

Pounds of Meat Produced Per Year

Animal	Average weight of dam	Parturitions per year	Young per litter	Total young per year	Average liveweight at weaning	Pounds (liveweight) weaned per year	Pounds weaned per year expressed as % of dam's liveweight
Cow	1,000 lbs.	1	1	1	400 lbs.	400	40%
Goat	150 lbs.	1	2	2	35 lbs.	70	46%
Rabbit	11 lbs.	4	8	32	4½ lbs.	144	1,309%
Sheep	150 lbs.	1	1.5	1.5	100 lbs.	150	100%
Hog	400 lbs.	2	8	16	25 lbs.	400	100%

These figures are obviously rough averages: a Jersey cow might only weigh 800 pounds while a Holstein might be closer to 1,500; many beginning rabbit raisers do not get eight in a litter or four litters a year; not everybody butchers goat kids at 35 pounds; and some sheep raisers believe in weaning lambs at 60 or 70 pounds or even lighter. But taken as averages, the figures do show the relative values of breeding stock on the self-sufficient homestead.

valuable based on other considerations. The small amount of time spent would be "wasted" anyway, in most cases. The value of such work to unemployed or underemployed people, young and old, should be obvious. But raising livestock has just as much value, or more, for the harried individual with job pressures who considers the few minutes spent with the animals a respite from the rat race: a daily minivacation.

TABLE 5–4

Anticipated Harvest Per Square Foot

(Based on minimum housing space:
does not include feed production area)

Animal		Space[1] (sq. ft.)	Annual harvest (lbs.)[3]	Harvest per sq. ft. (lbs.)
Beef	Confinement	25	800	32
	Dry lot	200	800	4
Dairy cow	Dry lot	100	5,000–20,000 milk	50–200
Dairy goat		20	1,500 milk	75
	Butcher kid	20	30	0.6
Rabbit	One doe	9	144	16
Feeder lamb		35	100	2.8
Feeder pig[2]		20	440	22
Chicken[2]	Meat	3	16	5.3
	Eggs	3	27.3 (8 per lb.)	9.1

Many people who are striving to produce their own food are somewhat cramped for space. This chart gives some indication as to how much space is required for various animal products. Note the high ratings for milk.

When adjusted for actual homestead operating conditions, rabbits are likely to surpass both beef cattle and swine in this category.

1. Most homesteaders will prefer to use more space than that recommended for commercial operations, particularly for confinement beef and feeder pigs.

2. These figures assume that four batches of chickens (and two of pigs) can be raised in the same pen space each year. Because this system is seldom followed in actual practice on homesteads, the net harvest figures must be adjusted downward.

3. Production figures can vary widely, dependent upon quality of stock and management. Good stock — and good management — will pay handsome dividends. Also, these figures are liveweight — not dressed — which gives milk a slightly unfair advantage.

TABLE 5–5

Feed Consumption of Common Homestead Livestock

Cow 2 lbs. good roughage per day per 100 lbs. body weight
1–25 lbs. grain per day (depending on hay quality, milk production, etc.)

Goat per day roughage (hay or pasture). About 3 lbs. depending on quality, waste, etc., fed free-choice
1 lb. grain per day, plus 1 lb. additional for each 2 lbs. of milk produced

Rabbit 5 oz. of pellets or equivalent per day; more for does with litters

Sheep A 55-lb. feeder will eat about 3 lbs. per day, half grain and half roughage. Figure 400 lbs. of grain and 500 lbs. of roughage to produce 100 lbs. of lamb

Hog 600 lbs. from weaning to 220 lb. slaughter weight; 900 lbs. total, including feed for boars and gestating sows, waste; nonbreeders, etc.

Chicken Laying hens: 7 lbs. per month. Broilers: 12 lbs. feed for 4 lb. body weight (12 weeks)

TABLE 5–7

Reproduction Information

Animal	Age at puberty	Heat interval	Heat duration	Gestation period
Cow	8–12 mo.	21 days	16–20 hrs.	284 days
Goat	7 mo.	21 days	36–48 hrs.	151 days
Sheep	7 mo.	14–20 days	30 hrs.	148 days
Rabbit	6 mo.	——	——	31 days
Hog	5 mo.	18–24 days	48–72 hrs.	113 days

These are averages, and individuals may vary widely.

TABLE 5–6

Feed Conversion Ratios

(How many pounds of feed it takes — with good stock and management — to produce one pound of meat)

Animal	Ratio	Comments
Cow		
Meat	15:1	This is mostly — and can be entirely — hay and roughage. If you have "waste" land, this ratio, though high, might actually be quite economical because feed *prices* are not reflected in these ratios.
Milk	3:1	This assumes a good milker. "Poor doing" animals eat practically as much as good producers, but obviously feed conversion ratio is less.
Goat		
Meat	15:1	This is based on range-fed animals kept for meat. Cull kids from a dairy herd could be charged just with the milk they consume, and the ratio could be as low as 3:1.
Milk	3:1	See comments on cow milk.
Rabbit	4:1	There is probably more variation here than among most other meat animals because of the wider variation in stock and feeding and management practices. Good stock and good management pay!
Sheep	9:1	This 9 includes 4 parts grain and 5 parts roughage. Many range sheep and some farm flocks do not get grain. See comments under "Cow, Meat."
Hog	4:1	Many modern producers are doing better than this, but few homesteaders can hope to match their achievements. On the other hand, much of this feed might be items that, without the pig, would be wasted: surplus garden produce, skim milk, etc.
Chicken		
Meat	4:1	Some broiler factories have brought this as low as 2.2:1. Ranging birds can pick up as much as 20% of their feed. Chickens can make use of garden produce.
Eggs	3.6:1	Ranging birds can pick up much of their nutritional needs, and kitchen and garden waste can reduce feed bills too.

TABLE 5–8

Incubation Periods for Selected Fowl

Chicken	21 days
Turkey	28 days
Duck	28 days
Muscovy duck	33–35 days
Goose	29–31 days
Guinea	26–28 days
Pigeon	16–18 days
Japanese quail	17–18 days

TABLE 5–9

Water Requirements for Livestock

Cow	12 gal. per day
Goat	1 gal. per day
Sheep	1 gal. per day
Hog	1 gal. per 100 lbs. liveweight
Rabbit and litter	1 gal. per day in warm weather
50 chicks	1 gal. per day
50 layers	3 gal. per day

Water has been called "the most important feed." Water consumption varies with type of feed, temperature, and other factors, and is especially important for lactating animals. A year-round source of good water, conveniently located, is of prime importance to the livestock raiser.

TABLE 5–10

Slaughter Ages and Weights for Common Homestead Livestock

Animal	Age	Prime* weight
Rabbit	2 mo.	4¹/₂ lbs.
Broiler	3 mo.	4 lbs.
Lamb	5 mo.	100 lbs.
Hog	6 mo.	220 lbs.
Beef	18 mo.	1,200 lbs.

*Meat animals fed past prime weight make expensive gains (feed is wasted) and quality suffers.
Veal calves are commonly butchered at about 4 months.
Prime weight for milk-fed goat kids is 20–30 pounds.
Cull breeding stock (and layers) are considered a homestead bonus.

TABLE 5–11

Amounts and Fertilizing Values of Manures

Animal	Tons excreted per year per 1,000 lbs. liveweight	% Nitrogen	% Phosphoric acid	% Potash
Rabbit	4.2	2.4	1.4	0.6
Sheep and goat	6.0	1.44	0.5	1.21
Swine	16.0	0.49	0.34	0.47
Chicken	4.5	1.0	0.8	0.39
Dairy cow	12.0	0.57	0.23	0.62
Beef	8.5	0.73	0.48	0.55
Horse	8	0.70	0.25	0.77

Manure can be an extremely valuable by-product of self-sufficient livestock production because of its role in building and maintaining soil fertility. However, it must be properly managed to realize the optimum fertilization value. Composting is the ideal way to conserve the value of manure.

TABLE 5–12

Animal Units

Horse	1
Cow	1
Calf	0.25
Sow	0.4
200-lb. pig	0.2
Sheep	0.14
Goat	0.14
Lamb	0.07
Kid	0.07
100 laying hens	1
200 broilers	1

This chart represents the common saying that one cow is equal to 6 to 8 goats. One divided by 7 is 0.142, which is the "animal unit" for a goat. A hundred laying hens eat as much as one horse, etc.

Summary

Managing your personal food supply implies making intelligent choices based on logic and the best information available, even though in practice most home livestock production depends to a large extent on sentiments and other irrational considerations.

But let's imagine for a moment that a family wants to be as self-sufficient as possible. What livestock should they be thinking of?

Eating habits have been changing rapidly in recent years due to such factors as changing prices and concerns over cholesterol and nitrates. However, in an average recent "normal" year, here is what the average American eats:

Food item	Average per person consumption per year	Average livestock units required for this production
Milk	75 gal.	.50 goat (1,500 lbs./yr.)
		.12 cow (5,000 lbs./yr.)
Butter	26 lbs.	.33 goat (1,500 lbs. milk/yr.)
		.10 cow (5,000 lbs. milk/yr.)
Eggs	30 doz.	1.7 hens (220 eggs/yr.)
Beef	113 lbs.	.22 steer
Pork	72 lbs.	.72 hog
Chicken	40 lbs.	16 chickens
Lamb and mutton	3.2 lbs.	
Veal	2.3 lbs.	
Rabbit	0.12 lbs.	

Egg production offers few choices except among breeds of hens, although increased numbers of people are showing an interest in Indian Runner ducks (which produce more eggs than most chickens) and quail. But these are largely personal choices.

Milk is perhaps the most important of animal products, and the major choice here lies between goats or a cow. There are many good arguments for each, so here again, personal preference is the deciding factor.

Of the meat-milk-egg group of foods, meat offers the most options. From the strictly practical standpoint, if eggs and milk are produced there will be cull animals and unwanted offspring to contribute to the meat supply, almost as a bonus added to the egg and milk production. Beyond that, many factors are involved.

From all of the foregoing charts there is little doubt that, based on space, labor, experience required, investment, feeding factors and others, the rabbit is the ideal choice for a homestead meat source. The pig probably rates second. Lamb and beef are better suited to marginal agricultural areas than to the land-intensive, labor-intensive homestead.

As mentioned earlier, the goose and the guinea (as well as ducks) can be ideal homestead livestock under certain conditions, but the difficulty of plucking, especially geese, necessarily downgrades them for most homesteads. Particularly in confinement or on limited range, meat chickens will be much more adaptable to most homesteads.

Therefore, considering all the information given here, the "ideal" home livestock production unit would probably include the following for a family of four:

```
 4  goats
50  broilers
 2  hogs
 4  breeding rabbits
12  laying hens
```
Miscellaneous as desired for variety.

An operation of this size could conceivably be contained in less than 200 square feet of barn space (exclusive of feed and equipment, storage and pasture, if any). It shouldn't take more than two hours per day. It will yield about 7 tons of manure exclusive of bedding. It would require roughly 5,000 pounds of hay and roughage and 5,500 pounds of grain and concentrate. On good farmland, this could mean as little as one acre of hay and two to five acres of grain.

Any family with such a setup would be well on the way to food self-sufficiency, making the most of their little corner of planet Earth, as well as good times and good eating.

Chapter 6

Buying
The Best Food

With a few exceptions, no matter how hard you try to become completely self-sufficient, sooner or later you will have to buy some part of your food supply. And for those who have neither the space nor desire to produce their own food, shopping is an everyday chore. However, like everything else, there are some good ways to buy food, and there most assuredly are some bad ways to buy it. This chapter will show you what to keep your eye out for when buying food to insure you not only get the best food for your body, but you protect your budget at the same time.

The wisest approach to buying food to supplement your food supply is to evaluate all the potential sources and decide which is most appropriate for your needs. Sometimes direct access to a grower or manufacturer is possible personally, or through a buying group or a co-op. In some circumstances mail-order houses which supply food in bulk or in household quantities are most convenient. Finally, there is the retailer which might be anything from a farm or roadside stand to a specialty store that sells just a few items like cheese or fresh produce or baked goods, or a neighborhood grocery, or the supermodern supermarket.

Where To Buy

There is no simple rule to determine where you will make your best purchases. Comparison shopping might reveal that grains, beans, nuts, and other items that can be stored conveniently over a period of time are best purchased from a reputable organic wholesaler like Arrowhead Mills or Erewhon, or a distributor who services your local natural foods store. Very often you can purchase these items in bulk directly from a store at cost or for a minimal service charge (10 percent), if you place your order in advance.

If you are in an area that caters to a specific ethnic population, there may be a local importer who can supply you with some otherwise hard-to-find items. Where there is a large Arab or Greek population, dried beans, dried fruit, tahini, imported oils, nuts, and other traditional staples are often available at very reasonable prices. Similarly, in Italian-oriented communities fresh pasta products, cheeses, and spices will be abundant, while in Oriental neighborhoods seaweed, bean curd, rice flour, mung and soy beans, and a wide variety of fresh and dried produce can be found. In short, a trip to a local "bodega," or specialty store, can be a rewarding experience both monetarily and in terms of new eating experiences that might open up for you.

There are times too when the supermarket will be your best source of economical foodstuffs. Despite the fact that there are so many middlemen between you and your supermarket shelf, a large store or chain has greater buying power and often negotiates foods at low prices. While some items enjoy from 60 to 100 percent markups, others are often sold at or below wholesale costs ("loss leaders") or for only a small profit, and here is where you can save money over what you would pay in a smaller grocery, or even by buying directly from the manufacturer. Most common among the loss leaders are paper products and canned goods, but sales extend this category to include eggs, butter, cheese, dry milk, and even meat and produce on occasion to attract customers.

Unprocessed Foods
Are Your Best Buy

As we saw in Chapter 1, foods fall into two general categories: *unprocessed foods,* or those foods which you buy pretty much as they exist in nature and which require further handling at home, and *processed foods* which have already been prepared for you so all you may have to do is minimal cooking or perhaps nothing at all. Which type of food is most economical for you will depend on your life-style and how much effort you are willing to expend to get the most for your food dollar, as well as on the particular item in question.

It has been asserted by the U.S. Department of Agriculture that "the majority of convenience foods are as cheap or cheaper than that made from scratch." Larry Traub, economist with the USDA, backs this claim with a USDA study conducted in January 1974 revealing that "59 percent (of convenience foods) had a cost per serving equal to, or less than, their home prepared or fresh counterparts." What Traub and the USDA neglected to mention was that this survey was concerned with *cost per unit weight* only, giving no consideration to the quality of ingredients or nutritional worth of the food. While according to Traub, "the lower cost of convenience meat items results, in part, from the fact that much more of the edible meat is used, enabling processors to more efficiently utilize a carcass," this saving is only a small part indeed. Actually it is the manufacturer's use of fillers such as modified food starch and flour, flavor enhancers such as MSG, disodium guanylate, sugar, and salt, the introduction of imitation ingredients like whipped toppings, dehydrated potatoes, fake cheese and soy analogs, and chemical additives, particularly artificial coloring, flavoring, and preservatives, that make processed foods cheap to manufacture.

If you were to consider the quantity of high quality food ingredients used by the manufacturer compared to what you might use in a home recipe, you would be surprised to find how nutritionally misleading most "convenience foods" really are. In evaluating the contents of commercial frozen beef pies, *Consumers' Research* magazine reported that in all samples the bulk of the package was crust, and in seven out of ten beef pies there was more gravy than beef. A breakdown of these ten pot pies is shown in Table 6-1.

The frozen pot pie is only one of a long list of prepared foods that charges you more for less. The Standards for Meat and Poultry Products present a partial listing of the percentages of meat, poultry, or other ingredients by weight which must be contained in a product to meet specific labeling requirements of the USDA. In order to be labeled with a

TABLE 6–1

Frozen Beef Pie Ingredients

	Percentage of ingredients by weight						
	Crust	Beef	Gravy	Potatoes	Onions	Peas	Carrots
Banquet	45	17	30	4	—	2	3
Farmdale	59	26	11	—	—	2	2
Grand Union	49	17	28	—	—	3	3
Morton	35	24	30	6	—	1	4
Myers	16	28	25	13	—	9	8
Pantry Pride	49	17	27	2	—	2	2
Stouffers	30	27	23	—	10	3	8
Sultana	49	10	22	8	—	7	4
Super Saver	51	8	30	—	—	5	5
Swanson	41	22	23	10	—	2	3

Compiled by Consumers' Research Inc.,
for *Consumer's Research* Magazine, August 1976.

particular name — such as "Beef with Gravy" or "Spaghetti with Meat and Sauce" — these products must include the noted percentages of ingredients. How do these rate compared to what you would add at home?

Standards for Meat and Poultry Products

(Percent of meat refers to uncooked weight unless otherwise stated)

Baby Food — High Meat Dinner — at least 30% meat; Vegetable and Meat — at least 8% meat; High Poultry Dinner — at least 18¾% poultry meat, skin, fat, and giblets
Beans with Frankfurters in Sauce — at least 20% franks
Beef with Gravy — at least 50% beef (cooked weight)
Gravy with Beef — at least 35% beef (cooked weight)
Breaded Meat — breading can't exceed 30% of finished weight
Breakfast Sausage — no more than 50% fat
Chili Con Carne — at least 40% meat
Chili Con Carne with Beans — at least 25% meat

Chop Suey Vegetable with Meat — at least 12% meat
Chow Mein Vegetables with Meat — at least 12% meat
Deviled Ham — no more than 35% fat
Goulash — at least 25% meat
Ham Croquettes — at least 35% ham (cooked weight)
Hash — at least 35% meat (cooked weight)
Lasagna with Meat and Sauce — at least 12% meat
Manicotti — at least 10% meat
Meat Balls — no more than 12% extenders
Meat Balls in Sauce — at least 50% meat balls (cooked weight)
Meat Pies — at least 25% meat
Spaghetti Sauce with Meat — at least 6% meat
Spaghetti with Meat and Sauce — at least 12% meat
Spaghetti with Meat Balls and Sauce — at least 12% meat balls
Stews — at least 25% meat
Veal Parmigiana — at least 40% breaded meat product in sauce
Poultry a la King — at least 20% poultry meat
Poultry Chop Suey — at least 4% poultry meat
Poultry Chow Mein — at least 4% poultry meat
Poultry Pies — at least 14% poultry meat
Poultry with Gravy — at least 35% poultry meat
Poultry with Gravy and Dressing — at least 25% poultry meat

Based on these percentages, a one-pound can of beef stew could contain as little as 4 ounces of meat (before cooking) or 2 ounces per serving. A typical homemade beef stew, based on a recipe in *The Joy of Cooking,* offers 5.3 ounces of meat per serving.

As mentioned earlier, to fill the rest of the package, food processors make frequent use of such commodities as modified food starch, cornstarch, wheat flour, and shortening. These ingredients not only cheapen the manufacturer's costs, but alter the nutritional make-up of the food as well. Such fillers tend to add carbohydrates, saturated fat, and calories to the product and little else. By replacing whole food with highly processed substitutes, the inherent fiber in foods is greatly reduced too, and thus as we saw in chapter 1 many people suffer from lack of roughage in their diets. The ubiquitous addition of salt and sugar adds to the growing incidence of hypertension, hardening of the arteries, and obesity in this country. Foods can be extended, but if you were to extend them in your own kitchen with whole grain flours and cereals, wheat germ, and dried bean products, you would get an increase in fiber, vitamin, and mineral content.

In canned products containing both liquid and solid ingredients, the problem of determining nourishing food content is further complicated by the fact that an indeterminate proportion of the package is liquid and the percent of solid food available differs from brand to brand. Thus, one brand may cost less per unit of weight, but actually cost more per edible portion.

Unfortunately the trend today on the part of the food industry is to discover low-cost fabricated foods to take the place of real ingredients. As Dr. Ross Hume Hall points out in his book *Food For Nought,* the object of the food industry is to develop "palatable products that sell well." And are they tasty? In a blind taste test conducted by Jean Hewitt of the *New York Times,* nine people, including four school children, compared four dishes made from dinner mixes (such as Hamburger Helper) and four homemade look-alike versions. The homemade versions were made from simple ingredients found in the average family kitchen, took only five to 10 minutes longer to prepare, and were made for an average of 10 cents less than the convenience dinners. In three of the four samples all nine testers preferred the homemade dinners.

But even if these imitation products were indistinguishable to the taste buds and eye, they do not go unnoticed by the body, which cannot make the same metabolic use of them as it would of the natural foods they replace. Additionally, while many of these additives have been subject to criticism as possibly adding harmful elements to the diet, none has any nutritional advantages.

Ecological Costs

Aside from lowering the nutritional quality of the diet, processing of food has a detrimental impact on the environment. The excessive packaging of most processed foods adds to the waste of resources and build-up of garbage. Dr. Priscilla Laws, associate professor of physics at Dickinson College in Pennsylvania, contends that if "U.S. production of paper for packaging purposes were cut in half, .2 million barrels of oil would be saved each day. This amount of energy is comparable to that which will be saved if all homes burning fuel oil cut oil consumption by 15 percent."

In the book *Energy and Food* prepared by the Center for Science in the Public Interest, the energy cost of food processing, including production, delivery, and marketing is revealed.

Here we learn, for example, that the energy cost of processing one pound of corn amounts to:

> 5,250 BTUs - fresh
> 10,300 BTUs - canned
> 12,750 BTUs - frozen
> 37,100 BTUs - dehydrated

Cost per Measure

Even if we were to discount the drain convenience foods place on the quality of foods and the quality of the environment, would the USDA statistics which appear to back up the claim that "the majority of convenience foods are as cheap or cheaper than that made from scratch" hold true?

Not according to consumer writer Sidney Margolius. He has calculated that the buyer "gives Lipton $.42 to combine $.30 worth of beef and $.07 worth of dried noodles in a package of Beef Stroganoff. Betty Crocker gets $.27 for combining $.12 worth of macaroni and $.10 worth of cheddar in macaroni and cheese, Uncle Ben gets $.12 for adding seasoning to his rice, and General Foods gets something like $1.70 a pound for adding seasonings to its Shake 'n' Bake."

Margolius is not the only one to disagree with the USDA findings. In evaluating the cost per pound of cereals, the Consumers Cooperative of Berkeley, Inc. in California came up with these cost comparisons:

Cereal	Cost per Pound/$
Whole Oats	.16
Cracked Wheat	.26
Brown Rice	.40

While prepared cereals which require less cooking revealed:

Cereal	Cost per Pound/$
Instant Ralston	.46
Rolled Oats	.30–.47
Wheatena	.49
Cream of Rice	.67
Cream of Wheat	.48–.57
Cream of Wheat, instant	1.04
Hominy Grits	.34
Instant Grits	.98
Maltex	.64

A similar situation exists for beans, where canned beans might be as much as three times the cost of an equal volume of beans cooked from the dried state.

The Price of Beans

Beans	Weight	Cooked Volume	Price/$	Price/Cup
Kidney, canned	1 lb.	2 cups	.39	.195
Kidney, dried	1 lb.	6.25 cups	.46	.072

Based on prices in Woodstock, New York, September 1975

Fresh fruit, when purchased in season, is usually less expensive than canned or frozen varieties which normally have sugar added, greatly increasing the cost. The USDA study of January 1974, on which much of their information on the cost of convenience foods is based, reveals the following:

Fruit Costs per Serving

Fruit	Fresh ¢	Frozen ¢	Canned ¢
Peaches	9.1	23.0	17.2
Grapefruit	4.5	26.4	14.3
Strawberries	15.4	34.6	30.0
Raspberries	16.8	36.1	23.8
Pineapple Chunks	12.0	12.5	11.1

Notice that pineapple, which is available unsweetened, shows the least price variation.

The one area in which the cost of processing is not so extreme is in terms of prepared juices versus fresh squeezed, and frozen and canned produce versus fresh. One reason these convenience items may represent a monetary savings is that the processor can contract for huge quantities or often owns the farm, thus saving on raw materials, and the processor has developed ways of using what the homemaker often discards as waste. Moreover, the high cost of fresh produce in most stores is based not only on the market value of the item, but includes an additional "surcharge" to cover spoilage. The savings afforded by processing of vegetables and juices, based on the January 1974 USDA study, conducted in one supermarket chain, is shown on the table which follows. Although these prices may not agree with those in your supermarket today, the pattern is universal.

Comparative Food Costs per Serving

Food	Fresh ¢	Frozen ¢	Canned ¢
Orange Juice	8.3	4.3	4.7
Lemon Juice	7.5		1.9
Corn on the Cob	16.7	12.5	
Corn Kernels	15.2	8.5	6.9
Green Beans	8.9	8.1	8.6
Spinach	26.3	8.5	12.5
Lima Beans	29.6	10.0	10.2
Asparagus	19.1	17.6	18.4
Brussels Sprouts	12.5	10.8	26.6
Carrots	5.5		8.1

   While some of these fresh vegetables may be more expensive than their frozen or canned counterparts, this is only true for unseasoned products. When vegetables are preseasoned or packed in a sauce, as is the current marketing trend, the price jump is significant. One finds:

When Someone Else Butters Your Beans

Food	Weight/ounces	Price/¢
Peas	10	33
Peas with Butter Sauce	10	49
Corn	10	29
Niblets Corn with Butter	10	49
Brussels Sprouts	10	37
Brussels Sprouts with Butter	10	65
French Style Green Beans	9	37
French Style Green Beans with Toasted Almonds	9	49
Broccoli	10	37
Broccoli with Cheese Sauce	10	59
Broccoli with Hollandaise	10	65

Based on prices in Woodstock, New York, September 1975

Some additional items which the USDA chose to evaluate in its study of cost comparisons between home prepared, frozen, and canned alternatives are listed below. If you were to compute the value of these foods strictly in terms of money perhaps you would agree with their conclusions that "the hypothesis that convenience foods contribute to higher prices may be questionable." You should understand, however, that what you are gaining in terms of less advance planning, less cooking and preparation time, and less clean-up, you are sacrificing in terms of nutrition, quality of raw ingredients, and potential adverse effects from chemical food additives. Strictly in terms of cost per volume through, the USDA supplies the following figures for January 1974:

Food Costs per Savings

Food	Home prepared	Frozen	Canned
Beef Patties	17.4 ¢	34.6 ¢	20.3 ¢
Meat Loaf	56.0	59.0	
Beef Pie	30.8	33.0	
Beef Stew	37.9		33.0
Fried Chicken	27.2	43.5	
Chicken Meat	20.0		32.5
Chicken Chow Mein	13.3	34.1	35.6
Turkey Sandwich	26.3	35.8	
Haddock Sticks	31.0	17.4	
Crab Cakes	39.4	39.5	
Shrimp Creole	69.8	74.0	
Shrimp, fried	47.2	81.4	
Spanish Rice	7.0		10.0
Pizza	31.8	56.1	

Buying in Bulk

Once you decide what it is you wish to buy, you can then determine the best approach for securing it. The most efficient way to buy food, strictly in terms of cost per unit, is to buy in bulk. But whether or not this is practical for your life-style is an important consideration before you begin to seek out bulk food suppliers.

When you have the opportunity to buy nonperishable items, like honey, maple syrup, peanut butter, dried beans, grains, dried fruit, nuts, etc., the saving of buying in bulk is easy to figure. The only real consideration is whether you have sufficient storage space.

It makes no sense to buy a basket of perishable produce, however, unless you can use it quickly or store it for the future. Although a small percentage of waste may not make the bulk purchase uneconomical, you must not exceed the point at which the spoilage will raise the cost above the current retail price.

The amount of spoilage you can absorb and still enjoy the advantage of bulk buying is known as "the margin of waste." To determine how much spoilage you can afford on an item, divide the current retail price (or nonbulk price per unit) into the bulk price. This will tell you how many units you must consume to make the purchase economically viable. The number of units beyond this that you obtain in the sale is your *margin of waste,* and even if this entire portion spoils you will not have lost money in the deal.

$$\text{Volume Equivalent at Current Retail Price} = \frac{\text{Total Bulk Price}}{\text{Nonbulk (or Retail) Cost per Unit}}$$

Margin of Waste = Total Amount Purchased — Volume Equivalent at Current Retail Price

Thus, if 1 bu. (30 lbs.) green beans sells for $6,00 and the retail price of green beans per lb. is $.29

$$\text{Volume Equivalent at Current Retail Price} = \frac{6.00}{.29} \text{ or } 20.7$$

Margin of Waste = 30 — 20.7 or 9.3 lbs.

Keep in mind that bulk produce is often sold by the bushel, an indication of volume, not weight, or cartons containing an average count of an item. Therefore, if you wish to figure the price per unit (be it one item or one pound) you must weigh the bushel or find the count per carton. In the absence of scales or someone who can answer your query, use the table of standard bulk units of food (Table 6-2) as a general guideline.

If you are not sure you can use at least the remainder of the food above the margin of waste, bulk buying will not be advantageous. But if you plan ahead, you can easily insure maximum usage. One important approach to maximizing a bulk purchase is menu planning. One of the biggest problems with bulk buying of perishables is the boredom that comes from seeing the same food on the plate day after day. Anyone who has grown zucchini can appreciate how depressing it is to hear the refrain "Oh no, not again!" after having strained his or her culinary genius to use the supply of such a prolific

TABLE 6–2

Standard Bulk Units of Food

Fruit	Approximate Weight/Volume
Apples	45 to 50 lbs./bu.
Apricots	48 lbs./bu.
Berries (not strawberries)	64 lbs./bu. or 24 qts./crate
Cherries	60 lbs./32 qts. (or crate)
Cranberries	55 lbs./bu.
Grapes	sold in quart baskets
Peaches	40 to 50 lbs./bu.
Pears	50 to 55 lbs./bu.
Plums	50 to 55 lbs./bu.
Strawberries	50 lbs./32 qts.
Tomatoes	50 to 60 lbs./bu.

Vegetables	
Asparagus	40 lbs./bu.
Beans, lima	32 lbs./bu.
Beans, snap	30 lbs./bu.
Beets	52 lbs./bu.
Beet Greens	15 lbs./bu.
Broccoli	25 lbs./crate
Carrots	50 lbs./bu.
Chard, Collards	12 lbs./bu.
Corn	36 lbs./bu.
Kale	18 lbs./bu.
Okra	40 lbs./bu.
Onions	52 lbs./bu.
Peas, in pod	30 lbs./bu.
Potatoes	60 lbs./bu.
Soybeans	60 lbs./bu.
Spinach	18 lbs./bu.
Summer Squash	40 lbs./bu.
Winter Squash, Pumpkin	40 lbs./bu.

Grains	
Alfalfa seed	60 lbs./bu.
Barley, hull-less	60 lbs./bu.
Buckwheat	50 lbs./bu.
Flax	56 lbs./bu.
Millet	48 lbs./bu.
Oats	32 lbs./bu.
Rice	45 lbs./bu.
Rye	56 lbs./bu.
Wheat	60 lbs./bu.

Compiled by USDA

vegetable. If you are considering a bulk purchase the first thing you should do is sit down with a pencil and paper, and perhaps your favorite cookbooks, and decide just how you can fit this food into the family menu. Consider its use as a main dish item (many vegetables can be stuffed, stewed, or simply steamed and served with a protein-rich sauce for a nourishing meal), a fruit or vegetable accompaniment, a soup, a salad, or dessert. By consulting a recipe you can gauge how much of the food you can consume in this way and still find it enjoyable.

In addition to bulk buying for present eating, there is another reason to secure produce in quantity at the height of the season. That is to preserve the food for use later in the year, when prices are up and quality is lower. Using the four basic methods of keeping food for the future — simple storage, freezing, canning, and drying — you will be able to make bulk buying go a long way. The details of food preservation are covered in the next chapter.

The Best Bulk Buys

Bulk purchases can be arranged in two different ways. For items which store easily over an extended period of time, such as grains, dried fruit, nuts, and beans, plus certain prepared foods, mail order bulk buying or buying directly from a distributor may be arranged. Several natural food wholesalers sell directly to consumers (often there is a minimum order), and depending on where you are located delivery may be free or pick-up arranged at an outlet which normally buys from the wholesaler. If you cannot buy directly from the warehouse, the distributor who services local stores may be willing to sell you items in bulk.

For produce and other perishable items — meat, dairy products, baked goods — local farms and food outlets are your best source of bulk food supplies. At harvesting time bushels of locally grown fruit and vegetables are sold at the most advantageous prices. Not only are these freshly picked foods at their best price, but they are generally of the highest nutritional quality. (Foods that are harvested for transport are usually picked before they are ripe and often before they are fully matured and do not have a chance to develop properly.) They are also less subject to fumigation, gassing, and other artificial treatment.

There are basically two ways to buy from a farmer in your area: you can either buy produce from him already picked and packed, or you can pick your own. In recent years more and more farms are trying pick-your-own marketing techniques. The operation is simple: customers bring containers and provide labor, and the farmer provides the produce. Prices are usually the lowest you'll find around, the quality is controlled by an expert — you — and the little labor involved provides an often needed break for the entire family. For gardeners with limited space, pick-your-own is a good way to get the freshest possible produce for your own home canning, jellying or freezing of those items you don't have room to grow yourself. To get the list of farmers in your area who sell by pick-your-own, contact the Direct Marketing Office of your State Department of Agriculture; they usually have complete brochures already made up.

The other way to buy in bulk is to have the farmer do the picking and packaging. The savings will not be as high this way, but you may be able to save some money over the wholesale market price. It is best to contact the person you wish to buy from a couple of weeks before harvest time to make sure you both are agreed upon on how much you will buy, the quality, price, and who will provide transportation and cleaning of the product. Some farmers are reluctant to sell directly, as they have found themselves holding out a few bushels for a customer from a shipment, and having the customer fail to show up. Many farmers ask for a guarantee if you want a large order, and often there are other complications. It is best to find someone you can deal with and trade with the same person every year.

If you cannot find a grower to buy from, locate the nearest wholesale produce market where the merchants in your area shop. Individuals are welcome here, but an orientation trip before you plan to buy is recommended. Visit the market early in the morning (around 5:30 or 6 a.m.) when restaurants and other buyers are shopping and watch them as they make their purchases. Inquire as to the bulk quantities available and the smallest bulk purchase you can make. Price similar items from several sellers and compare quality.

By subscribing to the *Fresh Fruit and Vegetable Market*

News for the terminal market nearest you, or *Food Marketing Alert,* you will be able to glean what the price and supply situation is for all items. These publications are prepared by the USDA and are available free from your local agriculture office. Have someone at the office explain the coding to you, and these publications can be very informative. When you go to the market to buy, get there as early as possible since sales are made on a first come basis.

Even without an official publication you can generally tell what is a good buy based on the season. When local farms are flourishing there will be an abundance of the foods they produce. Although the precise season for each vegetable varies throughout the country, during the cool spring growing season leafy green vegetables, broccoli, artichokes, radishes, peas, asparagus, pineapple, strawberries, and rhubarb are abundant. During the warmest months beans, tomatoes, okra, summer squash, corn, peaches, melons, plums, berries, and other fruits and vegetables dependent on warmth and sunshine are in good supply. Then, as the weather becomes cool again, the best prices and quality are found for cabbage, cauliflower, root crops, citrus, apples, pears, cranberries, grapes, greens, broccoli, pomegranates, sweet potatoes, and other fall harvested produce. For more details on harvest dates in your area consult Table 6-3 or your local county agent.

Prices for fresh produce coming from the terminal market will reflect the availability of these foods on a countrywide basis. The United Fresh Fruit and Vegetable Association in Washington, D.C. offers the guidelines in Table 6-3 on produce availability throughout the year:

TABLE 6–3

Monthly Availability Expressed as Percentage of Total Annual Supply

COMMODITY	Jan. %	Feb. %	Mar. %	Apr. %	May %	June %	July %	Aug. %	Sept. %	Oct. %	Nov. %	Dec. %
APPLES. all	10	9	10	9	8	5	3	4	9	12	10	11
" Washington	10	11	11	11	11	7	4	2	5	8	9	11
" New York	10	10	12	11	9	6	2	2	7	11	10	10
" Michigan	13	12	12	10	6	2	*	2	5	13	12	13
" California	6	6	7	5	2	1	4	15	26	15	8	5
" Virginia	9	8	8	5	2	*	1	2	16	19	17	13
APRICOTS					11	60	27	2				
ARTICHOKES	4	6	14	19	12	5	6	7	5	8	8	6
ASPARAGUS	*	6	28	31	20	10	*	*	1	1	1	
AVOCADOS, all	9	7	8	8	8	7	7	8	7	9	11	11
" California	7	8	11	10	10	10	8	8	6	6	8	8
BANANAS	8	8	10	9	8	8	7	7	7	8	9	9
BEANS, SNAP, all	6	4	6	9	10	12	12	11	9	8	7	6
" Florida	12	9	14	20	14	3	*		*	2	12	14

COMMODITY	Jan. %	Feb. %	Mar. %	Apr. %	May %	June %	July %	Aug. %	Sept. %	Oct. %	Nov. %	Dec. %
BEETS	5	5	6	6	6	12	14	13	12	10	7	4
BERRIES, MISC.**					2	30	39	14	8	5	2	
BLUEBERRIES					1	26	43	28	2			
BROCCOLI	10	9	12	9	9	7	5	5	7	9	9	9
BRUSSELS SPROUTS	13	13	12	7	4	*		2	6	14	17	12
CABBAGE, all	10	8	9	9	9	9	8	7	7	8	8	8
" Florida	17	15	19	22	15	3	*		1	*	1	8
" Texas	16	14	18	12	8	3	2	2	1	3	8	13
" California	10	9	11	9	11	11	7	6	5	7	7	7
" New York	9	7	5	3	1	1	7	10	12	16	17	12
" North Carolina	1			*	11	27	9	10	9	8	17	8
CANTALOUPES, all		*	3	4	10	20	25	22	11	4	1	
" California					*	15	28	33	16	6	1	*
" Mexico		1	17	32	43	7						
" Texas					23	47	19	9	1	*		
" Arizona					*	48	47	*		4	*	
CARROTS, all	10	9	10	9	8	7	7	7	7	9	9	8
" California	9	8	8	8	10	11	11	8	6	6	7	8

TABLE 6–3 *(Cont.)*

COMMODITY	Jan. %	Feb. %	Mar. %	Apr. %	May %	June %	July %	Aug. %	Sept. %	Oct. %	Nov. %	Dec. %
" Texas	15	16	18	16	8	3	*	2	2	3	7	9
CAULIFLOWER, all	9	6	8	7	6	6	5	6	9	15	14	9
" California	10	7	10	10	9	8	6	6	6	8	10	10
CELERY, all	9	8	9	8	8	8	8	7	7	8	10	10
" California	8	6	7	7	7	10	9	7	7	9	13	10
" Florida	15	15	17	15	14	8	1			*	3	11
" Michigan						1	20	29	30	16	3	1
CHERRIES, SWEET					11	41	43	5				
CHINESE CABBAGE	10	9	8	8	8	8	7	8	8	9	9	8
COCONUTS	9	7	9	7	6	5	4	7	8	8	11	19
CORN, SWEET, all	3	2	4	7	16	17	16	14	8	5	5	3
" Florida	5	4	6	11	27	24	5	*	*	5	7	6
" California					10	27	25	17	9	7	4	*
" New York							5	45	40	10		
CRANBERRIES									8	26	48	18
CUCUMBERS, all	7	5	6	7	11	12	12	9	8	8	8	7
" Florida	4	1	2	10	29	11	1		*	7	21	13
" Mexico	23	21	23	15	2	*					2	13

COMMODITY	Jan. %	Feb. %	Mar. %	Apr. %	May %	June %	July %	Aug. %	Sept. %	Oct. %	Nov. %	Dec. %
" California	*	*	1	3	12	15	21	17	13	10	6	2
EGGPLANT	10	8	8	9	7	7	8	10	9	8	8	8
ESCAROLE-ENDIVE	10	9	10	10	9	8	7	7	6	7	8	9
GARLIC	8	8	8	8	8	8	10	9	10	9	7	6
GRAPEFRUIT, all	12	12	12	11	10	6	4	3	3	8	10	9
" Florida	11	12	13	13	11	5	2	*	3	10	10	10
" Texas	18	18	18	11	4	*		*	*	5	11	14
" Western	5	5	6	7	12	15	17	16	10	2	2	3
GRAPES	4	3	3	3	2	6	11	17	18	15	10	8
GREENS*	10	9	11	10	9	7	6	6	7	8	8	9
HONEY DEWS	1	1	3	5	7	12	10	20	22	15	3	1
LEMONS	8	6	8	9	9	11	11	9	7	8	7	8
LETTUCE, all	8	7	9	9	9	9	9	9	8	8	8	7
" California	8	8	8	7	10	10	10	9	9	9	7	5
" Arizona	11	6	13	25	7	1	*	*	*	2	13	21
" Florida	16	15	20	16	9	*				*	8	15
" Ohio	6	6	9	7	6	8	12	12	9	9	9	7
LIMES	6	4	5	5	9	12	13	12	10	8	7	9

TABLE 6–3 *(Cont.)*

COMMODITY	Jan. %	Feb. %	Mar. %	Apr. %	May %	June %	July %	Aug. %	Sept. %	Oct. %	Nov. %	Dec. %
MANGOS	*	1	3	6	17	23	28	17	4	1		
MUSHROOMS	9	8	9	9	9	8	7	7	7	8	9	9
NECTARINES	*	*	*		1	19	36	30	12	*		
OKRA	2	3	6	7	11	14	17	17	11	7	3	2
ONIONS, DRY, all	9	7	8	8	9	9	9	9	8	9	8	7
" Texas	1	*	4	26	27	14	12	10	3	1	1	1
" California	3	1	1	1	11	21	23	17	8	6	5	3
" New York	12	9	11	6	2	1	1	8	14	13	12	11
ONIONS, GREEN	7	6	8	10	11	10	10	8	7	7	7	7
ORANGES, all	11	12	13	11	10	7	5	4	4	5	8	10
" Western	9	10	12	12	11	7	5	5	6	6	7	10
" Florida	14	15	14	11	9	6	3	1	1	4	9	13
PAPAYAS, HAWAII	6	6	6	7	10	10	9	8	8	10	11	9
PARSLEY & HERBS****	8	7	9	7	7	8	7	8	8	9	11	11
PARSNIPS	12	11	11	9	7	5	3	4	8	11	10	9
PEACHES, all	*	*			6	17	31	29	15	1		
" California					8	22	34	24	10	2		
" South Carolina					1	19	53	26	1			

COMMODITY	Jan. %	Feb. %	Mar. %	Apr. %	May %	June %	July %	Aug. %	Sept. %	Oct. %	Nov. %	Dec. %
" Georgia					5	42	45	8	37	1		
" New Jersey							8	54				
PEARS, all	**7**	**7**	**7**	**6**	**4**	**2**	**4**	**13**	**16**	**17**	**10**	**7**
" California	1	*	*	*			12	33	27	20	5	1
" Washington	9	9	8	6	2			9	16	16	14	11
" Oregon	16	16	13	7	1			*	3	15	16	13
PEAS, GREEN	**12**	**12**	**13**	**13**	**12**	**12**	**10**	**6**	**5**	**2**	**1**	**2**
PEPPERS, all	**8**	**7**	**8**	**7**	**8**	**10**	**11**	**9**	**9**	**8**	**8**	**7**
" Florida	15	9	10	14	16	14	1			*	6	15
" California				*	2	7	13	15	20	28	14	1
" Mexico	19	24	25	13	5	2	1	1	1	1	2	6
PERSIMMONS										33	48	19
PINEAPPLES	**7**	**7**	**11**	**10**	**12**	**12**	**9**	**7**	**6**	**5**	**7**	**7**
PLANTAINS	**7**	**7**	**6**	**8**	**8**	**9**	**9**	**11**	**10**	**9**	**6**	**10**
PLUMS-PRUNES	*	*	*		1	15	33	32	15	2		
POMEGRANATES								2	9	72	15	2
POTATOES, all	**9**	**8**	**9**	**8**	**9**	**8**	**8**	**8**	**8**	**9**	**8**	**8**
" California	5	5	5	4	9	23	23	9	5	4	4	4

TABLE 6–3 *(Cont.)*

COMMODITY	Jan. %	Feb. %	Mar. %	Apr. %	May %	June %	July %	Aug. %	Sept. %	Oct. %	Nov. %	Dec. %
" Idaho	13	12	13	13	13	7	1	*	1	6	10	10
" Maine	13	12	15	17	15	5	*	*	1	3	8	10
" Colorado	12	10	12	1	7	*	*	6	9	11	10	11
" North Dakota	15	13	14	12	5	1	*	*	2	9	14	14
PUMPKINS	1	1	2	2	2	2	*	*	3	83	2	1
RADISHES	8	8	10	11	11	8	8	7	6	6	9	8
RHUBARB	8	15	16	23	21	9	3	1	1	1	1	1
SPINACH, all	9	9	11	9	9	8	7	6	7	8	8	9
" California	9	10	12	10	9	7	7	7	6	7	8	8
SQUASH, all	8	6	6	7	8	9	10	9	9	11	10	7
" California	4	3	3	8	10	12	11	10	10	13	11	5
" Florida	11	9	11	15	15	3	*	1	1	6	14	14
STRAWBERRIES, all	3	5	8	18	29	16	7	5	4	2	1	2
" California		*	3	22	35	18	9	6	4	2	*	*
" Mexico	21	25	29	5						*	5	14
SWEET POTATOES, all	9	8	8	7	5	3	3	5	9	11	19	13
" North Carolina	9	8	10	10	7	4	1	1	6	12	19	13
" Louisiana	9	8	9	6	2	*	5	11	11	11	16	12

COMMODITY	Jan. %	Feb. %	Mar. %	Apr. %	May %	June %	July %	Aug. %	Sept. %	Oct. %	Nov. %	Dec. %
" California	8	7	8	8	5	4	3	3	7	10	20	17
TANGELOS	23	4	*			*			*	*	**33**	**39**
TANGERINES	21	8	7	4	**2**	11	11	**9**	7	**5**	**20**	**32**
TOMATOES, all	7	6	8	8	11	11	11	**9**	**7**	**8**	**7**	**7**
" California	1	*		*	1	8	17	16	16	22	13	5
" Mexico	13	17	22	20	16	5	*	*	*	*	2	3
" Florida	14	8	10	12	20	13	*	*		*	6	17
" Ohio			1	6	18	20	24	11	5	6	7	2
TURNIPS & RUTABAGAS	**12**	**10**	**10**	**8**	**6**	4	4	**6**	**7**	**11**	**13**	**9**
" Canada	11	10	9	7	3	1	1	4	10	12	19	13
WATERMELONS	*	*	1	**3**	**10**	**28**	**31**	**20**	**5**	1	*	*

* Supply is less than 0.5% of annual total.
** Mostly raspberries, blackberries, and dewberries.
*** Includes kale, kohlrabi, collards, cabbage sprouts, dandelion, mustard and turnip tops, poke salad, bok choy, and rappini.
**** Includes also parsley root, anise, basil, chives, dill, horseradish, and others.

By United Fresh Fruit and Vegetable Association by Charles E. Magoon

Supermarket Shopping

Although buying food in bulk is often the most economical way to shop, it is not always practical. Where storage space is limited, when additional supplies are needed, or when you are pressed for time, more traditional shopping strategies must be put into operation.

As a matter of convenience the supermarket cannot be ignored. Nowhere do you find such a large variety of foods under one roof. While many of the foods available in the supermarket are highly processed and heavily dependent on chemical additives, there are still items to be found that offer good nutritional value at a fair price.

In order to determine what is the best buy, you must learn to read labels not only for price comparison but to understand the nature of the food. All processed, packaged foods are required by law to contain the following information on the label:

1. The name of the product.

2. The variety, style, and packing medium in conjunction with the name, as *French style* string beans; *diced* carrots; pineapple packed in *pineapple juice.*

3. The net quantity, that is, the total weight of the contents.

4. Name, city, state, and zip code of the manufacturer, packer, or distributor.

5. A list of special dietary properties if applicable, such as *enriched, high protein, salt-free, artificially sweetened.* Where these involve nutritional claims the package label must also include the nutritional contribution the food can be expected to make to your diet as explained further on in the section on nutrition labeling.

6. Some indication if the product differs from government regulations, making the product "Imitation" or "Below Standard of Quality."

7. A list of ingredients in descending order of predominance. This applies to all foods, except those which have a preregistered "recipe" with the Food and Drug Administration (included in Title 21, Code of Federal Regulations), in which case only certain optional ingredients may be on the label. There are hundreds of foods thus exempted and they fall into the following categories:

Cacao (cocoa bean) products
Wheat flour and related products
Corn flour and related products
Rice and related products
Macaroni and noodle products
Bakery products
Milk and cream products
Cheeses, processed cheeses, cheese foods, cheese spreads, and related foods
Frozen desserts
Food flavorings
Dressing for food
Nutritive sweeteners
Canned fruits and fruit juices
Fruit pies
Fruit butters, fruit jellies, fruit preserves, and related products
Nonalcoholic beverages
Shellfish
Fish
Eggs and egg products
Oleomargarine
Nut products
Canned vegetables
Tomato products

There are several other points of note about labeling requirements. With the exception of butter, ice cream, and cheese, which do not have to list the use of artificial coloring, whenever artificial color, flavor, or preservatives are used it must be stated on the label. Also, if any ingredient itself contains one of these additives it will be evidenced on the label, as for example, "Vegetable oil with BHT."

Certain other chemical additions, like fumigants used in storage, defoaming agents added in production, or anticaking agents which are inherent in the salt added to the ingredients, will not be indicated on the label.

Many labels also offer the last date of sale or expected freshness, and while all this information by no means reveals everything you might like to know, it can be of value in helping you to purchase high quality, economical foodstuffs. If you are interested in educating yourself further in this area you should read Title 21 of the Code of Federal Regulations which sets forth most of the rules and regulations pertaining to commercial food manufacture, and *The Supermarket Handbook/Access to Whole Foods* by Nikki and David Goldbeck which, among other things, attempts to translate this law for the lay person.

To be more specific here, however, in terms of good, wholesome foods, what are the best choices you can make at the supermarket? To help you decide let's roam through the aisles of a store.

The Dairy Case

Eggs   If you cannot get eggs from a local farmer who raises free-running, grain-fed hens, you might as well get them at the supermarket. The official USDA grade shield on eggs is an indication of quality *at the time of grading.* Grade AA and A eggs have a high rounded yolk and compact white, all signs of freshness. As quality deteriorates rapidly at room temperature, only buy eggs from a refrigerated case. According to the USDA, to get the best egg buy per weight you must know the price of a dozen large eggs and the price difference between the various size eggs you are considering. With this information you can consult the following table for the most economical buy:

When the price of a dozen large eggs is: ¢	Buy the larger of two sizes if the price difference is less than: ¢
41–48	6
49–56	7
57–64	8
65–72	9
73–80	10
81–88	11
89–96	12
97–104	13
105–112	14
113–120	15

So if you go to the store and the price of a dozen large eggs is 85¢, and the next larger size, extra large eggs, costs 92¢, you will know the latter is a better buy. (According to the USDA, at 85¢ a dozen for large eggs it is more economical to buy the larger size when the price difference is less than 11¢.) Likewise, if medium eggs sell for 75¢, you will get more for your money if you spend 85¢ for the large size.

Milk and Milk Derivatives   Often "dairy" and "ice cream stores" offer milk at a better price, but if not, whole and skim milk, light, whipping, and sour cream, and yogurt are sold at most supermarkets. The quality of these items is comparable to all but those you get right from the farm. Be sure to read the label of yogurt in particular to see that all you are buying is pasteurized milk plus the culture. Many brands add unnecessary thickeners, preservatives, and coloring and flavoring agents. Located elsewhere in the store is dry milk powder which is an economical buy (most brands save you from one-half to one-quarter the price of fresh milk) and can be used for cooking where it will go undetected, and making homemade yogurt, in addition to drinking. Other processed milk products like evaporated and condensed milk are less desirable due to their dependence on emulsifying agents like carrageenan, and refined sweeteners.

In most parts of the country with local dairy herds you will be able to find a dairy product you cannot buy in stores, raw milk. This is milk that has not been pasteurized. Nutrition-wise, the best milk to drink is raw milk, as the temperatures needed for pasteurization have a harmful effect on vitamins A, B, and C. Most states allow raw milk to be sold if the farmer purchases a permit. Sanitation standards are strict, and almost constant testing procedures must be maintained to make sure bacteria counts are kept low. If your source has a permit, you need not worry, but if you are buying raw milk from a person without a permit, you should inspect the barns, milking parlor, and dairy yourself to see if things are clean and properly cared for. Raw milk is both cheaper and more nutritious, but you may have some problems finding a convenient and safe source of supply.

Cheese   There are two general classifications of cheese: natural and processed (including pasteurized process cheese, cheese food, and cheese spread). The latter group, identifiable by one of these terms on the label, contains a variety of additives including emulsifiers, stabilizers, artificial coloring and flavoring, and preservatives. Although natural cheeses may cost a few cents more, in terms of quality and wholesomeness they are the best buy. Be careful though. Some natural cheeses may contain the preservatives sorbic acid, sodium sorbate, or potassium sorbate; this will always be included on the label.

Butter   All commercially manufactured butter is subject to the same abuses. Often it is stored for a long period of time, it may be colored without indication, and it may be produced from stale recycled milk or cream. Since sweet butter is more likely to reveal mishandling than salt butter, and it is also lower in sodium content, this is your best butter buy. Most margarines are heavily laden with chemical additives, but if you insist on buying one, look for a brand which lists liquid oil rather than hydrogenated or hardened oil first on the label.

The Meat Case

It is probably more difficult to determine the quality of meat in the supermarket than anywhere else. The use of special lights, wrappings, blood, and (according to Jon McClure in *Meat Eaters Are Threatened*) toxic chemicals forbidden by law, all make a visual appraisal of meat unreliable. Here though are several tips which may be of help.

1. Buy unfrozen cuts since you have no way of knowing how long meat has been frozen or under what conditions it has been kept.

2. Use the date on the package as a guideline. Although different stores use different dating codes, the store manager is obliged to interpret for you.

3. If a choice of grades is available buy "good" rather than "choice" as it is less expensive, less fatty, and correspondingly higher in protein and minerals.

4. If you do have a chance to view the meat, remember that fresh meat is cherry red in color. The darker the meat, the older the animal. Texture should be velvety, not coarse; fat white, not yellow.

5. For ground meat select the cut of meat yourself and ask to have it specially ground. To reduce the cost per pound and increase the available nutrients have the butcher grind in a heart or liver at the same time.

6. In choosing organ meats, and liver in particular, it is best to choose those of young animals (calves over steers) for they have had less exposure to hormones and antibiotics in their short life.

7. Although it is costly, veal, which is the meat of a young calf, is among your best buys as the animal is slaughtered young and therefore avoids a long life of chemical feeding. Veal is low in fat, making it easier on your heart, and since there is very little waste, a small amount can go a long way.

8. Lamb also comes from young animals and thus has had

less chance of being mistreated with chemicals in its short life. One excellent buy in the lamb department is New Zealand Lamb since, according to The New Zealand Lamb Information Center, "in New Zealand all sex hormones and tenderizers are banned, and animal tranquilizers are not in use." In terms of nutritive content, leg of lamb has about half the fat of breast and shoulder cuts.

9. Stay away from frankfurters and other processed meats in general. The drawbacks to all these products are many. Firstly, almost all commercial manufacturers of processed meats rely on those cancer-causing nitrites that we discussed in chapter 2 to preserve and color their products. In addition, all these meat items are high in fat; corn syrup, a highly refined sugar extract, is present in most varieties; and even in "all meat" frankfurters as much as 45 percent of the weight may be fat, water, and additives. In pork and breakfast sausage fat alone may account for 50 percent of the contents.

10. Poultry may be less costly, less fatty, and higher in nutrients per calorie than other meats, but the specimens offered in the supermarket are not always of the most wholesome quality by organic standards. Chickens in this country are raised in enormous coops, and the bird may be housed in an individual box for its entire life. Antibiotics and arsenic are commonly added to the feed to improve the efficiency of food utilization, speeding growth and weight gain. Residues of these chemicals may be transferred to the meat and the eggs. If you do buy supermarket poultry you will generally get a better price on the whole bird than on cut-up birds or parts. Avoid "butterball" and self-basting turkeys which cost 5 to 10 cents more per pound for the addition of fat (usually saturated coconut oil) and water. Consider duck, which being less in demand is raised in a more natural setting.

11. Try to emphasize fish on the menu. Select ocean varieties over fresh water fish which are unfortunately exposed to more pollutants. Nutritionally fish is higher in protein and lower in fat and calories per pound than meat.

Cereals and Grains

With the enormous display of packaged, processed cereals of little nutritional value beyond the synthetically introduced vitamins, you probably wonder what could be a good buy on this shelf. If you look closely you will find an occasional brand of cold cereal based on whole grains which is devoid of sugar, artificial color and flavor, and the preservatives BHT and BHA. This is a good time to remind you that the ingredients are listed on the label in descending order, and if sugar is near the top of the list, that is mostly what you are paying for.

The supermarket can offer good buys on oats (not the instant kind), whole wheat and whole rye cereals, wheat germ, and in some parts of the country unbolted cornmeal (as opposed to degermed cornmeal which has had the germ removed). Other whole grains you may find include cracked wheat (bulgur), buckwheat groats (kasha), and brown rice. Semolina (couscous), found in some supermarkets, is a partially refined grain in that it retains the germ, but not the bran from durum wheat. Usually the prices on these items will be lower than those in the natural foods store, although the brown rice, for one, is rarely of as high quality. Most other grain products in the supermarket, including farina, grits, and corn flour, are highly refined.

While it is possible to find unbleached white and whole wheat flours in the supermarket, it is better to buy these from an organic supplier as the large commercial manufacturers fumigate these items. If economic factors or lack of choice dictate buying whole grain flours in the supermarket, check the label to be sure they are not "bromated" or "phosphated," both processes employed to "improve the baking qualities" of the grain.

Baked Goods

With the growing interest in "health foods" most supermarkets have taken on at least one line of whole grain bread. Do not be misled by packages that say "natural" or "old fashioned" — read the label. Select breads made with whole grains, honey or molasses, vegetable and nut oils, possibly milk and eggs, yeast, and nothing else. Look for crackers with the same qualities. You will undoubtedly recognize many crackers that are on the shelf of both your local natural foods store and the supermarket. Use the crackers and stale bread for making crumbs and you will save the purchase of this item and get better food value for less money at the same time.

Pasta

The best pasta products are those made with whole wheat flour, but these are not widely available in the supermarket.

Most commercial manufacturers use durum flour, semolina, or farina instead, all products of highly refined wheat. At least you should purchase those made with unbleached flour if this is specified.

Although many companies say on the package "no artificial color added," no pasta product on the market, by law, is permitted to add coloring agents. They may add the chemical disodium phosphate to reduce cooking time, and this will be specified on the label.

Enrichment of pasta products can come from synthetic vitamins as well as from wheat germ and food yeast. Naturally the latter is preferred, but the label will not necessarily help you determine how the enrichment was achieved.

The difference between macaroni products and noodles, both forms of pasta, is that noodles include the addition of eggs, either whole or just yolks, fresh or dried. While the eggs add nutrients, the quality of grain used in noodles is lower, so that macaroni actually has a higher protein content.

Beans

Dried beans are among the most economical sources of protein you can buy. On a pound for pound basis soybeans, for example, furnish more than twice the protein of sirloin steak at about one-sixth the price. Other cost/protein comparisons appear in Table 6-4. The price of dried beans in the supermarket is usually several cents lower per pound than elsewhere, but remember, these beans are not generally grown under organic conditions as they may be when purchased from a natural foods supplier.

Not only are beans an economical buy, they are a nutritious bonanza. Table 6-5 compares the nutritional content of navy beans to white rice, a baked potato, and spaghetti. As you can see, it is no contest: beans are a far superior food source.

The quality of beans can best be determined if you select a see-through package. The beans should have a bright uniform color, as fading is an indication of long storage and less tasty results. It is best to buy beans which are uniform in size, otherwise they will not cook evenly and by the time the larger beans are tender, the small ones will be mushy. You should also look over the package for defects, including many discolorations, perforations in the bag itself, cracked beans, and foreign matter, all of which indicate lesser quality.

For those who yearn for variety on the menu, you could

hardly find a category of food that offers more choices than beans. Each type of bean has its own characteristic flavor, making it particularly suitable to certain types of service, although in general one type of bean can be substituted for another in a recipe. Some favorites include:

Black beans — These are popular in South American dishes and are the basis of a thick, spicy Cuban soup that is laced with hot pepper and vinegar.

Black-eyed peas (or cow peas) — A mainstay of southern and soul food cookery accompanied by rice (brown) and greens. These beans are oval shaped with a small black spot on one side.

Chick peas (garbanzos) — Mideastern and Spanish cuisines feature many chick pea dishes, from dips to soups to bean croquettes. Chick peas have a distinct nut-like flavor.

Great Northern beans — Like pea beans, only larger, these beans are used primarily in soups and home-baked beans.

TABLE 6–4

The Money Saving Bean

Food	Cost/Lb.* $	Protein/Lb. (grams)	Calories/Lb.
Soybeans	.69	154.7	1,828
Split peas	.29	109.8	1,579
Lima beans	.65	92.5	1,565
Kidney beans	.49	102.1	1,556
Lentils	.37	112.0	1,542
Chick peas	.69	93.0	1,638
Eggs	.56	52.1	658
Cottage cheese	.69	61.7	481
Swiss cheese	1.79	119.8	1,610
Chicken	.79	57.4	382
Halibut	2.39	94.8	454
Tuna, canned	1.35	111.1	760
Ground chuck	1.03	81.2	1,216
Sirloin, bone in	2.29	71.1	1,316
Bacon	1.89	38.1	3,016
Frankfurters, all meat	1.29	59.4	1,343
Pork, loin chop	1.99	61.1	1,065
Veal, loin chop	2.39	72.3	681
Lamb, shoulder chop	1.99	58.9	1,082

*average supermarket price, July 1975

Beans make an excellent, nutritious substitute for rice, potatoes, or spaghetti. The National Academy of Sciences-National Research Council has set a Recommended Dietary Allowance for nutrients that children and adults need daily. Here's how navy beans (the most common kind) stack up against rice, potatoes, and spaghetti in providing the daily allowance of seven important nutrients.

TABLE 6-5

Why Not Use Beans Instead?

	Navy beans (1 cup cooked)			White rice (1 cup cooked)		
	Child 7-10	Male 23-50	Female 23-50	Child 7-10	Male 23-50	Female 23-50
Protein	41%	27%	32%	8%	5%	7%
Thiamin	36	31	43	13	11	16
Vitamin B-6	31	19	19	6	3	3
Iron	52	52	29	14	14	8
Calcium	12	12	12	2	2	2
Phosphorus	35	35	35	5	5	5
Magnesium	45	32	38	5	3	4

	Baked potato (1 large)			Spaghetti (1 cup cooked)		
	Child 7-10	Male 23-50	Female 23-50	Child 7-10	Male 23-50	Female 23-50
Protein	11%	7%	8%	20%	13%	16%
Thiamin	13	11	15	22	19	26
Vitamin B-6	31	19	19	3	2	2
Iron	10	10	6	16	16	9
Calcium	2	2	2	2	2	2
Phosphorus	12	12	12	12	12	12
Magnesium	20	15	17	12	8	10

Compiled by Consumers Union for *Consumer Reports*

Kidney beans — Red and shaped like a kidney, and particularly popular in South American favorites like chili and refried beans.

Lentils — Lentils, unlike other beans, do not require presoaking and are tender after about 45 minutes cooking. Lentils lend themselves to soups, salads, curries, and combination with grains, meat, and other vegetables as well as fruits. The cooking liquid is an ideal base for nonmeat gravies.

Lima beans — These broad, flat beans come in a variety of sizes. They make a welcome soup or stew on a cold, damp day.

Navy beans — This general title refers to all small white beans including Great Northern and pea beans.

Pea beans — These are the favored bean for baked beans since they hold their shape well even after hours of cooking.

Pinto beans — Part of the kidney bean family and suitable for all the same dishes. These beans are beige colored and speckled.

Pink beans — Another kidney bean variation that is more delicate in color and flavor.

Soybeans — Of all the beans soybeans have the highest quality of usable protein and are the only food in the vegetable kingdom that contains all the essential amino acids the body needs to build protein. Soybeans are mild in flavor and can be used in the same manner as all other beans. In addition, they can be ground with water to make soy milk and curdled to make soy cheese.

Split peas — Split peas, both yellow and green varieties, have had their skins mechanically removed, and this is responsible for their shortened cooking time. Like lentils they need no soaking and are cooked tender in about 45 minutes. Split peas are best suited to soups and curries and vegetable purees.

Whole peas — Whole peas are more akin to other beans in cooking techniques and should be soaked beforehand. One of the nicest ways to serve them is just plain boiled and seasoned with butter.

See chapters 3 and 9 for specific directions for cooking grains and lentils and combining them with other foods for low-cost dishes.

Canned, precooked beans are less economical, but are good in a pinch. In purchasing canned beans read the label to determine which brands do not add the chemical FDTA.

Fruit and Vegetable Juices

A large chunk of the food budget is spent on things to drink, particularly in households with children. The supermarket is a very important source of pure fruit and vegetable juices at rock bottom prices. Among the best buys are tomato juice, apple juice, pineapple juice, orange and grapefruit juices, prune juice, and carrot juice, all, of course, unsweetened. This is one aisle where there are frequent sales when you can stock up for several months. Note: Other titles given to juice-like beverages, including juice-drinks, ades, nectars, a..d punches, indicate the juice has been extended with water and sweeteners and more often than not artificial coloring, flavoring, and nutrients.

Oils

While cold pressed and unrefined oils are not available in the average supermarket, the minimally processed oils you can get include olive oil and peanut oil, both good buys if you cannot afford the high prices for oil elsewhere. While these two are free of preservatives and "winterizing agents," most supermarket safflower, corn, soy, and vegetable oils are not.

Fruits and Vegetables

Although some supermarkets have a pitiful display of wilting produce, there are equally as many with top choice, high grade items. If there are several supermarkets in your area, patronize the store with the best produce, even if you don't buy your produce there, since this is one sign that the store is conscientious. When your own garden is not producing you may be able to get fresh, but rarely organic, fruits and vegetables from Florida and California. If you stick to what is in season you can actually do quite well on supermarket produce and avoid having to resort to commercially canned and frozen alternatives. The Tips for Fruit and Vegetable Selection below will help you determine quality; seasonal abundance is summarized in Table 6-4, Fruit and Vegetable Availability, earlier in the chapter.

If you cannot shop regularly or find what you need, frozen produce can be economical. Be sure to read the label carefully and buy packages containing frozen produce only. You will notice it is getting harder to find items which do not have a sauce, or added chemicals to make them "quick cooking."

Tips for Vegetable Selection

Artichokes — Look for compact, tightly closed heads that are heavy in relation to size. Choose those with green, fresh-looking leaves. Avoid leaves that are very brown or show mold growth or worm holes. Spreading leaves indicate age and will be tough, dry, and bitter.

Asparagus — Look for firm, well-rounded spears with compact tips. Avoid flat stalks and tips that are open or decayed.

Avocados — See Fruits.

Beans, green and wax — Select pods that are crisp and snap easily. Color should be bright and fresh looking. Avoid beans that are limp, thick, and marked with brown rust spots.

Beets — Look for firm beets with a smooth surface and lush red color. If tops are intact they should be fresh looking. Badly wilted tops indicate lack of freshness, but the beets could still be satisfactory as long as they are firm. Beets that are soft and have scaly areas around the top are generally tough and bitter.

Broccoli — Stalks should be firm with a dark green cluster of compact buds at the top. Buds that are open, yellow, or wilted mean stalks that are tough and stringy.

Brussels sprouts — These miniature cabbages should have tight, firm leaves with a bright color and no worm holes. Avoid those with yellowing leaves that are soft, loose, or wilted.

Cabbage — The same rules govern cabbage as Brussels sprouts, and heads should be heavy with deep color and no obvious blemishes.

Carrots — Firm and well colored carrots are the tastiest, and those that have a regular shape are most economical as there is less waste. Carrots with large green areas at the top and those that are flabby are rarely sweet.

Cauliflower — The head of cauliflower should be compact with creamy white clusters. Many discolorations are a sign of mold and insect injury.

Celery — Buy celery with as many fresh green leaves as possible for soup making, and check to see the stalks are crisp and snap easily. Poor quality celery is limp and shows discoloration along the base.

Corn — Once corn is shucked flavor and nutrients dissipate rapidly. Therefore ears of corn should have the husks when bought, and they should be a good green color with silk ends that are neither discolored nor dried out. When you pull back the husk the kernels should be plump and milky. Color is no indication of quality since this varies with species; however, kernels that are extremely pale, underdeveloped or shriveled, or oversized are indications of poor flavor.

Cucumber — Look for unwaxed cucumbers with a uniform green color and a fairly even shape. Overgrown cucumbers, which have a dull color and show yellowing, have a bitter taste. So do those with withered ends or flesh that gives under pressure.

Eggplant — A regal purple skin and a vegetable that is heavy in relation to size are signs of a sweet eggplant. Avoid those with poor color, dark spots, and cracked or shriveled skin.

Garlic — Garlic bulbs should have a papery, unbroken casing. Those that are soft, with brown spots, are on the road to decay.

Greens — Greens should look fresh to the eye with bright color and no visible blemishes. Leaves that are wilted, yellowing, or soft in spots will spoil rapidly.

Leeks — Leeks that are crisp are fresh; leeks that are wilted, have soggy roots, or brown outer leaves are not.

Mushrooms — Young mushrooms are the tastiest and they are evidenced by caps that are closed around the stem or just slightly open revealing tan gills. White or cream colored species are best, although a light brown color is acceptable too. Those with wide open caps, serious discoloration, and soft spots will be spongy in texture.

Okra — Pods of okra should be blemish free, and the tips should bend under slight pressure. If the ends are stiff and won't bend, and if the pods are over 4½ inches long, they will more than likely be tough.

Onions — The outer scales of onion should be dry and papery and the bulb itself quite hard. Onions that are wet, beginning to sprout, or are excessively green should be discarded.

Parsnips — To avoid waste, even-shaped roots are suggested. They should be smooth, firm, and free of surface decay. Extremely large parsnips and those that are flabby remain tough, even after cooking.

Peas — Fresh pea pods feel velvety and plump, without being swollen. Once they are swollen, flecked with gray, and pale the peas are past their prime.

Peppers — Although firm bright color is an indication of good quality, a shiny surface on peppers can be misleading, a product of waxing rather than quality. Peppers should be heavy for their size; if the walls are thin they will be lightweight and flimsy. While shape does not affect flavor or wholesomeness, a very crooked pepper may have greater waste.

Potatoes — Again, to avoid waste potatoes should be fairly uniform in shape. They should be firm and free of eyes, or sprouts. Soft spots, bruises, or cuts lead to decay. Large areas of green impart a bitter taste.

Pumpkin — Pumpkins should be firm and heavy for good eating quality.

Radishes — Choose medium size radishes that are firm and of good color. Radishes that are overgrown, with yellow or decayed tops, are bitter. Undesirable sponginess can be detected by slight pressure.

Summer squash — Again, this vegetable should be heavy for the size, with a rind tender enough to puncture with a fingernail. Soft spots, dull color, and tough surface mean many seeds and a dry, stringy pulp.

Sweet potatoes and yams — Like other potatoes these should be firm and evenly shaped to avoid waste. Color can be misleading since these potatoes may be waxed or artificially colored. Any injury to the surface, including cuts and worm holes, will lead to waste and rapid decay.

Tomatoes — Actually a fruit, but considered by most in the vegetable category, tomatoes should be firm, plump, with good color and a tomato smell. It is better to do without than to buy hard, tasteless tomatoes out of season.

Turnips and rutabagas — Once again, choose those that are heavy in relation to size with no surface defects.

Winter squash — Look for a hard, tough rind and a hefty weight.

Tips for Fruit Selection

Apples — To be rich in flavor with a crisp interior apples must be picked after maturity is reached. Although waxing may enhance their appearance, only those of high color are mature. Apples that yield to pressure will have a soft, mealy flesh.

Apricots — Ripe apricots yield to gentle pressure. Overripe ones are mushy. Choose only those with a uniform golden-orange hue and pass by those that are pale yellow or greenish in hue. These are either underripe or overmature.

Avocados — For immediate eating choose avocados that yield to gentle pressure. For the future buy firm fruit and ripen at room temperature. The skin should be of even color with no cracks. Irregular brown markings do not affect interior quality, but avoid fruits with dark sunken spots and a cracked surface.

Bananas — The stage of ripeness is indicated by the color of the banana peel. When the yellow jacket is speckled with brown the fruit will be tender, sweet, and easy to digest. It is better to buy fruits with some signs of green and ripen them at home, however, so you can be sure they haven't been gassed into phony ripeness. The skin should be intact and free of bruises.

Blueberries — All berries should be plump, firm, and of deep color. Berries that lack color lack flavor.

Cherries — A very dark color for the variety is the most important sign of maturity and sweetness. The surface should be bright and glossy and should not be obscuring any soft leaking spots, common signs of decay.

Cranberries — The same rule holds here: plump, firm fruits with good color and sheen. Before you use cranberries remove any shriveled or leaking intruders.

Figs — Ripe figs are soft, without being mushy. While minor bruises are unimportant, a break in the skin will bring rapid deterioration.

Grapefruit — With all citrus a heavy fruit is a sign of juiciness. The thinner the skin, the juicier the fruit is likely to be, but even thick-skinned varieties can be quite tasty. Wrinkled or rough skin, however, means tough, dry fruit inside. If the skin breaks easily with pressure there is probably internal decay.

Grapes — Color, again, is the best criterion for judging grapes. Green grapes are sweetest when they exhibit a yellowish cast. Red grapes should be deep red. Avoid grapes that are soft, wrinkled, and leaking.

Lemons — For the most juice choose heavy lemons. Those with a rich yellow color will be less acidy than their paler cousins.

Limes — Just like lemons the heavier fruits are the juiciest. Avoid those with dull, dry skin and surface irregularities.

Mangoes — A ripe mango will range from orange-yellow to red and the flesh will yield to slight pressure. The green fruit should be left at room temperature to ripen.

Melons — A melon that is picked before maturity will never be sweet. If part of the stem base remains, or the stem scar is jagged, the melon was not yet mature at picking time. Ripeness is not the same thing as maturity.

A mature, ripe cantaloupe will yield to pressure at the blossom end (opposite the stem end) and will have a pleasing, sweet fragrance. If the entire surface is soft, however, and the color bright yellow between the netting, the fruit will be over-ripe and thus tasteless and watery.

Ripe honeydews have a faint aroma and a slight softening at the blossom end. A soft velvety surface is a sign of maturity; a dull white color and hard, smooth feel indicate immaturity.

Watermelons are best judged by their flesh, which should have good color and no white streaks. Seeds should be black or brown. White seeds, white streaks, and pale flesh indicate immature fruit. Dry, mealy texture or stringy flesh indicate over-maturity.

Nectarines — Sweet nectarines have good color, are plump, and show slight softening along the "seam." Very hard or dull colored nectarines, and those that show any shriveling, will never be up to par.

Oranges — Since many growers dye the skins to make oranges appear mature, color cannot be relied on to judge the quality. Samples which are light or have a very rough surface have little juice inside. Firm heavy fruits are best.

Papayas — Ripe papayas yield to gentle pressure and range in color from golden yellow to orange. Those with dark patches and soft spots are beginning to show signs of decay.

Peaches — Very hard peaches with green tones have been picked immature and will never ripen properly. Choose those which show some red against a yellow or cream colored background if you want the flavor to meet with your expectations.

Pears — No matter what variety of pear you choose it should be firm when purchased. Pears should not be hard, however, and to insure proper ripening you might want to select those which indicate a bit of softening. If pears are shriveled near the stem, assume they were immature at picking time and will never ripen properly. Spots on the sides or near the blossom end are signs of a mealy interior.

Pineapple — Like many other fruits, unless the pineapple is picked at maturity it will never be sweet. When pineapples are mature they are dark green. As they ripen the green is replaced by oranges and yellows. The fully ripe fruit is gold, orange, or red depending on the variety. It should have a fragrant odor and a slight separation between the eyes. The leaves should pull out with a gentle yank. If the eyes are pointed or sunken, or the color yellow-green, the pineapple is immature. Dark eyes, soft spots, and an unpleasant odor usually mean internal damage.

Plantains — Referred to as "cooking bananas," ripe plantains are yellow or speckled with brown, while those that are green must be ripened at room temperature for a few days.

Plums — The plums you choose should have a good color for the variety, a glow to the skin, and when ready to eat they should yield to gentle pressure. Avoid fruit with skin breaks or discoloration, plums that are very hard and poorly colored, and those that are soft or leaking.

Raspberries — Whether black or red, the color should be bright and the individual bumps on the berries plump and tender without being mushy. If the container is wet or badly stained, the berries at the bottom are probably overripe.

Rhubarb — The stalks of rhubarb should be firm and crisp, like celery, with a deep red or cherry red color. Hothouse rhubarb is lighter in color than field grown. Do not buy rhubarb that is wilted or grossly over- or undersized.

Strawberries — Again, full, rich color and firm flesh are the signs of good strawberries, while berries with large uncolored areas, lots of surface seeds, a dull shrunken appearance, or extreme softness are of lesser quality.

Tangerines — Unlike other citrus fruits the skin of a tangerine is loose fitting, and therefore the fruit will never feel firm. Ripe tangerines are yellow-orange in color, although small areas of green are not detrimental and may indicate that the fruit was not dyed. Skin punctures, on the other hand, cause rapid deterioration and drying of the fruit.

Sweeteners

Some brand of molasses and honey is sold in every super-market. While the honey may be of undistinguished origin, if it is raw it is of greater virtue than the other choices around you. Molasses is available in two strengths — blackstrap and unsulfured. The blackstrap is thick, dark, and borders on bitter in taste. It is a valuable source of calcium and iron. Unsulfured molasses is milder in color and flavor, giving a taffy-like taste to the foods it is added to. Unfortunately, unsulfured molasses offers less iron and about one-third the calcium of blackstrap. Pure maple syrup is sold in many supermarkets, although the small quantities it is packaged in may not be the most economical. Raw or turbinado sugar is a relatively new item in the supermarket but it is rarely a wise buy; while it is minimally superior to refined sugar, it is still not good for you and never warrants the high price placed on it.

Other Assorted Items

Other good food buys you may encounter in the super-market include dried fruit (not all brands are sulfured), nuts in the shell, popping corn, roasted soybeans, and unflavored gelatin. In some stores you may also find pure peanut butter, but more often this excellent source of nourishment is coupled with hydrogenated shortening and sweetening. Read the label.

Is Bigger Better?

To find the most economical size package for any of these items look for the unit price on the shelf. While larger packages are usually the better buy, this is not without exception. In addition, a visual estimate of a package can often be misleading, since overpackaging can make a box look like it contains more inside than it really does. Be sure to note the actual weight of contents on the label and divide this by the package price if the unit price is not visible. Although this may be time consuming, it probably will be an eye-opening experience.

Nutrition Labeling

On many packaged food labels you will find some indica-tion of the nutritional value of the contents. Presently this information is only mandatory for certain foods, specifically those products that are "enriched," "fortified," or contain any references to protein, fat, calorie content, or any specific dietary uses on the package. But even when it is not required many food companies offer this information voluntarily.

Federal requirements for nutrition labeling call for the inclusion of:

the size of a serving,
the number of servings per container,
the number of calories per serving, and
the amount in grams of protein, carbohydrate, and fat.

If the manufacturer wishes, the amount of saturated fat, unsaturated fat, and cholesterol may also be specified. In addition, the label must state the percent of the U.S. Recommended Daily Allowance (RDA) supplied by one serving for each of the following nutrients: protein, vitamin A, thiamin, riboflavin, niacin, vitamin C, calcium, and iron. These values are based on the recommendations for "Adults and Children Four or More Years of Age" and are very similar to those established by the National Academy of Sciences shown on pages 62-63.

The purpose of nutrition labeling is to help the buyer determine the value of certain foods. In this manner one food or brand can be compared with another and judged for nutritional superiority.

There are many drawbacks to this procedure. Often the nutrients cited on the package are not there inherently, but are in the form of synthetic vitamins and minerals added by the manufacturer. Very little care is taken to see that nutrients which are dependent on each other for proper use are added in the most assimilable quantities or form. As a consequence of this synthetic fortification many people are getting an oversupply of some nutrients at the expense of others.

Many people are also being misled, believing they are eating well because they have consumed foods which add up to 100 percent of the RDA for the given nutrients, while there are actually many more essential vitamins and minerals found in food that are not included in this assessment. Additionally, foods which contain too much salt and sugar and too little roughage may appear to be better than their actual worth since there is no measure of counterproductive ingredients on the nutrition label.

Due to these drawbacks, the value of nutrition labeling is greatly diminished and the information should be used only to determine the relative value of foods in the diet and not to plan a sound eating scheme.

Open Dating

Another area of marketing that is sadly deficient is the dating of foods for freshness. Practically all packaged foods sold in the supermarket are coded with either the date of processing or their expected life span. In most cases, however, the key to this coding is reserved for the manufacturer and the distributor; rarely is it shared with the buying public. Moreover, the code changes from item to item and store to store with unrelated numbers or letters frequently added, generally having to do with where the food was processed or by whom. Even if you did learn to interpret the symbols, you would still have to determine if this was the day the item was made, the last day it should be sold, or the date when the product was no longer edible.

To avoid much of the confusion many states have passed "open dating" requirements. Open dating means clearly indicating when the product was prepared or how long you can expect it to maintain quality. For dairy products, eggs, fresh meat, produce, and frozen foods which do not have an unlimited life span this is highly valuable. There is still, however, a lack of uniformity, as general consensus varies as to when certain foods are no longer fresh. In some states bread that is more than 48 hours old must be considered "day old." In other places it is given a life span of a week. While New York City law requires milk to be sold within 66 hours of pasteurization, in other areas of the state the time lapse is left to the discretion of the dairy and may be as long as ten days. Some manufacturers think yogurt is still saleable three, four, and five weeks after the culture is made, while others place a limit of two weeks and only guarantee quality for one week after that. Frozen food manufacturers hardly ever clue you in on the date of freezing, although the USDA firmly agrees that foods deteriorate after prolonged storage, and one year is the maximum recommendation for any frozen food if high quality eating is expected. Thus, unless you know when the food was placed in cold storage, you have no idea how long you can wait before using it.

Other problems are inherent in open dating. Once a package is opened the life span of the food can no longer be guaranteed. The way in which the food was handled during processing, shipping, and display also affects the rate of deterioration, and thus cheeses, dairy products, eggs, meats, and produce left unrefrigerated will degenerate more rapidly than those properly handled. The same holds true for frozen foods, which frequently defrost during shipping and while waiting to be transferred to the store freezer.

In the end, it is the responsibility of the buyer to make the seller aware of consumer needs and dissatisfaction. If you purchase any item that does not suit your standards for quality or freshness be sure to return it to the store and register your complaint with the manager.

Buying from a Co-op

A compromise between buying food direct from the producer and buying in the supermarket is buying at a consumer co-op. A co-op is nothing more than people working together to beat inflation, overprocessed foods, food-handling monopolies, price fixing, and the many other ills of today's supermarkets. For this reason, co-ops know no geographical, cultural, economic, or racial boundaries — they're everywhere and involve all kinds of people.

In the simplest sense a co-op happens when a group of people get together and pool their food needs, contact a supplier, order food in bulk, and divide the order among themselves when it is delivered. Variations range from this simple "buying club" to incorporated cooperatives returning yearly dividends to members.

The economic theory behind a co-op is that members volunteer their labor and give up some of the plushness and convenience of the supermarket to drastically cut the prices they pay for food. By doing away with the middlemen, co-opers usually save upwards of 30 percent on their food bills.

A co-op buys at about 40 percent discount. On such items as produce, where supermarkets have a very high markup to cover spoilage, co-ops often save up to 75 percent. A co-op's overhead usually runs only about 5 to 15 percent of the retail food value. When this is compared to the standard middleman's overhead of 60.3 cents out of every food dollar spent, you quickly see why co-ops are enjoying a phenomenal revival.

Through a co-op people become an integral link in their food supply chain, and they like the newfound feeling of responsibility as opposed to being pushed around by large impersonal food processing cartels. For others, co-ops offer a constructive outlet for their energies. Many join just to save money, others in pursuit of better food. For people who depend on their garden for the majority of their food, a co-op is the best place to get those items you have neither the room, inclination, nor ability to grow.

A look at the past of the co-op movement should prove that, as Ralph Nader told Consumer Assembly '75, "They're (co-ops) American as apple pie, and it's a misreading of history to say we can't bring them back again."

Co-ops usually start small, and then either die out or grow. Those that grow usually do so in a pattern. A good example of how a co-op network grows is covered in the *Food Conspiracy Cookbook* by Lois Wickstrom, as she recounts the growth of the co-op movement in Berkeley.

In July 1969, three Berkeley residents met to figure out how they could buy food cheaply. They started to post ads asking people to join them in a food conspiracy. At first they were limited to produce only, and quickly found they had grown to a size where one truck could not handle the weekly run, and the members could not all fit in one living room for meetings. By December of the same year, the conspiracy split north and south.

After the December split, each conspiracy split twice again, giving them a total of eight, each with complete autonomy. The groups usually chose to order with the other groups, to increase purchasing power as they began to branch into other food items. Shortly, a headquarters for the eight groups was set up, and one person began to distribute a list of dry goods to be sold to the eight groups.

Soon the branches began to get authorization to accept food stamps, followed quickly by tax licenses and other government requirements. Now the entire setup has over 2,000 members in 60 conspiracies.

For every success story such as Berkeley, there are probably twice as many stories of co-op efforts that never really got off the ground. Basically there are only three essentials for a good food co-op: good food, cheap prices, and good people. Likewise, success of a co-op should be measured in three ways: by the interest of the people involved, by the co-op's economic strength, and by the co-op's ability to survive for a long time.

Once you have decided a co-op is for you, the next step is to find out if there is a co-op in your area, or whether you have to start up a new co-op.

The clearinghouse for information about food co-ops in the United States is the Food Co-op Project (Loop College, 64 E. Lake St., Chicago, Ill., 60601). They issue a biannual, computerized nationwide *Directory of Food Co-ops* and *Food Co-op NOOZ,* a bimonthly co-op newspaper. A typical issue of the *NOOZ* might include aids on finding co-op sources, advice to those ambitious enough to want to start a regional warehouse, and comments on the political role of co-ops as an alternative to the present economy. The *NOOZ* is geared more for large, well-established store front co-ops than for small neighborhood co-ops.

Another way to locate an established co-op is to visit wholesale warehouses and keep an eye out for people loading food into station wagons or vans. Ask wholesalers whether they sell to any area co-ops. You can post a notice on bulletin boards in area colleges or churches. Sometimes the local newspaper's news editor will be able to tell you of area co-op activity and whom to get in touch with. If you have a small community newspaper you could try to have a notice put in, telling of your planned co-op. A word of caution: ads in the classified usually don't attract much of a response.

Because of their very nature, most co-ops have a very low profile. It may take a little searching out, but if you live in an area of any size, chances are good that sooner or later you'll find one.

For those interested in starting a co-op, a little planning goes a long way. The first step is to get together a group of people with something in common, be it a church, a neighborhood, a university, work, or what have you.

Once you get some feedback from people, organize a meeting as soon as possible before interest dies out. At your first meeting you should explain what a co-op is, why you want to form one, and then discuss what type of co-op the group would like to form. There are basically three forms a co-op can take.

Buying Club

Everyone pays an agreed-upon figure to the purchaser who then makes what he considers the best buys, to be distributed equally among members. This form is usually limited to produce and perhaps dairy products.

Advantages: Ease of bookkeeping and distribution, and there is no storage of waste or perishable goods.

Disadvantages: Inability to choose what you want unless you're the purchaser for a particular week. This system presupposes that all members tend to eat in about the same patterns and amounts. Sometimes you get a food you or your family doesn't like.

Preorder Buying Club

Everyone preorders from an order sheet and pays in advance. Volunteers divide the purchase into individual orders. Members pick up orders and order forms for the next purchase at the same time. Probably the most common type of co-op in existence, this form abounds in both suburban neighborhoods and rural areas.

Advantages: You usually get exactly what you want, the group has a lot of flexibility, and there is no storage needed.

Disadvantages: Orders may have to be adjusted because wholesalers sell in set amounts, i.e., grains in 50-pound bags, beans in 25-pound bags, bottles of oil in case lots of twelve; either members must adjust their orders accordingly, or you need storage facilities. Also bookkeeping is a little tricky because items ordered often are out of stock and prices change, necessitating adjustments of members' bills.

Store Front

If you have the physical area, enough members, and enthusiasm, you may be able to support a store front. Members pay a joining fee which covers the initial expense of opening and stocking a store. They shop and purchase what they want at wholesale prices plus a slight markup to cover operating overhead. Nonmembers are allowed to shop, but at a higher markup.

Advantages: The attraction and ease of shopping rather than preordering; you don't have to know what you'll need a week or more in advance.

Disadvantages: The expense of keeping up a store; co-ops able to operate this way are often backed by a company (membership open to employees only) or are affiliated with a university or civic group and have access to a store front without having to pay rent. Someone usually has to be paid to manage this type of setup. Although it may vary, a store front usually requires over 300 active members to be open five or six days a week.

Discuss these possibilities at your meeting and decide what form the co-op will take, usually dictated by your resources and circumstances. The determining factor in what type of co-op you have will be the number of people interested in joining. A good number for a buying club is usually five to ten, and for a preorder buying club, ten to 16. Any more than that and you may find yourself with more food ordered than you can easily pick up in a station wagon. Any less and you will have to restrict your activities to occasional buying in order to meet the minimum order requirements of wholesalers.

If you are going to have a buying club, decide at that first meeting how much money members want to put in each week. Agree on what types of foods will be bought and when the co-op will start. If you are trying a preorder buying club, it is good to have order forms at the first meeting, or as soon as possible after the meeting to get people committed while enthusiasm is high. People are skeptical of ways to save money, so things have to get rolling fast — once the co-op is working, it will stand on its own merit.

In most cases, your co-op will take the form of a buying club or a preorder buying club. These forms require limited work, especially when located near cities with easy access to the big wholesale markets. If you live in the country, your strong point will be buying directly from area farmers, or-chards, and dairies.

Most store front co-ops evolve from large, successful buy-ing clubs and thus already have a large membership available and interested. With a store front, your savings are somewhat reduced, and your work load may be increased, but con-venience is greatly increased, as is the available inventory. These things should all be carefully weighed before undertak-ing the opening of a store front. It's a business owned by its members and must successfully compete with other busi-nesses, while a buying club is basically a neighborhood project that can be stopped any week the members wish with no major financial liability.

The first problem your co-op is likely to encounter is deciding what types of food to handle. Some may want only organic, while others will call for processed convenience foods. Economics will play a role here, as your largest savings will be on unprocessed perishables such as produce, fruit, and dairy products. Savings on such things as canned goods will be little, if any, as there is little markup on these items from producer to supermarket.

By featuring natural foods, those that have not received much processing on their way from farm to you, the best monetary and nutritional savings will be realized. By not limiting your buying solely to organic foods the co-op will be able to deal directly with area farmers in addition to wholesalers to get the best food at the best prices.

Getting Started

Once your co-op has decided what form it will take and what types of foods you will handle, you're on your way. Each co-op will adapt to its own circumstances, and no two ever seem to operate quite the same, but here are some suggestions to help you over those first faltering steps:

1. **Finding a distributor.** You may be able to buy in bulk from local stores with a special price for full bags and case lots. This might be the simplest way to get established. If stores do not want to sell in bulk, find out who supplies them or check the yellow pages under wholesalers, and deal direct. Contact distributors and get their wholesale price lists. Find out how much each wants for a minimum order, when orders have to be in, when and where orders will be delivered or have to be picked up, and whether they require tax and licensing information about your group. In some states distributors need a copy of your resale permit or other permits and licenses. If your distributor indicates that permits are required, consult your state or city tax office.

Some of a co-op's best buys will be on dried products like grains, seeds, and nuts. Usually your best source of supply will be from a natural foods distributor. If you can't find one in your area, check with local health food stores, or write to some of the major natural food producers asking who handles distribution in your area, but be sure to stipulate that you are talking about wholesale distribution. Because dried items are usually limited to bulk orders of 25 or 50 pounds, members will have to divide a bag and store more of the product at home than they normally would.

2. **Bookkeeping.** If no one in your group has any book-keeping experience, get a basic bookkeeping ledger to use instead of trying to figure it out on your own. The basic types of co-ops all present different bookkeeping problems. All of them could probably benefit by opening their own checking ac-counts. You'll probably be able to get an account as a nonprofit organization, thus getting your checks without charge. Many people feel the buying club type of group is best, as it requires very little carry-over bookkeeping: when you've paid the week's bills, you should be out of money.

3. **Labor.** Co-ops deal with getting members to work in a variety of ways: having a work manager assign jobs, posting a sign-up sheet, charging a sliding markup fee based on who works and who doesn't. You'll have to experiment a little to see what works best for your organization. It is advisable to have at least an initial rotation of all jobs for two reasons. You'll be able to weed out those who really aren't suited for keeping the books or tallying the orders and those whose schedules or other responsibilities don't allow them to perform certain jobs. Also everyone will have a basic idea of how the co-op works; if one member must withdraw he won't leave an unfillable gap. The most common co-op problem, known as burnout, seems to result from letting one person do all the work because he/she "really does it better" or "really has more time." When this one person has to leave or just gets tired of doing all the work, the co-op collapses.

In the beginning you may not even realize how many jobs a co-op entails. In addition to the bookkeeper and order taker, you may need someone to receive and check deliveries, people to break the purchase down into individual orders or to ar-range it on shelves and price it, a person to make sure all the members know when and where to pick up their orders, a clean-up crew, cashiers, and possibly babysitters. When you begin to deal with individual farmers you may need people with a truck or van to pick up your order and bring it to your distribution point.

As some co-ops progress and diversify they divide the labor according to items purchased. For example, your co-op might have a produce coordinator, a cheese coordinator, and a bulk foods coordinator. Each takes charge of ordering and distributing one type of food.

Many people view co-ops as a tool of social change, so be prepared for the possibility of subtle changes in your way of living, beyond the savings in food dollars. First of all, produce obtained through a co-op should be better and fresher than any you've ever bought in a store, and you may find yourself using many more fresh fruits and vegetables and fewer frozen, canned, and highly processed food and snack items. Next, you may find that some items previously stuck with prohibitive price labels are suddenly affordable. You'll find yourself experimenting with unfamiliar or unavailable grains, sprouting some uncommon beans and seeds, and learning to control more of your food supply.

Chapter 7

Preserving Your Food

If after careful planning, buying, and gardening you have laid in a supply of good whole food — whether from a natural foods store, a food co-op, or your own backyard — your first consideration will be to store it in a way that retains as much as possible of its original goodness.

Vitamin loss is accelerated by high temperatures and exposure to light and air. Dampness encourages spoilage. Open or easily penetrated containers invite insects and rodents, for, as one natural foods company states on its bags, "They know what's good!" Long shelf life is not one of the selling points of natural foods. It is therefore up to you to store these foods carefully to keep as much of their vitamin and mineral value as possible intact. Freedom from chemical antioxidants, emulsifiers, and stabilizers is surely worth a little extra effort spent in preparing whole foods for storage.

Storing Food Fresh

For short term storage of such perishables as eggs, cheese, butter, and milk, refrigeration is generally taken for granted. Such foods as flours, nuts, oils, and seeds are often considered staples and are kept on any handy shelf. If you've put special effort, time, and money into tracking down and raising the most nutritious foods possible, though, you will want to find out more about the special needs of these often neglected foods.

Perhaps you have noticed that good natural foods stores keep all their wheat germ, nuts, and seeds that are not canned or vacuum packed in jars, under refrigeration. The most responsible millers of flour refrigerate the grains and grind the flour in small batches. There is a reason for all of these precautions. Oxidation of flour begins with the milling process in which the whole grain is broken up into many fine particles, exposing much more surface to the air. Whole grain flours containing oil-rich wheat germ oxidize (become rancid) more quickly than less nutritious, degerminated flours. Cold temperatures help to retard this oxidation process. Opened containers of oils and nut butters likewise soon become rancid at room temperatures. They should be refrigerated as soon as the seal has been broken. According to nutritionist Adelle Davis, no open container of cooking oil should be left at room temperature even overnight. Shelled nuts and seeds, being rich in oils, also require refrigeration when kept for more than a few days.

All of these requirements can lead to a traffic jam in the refrigerator. How can you do justice to the special requirements of these whole foods without buying a new, larger refrigerator?

Perhaps the following hints will help you to find space for all the good things you want to keep on hand for your family:

1. Ruthlessly eliminate from your refrigerator all "freeloader" foods that don't pull their weight nutritionally, like jam, soda, packaged dessert toppings, and sweet cakes.

2. Buy perishable staples like nuts and oils in small containers, especially in warm weather. The nutritional and space savings may be worth the few extra pennies you spend.

3. Make use of cool sheds, summer kitchens, porches, and basements for cool weather storage of perishable flours, nuts, and seeds.

4. Store flours, shelled nuts, and seeds in the freezer when you have the space there. For those who raise their own produce and meat this is often the period from February to July or August.

5. Use the food you do have on hand. Rotate it. Keep it

moving. If you have bought a new kind of nutritious food to try, sample it promptly rather than letting it gather dust on the shelf for a month.

6. Always use fresh, opened, or unpackaged food in preference to canned or jarred.

7. Go over the contents of the refrigerator once a week to be sure that no good foods are lost in the back corner and to remove spoiled or questionable food.

8. Buy unshelled nuts. They keep longer without refrigeration.

The right kind of protective packaging can lengthen the shelf life of stored foods too. Foods dried at home or purchased in bulk from a food co-op — raisins, grains, seeds, and such — need more protection than a paper bag. They should be stored in cans with tight fitting lids or in jars with screw tops as soon as possible after purchase to protect them from moisture, insects, and rodents. Gallon jars that have been emptied of their mayonnaise or pickles may often be obtained free of charge from restaurants and diners. Plastic containers with sealing lids would be a second choice. At least they can be reused, unlike most plastic bags. Stores that sell ice cream by the half-gallon in plastic tubs will sometimes sell the tubs to you at cost. If you use plastic bags in your storage program, remember that each bag requires a lot of energy for its manufacture. Washing, rinsing, and reusing the bags helps to prevent some of this waste of energy. Cardboard oatmeal cartons may be reused and resealed with masking tape for storage of dry grains and legumes.

Storage around the House

Over the long run, you will want to develop a variety of different storage areas around your home to accommodate the requirements of different kinds of foods. Once you start to look, you will probably find a number of good food hideaways, some perhaps unique to your own home. Figure 7-1 may give you some ideas.

Many older homes have an unheated pantry or summer kitchen in which food will stay cold without freezing. These are usually fairly dry areas. Breezeways and unheated "Florida rooms" in newer ranch homes are also useful for cold storage. An unheated attic provides cold, usually dry storage, but the

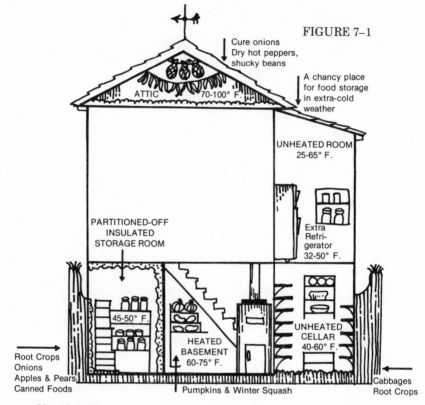

FIGURE 7-1

Cure onions
Dry hot peppers,
shucky beans

A chancy place
for food storage
in extra-cold
weather

ATTIC 70-100° F.

UNHEATED ROOM
25-65° F.

PARTITIONED-OFF
INSULATED
STORAGE ROOM

Extra
Refri-
gerator
32-50° F.

45-50° F.

HEATED
BASEMENT
60-75° F.

UNHEATED
CELLAR
40-60° F.

Root Crops
Onions
Apples & Pears
Canned Foods

Pumpkins & Winter Squash

Cabbages
Root Crops

Use this diagram as a rough guide to the appropriate places in the home for storing fresh garden produce. Room temperatures will vary according to the house's construction, location, type of heating, and placement of doors, windows, and vents.

temperature will vary more because of direct heat from the sun during many fall and spring days.

The Attic

Food stored in the attic is less likely to be noticed in passing than that kept in or near the living area. It is necessary, therefore, to cover and where possible seal the food against raids by mice, and to establish a regular schedule for checking the food for spoilage or other damage. The northeast corner of the attic will no doubt be the coolest, subject as it is only to mild morning sun. Overhanging trees can, of course, further reduce the temperature rise caused by the sun hitting the attic roof. It would be well to keep a record, either on the door to the attic or in the kitchen "nerve center," of just what food has been put in attic storage. It is always nice to find something you didn't realize you had, except when it's a two-year-old squash.

Unheated Areas

As more homeowners adopt wood burning stoves to heat their homes, extra rooms, hallways, and other unheated areas become available for storage of food. Check the temperature and moisture conditions in these areas of your home, if any, and choose foods that will keep well under those conditions.

For example, in a certain small home in which an efficient wood-burning stove in the kitchen is the source of heat for the whole house, heat rises to the bedrooms by way of the stairway in a corner of the kitchen. This house has several cool downstairs rooms which are not heavily used during winter months. These rooms are good places in which to stockpile some neat stacks of stored goods. Closets that are set into walls on the northern exposure of the house make good cold storage areas. The space above the basement stairway is cool and usually dry in a house that doesn't use central heating.

Basements

Basement storage is usually the first choice for canned goods, which are already sealed against air and dampness. The temperature here is usually cooler than that in the upper rooms, even in a centrally heated house. Many basements, though, do tend to be damp. For this reason, canned goods should be thoroughly cleaned of all food residue that might remain on the jar surface after canning, in order to prevent mold forming on the outside of the jar. Such mold does no harm to the contents of the jar unless allowed to contaminate the rim when the jar is opened, but it is unsightly.

If a basement or other food storage area is ever flooded, food that is stored there unsealed (in cardboard boxes, jars with screw-on lids, storage bags) must be considered contaminated and should be discarded. Canning jars that are immersed in flood waters should be thoroughly washed in hot, soapy water before using the contents.

In older homes, there is usually at least one basement room that is walled away from the furnace in order to maintain a cooler temperature. Such a room was often left with a dirt floor, perfect for maintaining the necessary humidity for stored vegetables. If the room has a window, you can open it on cold fall evenings to keep the room chilled within the proper range.

Enclosing a Basement Storage Area

If your home, like many others, lacks such a ready-made room for food storage, you may be able to enclose part of your basement area for this purpose. For an evenly cool temperature, the north side of the house is usually best. If you choose a corner with a window, you will have only two walls to put up and the window will be an invaluable help in maintaining an even temperature. Any window into a food storage room, though, should be shaded to exclude sunlight and screened against hungry mice and other varmints.

Most vegetables that you would store in a root cellar keep best at a temperature just above freezing. In practice, though, since it is difficult under home conditions to maintain a temperature that low, but no lower, the best temperature range to aim for would be between 35 and 40°F.

Suppose that you decide to enclose a corner of your basement for vegetable storage. You can store about 30 bushels of produce in a space 40 feet square (a room 5 by 8 feet, for example). First, frame the storage room with 2-by-4 lumber, leaving space for a door. For most effective insulation, sheath both sides of the studs, putting batts of insulation in the space between the double walls. Naturally, the door to the room should also be insulated. The outside walls, of course, should remain in their original condition so that they can transmit cold air from the surrounding cooler ground. A slatted ventilator may be installed if there is no window. Circulation of air and cool, steady temperatures are essential for success in keeping root vegetables in basement storage.

In homes where central heating is lacking or not used, the whole basement may remain cool enough for food storage during the colder winter months, although it is likely to be too damp for keeping grains, seeds, and some vegetables and fruits.

Many apartments provide basement storage space for renters to keep luggage and other goods. With careful planning and some shelving made of scrap wood, such a space might serve very well for limited storage of home canned goods. It would not be cool or damp enough for foods requiring root cellar conditions, obviously.

Stairs and Window Wells

Basement stairs may be utilized for winter cold storage of potatoes, apples, and other vegetables. The simplest way to go about this is to stand baskets of produce on the middle and lower steps. Upper steps may be warmed by the sun during the day and subject to freezing at night. Some clever homeowners with solid, well-built basement entrances rebuild the stairs into storage steps, in effect making each step a long, narrow drawer or else a wide box with the opening where the riser would be. Time and carpentry skill are required, but this is a good way to create storage space where none existed before.

Basement window wells also make good, if small, cold-storage areas. Open the window from the basement into the window well, box it in with scrap wood, old windows, or crates, and cache your produce there where outside air will keep it cool and warmth from the house will prevent freezing.

Porches

Enclosed porches, if not too sunny, can hold produce in baskets, clean garbage cans, and big jars. If sun does heat up the porch on warmer days, keep the produce on the north side and cover it with blankets to retain the cold.

Exposed porches offer less protection from freezing, but during much of the fall and spring they are cooler than the house for short term storage of fruits, vegetables, and some nuts.

One resourceful apple grower we know has a cottage in which there is a walk-in storage space under the elevated main floor porch. He suspends half-bushel baskets of apples on hooks attached to the floor joists using coat hangers. Since heat rises, the high hanging apples are protected from frost until early winter.

Other Odd Places

Utilize space under beds, corners beside appliances, and even space under one of those fashionable decorator tables with a floorlength skirt. Such tables are often cardboard forms with an attractive cover thrown over them; what is to prevent you from making a round plywood bin that could hold a solid stack of canned goods, especially those put up in tin cans, and then covering the whole cylinder with an attractive skirt. The space above kitchen cabinets is often wasted. This is usually a warm area, of course, but for short-term storage of canned goods it would be better than none.

Inside the Storage Area

The usefulness of any storage area will be more than doubled by the construction of sturdy shelves. Canned goods are heavy. One-inch lumber, well supported, should be used for jar storage shelves. Plan the shelf spacing to allow for a standard quart jar plus clearance of about 1 inch, with perhaps a lower shelf allowing more depth for rows of half-gallon jars. Good sturdy shelves for canned goods may be made by setting strong old barn planks or other sturdy boards between concrete blocks. The blocks space the shelves efficiently for quart jar storage. For shelves attached to a wall, be sure that the wall is strong enough to support the potential weight and be sure also to nail the shelf to the studs behind the wall, not just to the sheathing.

You will want to develop a system so that food left from one year is set aside in a separate place at the beginning of a new canning season — either on a certain section of your shelves or on another, separate shelf. Labeling the jars is important too, for it is easy to forget which peaches you canned with honey, which pickles are extra hot, which pears are spiced rather than plain.

Allow space also for bins, baskets, and boxes of unprocessed produce. In a dirt floored area it is wise to elevate these containers on planks or bricks so that they are not directly in contact with the floor. Bins and boxes should be slatted rather than solid to allow circulation of air around the produce they contain. It is helpful to keep a few empty baskets handy too to hold vegetables when you're checking and sorting at intervals during the winter. Expect some waste and don't let it upset you. You're still way ahead with your own good produce.

The majority of root crops grown for winter eating require cold, very moist storage conditions — conditions that are very difficult to maintain inside the house unless you have a special basement root cellar or insulated room. For this reason, they are good candidates for outdoor pit, root cellar, or in-the-row storage. The necessary high humidity and low temperature are more constant under those conditions.

The classic root cellar, dug into the side of a north-facing hill, is the dream of many homesteaders. A well-built root cellar is a lifetime investment that will keep your storage vegetables under the best possible conditions: moist (80–90 percent humidity), with good ventilation, dark, and as close to 32°F. as possible without actually freezing.

Root cellars may be constructed of concrete blocks, native stone, reclaimed bricks, old truck bodies, and logs, to name a few possibilities. Thick walls, sturdy support, protection from temperature fluctuations caused by solar heating, and good ventilation are some root cellar musts.

Not too many of us, though, have the place, let alone the time and materials, for a real dug-in root cellar. What other options are there?

In the Garden

One of the easiest of all storage methods, indoor or outdoor, is that of leaving root crops like carrots, parsnips, salsify, turnips, and some beets right in the garden where they have been growing. After frost has stopped their growth for the season, but before the ground freezes hard, mound hay, leaves, cornstalks or other loose insulating material over the rows of vegetables. Some gardeners use old boards or heavier cornstalks or sunflower stalks to hold down loose leaves that might otherwise blow away.

Parsnips and salsify develop a finer flavor after having been subjected to several good frosts. Well-buried beets should winter well in areas with moderate winters, although the beet is somewhat more cold-sensitive than the carrot and parsnip. Cylindra beets, which carry their shoulders well above the ground, should not be left in the row unless winters are very mild. Be sure to mark your rows of buried root crops, especially if you have left more than one crop in the ground to winter over. Drive stakes in each end of the row before the ground becomes hard.

In a Drain Tile or Barrel

Past generations of gardeners have worked out other good alternative storage methods. Underground pit or container storage also makes use of the earth's natural insulating ability. Two dependable versions are the drain tile and the barrel.

A large (18 × 30-inch or 24 × 24-inch) porous drain tile may be buried in a well-drained, shaded area and filled with fruit and vegetables. A few boards or stones placed in the bottom of the tile or under the barrel will give further assurance against seepage of water into the produce. It is a good idea to fill in around the vegetables and separate the layers with some kind of packing material such as sand, straw, or leaves. Remember that air itself is a fairly good insulator. The barrel should be buried in the earth at a 45-degree angle. First put rocks in the hole, then set the barrel in position with the lower rim meeting the level of the soil. Next cover the barrel with about 2 feet of earth. When the barrel is full of your good produce, set the lid in place and pile on at least a foot of straw or other insulating material, held down with a board and large stone. It is important to be sure that the barrel is tightly closed, or mice may have a cosy and well-fed winter! At the same time, though, you want to make sure that the cover to the barrel doesn't freeze shut, so that you can readily retrieve your garden bounty when you need it throughout the winter.

We have heard of at least one ambitious gardening family who buried a defunct refrigerator in the ground to store their winter vegetable supply. They removed the lock (for safety) and the shelves and piled straw over the door, held down by boards and rocks. An instant root cellar — once the hole is dug!

Outbuildings

Sheds, barns, and other outbuildings offer room for storage and protection from frosty nights in early spring and late fall. When the ground outside starts to get hard, though, produce kept in unheated outbuildings will need more protection. Covering the baskets with blankets will give you several more degrees of frost protection. Sometimes it is possible to keep a garage adjoining the house at above-freezing temperatures by running the stovepipe from cooking range or other wood-burning stove out through the garage on its way to the outside air, or — more simply — by venting a room heated by a wood-burning stove directly into the garage. If this latest procedure is followed, the car should never be idled in the garage with the motor on, for fear of sending carbon monoxide fumes into the house.

Guidelines for Fresh Storage

No matter what method you choose for storing your unprocessed fruits and vegetables, you will obtain the best results by following these guidelines:

1. Store only your very best produce — ripe, unblemished, unbruised. Blemished vegetables may be cut for drying, cooking, or preserving but should not be put in the root cellar. They will not keep well and may cause other food to rot.
2. Remove tops of root vegetables to within an inch of the crown.
3. If you do wash the vegetables before storing, and many gardeners don't, be sure that they are thoroughly dry before putting them away.
4. Check and sort the vegetables regularly. A certain amount of spoilage is to be expected; if you catch it in time, though, it won't ruin other foods.
5. Handle fruits and vegetables carefully when packing to prevent cutting and bruising — sure invitations to spoilage.
6. To prevent shriveling of vegetables, keep storage air moist enough by sprinkling the floor of the storage area with water or by covering the vegetables with damp rags or burlap bags.
7. Harvest the vegetables you plan to store as late as possible, when the weather is as cool as possible.
8. When ordering your seeds, select varieties that are known to keep well.
9. Harvest produce when soil is very dry, if possible, so that less soil will cling to the roots.
10. Rather than scrub vegetables to be stored, just shake off excess dirt. Scrubbing bruises and breaks the skin, inviting bacteria and mold to grow.
11. Keep a record, in the house, of what you have stored and where, lest you overlook some of your buried treasure, as most gardeners will confess to having done at one time or another.
12. Use stored root vegetables, when possible, before digging too deeply into frozen and canned supplies, with due allowances, of course, for menu variety.

Organically grown produce, because of its superior quality, flavor, and nutrition, is worth storing under optimum conditions. Some gardeners, in fact, state that their organically raised produce keeps better than comparable crops grown with chemical fertilizers only.

How do you know what storage temperature and humidity are best for a given vegetable? Here is a table outlining the requirements of some good storage vegetables:

Vegetables That Keep Well When Warm and Dry (50–55°F.
60–70% humidity)

Pumpkins
Squash
Sweet potatoes
Ripening tomatoes

Vegetables That Keep Well When Cool and Dry (35–40°F.
60–70% humidity)

Onions
Garlic
Soybeans in the pod (keep 2–4 weeks)

Vegetables That Keep Well When Cold and Moist (32–40°F.
80–90% humidity)

Potatoes
Cabbage
Cauliflower (2–4 weeks)
Apples
Grapes (40°F.)
Oranges
Pears
Quince

Vegetables That Keep Well When Cold and Very Moist (32–40°F.
90–95% humidity)

Carrots	Salsify
Beets	Winter radishes (in sand)
Parsnips	Kohlrabi
Rutabagas	Celeriac
Turnips	
Celery	
Chinese cabbage	

Harvest and Fresh Storage Tips, By Fruit and Vegetable

Here is a run-down on individual vegetables and fruits commonly stored by home gardeners:

Apples — For highest vitamin content and best keeping qualities, pick the apples when fully ripe. When picking, leave the stem on the fruit to prevent small skin breaks which would impair the keeping quality of the fruit. Shallow layers of apples keep best; many apples heaped high are likely to bruise those on the bottom, resulting in decay. Containers no larger than one half bushel should be used for apple storage. Slatted lugs or crates offer more ventilation and a wider surface area on the bottom. Avoid storing apples with potatoes, because the apples give off ethylene gas which induces sprouting in white potatoes.

Some apples that keep well are: Stayman, Winesap, Northern Spy, York Imperial, Baldwin, and Rome Beauty, all good for four to six months in storage under good conditions. Jonathan, MacIntosh, Cortland, and Delicious keep for two to four months under good conditions, less if conditions are less than ideal.

Cabbage — For storage, grow a solid headed cabbage and a good keeper like Danish Ballhead, Penn State Ballhead, or Premium Flat Dutch. Let the cabbage continue to grow in the garden row during the early fall. Light frosts improve its flavor. When black frost threatens, pull the plants, retaining the roots, and store them head down in a cool, moist place, covered with straw or leaves. If winters aren't too severe, the cabbages may be stored head down in a trench in the garden, mounded over with a well-packed covering of soil topped by leaves or other insulating material. Cabbage in storage can give out a strong odor that makes it unwelcome in most home pantries and basements. Even in the root cellar, cabbage flavor may influence more delicately flavored fruits and vegetables if placed too close to them. For barrel storage, many gardeners place their cabbage along with other cole crops like turnips and rutabagas which also tend to develop strong odors in storage.

Any cabbages that do freeze while still in the garden should be left in place until thawed naturally by milder weather, and then picked for use. Don't handle them while they are frozen.

Cauliflower — Only the best, good solid heads, not "riced" or overmature, should be stored. Make pickle of the imperfect ones; storage will do nothing to improve them. To keep cauliflower, pull it up with the root intact and store it in a cold, moist pit or cellar. It will keep for two to four weeks under these conditions.

Carrots — The best keepers are those with a large, solid core like Danvers and Chantenay, rather than the thin-cored gourmet kind described in seed catalogs. They'll taste good enough for a gourmet, though, when you unearth a bucket full of golden carrots in the midst of a January thaw. If not left in the ground to winter over, carrots keep best surrounded by moist sand or peat moss in a cold pit or root cellar. This might be the method of choice for far northern gardeners who might not be able to unearth their buried carrots, even if the row is well mulched and insulated. Watch the carrots for shriveling; sprinkle with water or top with a damp burlap bag to replace the water they have lost.

Celeriac — Start right, back in the growing season, by making a special second planting so that you will have tender, fleshy roots for storage in the fall. Old, woody roots aren't worth keeping. Celeriac may be stored in sand in sturdy boxes set in a cool, moist cellar. Use them along with carrots and potatoes when you make a winter stew.

Celery — Where weather extremes are not severe, celery may be left right in the garden row until well into the winter. If the celery row has become weedy, just leave the weeds there; they'll help to protect the celery. Some gardeners mound 6 inches of soil around the plants and cover them with leaves or straw held down with old boards, to further extend the garden life of their celery plants. To store celery inside, lift the plants roots and all, and replant them in a sand-filled box in the root cellar. Place them close together in the box. Be sure to dry some of the celery leaves. They give good flavor to winter soups and stews.

Chinese Cabbage — Like regular cabbage, Chinese cabbage should be harvested as late as possible after the first frost, but before a hard killing frost. Pull the plants up root and all, remove the largest outer leaves, and pile the heads carefully in a cold pit or cellar. Heap dry straw over them and cover the mound with soil. They will keep this way for one or two months. They may also be brought into the cellar in soil-filled boxes like celery.

Garlic — Let the tops dry and yellow before you harvest; the bulb will not be likely to rot then. Shake the bulbs free of loose earth and brush off excess papery sheath that may cling to them. Cut the roots close to the bulb. Garlic will rot if kept too damp, and it will shrivel in too warm and dry a temperature. When you hit the right combination of temperature and humidity (35° to 40°F. at 60 to 70% humidity), it will keep until the next growing season.

Grapefruit — When kept as near 32°F. as possible, grapefruit will last about four to six weeks.

Grapes — Let your grapes ripen on the vine until the stem begins to turn brown. Cut the clusters from the vines when they are free of dew or rain, holding the steins to prevent bruising the grapes. Cool them immediately and store in shallow trays in a fairly moist place at 40°F. Catawba grapes keep especially well. Consider also drying some grapes if you have an especially large crop.

Horseradish — Like other root crops, horseradish keeps well in damp sand or in a storage pit. Roots make their main growth during the cool months, so harvesting of horseradish roots should not begin before September. Digging may continue until hard frost makes ground impenetrable. Horseradish is said not to freeze well; most homemakers grate the roots and keep them in jars with vinegar in a cold place, grating a few weeks' supply at a time.

Jerusalem Artichokes — Their thin skin limits their indoor keeping time, even in the refrigerator. They keep beautifully in the ground, though, and may be dug whenever the soil is soft enough. To make things easier for yourself, cut down the tall stalks of the plant when frost has blackened them and set bales of spoiled hay or heap mounds of leaves over the plants, so that the soil can be dug for another month or so. Don't worry about digging up all the tubers and eradicating the planting; it is next to impossible to do so. Some small eyes always remain.

Kohlrabi — This is another frost-hardy Brassica that can be pulled up root and all and stored much as you would cabbage. The best kohlrabi for storage is a late planting that has grown quickly in the fall rains; tough specimens only get tougher.

Leeks — To survive mild winters, leeks may be mounded with soil or dug and set in boxes of sand in the root cellar if winters are very cold.

Onions — Harvest the onions when the tops are dry, cure in the sun for two days to toughen them, and clip the tops off an inch from the bulb. Spread the onions in a shallow box or tray or on a heavy screen for a week or so. Leave the skin on until you are ready to use the onions. Onions don't belong in the damp root cellar. They survive best in a cool but dry place, at temperatures of 32 to 40°F. and a humidity of 60 to 70%.

Oranges — Often purchased in bulk by those who live where they won't grow, or ordered by mail from organic suppliers in the South. Oranges do best in storage at 30 to 32°F. with a humidity of 85 to 90%. Florida oranges will last for eight to ten weeks at this temperature and humidity. California oranges require a slightly higher temperature, 35 to 37°F., and they will keep for six to eight weeks.

Parsnips — Like salsify, parsnips improve after a few

frosts and winter very well in the ground. If your winters are too severe to permit midwinter digging in the garden, even if the row is heavily mulched, you may want to leave some parsnips in the row under heavy mulch for a spring treat and keep the rest in a pit under soil and insulation such as straw or leaves. Parsnips shrivel quickly when removed from the cold moist ground, so they do better in outside underground storage than in even a cold root cellar.

Pears — Pick pears from the tree before they are fully ripe to prevent the formation of grit cells. Keep the stem on the fruit and pick it when the skin changes from medium to light green. Keep them well spread out in a cold, humid place and ripen a few at a time in the house. For especially good results in long term storage, wrap each pear in paper as you set it away.

Peppers — Bell peppers, picked with the stem intact, may be kept in a cold, damp place for a month or so, less than that if humidity is much lower than 95%. Red hot peppers, especially the long, slim varieties, are customarily dried either on screens or strings.

Potatoes — They may be left in the hill until the weather turns consistently cool but should not be allowed to freeze or to resume growth in a period of mild rainy weather. Cure the tubers by air-drying them for a few hours, then keep them in a dark, humid spot at 36 to 40°F. They need to be allowed to develop tough skins in order to store well. Exclusion of light is important to prevent development of unwholesome green skin. Warmth and light encourage sprouting, although most stored potatoes will sprout by spring. Cold storage temperatures cause some of the starch in the potato to turn to sugar, resulting in a slightly sweet flavor that some people find objectionable. The best way to combat this problem is to bring a few pounds of potatoes at a time into warmer storage. When this is done, some of the sugar will revert to starch. Keep your potatoes separate from stored apples because the ethylene gas normally given off by apples causes white potatoes to sprout.

Pumpkins — May remain in the garden until the first frost. Be sure to keep the stems on when you harvest the pumpkins. They have a more tender rind than squash and consequently don't keep quite as well. Curing them in the field for several weeks, as long as hard frost doesn't hit them, extends their keeping time. They should last two or three months at 70 to 75% humidity and a temperature of about 50°F. After long storage in warm temperatures, they become stringy. When storing pumpkins, don't let them pile up or rest on each other. Small bruises encourage rot.

Quince — Well spread out in containers, quince that is not bruised will keep under the same conditions as apples for two to three months in a cold, damp place.

Radishes (Winter Variety) — For storage, plant seed of one of the large good keepers like China Rose in early August. Leave the roots in the ground until hard frost, then store them in a box of sand in a cold cellar or in an outdoor pit, barrel, or can.

Rutabagas — The first light frosts of fall don't bother the rutabaga, but they should be pulled before hit by killing frost. They do well when stored in moist sand to prevent shriveling.

Salsify — Well mulched, the oyster plant, as it is commonly known, will survive the winter in most temperate zone areas. It may be dug whenever the ground will admit a fork. Its flavor is actually improved by a good frost or two. The roots are thin and they shrivel readily when exposed to the air, so any salsify that you dig up should be promptly used or stored in sand in the root cellar or in damp covered pits.

Squash — The harder skin of the squash makes it possible to store this vegetable for up to six months. It prefers a lower humidity than the pumpkin, about 50 to 60%, and a temperature, likewise, of 50 to 60°F. Large squash keep best. Small varieties like acorn sometimes shrivel inside after several months of storage. Leave the fruit on the vine until frost is near. Letting it cure in the field will further toughen the skin. You can spread the squash on a shaded porch during the early days of fall and then winter them indoors in an unheated room.

Sweet Potatoes — Uncured sweet potatoes shrivel and spoil within a few weeks. They have a very tender skin, which must be toughened by exposure to temperatures of about 85°F. at 90% humidity for about ten days. Then they will keep better, for a few months or even until spring, if you've hit on just the right combination for curing. Keeping time for uncured sweets may be extended somewhat by keeping them in moist sand. Cured sweets keep best at about 55°F. in 80 to 85% humidity. Be sure to save and use the tiny sweet potatoes. They are tender and delicious. Storage temperatures below 50°F. damage the sweet potato.

Tomatoes — For ripening in storage, tomatoes should be picked without stems. Ripe tomatoes, of course, have a very brief storage life but those that are a good strong green will ripen well over a month or more if kept at 55°F. They will be ready to eat in about two weeks if kept at 65 to 70°F. Tomatoes that are still white will not be as solid or juicy when ripened indoors as those that have advanced into the green stage. Spread out the fruits in a single layer and, if time permits, wrap the most promising specimens in paper. As they develop color, bring them into the house to complete ripening at a sunny window. Avoid extremes of dampness that might encourage decay, or dryness that will shrivel the tomatoes before they ripen.

Turnips — If at all possible, store turnips, kohlrabi, and cabbage separate from other more delicately flavored fruits and vegetables such as celery, apples, and pears, since they may transmit a strong flavor to these and other foods in storage.

Methods of Processing

Other home storage methods, requiring more processing and sometimes special equipment, are more suitable for the quickly perishable foods like berries, soft fruits and vegetables, meats, etc. These methods include canning, drying, salting/fermenting, smoking, and freezing. Each of these methods, in different ways, preserves food by preventing activity of the four causes of spoilage: molds, yeasts, bacteria, and enzymes. Molds, yeasts, and bacteria are everywhere: in the air, soil, and water on which we depend. We couldn't do without them, but when they live on food they cause spoilage and some kinds cause sickness.

Mold and yeast growth stops at temperatures below 32°F. and is most active at temperatures between 50° and 100°F. Most molds are destroyed by several minutes exposure to temperatures of 212°F. Yeasts don't tolerate temperatures above 116°F. Bacteria are generally inactive under 32°F., beginning to stir at temperatures up to 50°F., most active at temperatures of 50 to 120°F., and the majority begin to be destroyed at 140 to 190°F. To be considered safe, though, food should be subjected to 212°F. in processing for canning. Spores and toxins may survive considerably higher temperatures.

Enzymes in fruits and vegetables are active even after picking, and this continued activity causes a degeneration in flavor, texture, and color of the food. Most active at 80 to 120°F., enzyme action is halted by exposing the food to temperatures above 140°F.

Canning

Canning destroys the spoilers (bacteria, molds, yeasts, and enzymes) by heat and seals out air, thus preventing entry of new bacteria, molds, and yeasts from surrounding air. Always wash food well before canning; *Clostridium botulinum,* which in the absence of air can produce a fatal toxin, lives in the soil.

Fruits and vegetables for canning should be as ripe and sound as possible. Many people prefer to cut out small blemishes and insect evidence, though, rather than eat produce that has been sprayed with pesticides and fungicides. All food should be thoroughly washed to cut down on contamination by *C. botulinum,* which is commonly found in soil.

Foods that are strongly acid, such as pickles, rhubarb, plums, apricots, apples, peaches, pears, cherries, grapes, and tomatoes may be canned using the water bath method, boiling the filled and sealed jars of food in water to a depth of 1 or 2 inches above the jar tops. A temperature of 212°F. must be maintained for the recommended time for the particular food being canned. Dense food like applesauce should be packed hot into hot jars, since the heat is slow to penetrate the solid mass. See Table 7-1 for processing times and methods recommended for each acid fruit.

TABLE 7–1

Timetable for Processing Fruits, Tomatoes, and Pickled Vegetables in Boiling-Water Bath

Product	Raw pack or hot pack foods following directions. Check jar rims and discard any nicked or cracked jars. Use new lids only. Put filled glass jars into canner containing hot or boiling water. For raw pack have water in canner hot but not boiling; for all other packs have water boiling. Add boiling water to bring water 1 or 2 inches over tops of jars, but don't pour boiling water	Pints	Quarts

TABLE 7–1 *(Cont.)*

Product		Pints	Quarts
Product	directly on glass jars. Put on cover of canner. Count processing time when water in canner comes to a rolling boil. When processing time is completed, remove the jars from the kettle and put them in a draft-free place to cool. Test for seal after 12 hours and reprocess any unsealed jars or use them promptly.		
Apples	Hot Pack 1. Pare, core, cut into pieces. To keep from darkening, place in water containing 2 tablespoons each of salt and vinegar per gallon. Drain, then boil 5 minutes in thin syrup or water. Pack apples in jars to ¹/₂ inch of top. Cover with hot syrup or water, leaving ¹/₂ inch at top.	Min. 15	Min. 20
	2. Make apple sauce, sweetened or unsweetened; pack hot to ¹/₄ inch of top.	10	10
Beets, Pickled	Hot Pack Cut off beet tops, leaving 1 inch of stem and root. Wash beets, cover with boiling water, and cook until tender. Remove skins and slice. For pickling syrup use 2 cups vinegar to 1 cup honey. Heat to boiling. Pack beets in jars to ¹/₂ inch of top. Add ¹/₂ teaspoon salt to pints, 1 teaspoon to quarts. Cover with boiling syrup, leaving ¹/₂ inch at top.	30	30
Berries, Except Strawberries	Raw Pack Wash berries and drain. Fill jars to ¹/₂ inch of top, shaking berries down gently. Cover with boiling syrup (thin or medium recommended) leaving ¹/₂ inch at top.	10	15
	Hot Pack Wash berries and drain well. Add ¹/₄ cup honey to each quart fruit. Cover pan and bring to boil. Pack berries to ¹/₂ inch of top.	10	15
Cherries	Raw Pack Wash; remove pits if desired. Fill jars	20	25

Cherries	to ¹/₂ inch of top, shaking cherries down gently. Cover with boiling syrup (thin or medium) leaving ¹/₂ inch at top.		
	Hot Pack Wash; remove pits if desired. Add ¹/₄ cup honey to each quart of fruit. Add a little water to unpitted cherries. Cover pan and bring to boil. Pack hot to ¹/₂ inch of top.	10	15
Figs	Wash and drain ripe but firm figs, leaving stems on. Bring to boiling in hot water and let stand five minutes. Drain. Put fruit in hot jars. Leave ¹/₂ inch head space. Cover with boiling light syrup made with honey.	85	90
Fruit Purée	Hot Pack Use sound, ripe fruit. Wash; remove pits if desired. Cut large fruit in pieces. Simmer until soft, add a little water if needed. Put through strainer or food mill. Add honey to taste. Heat to simmering and pack to ¹/₄ inch of top.	10	10
Peaches or Apricots	Raw Pack Wash peaches or apricots and remove skins. Remove pits. To keep from darkening place in solution (same as apples). Drain, pack fruit in jars to ¹/₂ inch of top. Cover with boiling syrup (light or medium) leaving ¹/₂ inch at top.	25	30
	Hot Pack Prepare fruit as for raw pack. Heat fruit through in hot syrup. If fruit is very juicy you may heat it with ¹/₄ cup of honey to 1 quart of raw fruit adding no liquid. Pack fruit to ¹/₂ inch of top.		
Pears	Peel, cut in halves, and core. Follow directions for peaches either raw pack or hot pack using same timetables.		
Plums	Raw Pack Wash. To can whole, prick skins. Freestone varieties may be halved and pitted. Pack fruit in jars to ¹/₂ inch of top. Cover with boiling syrup, leaving ¹/₂ inch space at top.	20	25

TABLE 7-1 *(Cont.)*

Product	Hot Pack	Pints	Quarts
Plums	Hot Pack Prepare as for raw pack. Heat to boiling in syrup or juice. If fruit is very juicy, you may heat it with honey, adding no liquid. Pack hot fruit to ½ inch of top. Cover with boiling syrup, leaving ½ inch at top.	20	25
Rhubarb	Hot Pack Wash and cut into ½ inch pieces. Add ¼ cup honey to each quart rhubarb and let stand to draw out juice. Bring to boiling. Pack hot to ½ inch of top.	10	10
Sauerkraut	Hot Pack Heat well-fermented sauerkraut to simmering (185°–210°F.). Pack hot kraut to ½ inch of top. Cover with hot juice, leaving ½ inch at top.	15	20
Tomatoes	Raw Pack Use only perfect, ripe tomatoes. Scald just long enough to loosen skins; plunge into cold water. Drain, peel, and core. Leave tomatoes whole or cut in halves or quarters. Pack tomatoes to ½ inch of top, pressing gently to fill spaces. Add ½ teaspoon salt to pints and 1 teaspoon to quarts, if desired.	40	50
	Hot Pack Quarter peeled tomatoes. Bring to boil and pack to ½ inch of top. Add salt as for raw packed tomatoes.	35	45

Low-acid foods like okra, peppers, pumpkin, squash, carrots, cabbage, corn, turnips, beets, snap beans, greens, cauliflower, peas, all other vegetables, and nonacid foods like meats, poultry, and seafood must be canned at 240°F. under pressure to kill the spores of the bacterium *C. botulinum,* which produces its highly poisonous toxin under low-acid, airless conditions. Processing times vary with the acidity of the vegetable and the size of the jar. Table 7-2 will give you an idea of these times. Old methods of processing of low-acid vegetables in a water bath for long periods of several hours have been shown to be unreliable. Authorities recommend boiling all low-acid foods for 15 minutes before serving as an added precaution.

TABLE 7–2

Timetable for Processing Low-Acid Vegetables

Product	Work rapidly. Raw pack or hot pack foods following directions, adding if desired ½ teaspoon salt for pints and 1 teaspoon for quarts. Check jar rims and discard any nicked or cracked jars. Use new lids only. Place jars on rack in steam pressure canner containing 2 to 3 inches of boiling water. Fasten canner cover securely. Let steam escape 10 minutes or more before closing petcock. When processing time is completed, remove the jars from the kettle and put them in a draft-free place to cool. Test for seal after 12 hours and reprocess any unsealed jars or use them promptly.	Use 10 Pounds Pressure Pressure Canner	
		Pints	Quarts
Asparagus	Raw Pack Wash asparagus; trim off scales and tough ends and wash again. Cut in 1-inch pieces. Pack asparagus tightly as possible without crushing to ½ inch of top. Cover with boiling water leaving ½ inch at top.	Min. 25	Min. 30
	Hot Pack Prepare as for raw pack; then cover with boiling water. Boil 2 or 3 minutes. Pack asparagus loosely to ½ inch of top. Cover with boiling water leaving ½ inch at top.	25	30
Beans, Dry with Tomato or Molasses Sauce	Hot Pack Sort and wash dry beans. Cover with boiling water; boil 2 minutes, remove from heat and let soak 1 hour. Heat to boiling and drain, saving liquid for sauce. Fill jars ¾ full with hot beans. Add small piece of salt pork, ham, or bacon. Fill to ½ inch of top with hot tomato or molasses sauce.	65	75

TABLE 7–2 *(Cont.)*

Product			
Beans, Fresh Lima	Raw Pack Shell and wash beans. Pack loosely small type to 1 inch of top of jar for pints and 1½ inches for quarts; for large beans fill to ¾ inch of top for pints and 1¼ inches for quarts. Cover beans with boiling water.	40	50
	Hot Pack Shell the beans, then cover with boiling water, and bring to boil. Pack beans loosely in jar to 1 inch of top. Cover with boiling water, leaving 1 inch at top.	40	50
Beans, Snap	Raw Pack Wash beans. Trim ends and cut into 1 inch pieces. Pack tightly in jars to ½ inch of top. Cover with boiling water, leaving ½ inch at top.	20	25
	Hot Pack Prepare as for raw pack beans. Then cover with boiling water and boil 5 minutes. Pack beans in jars loosely to ½ inch of top. Cover with boiling-hot cooking liquid and water, leaving ½ inch at top.	20	25
Beans, Soybeans	For green soybeans, follow directions for lima beans.	55	65
Beets	Hot Pack Sort beets for size. Cut off tops, leaving 1 inch stem, also root; and wash. Boil until skins slip easily. Skin, trim, cut, and pack into jars to ½ inch of top. Cover with boiling water, leaving ½ inch at top.	30	35
Carrots	Raw Pack Wash and scrape carrots. Slice, dice, or leave whole. Pack tightly in jars to 1 inch of top. Cover with boiling water.	25	30
	Hot Pack Prepare as for raw pack, then cover with boiling water and	25	30

Carrots	bring to boil. Pack carrots in jars to ¹/₂ inch of top. Cover with boiling-hot cooking liquid and water, leaving ¹/₂ inch at top.		
Celery	Wash and chop celery into 1 to 2 inch lengths. Boil 3 minutes. Put into hot jars, within 1 inch of top. Cover with boiling water leaving 1 inch head space.	30	35
Corn—Cream Style	Raw Pack Husk corn and remove silk. Wash. Cut corn from cob at about center of kernel and scrape cobs. Pack corn loosely in pint jars to 1 inch of top. Cover with boiling water.	95	
	Hot Pack Prepare as for raw pack. Add 1 pint boiling water to each quart of corn. Heat to boiling. Pack hot corn to 1 inch of top.	85	
Corn—Whole Kernel	Raw Pack Husk corn and remove silk. Wash. Cut from cob at about ²/₃ the depth of kernel. Pack corn loosely to 1 inch of top and cover with boiling water.	55	85
	Hot Pack Prepare as for raw pack. To each quart of corn add 1 pint of boiling water. Heat to boiling. Pack loosely to 1 inch of top with mixture of corn and liquid.	55	85
Mushrooms	Hot Pack Select tender, young mushrooms. Discard any that have opened. Wash thoroughly and trim off tough stalks. Cut in slices or leave small mushroom caps whole. Steam mushrooms for 4 minutes. Pack into hot jars, leaving 1 inch at top. You may add ¹/₂ teaspoon salt. Cover mushrooms with boiling water.		
Okra	Can okra pods whole unless they are to be used for soup. Slice pods for soup. Wash and drain. Remove	25	40

TABLE 7–2 *(Cont.)*

Product			
Okra	stem and blossom ends. Boil two minutes. Pack into hot jars. Cover with boiling water, leaving 1 inch head space.		
Peas, Green	Raw Pack Shell and wash peas. Pack peas loosely in jars to 1 inch of top. Cover with boiling water, leaving 1 inch at top.	40	40
	Hot Pack Prepare as for raw pack. Cover with boiling water and bring to boil. Pack peas loosely in jars to 1 inch of top. Cover with boiling water, leaving 1 inch at top.	40	40
Sweet Potatoes	Wash and steam newly dug potatoes until skins rub off readily. Do not prick potatoes. Pack into hot jars. Press potato to fill spaces. Add no liquid.	65	95
Pumpkin or Winter Squash Cubed	Hot Pack Wash pumpkin or winter squash, remove seeds, and pare. Cut into 1 inch cubes. Add just enough water to cover. Bring to boil. Pack cubes in jars to ½ inch of top. Cover with hot cooking liquid and water, leaving ½ inch at top.	55	90
Pumpkin or Winter Squash Strained	Hot Pack Wash pumpkin or winter squash, remove seeds, and pare. Cut into 1 inch cubes. Steam until tender (about 25 minutes). Put through food mill or strainer. Simmer until heated. Pack hot in jars to ½ inch of top.	65	80
Spinach and Other Greens	Hot Pack Pick over and wash thoroughly. Cut out tough stems and midribs. Place about 2½ pounds of spinach in cheesecloth bag and steam about 10 minutes or until well wilted. Pack loosely to ½ inch of top. Cover with boiling water, leaving ½ inch at top.	70	90

Oven canning is unreliable at best and potentially dangerous, since the jars may explode. Besides using more fuel and offering no saving of time, this method may be hazardous to people and property. It cannot be recommended.

Seedy berries, although they may safely be canned, are usually of better quality if frozen. Canned applesauce is often preferred to frozen. Greens take up little space when blanched and frozen and retain more food value when well frozen than when canned. Low-acid foods like beets, peppers, snap beans, and cabbage may be preserved by pickling, in which case the higher acidity makes it possible to safely use the water bath canning method. Such pickles should have a pH of 4.6 or lower. Use only standard 5 percent vinegar, not homemade vinegar of uncertain strength, in a dilution of at least 1 cup of vinegar to each cup of water or juice.

Canning Tips

The gardener who is canning produce is doubly busy because harvesting, washing, and sorting the fruits and vegetables takes as much time as preparation for canning. Many gardeners try to put up a few jars of something each day from midsummer on, to build up the larder gradually. Still, there will be days when pecks of peas and bushels of tomatoes and apples, grapes and pears must be dealt with. Perhaps some of the following tips will save you time and trouble:

1. Grape juice may be made right in the jar by pouring boiling water over the washed, sweetened, uncooked grapes, then processing the jars in a boiling water bath for 10 minutes.

2. If at all possible, use unsprayed apples (if you are buying apples; we assume you will not spray your own) to make applesauce, so that you needn't peel them. Alternatively, wash sprayed fruit in a vinegar and water solution; use about 1 cup of vinegar to 3 gallons of water to remove as much as possible of the chemical residue.

3. If cucumbers are ripening slowly, you may want to make a jar or two of pickles at a time. Small quantities of small jars of acid foods may be canned in any deep pan. Put old canning jar rings on the bottom of the pan to assure circulation of the boiling water and be sure that at least 1 inch of water covers the tops of the sealed jars.

4. To loosen skins of tomatoes and peaches for quick peeling, steam them for a few minutes. (Lye is commonly used for

this purpose in canning factories; another good reason for doing your own.) Consider, too: is it necessary to peel your tomatoes? Canning them with the peel on can save a lot of time and vitamins, although they get tougher in the process.

5. Assemble needed supplies before cutting the vegetables or fruits. It is discouraging to have a canning rack full of jars packed to the top with food to be processed, and then to find that you haven't the right size lid for that jar on hand!

6. Invest in a ladle, a canning funnel, and a timer. They will save you time and trouble.

Checklist for Canning Problems

If you notice puzzling changes in some of your canned goods, you may want to check the following list to see what might have gone wrong. Any mushy, bubbling, moldy, or slimy food should be considered spoiled.

1. Fruit floats — because it is lighter than the syrup. Heating the fruit first and packing it tightly may help to prevent floating.

2. Yellow crystals on canned green vegetables — are glucoside which occurs naturally and does no harm.

3. Crystals — on grape products are tartaric acid, a natural component of grapes. Put into clean jars and reprocess.

4. Shriveled pickles — too much salt, sugar, or vinegar was added to the pickles at one time. Add these substances gradually, working up to the full amount.

5. Hollow pickles — cucumbers were too old when processed. Ideally, pickles should be made within one day of picking.

6. Fruits darken after removal from jar — processing time was too short to destroy enzymes.

Canning Equipment

The following equipment isn't all necessary, but will make your home canning of fruits and vegetables easier. The items marked with * can be considered optional:

Water bath canner for acid foods
Pressure canner for low-acid foods

Jars, sealing discs, bands and/or rubbers, glass tops to use with rubbers as needed, screw lids
*Ladle
*Wide mouth funnel
*Jar tongs to lift jars into and out of hot water
*A small timer
*Long-handled stirring and slotting serving spoons

Also optional, but nice to have, are a household scale, a strainer, and a blender or food mill. Quilted mitts handle hot jars more easily than small potholders.

Although canned foods will keep for years, their flavor and food value deteriorate under exposure to light and high temperatures. *C. botulinum* is more likely to be active at temperatures above 60°F. Keep your canned goods in a cool (45 to 60°F.), dry, dark place to preserve all the goodness that you have put into them. Food quality and nutritive value are highest during the 12 months after processing.

Freezing

Freezing does not destroy the microorganisms responsible for spoilage as canning does; it merely inhibits them by chilling the food below their range of activity. For that reason, thawed foods in which the temperature has risen to or near that at which microorganisms grow, should not be refrozen.

Only the very best ripe, unblemished food should be frozen, since freezing can preserve but not enhance food quality. An hour or two from garden to freezer is the goal to aim for. Produce that must be held longer than that should be chilled; in fact, if the food is to be cut for freezing, prior chilling will help to cut vitamin losses. Freezing is a good way to preserve small amounts of food as they become available. Root vegetables like carrots and beets should be cooked before freezing. Potatoes do not freeze well; they develop a different texture that many people find unappetizing. Freezing is usually the method of choice for preserving meats.

For highest quality, food put into the freezer should freeze rapidly. If too much food is put into the freezer at one time, the overloaded freezer will not be able to freeze the additions as fast as necessary. About 2 or 3 pounds of new food for every cubic foot of freezer space can be frozen in a 24-hour period. Adding too much unfrozen food to the freezer can reduce the quality of the food already stored there by raising the temperature above the minimum necessary to maintain quality.

Vegetables

Vegetables to be frozen (except for bell peppers and tomatoes) must be blanched to destroy enzymes that would lower quality. See Table 7-3 for times. To steam blanch, place no more than 2 pounds of a vegetable (preferably less) on a rack above 1 to 2 inches of boiling water in a kettle with a tight fitting lid. Vegetables that tend to pack together, like sugar peas, may not heat evenly when done in this way, but steam blanching is effective for most other vegetables. Vegetables should be cut in small pieces to allow quick penetration by the steam. As soon as blanching time is up, cool the vegetables in cold running water or ice water. Blanching by steam results in less vitamin loss than the boiling water method. To blanch food in boiling water, submerge 1 to 2 pounds of vegetables in at least 4 quarts of boiling water in a large kettle. Use a wire basket or special enameled blancher sold in hardware stores. Cool quickly and package immediately, pressing out as much air as possible if using plastic bags.

Fruits

Fruits that are frozen in syrup are usually treated with an ascorbic acid preparation to prevent darkening. Follow the directions given by the manufacturer of the commercial preparation. Or you can use vitamin C tablets, crushed and dissolved in water. One half to three-fourths of a teaspoon of ascorbic acid to each quart of syrup is the usual recommendation.

Meats

When freezing raw meat, do not salt it; salt tends to cause rancidity in fats. For this reason, salt-cured ham and bacon and seasoned sausage have a short freezer storage life: about two to three months.

When freezing cooked meats or combination dishes, especially those containing meat products, sea food, milk, and/or eggs, the food should be cooled and frozen as soon after cooking as possible. Setting the pan of food in ice water or in cold running water will speed the cooling process. Skim extra fat from the gravy if you expect the dish to remain in storage for more than several weeks.

To save freezer space, cook bones in water to cover and make a concentrated stock, which may be frozen in small portions. Avoid stuffing poultry before freezing since the solidly packed cold stuffing may heat too slowly during the roasting process to prevent growth of undesirable microorganisms.

Cheese

Cheese may be frozen too, although it often becomes crumbly. If it is to be used in cooking, the change in texture will not matter. For best results in freezing cheese, wrap it tightly in moisture-proof material and freeze it rapidly in small amounts of approximately ½ pound. When cheese is frozen slowly, it becomes crumbly. Moist cheese generally retains better quality when frozen than hard cheese, since it is less affected by dehydration that naturally occurs during the freezing process.

Butter

Salted butter keeps for several months in the freezer. Unsalted butter is more perishable, but keeps best in the freezer, since its refrigerator life is short.

Milk

Milk has a freezer life of about three months, but in milk that isn't homogenized the cream separates into small particles and won't mix in again. This is less of a problem with goat milk, which is naturally homogenized. Milk that does develop cream particles can be used for cooking or well-blended for milkshakes. For best quality, freeze milk in amounts of 1 quart or less; larger volume freezes too slowly and often sours on thawing.

Eggs

Eggs may be frozen for use in cooking during short winter days when hens aren't laying well. To freeze whole eggs, mix the yolks and whites with a fork, taking care not to introduce air that would have a drying effect. Package the stirred eggs in containers, adding 1 teaspoon salt for each 2 cups of mixed egg,

TABLE 7–3

Preparation for Freezing

Blanching Time in Minutes

			Water	Steam
Artichokes	Remove and discard outermost leaves. Trim stalks to 1 inch and cut across the vegetable to expose the tightly packed inner leaves to blanching. Scald. Chill.	Small Large	3 5	— —
Asparagus	Sort stalks according to thickness. Wash thoroughly. Cut in jar-size or 2-inch lengths. Scald. Chill. Pack, leaving no head space.	Small Medium Large	2 3 4	4
Beans, Lima or Butter	Shell. Wash. Sort according to size. Scald. Chill.	Small Medium Large	2 3 4	3
Beans, Snap, Green or Wax	Wash. Remove ends. Cut as desired. Scald. Chill.		3	3
Beets	Wash and sort according to size. Trim tops, leave 1/2 inch of stems. Cook until tender. Chill. Peel and cut as desired.	Small Medium	30 45	—
Broccoli	Wash, peel stalks, and trim. To remove insects, soak for 1/2 hour in salt-water (4 tsp. salt, 1 gal. cold water). Split lengthwise. Scald. Chill. Pack, leaving no head space.		3	5
Brussels Sprouts	Trim, removing coarse outer leaves. Wash thoroughly. Sort. Scald. Chill. Pack, leaving no head space.	Small Medium Large	3 4 5	5
Cabbage	Trim off outer leaves. Shred for tight packing or cut into wedges. Scald. Chill.		1 1/2 3	3 4
Carrots	Remove tops. Wash and peel. Leave small carrots whole. Cut others into slices or strips. Scald. Chill.	Whole Cut	5 2	5 4
Cauliflower	Trim and cut in pieces 1-inch across. Wash well. To remove insects, soak for 1/2 hour in salt-water (4 tsp. salt, 1 gal. cold water). Drain. Scald in salt-water (4 tsp. salt, 1 gal. water). Chill. Pack, leaving no head space.		3	4

Celery	Strip any coarse strings from young stalks. Wash and trim, cut across the rib into 1-inch pieces. Scald. Chill.		3	4
Corn, Whole-kernel	Husk, silk, and wash. Scald. Chill. Cut kernels at about ²/₃ the depth of the kernels.		4	—
Cream-style	Husk, silk, and wash. Scald. Chill. Cut kernels at about the center of the kernels. Scrape cobs to remove juice and heart of the kernel.		4	—
On-the-cob	Husk, silk, and wash. Sort according to size. Scald. Chill.	Small Medium Large	7 9 11	—
Greens, All Kinds	Wash thoroughly. Remove tough stems and imperfect leaves. Scald. Chill.		2–3	4–5
Kohlrabi	Remove tops and roots. Wash, peel, dice in ¹/₂-inch cubes. Scald. Chill.		1	3
Mushrooms	Use firm tender small to medium size. Wash and cut off lower part of stems (cut large mushrooms into pieces), add ¹/₃ tsp. lemon juice to 1 gal. water. Scald in boiling water. Chill.	Small Large	2 4	— —
Okra	Wash. Remove stems; do not break seed pod. Scald. Chill.		3–4	5
Parsnips	Remove tops. Wash, peel, cut into ¹/₂-inch cubes. Scald. Chill.		2	4
Peas, Green and Blackeye	Shell. Discard immature and tough peas. Scald. Chill.		1¹/₂-2	1¹/₂-2
Peppers	Wash and halve, remove seeds and pulp, slice or dice. Peppers do not require blanching.		—	—
Rutabagas and Turnips	Remove tops. Wash, peel, cut in ¹/₂-inch cubes. Scald. Chill.		2	4
Squash, Summer	Select squash with rind still tender. Wash, and cut without peeling in ¹/₂-inch slices. Scald. Chill.		3	4
Squash, Winter and Pumpkin	Wash. Cut in pieces and remove seeds. Cook until soft. Remove rind. Put pulp through sieve. Cool by placing pan containing purée into cold water. Stir puree occasionally to hasten chilling.		20	—

Preparation for Freezing	Blanching Time in Minutes
Sweet Potatoes Freeze mature sweet potatoes which have been cured. Wash. Cook until tender. Cool at room temperature. Peel; cut in halves or slices, or mash. To prevent darkening: dip halves or slices for 5 seconds in lemon-water (1½ cup lemon juice, 1 qt. water); mix 2 tbsp. orange or lemon juice with each quart of mashed.	

or 1 tablespoon honey for each 2 cups of egg, depending on future use. Label them well or use a different kind of container for each. (But record your code!) Eggs keep their quality for about eight months in the freezer.

Packaging for the Freezer

According to home freezing expert Hazel Meyer, author of *The Complete Book of Home Freezing,* "About 85 percent of food failures in freezing are caused by inadequate packaging materials and methods." The remaining 15 percent is due to slow freezing, poor food quality, mistakes in preparation, and poor choice of foods.

Packaging, then, is as important as blanching in preserving food quality. Your objective is to seal the food as well as possible, keeping air out and using a package that is strong enough to withstand jostling in the freezer without splitting and breaking. Dehydration, or freezer burn, is caused by the evaporation of food juices by exposure to air. Oxidation is another freezer problem to guard against. Oxidized food has been invaded by oxygen, lowering the vitamin content and causing rancidity of meats and fats, and often trading flavors with other stored foods. For an idea of how long you can safely keep frozen foods that are properly packaged and prepared in a freezer at 0°F., see Table 7-4.

Equipment for Freezing

Equipment necessary for freezing (in addition to the freezer!) includes the following: (Items marked with * are not needed, but will make the job easier.)

Blanching kettle or wire baskets and large kettle
Rack for steaming vegetables

Plastic sealed containers, polyethylene bags, cans, jars, and other *well-sealed* containers
Freezer paper and tape
Wax marking pencil
*Minute timer for blanching
*Wire basket or colander for cooling vegetables
*Trays or cookie sheets for quick freezing
Guard against splitting and tearing of freezer packages by:

    1. Double-bagging irregularly shaped foods.
    2. Protecting sharp meat bones with padding of extra freezer paper or old plastic bags.
    3. Using heavy paper especially made for freezer use, with a moisture-vapor barrier, and sealing it with special freezer tape.

TABLE 7-4

Maximum Storage Times
for Frozen Foods

Baked breads ....2–4 mo.
Unbaked breads....................................about 7 days
Cookies ....4–6 mo.
Ice cream ....2–4 mo.
Pies...2–4 mo.
Raw meat
    Beef ....6–12 mo.
    Pork ....3–6 mo.
    Lamb ....6–9 mo.
    Veal ....6–9 mo.
    Ground meat ....3 mo.
Combination dishes ....2–3 mo.
Poultry
    Chicken, turkey.................................12 mo.
    Duck, goose ....6 mo.
Seafood
    High in fat.....................................6–8 mo.
    Low in fat ....10–12 mo.
Wild game, animals, and birds ....9 mo.
Vegetables
    Cooked ....about 4 mo. at 0°F. (only 6 mo. at 5°F.)
    Blanched, raw ....10 mo. at 0°F. (only 6 mo. at 5°F.)
Fruits, purées, juices ....1 year at 0°F., 8 mo. at 5°F.
    Cooked fruits ....4 mo.

4. Avoiding using rubber bands to fasten packages. They lose their elasticity and often break in the freezer.

5. Avoiding aluminum foil as an outer wrapping. It tears very easily, exposing the contents.

6. Lining coffee cans with plastic bags and topping with their lids, to hold frozen nuts, berries, and individually frozen vegetables.

An easy way to make fruits and vegetables readily available is to spread them on trays and quick freeze them. When they are individually frozen solid, store them in your regular freezer containers or improvised cans as above. They won't adhere to each other and you can remove as many as you need at one time. This works especially well with figs, blueberries, cranberries, rhubarb, mushrooms, peas, beans, soybeans, carrots, limas, and Brussels sprouts. You have to be careful not to let the individual pieces stay on the sheet too long or they will get freezer burn or form ice crystals. Always leave ½ to 1 inch head space at the top of a container of liquid to allow for expansion during freezing.

The freezer should be kept in a dry, cool place, preferably between 50 and 70°F. If kept in a damp spot, it is a good idea to elevate the freezer on blocks to keep it off the damp floor. In case of a power outage, a 50-pound block of dry ice will keep food in the freezer for two or three days, as long as the freezer door is kept closed.

Brining

Salt preserves food by reducing bacterial growth. In addition, the fermentation of vegetables in their own juice, as is done with cabbage, rutabagas, beans, and even sweet corn, results in a product with a special taste appeal of its own. Healthful lactic acid is developed when cabbage ferments. Vitamin loss is greater in this method than in canning and freezing, but generally the vegetables so prepared are considered a relish or appetizer rather than the mainstay of the meal.

To brine foods, use only fresh, sound vegetables. Fifteen pounds of kraut will fit in a 2-gallon crock. Shred the cabbage (or turnip or rutabaga). Sprinkle with salt at the rate of one tablespoon of salt to three pounds of cabbage. (Authorities and experienced sauerkraut makers differ on the amount of salt. Some use less than this; many use a bit more — 3 tablespoons salt to 5 pounds cabbage.) Tamp the salted cabbage until juice rises. Top with clean large cabbage or grape leaves. Weight the cabbage to keep it submerged in liquid. You'll need a weight of about 10 pounds to take care of a 5-gallon crock.

The best kraut is made slowly at temperatures of about 60°F. or under, taking as much as a month to ferment. Faster fermentation will take place at higher temperatures. Check on the progress of fermentation, rap on the side of the crock with your hand, and remove the top layer of scum every now and then. If no bubbles rise to the surface, fermentation is complete. Store the kraut at 40°F. or less, or can it in a boiling water bath for 25 minutes. It can be frozen, but no doubt freezer room is needed for more perishable foods.

Kraut may also be made by this same method in wide-mouth gallon jars, or even quart jars, in small amounts.

Green tomatoes and cucumbers may be preserved in crocks or jars in a salt, water, and vinegar solution, often with added spices. See your favorite cookbook or canning book for directions. *The Ball Canning Book,* available from Ball Corp., Muncie, Indiana, 47302, has a number of good recipes for putting down cucumbers in crocks. The same recipes may be used for pickling green tomatoes.

Equipment needed for brining and fermentation of vegetables would usually include:

Grater, shredder, or slaw cutter

Household scale

Crocks or large jars

Weights (stones or water-filled jugs), clean cloths, and odd spare plates

Measuring spoons

Smoking

Meat, fish, and game may be smoked to preserve it from bacterial spoilage and give it a distinctive flavor that adds variety to the menu. Actually, the salt and sugar used to prepare the meat for smoking are largely responsible for the preservation. Meat is cured in a sugar/salt solution for two or three days per pound before smoking. Meat and brine should be at about 38°F. when combined. Below 36°F. the meat won't absorb the brine, and above 42°F. activity of spoilage organisms begins. A meat pump will carry the cure to the interior of the meat and insure more thorough and even curing.

Brine proportions recommended by the U. S. Department of Agriculture are: 8 pounds of salt, 2 pounds of sugar, 2 ounces of saltpeter, and 4½ to 6 gallons of water to each 100 pounds of meat. This brine is very salty. Meat that will be refrigerated can be cured in a slightly weaker brine, using about 6 pounds of salt with the other proportions remaining the same. Since one important reason for preparing your own meat is to assure its wholesomeness for your family, you may want to use honey instead of sugar, and will probably want to omit the saltpeter, which serves only to preserve the color of the meat, hardly worth the damage it does to your body. Saltpeter is a form of nitrate that changes to toxic compounds in combination with amines in many common foods. These compounds — nitrosamines — have been shown to cause cancer in experimental animals. They are highly suspect as a cause of human cancer. Ingestion of nitrates, therefore, should be avoided. Read labels of commercial curing preparations carefully, for most contain nitrates (saltpeter) which should be avoided.

The meat should be submerged in the brine and turned weekly to expose all surfaces equally to the cure. If the meat will be smoked for flavor rather than for long-term preservation, or if it will be frozen when finished, a curing period of two weeks for bacon and three weeks for ham is sufficient. For meat to be kept in a cold place, but not frozen, a longer period of curing is necessary: two days per pound for bacon and three days per pound for ham.

There are no hard and fast rules for the length of time meat should be smoked. This is a matter for experiment since individual tastes and smokehouse conditions vary. In general, you should count on smoking a piece of bacon for about 48 hours and a ham for around 72 hours. A shoulder — thicker than bacon but thinner than ham — requires about 60 hours. Try smoking your meat for about two-thirds of the expected time and then sample some. If it is not as highly flavored as you want it to be, simply return it to the smokehouse for additional smoking.

Keep smokehouse temperatures between 90 and 150°F. A temperature on the low side — near 90 — would probably be best. Meat dries readily at temperatures above 110°F. and pork fat begins to melt at 120°F. Many commercial smokehouses raise the temperature to 140°F. during the process to kill any trichina larvae that might be present.

Remember that wild game can carry parasites like

trichina (that causes trichinosis in humans), so be sure to cook it thoroughly before eating it. Meats that have been smoked should reach an internal temperature of 180°F. for at least 30 minutes during cooking.

Meat should be smoked when weather is cold enough to discourage bacterial spoilage. Daytime temperatures between 30 and 50°F. are about right.

Directions for building and maintaining a smokehouse or an improvised smoker may be obtained from government pamphlets and from books on home butchering. The traditional smokehouse is a tall, narrow, square, ventilated but windowless building, but simpler variations, ranging from 55-gallon steel drums to discarded refrigerators (remove all galvanized fittings) to old car bodies have been used successfully. Green hardwood makes the most satisfactory smoking fuel, since it smolders rather than flames. Hickory, oak, maple, ash, and fruitwood are good meat smoking fuels. Corncobs of a hard, flinty type of field corn or popcorn make good smoke. Avoid using softwoods, though. Pine, spruce, and other softwoods produce an unpleasant tasting resinous smoke.

Bank the fire with wood shavings or sawdust when it is necessary to cool it.

It is important to remember that the smoke that gives flavor to ham and bacon deposits coal-tar derivatives — another suspected carcinogen — in the meat. The most wholesome way to preserve meat would be to freeze it or can it, if facilities are available.

Drying

Drying preserves food by removing 80 to 90 percent of the water. Destructive microorganisms can't thrive without moisture and find the more highly concentrated sugar and acid environment inhospitable. Bacteria need 18 percent moisture; yeasts at least 20 percent, and molds only 13 to 16 percent.

Home dried foods shrink to one-sixth to one-third of their original bulk, depending on the food. The following fruits are good candidates for drying: apples, bananas, apricots, cherries, figs, grapes, plums, peaches, and pears. Fruit leather, made of puréed fruit, may be dried in thin layers on trays. Vegetables that may be successfully dried include corn, lima beans, snap beans, celery, carrots, herbs, mushrooms, peppers, pumpkin, sweet potatoes, and tomatoes. Tomatoes are a bit tricky, though. They should be dried in an efficient dehydrator rather than an oven. Use tomatoes that are not overripe and slice them ⅜ to ½ inch thick.

Drying is a low-energy method of food preservation next in line, perhaps, after root cellar storage and just ahead of smoking. Some kinds of effective drying arrangements include the following:

Solar dryers

Wood frame holding trays over space heater or hot plate

Oven (leave door open for air circulation)

Sun

Shade-drying in hot, dry climates

Racks over wood stove, hot water heater, or refrigerator. Hot air registers are effective but likely to carry fine dust and fuel fumes.

Small light bulb in a foil-lined box

Although drying is an ancient traditional method of food preservation, it is still being studied and improved on, and there is room for all kinds of experiment and improvisation. The result is what counts.

Important steps in the process:

1. Cut food in small, uniform pieces about ¼ inch thick.

2. Provide good air circulation for quick, complete drying.

3. Avoid metal trays or screens since they may react with moist acid foods.

4. Cloth netting, dowel, fiberglass screening, and strong old sheets are some recommended screening bases for use in making drying trays.

5. Vegetables, unlike fruits, should probably be steamed to blanch them before drying in order to inactivate enzymes and kill spoilage organisms. Remember that vegetables have less acid than fruits.

6. Temperatures of at least 140°F. should prevail for at least half the drying time, again to kill spoilage organisms. For the remainder of the time, maintain a temperature of 95 to 110°F.

7. Avoid high temperatures that would cook the food or prematurely harden its surface, preventing the interior from releasing moisture.

8. Protect foods from dust, birds, and insects while drying.

9. Many fruits don't need to be peeled. Experiment and see which ones you like unpeeled. Save vitamins, minerals, and time!

How do you tell when food is dry enough to store? There is no foolproof test to use at home, but you can be guided by the consistency of the food. Vegetables may be brittle. Fruits will be tough, leathery, and pliable, while warm from the drier; some of them may become somewhat crisp when cooled. Generally, fruits should retain no more than 20 percent of their water, vegetables 10 percent. You can also weigh samples of your dried and fresh produce to determine roughly how much dehydration has taken place. Food that weighs half as much as it originally did retains about one-third of its original moisture.

Some foods will stick to the trays during the drying process, but release readily once they are thoroughly dry.

The whole idea in drying is to remove the moisture from the food without cooking it. Maintaining good air circulation and thorough daily stirring and turning of the drying food, for the first four days or so, hasten drying at low temperatures. Vegetables usually require four to 12 hours of treatment in a dehydrator for complete drying. Fruits usually need at least six hours of drying time; allow more time for coarser pieces arranged very close together. Remove and package individual pieces of food as they become sufficiently dry. When using auxiliary heat, not just solar or hot attic drying, it is possible to scorch thin, almost dried food by overheating, so keep an eye on food that is nearly dry.

Food that absorbs air moisture or develops insect infestation during storage may be reprocessed by heating the pieces in a single layer in a 300°F. oven for 20 to 25 minutes.

All dried foods should be stored in a cool, dark place in tightly covered containers and checked regularly for evidence of mold or other spoilage. Keeping time for dried fruits and vegetables is up to three or four years, although as with other foods, nutritional value is highest during the first year after processing, so try to use your dried food in its first year. Be sure to label the food; it may be hard to recognize when dehydrated!

Guidelines for Preserving Taste, Appearance, and Food Value for Foods Stored around the Home

Grains

Grains must be protected from insects, rodents, and mold, but keep exceedingly well if stored in a tightly closed, clean container in a cool, dry place. Buy no more than you can use in a year since fresh supplies of grain will be available after the next harvest season.

Insect infestation can originate at many points in the production, shipping, and storing of grain. Insects may deposit eggs on unharvested grain. Storage containers may already be infested with eggs or larvae, especially in cracks and crevices. Or adult insects may enter loosely covered grain containers. Eggs of insects that prey on grains are usually tiny and difficult to detect. Buying grains directly from the grower avoids storage and shipping contamination, although the grain may still be infested on the farm.

The following insects may be found in wheat and corn:

Granary weevil — does commercially important damage, especially in the south, by pulverizing corn kernels.

Lesser grain borer — a tiny beetle whose eggs develop inside the grain. As the hatched beetles work their way to the outside, they destroy much of the grain.

Meals, flours, and other mixed grain products may contain the following pests:

Mediterranean flour moth — the larvae leave a characteristic mass of matted threads that make the flour grains, rice, etc., clump together. Also found in dried fruit and nuts.

Confused flour beetle — a worldwide inhabitant of mills, warehouses, and granaries.

Saw-toothed grain beetle — both the larva and the adult damage stored grains and flours.

A convincing argument for buying grains directly from the grower or from a dealer in natural foods whom you trust is the fact that most ordinary grain warehouses use chemical controls to assure "clean" grain.

Defend your stored grain against invaders by taking the following preventive measures:

1. Store grains in tightly closed containers. Tiny larvae easily work their way into opened boxes or plastic bags closed with wires, and even lurk under screw-cap edges of jars. They may hide in storage can crevices and remain to infest another batch of food.

2. Keep food in a clean, dry place and on a shelf rather than on the floor where the possibility of contamination is greater.

3. Cool, or better yet, cold storage areas discourage insect life.

4. Don't allow spilled food to remain in storage areas to attract unwanted insects.

5. If insect infestation is a problem, treat grain by:
   a. Heating it in an oven at 135°F. for 30 minutes. Then turn off the oven and leave the grain in for an hour, or
   b. Cooling at 0°F. for three or four days.

Since heating destroys some vitamins, it should be done only if necessary.

The insects mentioned above are unappetizing and destructive, but pose no threat to health if consumed. Rodent damage, however, is a health hazard, since mice and especially rats often carry diseases which can be transmitted to humans through their saliva or droppings.

Rats are capable of chewing through fabric, plastic, cardboard, wood, and even thin aluminum; to exclude them, grain must be stored in glass, heavy metal cans, or wood reinforced with hardware cloth. Concrete blocks form impenetrable storage receptacles for large amounts of grain. Avoid leaving spilled grain around to attract rodents.

Mold damage to grains cannot be undone; it can only be prevented. Molds are everywhere. Their spores are readily disseminated and impossible to keep out. Since molds require warm, moist conditions in order to grow, keeping grain in a cool, dry place will discourage most mold growth.

Nuts

Shelled nuts, with their high oil content, quickly grow rancid at room temperature. They must be protected from heat, light, air, and extreme dampness. Shelled nuts should be refrigerated in convenient amounts, with the bulk of the crop, if it is a large one, kept in the freezer at 0°F. Shelled nuts will keep in the refrigerator for six months; up to two years in the freezer. Nuts in the shell should be kept in a cold place (32 to 36°F. at 65 to 70 percent humidity is ideal) and used within a year. Coffee cans with plastic lids make good storage containers for shelled nuts.

Peanut butter is not a shelf staple, but a perishable. It is high in oil, which is readily oxidized to the point of rancidity. Opened containers of peanut butter should always be refrigerated. Other nut butters like sesame butter, cashew butter, and such should be treated the same way.

Seeds

Seeds, like nuts, are vulnerable to deterioration on account of their high oil and protein content. All shelled pumpkin, sunflower, sesame, and other seeds should be refrigerated and toasted, if at all, in small amounts. It is important too to notice how your health food store treats these nut and seed perishables. Serious, professional natural foods stores refrigerate all unshelled seeds and nuts not packed in cans or other airtight containers.

Oils

Oils deserve the same treatment, cold storage in the refrigerator. This is one food that is best purchased in small amounts to assure freshness and save refrigerator space. For the average family, pint and quart units are best. Although oils may be purchased by the gallon, the whole gallon must then be kept cold once the seal has been broken, and the larger oil surface exposed to the air in the large can will oxidize more rapidly than that kept in a tall, thin bottle.

Legumes

Legumes may be guarded against weevil infestation by heating them in an oven at 135°F., then leaving them in the closed oven for an hour after turning the heat off. Here again, tightly covered containers kept in a cool, dry place (not over 70°F.) will retain quality longer. Beans that have been stored for a period of months will take longer to cook than freshly dried beans, so it is a good idea not to mix batches of different age when cooking.

Flours

Flours, especially whole grain flours, are likely to become rancid at room temperatures since so much of their surface is exposed to the air. It is especially important to store flour in the proverbial cool, dry place in tightly sealed containers. Whole wheat flour to be kept more than a week or so should be stored in the refrigerator or freezer, as should wheat germ, which because of its high oil content is even more likely than flour to spoil. Flour that has been stored long enough to evaporate some of its natural moisture may absorb more liquid than expected, necessitating the adjustment of recipes.

Fruits

Use fruits fresh as much as possible. Avoid bruising and crushing, which breaks down tissue and invites spoilage. To store fresh, whole fruit, arrange it carefully in slatted boxes and bins, spread out as much as possible to avoid crushing, and allow air to circulate. Ripen at 60 to 70°F. If ripe, keep at 32 to 40°F. if possible.

Meats

Meats are highly perishable, of course. Ground meats and variety meats should be refrigerated no more than a day or two; cured meats, up to seven days. Leftover meats should be refrigerated promptly and used within two days if possible, or frozen for later use. Cooked meat and combination dishes may be kept in the freezer for two or three months. Meat, poultry, and fish should NEVER be canned by the boiling water bath method, but always in a pressure canner. It is possible to salt and dry meat and fish, but in practice the majority of householders choose freezing as the safest, most convenient method of storing meat.

To keep fish, clean and freeze it immediately if possible; if not, it may be refrigerated, but never for more than 24 hours. Shellfish tend to become tough if kept frozen for more than four months. Fish of two pounds or under may be frozen whole after cleaning. Larger fish should be filleted and/or cut into steaks, which should be separated by moisture-proof paper.

Eggs

Eggs for short term storage should be kept, large end up, in a closed container in the refrigerator. Exposure to air robs the egg of flavor and moisture, since the shell is porous. Fresh eggs will keep in the refrigerator for several weeks, but they lose flavor and quality after a week.

Storage Management

Record keeping is important when storing food. All canned foods should be labelled with the date processed and other pertinent information such as whether honey was used in sweetening, which tree the peaches came from, etc. — information that will help you to evaluate your efforts and to plan even better for the following year. Some central record should be kept, in a notebook or on the family calendar, of amounts processed and stored, as well as amounts planted and harvested, to help in planning the next gardening season. You want to know how much is enough! Many people keep a freezer inventory showing amounts and kinds of food frozen, and when.

Once the vegetables are stored, they can't be forgotten. It is important to check periodically to make sure that spoiled produce isn't affecting other sound produce in storage. The most likely areas of spoilage will be in those vegetables and fruits exposed to the air in root cellar, attic, porch, or garage. Canned vegetables should be checked too, as other jars are removed from the shelves, to make sure that moldy or otherwise obviously spoiled food is disposed of. Frozen food is less vulnerable to deterioration, but freezer burn can occur. (Food will look dried out on the surface.) Such foods should be used promptly; they are not spoiled, just not of the best quality. Meats that have had freezer burn may taste better if stewed or braised or otherwise prepared with moist heat. Dried food too should be checked for mold, especially in the first weeks of storage when enough moisture may remain in the food to support the growth of mold.

If you keep a compost pile, you will not feel so downhearted when you must discard a few spoiled vegetables. They'll rot down to make next year's garden better!

Alternatives to Your
Own Storage Spaces

Rental Freezer Lockers

Rental of a freezer locker, while less convenient than a home freezer, offers safe, temperature-controlled freezer storage that may be no more expensive, in the long run, than owning and maintaining your own home freezer. Most freezer lockers have a quick-freeze service that will rapidly chill your food to storage temperature. Many homeowners who already have one freezer rent space in a freezer locker for the part of the year — usually August through February — when they have a lot of vegetables and fruits and possibly fall-butchered meats to store. By late winter, there is enough space free in the home freezer to accommodate all the frozen food the family has stored. Many families, too, rent a second freezer (locker space) for the entire year.

Community Canning Centers

Use of community canning centers is now opening in many areas. These centers are supplied with everything you need in order to can by pressure cooker or boiling water bath and, in many cases, with tin can sealing and processing equipment. It is usually necessary to make an appointment to use the facilities. The disadvantage of lugging your produce over to the center may be more than offset by the opportunity to use first-rate equipment under ideal conditions, and often to have a good sociable time and possibly get some good advice while processing your food.

The Ball Corporation has designed and made available for sale prefabricated canning units described in their terms as "community nutrition centers." These prepackaged canneries are especially designed for use by families, co-ops and other small groups of people who want to do their own custom canning. The special equipment in the unit, which includes four 16-quart pressure cookers, a steam-jacketed kettle, an atmospheric cooker, a blancher/sterilizer, a pulper/juicer, table carts, safety controls, and other necessary equipment, makes possible safe and convenient canning of low-acid foods.

Since the canning units are locally owned and supervised, they differ considerably in operating procedure, cost to users, and amount of instruction available. The important thing is that they meet the needs of people in the area.

As of this writing, 140 of the Ball canning centers have been set up in 30 states. No doubt there will soon be more. To locate the center nearest you, write to:

Food Preservation Program
Ball Corp.
1509 Macedonia Ave.
Muncie, Indiana 47302
(phone 317-284-8441)

Your county agricultural extension office should have information about any community canning centers in your area.

Communal Storage Areas

The community root cellar is an old concept that is currently being reexamined. In Vermont the National Organic Farmers Association has set up several experimental units. They use old buildings that are renovated to provide proper storage conditions for root crops. Area farmers, gardeners, and co-ops who participate in the planning and renovation of the building are free to use the root cellar to store food over the winter. In its second year the program is showing promising results, and future plans call for testing the concept in cities. People would buy their goods in bulk and would use the central storage facility, possible for a fee. The rationale is simple: Why should everyone have his or her own root cellar, let's all get together and use one large, specially built facility.

Chapter 8

Turning Your Kitchen Into a Food Processing Center

If you're going to be taking a bigger say in your food supply, you'll be spending more time in the kitchen. This shouldn't
scare you off, it should serve as an invitation. If you don't already know it, you'll soon learn that processing food is just as
creative an act as growing it.

Due to modern food processing, cooking in most cases has
been reduced to a boring routine of opening cans, unpeeling
wrappers, and popping tops. For the person creating food from
raw ingredients, churning butter or turning a bushel of
peaches into a thick marmalade is as much an art form as play-
ing the piano or painting a portrait.

With this in mind, you should look at your kitchen more as
a studio than as a dungeon. For it is in this room that you
transform raw materials into a dinner that will not only delight eyes, noses, and tastebuds, but also nourish you and those
close to you.

Like any other art form, cooking calls for special equipment, and cooking natural foods places a much higher value on

267

having proper equipment. The person who lives off TV dinners can get along quite well with a set of silverware and maybe a paring knife. Likewise, the person who buys most food already prepared doesn't require much kitchen equipment outside the normal set of pots and pans, a few knives, and maybe a blender for mixing drinks. But for those of us who are going to be spending more of our time in the kitchen, proper equipment is a must. Cooking from scratch is very similar to gourmet cooking, only your emphasis is on practicality, nourishment, and low cost, not fancy displays of exotic dishes laden with calories.

Counter Space

If you should ever be lucky enough to start from scratch and design your own kitchen, the one thing you'll want most is space: plenty of counter space, storage space, cooking space, and floor space. The one main rule to follow in designing a kitchen is to have the sink and the stove in good working proximity. These two should be separated by about 3 feet of counter space, with additional counters on both sides.

Today's kitchens are seldom designed with food preparation in mind. Instead the goal is efficiency for preparing processed foods. The can opener is always located next to pan storage and on the way to the stove. The garbage can is well hidden between the sink and the stove, but there just isn't enough room to let a dozen jars of canned vegetables fresh out of the pressure canner cool off.

If you aren't starting from scratch and designing your own kitchen you'll have to make do with what you have; learn to improvise. When you do your canning, the jars may end up cooling off in the dining room or living room, and stored in the basement or den. If you don't have a lot of space, your kitchen must be flexible so areas can do double duty.

The main reason for having as much counter space as possible is to keep items like your blender, seed grinder, vegetable shredder, and flour mill out in the open where you can see them. If your space is limited, you're liable to pack these items up and store them in a closet someplace, vowing to use them regularly; but when faced with unpacking and repacking, they just don't seem to get used as often.

The goal to shoot for is to use as much of your counter space as you can for everyday chores, and when a big project comes along, clear the counter and get to work. Some counter space will also be needed for the daily jobs of cutting, chopping, kneading bread, and drying things. If at all possible, one counter should extend out from the cabinets several inches more than normal. This will allow you to easily clamp on grinders, food mills, juicers, and what have you.

Cutting Boards

When looking at counter space, many people feel the need for a chopping block of some sort. Natural foods cook and author Beatrice Trum Hunter has a unique outlook on this, as she prefers three separate portable cutting boards of closely-grained durable hardwood. One board is used for dry materials such as slivering almonds or slicing bread. This board is brushed dry. The second board is for cutting fruits and vegetables, and is washed and air dried. The third board is reserved solely for cutting and trimming raw meat and poultry. This board is scoured thoroughly to prevent spreading of food infections such as salmonellosis and trichinosis.

You may wish to add a pastry board for kneading bread and rolling out biscuits and such to this collection. With such a system you need not have any of your counter space permanently tied up in a cutting board, yet you have all the cutting surfaces you'll ever need at your disposal.

A Pantry

Next to counter space, you will also want lots of storage space. A good old-fashioned pantry of course is ideal. An unused closet can be easily converted into a pantry with the addition of shelves. The goal of your pantry is to have a place close to the kitchen to store items used for cooking. You don't want to store all the fruits and vegetables you canned in the pantry, but you might want to keep two jars of each at the ready.

Of course you can easily get by without a pantry, by efficient use of your cabinets. Many things that people put in cabinets have no business there. All of those cute little electrical gadgets that seem to find their way into your kitchen from past weddings, anniversaries, and Christmases should be seriously evaluated. If you don't use it once every two weeks, get it out of the kitchen and into some other storage area. The kitchen is for business, not long-term storage.

Your third space need will be for long-term storage. There is where you keep all those beautiful jars of preserves, safely out of the sunlight. View this area as your personal super-market, as you may only visit it once a week to restock your kitchen shelves and to make sure everything is all right and you don't have any insect problems. It could be in a heated garage, your cellar, the attic, or any other place that does not have freezing weather, is out of the way, and has ample space, where you can control the humidity.

Refrigerators and Freezers

When talking about storage areas, don't forget to include a refrigerator and freezer. Cooking from scratch will have you handling a lot more perishable foods than the traditional kitchen is designed to cope with, and your cooling facilities will need to do extra duty.

The ideal perishable food storage set-up would have a freezer for long-term storage, a refrigerator for semiperishable items like cooking oils, whole wheat flour, and dried fruits, and another refrigerator for day to day perishables including dairy products, fresh fruit, meat, and vegetables. This three-pronged attack would not only greatly simplify your food storage plans, but in the long run it would be less costly, energywise.

For your freezer you would want a large chest freezer, un-less you have back problems or limited space that requires an upright freezer. Uprights use more energy than chest freezers, but are a bit easier to use. A chest freezer usually holds more food than an upright, and its temperature is less affected by door openings. The last thing you want in a freezer is a no-frost upright unit. Not only do these units cost more initially, they consume about 60 percent more electricity than a typical manual-defrost upright and more than twice the electricity of a good chest unit.

A word of caution: When looking for a freezer ignore the standard advice of how large a freezer to get depending on how many people in your family. These guidelines are for those people not growing and preparing their own food. You'll need as large a freezer as your room or economics allow.

Having a large freezer humming away in the basement provides a lot of motivation to put in an extra row or two of vegetables to keep the larder full in winter. A large freezer makes it possible to enjoy the extras, such as strawberries in

December, that a small freezer and a large garden don't permit. You also have to remember that your freezer has to be large enough to handle the peak loads when you get a half side of beef, or just after your garden has been put to bed for the winter.

When looking for a refrigerator your first decision will be between a no-frost unit and a manual defrost unit. The most energy conserving unit would be manual defrost with a top freezer. Unfortunately, in the name of progress it is now almost impossible to buy a manual defrost refrigerator in the 17 to 20 cubic feet range, but you may be able to find an old model. If so, snap it up.

Faced with the decision of a side-by-side unit or a top freezer, we suggest you go for the top freezer unit. Side-by-sides offer more freezer space, although usually at the expense of refrigerator space, and they are more convenient to use. However, they cost more to purchase, do not accommodate large items easily, take up more floor space, use more energy, and tend to need more repairs.

Consumers Union studied refrigerators and found that no-frost top freezer units use an average of 133 kwh. a month, while side-by-side units averaged 162 kwh. a month. This amounts to a monthly electric bill difference of almost two dollars. To help you in finding a machine that makes good use of its energy, the Association of Home Appliance Manufacturers is currently developing an energy use labeling program for refrigerators. With these new labels, you will be able to tell which unit uses the most and which the least amount of energy.

If you are lucky enough to be able to set up a two-refrigerator operation, the unit for long-term perishables should by all means be a manual defrost, probably of a secondhand nature, but for the unit in your kitchen for everyday use you may wish to get a no-frost model. This refrigerator will be getting the brunt of your business, so the extra convenience may be worth its high cost.

Extra Equipment

When it comes to equipping your kitchen, anything goes. It's your kitchen, and if you want something and really need it, try to get it. This often calls for a lot of soul searching, a few costly mistakes, and a lot of overstuffed cabinets. However, there are a few general guidelines we can give you to make this task a bit less painful.

Probably the key question facing people who do a lot of cooking is how much are they going to do by hand and how much by machine. For those cooking with processed foods, their equipment needs are minimal. But when you start talking about baking all your own bread, maybe doing a little butchering, canning vegetables and fruits, freezing fresh from your garden, and so forth, you begin to quickly seek out specialized tools.

There is a great deal of debate on whether you want to make one large cash investment and get one of the currently popular super machines for your kitchen, or get a series of smaller (cheaper) items to do each individual job. Some of the questions you should ask yourself include the initial cost, do you have storage room for a lot of small machines, will a food processor do everything you want of it and to what degree of satisfaction, and lastly, does such a machine fit in with your life-style?

Kitchen Food Processors

The Cooks Catalog, a compendium of kitchen utensils and equipment put together by a group of America's more famous gourmets, comes out strongly in favor of the super machines for people who do a lot of cooking. Not to be confused with a grown-up blender, these machines will do everything from beating and mixing to puréeing, kneading bread, grinding meat, juicing, peeling, slicing, and in a few cases grinding coffee and grains.

The obvious benefit of these machines is time saved. Another benefit that's not as obvious is that with such a machine you may begin to do things you ordinarily wouldn't have the time or ability to attempt. Many people truly love home baked bread, but for one reason or another don't get around to making it as often as they would like. With a large, heavy-duty mixing machine that kneads as well, they may find themselves baking all their bread, an obvious improvement. This logic carries over into many other areas of cooking. The point is that sometimes these large machines, usually costing around $200, will free up a cook to attempt many more food processing steps in the kitchen.

The main argument is that everything these machines do

you can usually do by hand, not necessarily better, but certainly cheaper. The decision is yours to make, but you may want to give it serious thought early in your kitchen equipping process, before you buy many other pieces of equipment.

Blenders

A few notches below the large food processors you'll find America's favorite machine, the blender. Serious cooks often say of blenders, "There is not much a blender cannot do, and not much it can do right." This refers both to the blender's versatility and its limitations.

Blenders have small capacities, usually about half or two-thirds the size of the jar, the chopping action is limited, the blades run at too fast a speed to work air into a food, and blenders cannot take on tough assignments like kneading bread or mashing potatoes without endangering the motor.

However, blenders are superior at liquefying and puréeing foods. For small jobs they do a very good job of chopping nuts, making bread crumbs, and mixing liquids.

When buying a blender, all you really need is two speeds and an on/off switch. As blenders have grown in demand, they have become more and more complicated. You can buy a machine with up to 20 speeds, a timer, lighted controls, a pulsing action, and who knows what else.

However, some improvements have been beneficial to the cooking process. Look for a blender with a removable bottom to help you empty the finished product. Some come with special tops to allow you to add ingredients while the machine is running. If you look around you may be able to find one of the several models that offer miniblend containers. These half-pint jars screw onto the base in place of the regular container and are ideal for making baby food, salad dressings, or for other small jobs. Check to see if you can find a unit that accepts canning jars in place of its own special, small, expensive jars.

Probably the biggest argument in favor of blenders is price. You can get a machine that doesn't use a lot of power, does a variety of jobs with some degree of proficiency, and usually will cost you less than $50 for a deluxe model. However, you must be careful when running a blender, as most jobs are done in about one or two seconds, and a couple of extra seconds turns chopped walnuts into powdered walnuts with no extra trouble. If you were to be limited to only one machine in your kitchen, it would probably be a blender.

Home Mills

Shortly after you get bitten by the home baked bread bug, you'll begin to look for a source of quality whole wheat flour. Look no further than your own kitchen. All it takes is a home grain mill.

If you live close to a natural foods store that grinds its own flour and you don't mind the cost, you don't really need a mill. But the reason whole wheat flour is so good for you is because it has the germ ground in it, not removed, and this causes storage problems. The germ naturally has wheat germ oil in it, and once this is ground and mixed with the flour it quickly begins to turn rancid unless refrigerated. It even goes bad when chilled, but not as quickly.

Dr. Ross Hume Hall, professor of biochemistry at McMaster University in Ontario, Canada and author of *Food for Nought,* notes that the prepackaged whole wheat flour you find on supermarket shelves needs an extra dose of preservatives to compensate for the germ being ground into the flour. When you grind grain at home you have the benefit of only grinding as much flour as you'll need, so there are no storage problems and you know your flour is always fresh.

Grain mills come in three types: large electric units, a unit that attaches to another machine, and small hand units. These three styles are available with either stone grinders or steel grinders. Your first decision to make in buying a mill should be whether you want stone or steel grinding.

Stone has a reputation for making finer flour and has a certain old-time goodness about it, but also has a drawback. If you grind high-moisture grains, like soybeans, sunflower seed, or peanuts, the stones will clog and you have to disassemble the whole thing and either clean the stones or reface them, a tough job. Steel mills don't have this problem; they'll even grind peanut butter, but they don't grind grain as fine. When using steel mills, especially the hand-powered types, you may have to sift the flour before using it. Unless you are willing to run flour through a hand mill five or six times, you won't be able to grind pastry flour at home, but you will be able to make whole wheat flour for bread and cookies with no problems.

Unless you do an awful lot of baking, you'll probably not be interested in the large electric mills that sell for about $200. They do a really fine job of everything from cracking wheat and corn to making very fine pastry flour and cornmeal, but they are a little hard to clean up, and cost a bundle.

Costwise, the next step is a grain grinding attachment that runs off another appliance, usually one of the large kitchen food processors mentioned above or an electric mixer. These seldom cost over $50, do a good job, and are versatile. They are almost always made with steel rollers and not stone. These attachments grind slower and not quite as fine as the larger grain mills, but will grind and crack any grains you wish. These units are relatively easy to clean and store, and for most people will be the best answer to grinding grain at home. Be sure to check if any appliances you already own have a grain mill attachment you can order.

The last type of home mill is the small hand mill. These are available in a number of sizes and prices and with both stone and steel grinders. Their biggest drawback is the amount of physical work involved. It takes a devoted soul to turn the handle of a mill for 30 to 40 minutes every time you want to bake bread. We feel that in the long run these small machines will discourage a cook by the sheer amount of physical work involved in their operation. With many of these mills you have to run your flour through several times to get it fine enough for baking.

However, the small mills are versatile and you can do more than just grind grain with them, except for the stone grinders which are limited only to low moisture (below 12 to 14 percent) grains. The small steel mills can handle seeds, spices, peanut butter, and some even claim to be able to grind coffee.

It's hard to lay down a cut and dried rule of who should buy a home grinder and what kind they should buy. For people out in the country away from a store that grinds flour, such an appliance is almost a must, yet it's hard to say which kind would be best. All have their advantages and disadvantages.

The ideal mill has yet to be marketed, but several firms are working on a stone or steel mill that is powered by bicycle. With this unit a family could easily grind a week's supply of flour in less than an hour and get some beneficial exercise at the same time. If you're thinking about getting a mill, look around well and consider your selection carefully, for a mill will last you many a good year.

Shredders and Grinders

Two items you'll probably decide you absolutely must have, unless you buy a food processing center, will be a meat grinder and a vegetable shredder. With a shredder you can quickly reduce a head of cabbage to slaw, shred a bunch of raw beets, grate cheese, dice carrots, or what have you.

Chopped vegetables taste delicious in a salad, and quickly steamed or cooked briefly in a broth or a soup they give far greater nutritional value than whole vegetables because of the shorter cooking times. If you don't want to invest in a shredder, pick up a set of flat metal graters in varying sizes and use those. They may not look as nice, but they'll do almost as good a job.

A meat grinder has almost as many economical points in its favor as nutritional benefits. This isn't anything fancy, just a good, old-fashioned cast-iron grinder that clamps on the end of a table. Meats bought in one piece and ground at home give you a better assurance of quality than picking up a pack labeled ground chuck in a store. You'll be able to control how lean or fat your ground meat is without depending on a label. One thing to remember: commercially ground meat is usually derived from old dairy cows and bulls and gets a great deal of its flavor from the addition of fat from feedlot raised beef animals. If you want to try to match that same flavor (although it isn't nutritionally beneficial) ask your butcher for some fat trimmings to add in with the meat you grind at home.

A far better way to get more for your ground meat dollar is to use your grinder to add organ meats to the ground meat. Unfortunately, the most nutritious meats are usually those least palatable to the average family. They are the ones richest in minerals, vitamins, and nucleic acids. A grinder enables you to grind kidneys, brains, heart, and sweetbreads (thymus) and add them to your usual ground meat. Using about 1 pound of organ meat to every 3 pounds of ground meat will boost the nutritional value of your meat loaves, hamburgers, and meatballs and will go undetected by people who usually shun them.

Grinding organ meats will help your budget because they usually cost less than other cuts. Some states prohibit the sale of certain organs, but check with your butcher — just because you don't see it displayed doesn't mean you can't buy it, it just means it doesn't sell well.

Yogurt Makers

If you like yogurt and eat a pint or more a week, you might want to consider getting a yogurt maker. As you'll see on page 285, making your own yogurt instead of buying it can save you a considerable amount of money.

A yogurt maker is nothing more than an electrically heated base that maintains a temperature of 95°F. to 115°F. and that has four or five glass or plastic containers with lids that sit on top of this base. The makers are reasonably priced; they run from about $10 to $20. Those in the upper price range have thermostats and timers and plastic covers that have little purpose except to maybe keep the dust off the already covered containers underneath. Neither the covers nor the timers are necessary, and you're obviously paying more for them. If you take yogurt to work or wherever, get a yogurt maker that comes with containers that have screw-on lids. And if your refrigerator space is at a premium, you'll appreciate the yogurt-maker containers that are designed to stack nicely, one on top of another.

You can make yogurt without a yogurt maker, as we explain later in this chapter, by improvising with a warm oven, radiator, or cookstove, or thermos or electrical warming tray, but most such devices will not give you consistently rich and creamy yogurt.

Pots and Pans

What we all need in our kitchen is a good set of pots and pans. All you have to do is find the right type. Unfortunately there is no ideal pot. Cast iron probably has the most appeal, until it comes to upkeep. Copper and aluminum are the best heat conductors, but both form poisonous substances when they interact with different foods if exact cleanliness is not followed. Stainless steel has the easiest upkeep, but does not transfer heat very well. So what is a cook to do? Pick and choose carefully.

A nice matching set of pots and pans is ideal, if you want a wall covering and not something to cook in. The person who uses his or her pots and pans will end up with a wild combination of cast-iron fry pans, copper clad stainless pots, an aluminum canner or pressure cooker, and probably a few fancy tin-lined copper pans.

Briefly, here is a rundown of the qualities of the different materials pots are made of:

Cast Iron — Absorbs heat slowly and evenly and retains

it well. An excellent conductor, if not carefully cared for, it rusts, stains, and pits with time. Cast iron must be well-seasoned before its first use and wiped clean after each use. Washing in soap and water or scouring destroys the seasoning and leads to rust. These pots have no interaction with foods, with the possible exception of a slight beneficial imparting of iron.

Stainless Steel — The perfect material for cooking, with only one major drawback: it is a very poor conductor of heat. Stainless does not interact with food acids or alkalies and is completely nontoxic. It keeps bright and shiny and is strong enough to ward off dents, but its heat transfer properties makes it undesirable as a pot unless it is combined with another material like aluminum or copper.

Copper — An excellent conductor of heat, but it corrodes easily, forming a poisonous substance. Copper pots must be kept absolutely clean to avoid this danger. Any copper pot should have a tin, silver, or stainless steel lining before it is used for cooking.

Brass — A good conductor, but not as good as copper. It tends to discolor with age. Brass is more expensive and brittle than copper; thus you will seldom find a brass pot any more.

Aluminum — An excellent conductor of heat, second only to copper. It interacts with acid foods to darken them and destroy most vitamin C, changing the taste of foods. Since it is an excellent conductor of heat, it is desirable as a bottom on a pot of another material, or as a sandwich as noted below.

Tin — A very soft material, it is not strong enough to be used by itself. Since it is completely unaffected by moisture, is nontoxic, and does not corrode, rust, or pit, it is used as a coating for the inside of pots. Most well known are the beautiful French copper pots that are tin lined. Tin will become darkened by food acids, but this tarnish is a protective coating and should not be removed. As tin coatings are often very thin, care must be taken when using these pots and in cleaning.

Sandwiched Materials — This would include the now classic copper-bottomed cookware. Probably the best combination is a copper or aluminum-bottomed stainless steel pot. A heavy bottom layer is necessary to insure proper heat transfer, and some pots do not extend the coating material high enough up the sides of the pot, giving cold sides and a very hot bottom, a condition to avoid.

Ceramic Coatings — To take advantage of the heat conducting properties of materials like copper and aluminum, yet not cook in them, calls for coating the pot with a nonmetallic material. Usually this is a porcelain enamel coating over a cast-iron, copper, or aluminum pan. Sometimes the porcelain chips or cracks, or may develop hot spots causing food to scorch and stick in spots. Modern chemical nonstick surfaces should be avoided, as they do not do a very good job for very long. These finishes are rather fragile and scratch easily. With age they lose some of their effectiveness, and there are serious questions about toxic materials being released by these coverings.

Pressure Cookers and Canners

Another piece of equipment you ought to consider is the pressure cooker. Some people have hang-ups about such cookers — they have usually heard some horror story about a cooker that literally blew its top and its contents all over the kitchen, and they're afraid to take a chance.

But consider the advantages: they save both time and fuel. They're especially good for cooking grains and beans, because these foods tenderize best and in much less time when cooked under pressure. The beans really get soft, and they don't have to be soaked before cooking. Soy beans and black beans take 20 minutes (instead of two to three hours), and garbanzo beans — which can simmer for three hours on top of the stove and still be crunchy — are tender in 45 minutes.

In a pressure cooker, it is entirely possible to cook foods which tend to froth (like some beans) without fear. Simply put the food to be cooked in a stainless steel or other heat-resistant bowl, add the required amount of water, and cover tightly with foil. Then place the bowl in the cooker, adding water to a depth of about 2 inches, close the cooker and proceed as usual. You can even cook a grain in the water which surrounds that bowl, thus preparing beans and, for example, rice at the same time.

There is one inconvenience with the pressure cooker, and that is that you do have to stay in the vicinity of the cooker so that you can be sure that the pressure regulator is acting properly. It sometimes takes a little while to adjust the temperature of the stove burner in order to save electricity or gas. The way our Fitness House kitchen found most satisfactory is to place the closed pressure cooker on the largest burner, turn the heat on high, and wait until the pressure regulator starts to rock back and forth. (That is contrary to most manufacturers' instruction booklets, which recommend using the smaller burner and medium heat if the pressure cooker is made of stainless steel.) Then turn down the heat to medium, being sure that the regulator continues its motion, and set your timer for the correct number of minutes. After a little while, turn the heat down still lower, maintaining just enough to keep the regulator rocking.

If it stops, don't panic. One of two things has happened. Either there's not enough heat below the cooker, or, if you are cooking soybeans, brown rice, split peas, or applesauce — all foods which tend to become frothy — there's a chance that the vent pipe is blocked. Just remove the cooker from the heat, and cool it down by holding it under the cold water faucet, letting water run over the outer portion of the lid but not over the vent pipe. When the lid is cool to the touch and no more steam is escaping — *then and not before then* — lift off the pressure regulator and open the cooker. Check the automatic air vent and the vent pipe. Wash the lid to remove any clogged material, close the cooker, replace the pressure regulator, and resume cooking.

This may sound complicated, but it isn't at all. Once you've done it, it will seem very simple and safe, and for those of us who must prepare dinner quickly after a day's work outside the home, this way of cooking beans and grains opens up a wide new range of menu possibilities. Meats like pot roasts, beef stew, Swiss steak, roast pork, and soup stock, as well as vegetables, can all be cooked in a pressure cooker too. However, lots of people don't like the flavor and texture of pressure cooked meat, and vegetables get mushy very quickly, no matter how carefully you're watching the pot.

While we're talking about pressure cookers, we should also mention pressure canners. Anyone who wants to can low-acid vegetables and meats must use a pressure canner for the processing, because, as was explained in the last chapter, a higher temperature than that of boiling water is required to destroy any potentially harmful microorganisms. These canners, because of their large size, would be ideal for large-quantity pressure cooking — except for the fact that they all seem to be made of aluminum. We can't recommend using any aluminum for cooking because of the possibility of aluminum migrating into the food as it is cooked. But there are a number of nice stainless steel pressure cookers in 4-quart, 6-quart, and 8-quart sizes.

Knives

There is one item you'll use for almost every operation you perform in your kitchen — a knife — and the importance of good knives cannot be overestimated. Not only do good knives make a job easier, they are much safer than dull knives. Knives are the most used, and usually the most abused, utensils found in the kitchen.

Because you will be using your knives so much, here more than anywhere else in the kitchen, quality counts. Cheap knives don't sharpen well, they quickly lose whatever edge they have, and they often break.

Take one look at a cutlery counter and you'll think you're in for an expensive visit to get a good set of knives, but it needn't be so. A good set of knives can be bought for less than $50. All you really need is a chef's knife, a slicer, a boner, a paring knife, and a vegetable peeling knife. You may want to add a good bread slicing knife to this list if you're doing much baking.

The arguments over whether you should buy stainless steel or carbon steel knives are almost legion. To some extent the old points in favor of carbon steel are no longer valid due to the recent invention of high-carbon stainless steel. This new material combines the cutting properties of carbon steel with the maintenance features of stainless, a highly desirable combination. However, these knives are relatively unproven.

Briefly put, carbon steel knives take a sharper edge, stay sharper longer, are easier to sharpen, and normally cost less than stainless steel knives. Carbon steel also rusts, pits, and discolors with age, although with proper maintenance it will stay in beautiful shape indefinitely. In some cases the fine points of the above arguments are made by expert chefs, and to the average person the difference between a carbon steel edge and a stainless steel edge is somewhat like the proverbial gnat on an elephant's back.

In looking for a good knife keep in mind these points. A first-rate knife will have a large tang running all the way through the handle. The tang is nothing more than an extension of the blade, proving to you that the knife and handle are one piece. If you can't see the tang running through the handle, don't buy it.

The handle should be riveted into the tang with large rivets. The knife should be balanced and the handle should feel comfortable in your grip. Buying a knife is somewhat like buying shoes: you know what it should have, but it's hard to find one that's really comfortable, so be sure to try it out.

Here are a few pointers to look for in buying a good beginning set of knives.

The chef's knife can measure anywhere from five to 15 inches, and is used for chopping, mincing, and slicing. It should be triangular in shape to give you a good rocking motion when chopping. Be sure the handle is high enough for your knuckles to clear the cutting board when chopping. This knife should be heavy to help your chopping.

A boning knife is used to pry or cut meat from bones or strip the skin from the meat of animals. It is usually 5 to 7 inches long with a thin, flexible blade. The action of the blade enables the knife to get into hard to reach spots and scrape out good meat.

The paring knife looks very much like a chef's knife but on a smaller scale. Such knives are sold by the hundreds in dime stores, and the temptation to get a cheap one is great. Remember a cheap knife with a bad blade and uncomfortable handle isn't worth a dime. You'll probably use your paring knife more than any other, so get a good one. You'll be using this knife to do small chopping and slicing, and it should act as an extension of your hand.

A slicing knife is used to make long thin cuts in meat. It is often confused with a carving knife, and is much the same. These knives vary a great deal as to the flexibility of their blades, their length, and whether they have curved or pointed points and flat or hollow-ground modulated blades. Again, look for a comfortable knife that is flexible and long enough to cut all the way through the largest roast you usually fix.

The vegetable peeling knife should be of stainless steel because of its constant contact with acid foods. Fruits and vegetables with a high-acid content will become discolored within 15 to 20 minutes after being sliced or peeled with a carbon steel knife. Some vegetable knives are serrated to help get through the tough skins without mushing up the insides of things like tomatoes.

Gadgets

After the big investments for pots and pans and the like, all you have left is the myriad of small gadgets that often turn impossible chores into two-minute jobs. It's safe to say that there is a gadget made for every purpose you'll ever think of.

We've found that your best bet is to go to old-time country stores, hardware stores, house auctions, and lastly department stores after rifling through mail-order catalogs. When you get into the gadget buying business, you'll get burned sooner or later with a piece of junk, but likewise you stumble across what may well be the world's best peeler or scrub brush.

When we talk about gadgets, we include everything from a pot holder to a scrub brush or a meat thermometer. For some people the list of necessary gadgets is extremely short; for others it would take volumes. You will probably fall somewhere in the middle.

Beatrice Trum Hunter once listed kitchen items she felt a beginning cook would need. Her list included a vegetable shredder, one or two steamers, a timer, a wall magnet to hang knives, at least one good paring knife, a bread knife, a potato peeler, a rubber spatula, a blender, and a seed grinder. Most people would find this list a bit lacking, but it does show how simple this sort of thing can really be.

There are a few gadgets that are inexpensive, and not only save you some time, but produce meals that are nutritionally superior. One of these little wonder tools is the lowly vegetable scrubbing brush.

Recipes usually tell you to peel before using, and few people question that logic. But most of the vital nutrients are concentrated just below the outer covering of fruits and vegetables. Unless they are waxed or artificially colored or you know their chemical history, there is no reason to cut off all these nutrients. All you want to remove is the dirt.

A good scrubbing brush should be coarse enough to dislodge dirt, but not so abrasive that it cuts into the surface of the food. The brush should not be bleached or dyed with any chemicals that might be transferred to the produce. A good brush is made of medium-length natural bristles, so you can easily spot any that come loose before they end up on the dinner table.

To extend the life of your brush, always hang it from a hook in an area with good ventilation. This will allow good drying and prevent mold or mildew from forming. Hanging the brush over the sink is a good way to ensure that it gets plenty of use.

Another nutritional friend for your kitchen is the vegetable steamer. A stainless steel collapsible steamer is excellent for cooking vegetables whole, retaining their bright color, crispness, flavor, and nutrients. Although aluminum steamers are available and cheaper, invest in a stainless steel unit that will fit any size pot.

A good alternative to a steamer is a collapsible colander or metal basket. These collapsible units are also ideal for washing off salad greens without exposing the greens to too much water. You want something with openings large enough to let dirt and water pass freely, while retaining the smallest vegetable pieces you may be washing.

For those wishing to cut back on electricity use, a food mill is ideal. It does many of the jobs a blender does and a few a blender can't do. A food mill is best suited for puréeing fruits and vegetables.

Some mills have interchangeable blades to adjust for a coarse or fine purée. All food mills come apart easily for cleaning and usually cost less than $10.

Perhaps a food mill's biggest advantage is that it requires no water to be added and so produces a thicker, richer finished product when making purée. All a mill does is force food between a stationary disk and a movable disk powered by your arm. It doesn't require much strength and is easy to operate.

Of course there is a whole area of special materials you'll need for butchering, canning or freezing, and drying, and almost any good book that tells how to do these chores will cover equipment needs.

Make It Instead of Buying It

One very good way to turn your kitchen into more of a home food production center is to find out what prepared or processed foods you can make instead of buy. There are several that come to our minds, but to decide which ones would be practical for you, pick a food and ask yourself these three questions:

1. Does it require little time, effort, skill, and equipment to make at home?

2. Can I save money by making it instead of buying it?

3. Can I make a comparable or a superior product (that

contains higher quality ingredients and avoids artificial additives) than one I would otherwise buy?

If you can answer "yes" to all three questions, then there's no doubt about the advantages of the homemade version. Answer "yes" to two, and you still could benefit by making it yourself. Only one "yes," and the advantages of making it at home may be questionable, unless you're the kind of person who just enjoys doing more for yourself when it comes to good food.

To get you started, we'll go through some of the foods that we feel are worthwhile making at home. You can probably think of more.

Yogurt

One of the first foods we think of is yogurt.

Question #1: This one gets a definite yes from us. A quart batch of yogurt takes all of three to five minutes of preparation time, very little skill, and hardly any effort. All you need is a quart of fresh milk or dried milk and water, a little fresh yogurt or a yogurt starter culture, and either a yogurt maker or thermos bottle or container and a warm place (like a warm radiator, heating pad, plate warmer, or an oven).

Question #2: Another yes, especially if you can get hold of raw milk or use nonfat dry milk powder, both of which are cheaper than homogenized, pasteurized milk. At the time of this writing an 8-ounce carton of unflavored yogurt in a Pennsylvania supermarket costs anywhere from 33 to 41¢. Homemade, plain yogurt made from milk and two tablespoons of yogurt saved from the last batch costs from 6½ to 11¢. (We're not considering the cost of electricity and your investment in a yogurt maker — only the cost of the ingredients. Many people make fine yogurt without any special equipment. Anyway, the cost of electricity and the cost of a yogurt maker spread over a few years or so is quite small.) Here's how we arrived at these figures:

Question #3: We answer this with a yes, usually. The quality ingredients of store-bought versus homemade yogurt

Homemade Yogurt Made With Homogenized, Pasteurized Milk and Your Own Starter Yogurt

Cost per quart	$ .43
Cost of 2 tablespoons yogurt from last batch	.01½
Total cost for 32 ounces (1 quart) yogurt	.44½
Cost for 8 ounces yogurt	$ .11

Homemade Yogurt Made With Nonfat Dried Powder

Cost per quart	$ .27
Cost of 2 tablespoons yogurt from last batch	.01
Total cost for 32 ounces (1 quart) yogurt	.28
Cost for 8 ounces yogurt	$ .07

Homemade Yogurt Made With Raw Milk*

Cost per quart	$ .25
Cost of 2 tablespoons yogurt from last batch	.01
Total cost for 32 ounces (1 quart) yogurt	.26
Cost for 8 ounces yogurt	$ .06½

*The cost per quart here is based on roadside stand prices in the Lehigh Valley, Pennsylvania; if you have your own goat or cow, cost of the raw milk to you may be different.

can differ greatly. With only a few exceptions, most commercial yogurts contain preservatives. The flavored ones often have artificial coloring and flavoring in them and more sweetening than you might find necessary. If you want flavored yogurt, you can quite easily add your own fresh fruit, fruit butter (like apple or prune), vanilla extract, honey, or other natural flavoring to your homemade yogurt.

The How-To's The ingredients and equipment you're going to need include:

> 1 quart of milk, either raw, homogenized and pasteurized, or reconstituted nonfat dry milk powder
> ¼ cup nonfat dry milk powder — although not necessary, the additional dry milk makes for a thicker, creamier yogurt
> 2 tablespoons yogurt from your last batch
> A quart-sized thermos bottle, a quart-sized bowl (earthenware is best because it retains heat so well), or a yogurt maker

1. If you're using raw or homogenized and pasteurized milk, heat it to the simmering point — just below boiling. However, this need not be done to reconstituted dry milk, because the milk has already been processed and any unwanted strains of bacteria have been killed. Just add lukewarm water to reconstitute the dry milk, and skip step Number 2.

2. Cool the milk to about 115°F. A thermometer is not necessary: just place a few drops on the inside of your wrist; if it feels pleasantly hot, it is about right. You can speed up the cooling process by placing the hot milk in the refrigerator for a few minutes. But don't let it get cold.

3. Inoculate the milk with two tablespoons of fresh yogurt, either from your last homemade batch or from a store-bought variety. For a yogurt starter it's best to buy plain yogurt or a kind that has natural fruit preserves on the bottom of the carton. You will be able to skim enough yogurt off the top of the carton to use as a starter. The kinds of yogurt that have the preserves and flavorings blended throughout the product can also be used, but even in a small amount the flavoring can permeate the final product to a surprising degree.

4. Mix the yogurt and starter well and then strain into your thermos bottle, earthenware bowl, or yogurt-maker containers.

5. If you're using a yogurt maker, cover the container, and plug in the yogurt maker for about 6 hours.

If you're using a thermos bottle (and it should be one of the wide-mouthed kinds), pour in your lukewarm yogurt mixture, screw the lid on tightly, and leave it in a draft-free place for 4 to 6 hours.

If you're using a bowl and a warm place, cover the bowl with a tea towel or some kind of food wrap, and place it in a warm spot, like the top of a warm radiator, or in an oven that has a pilot light. (Don't turn the oven on unless it's very cold inside. Then turn it on for only a few minutes, just to warm it up.) If your oven is an electric one, turn it on to the lowest setting for about 3 to 5 minutes, then turn the oven off completely and put your covered bowl inside and close the oven door. Leave the yogurt in the oven or on the radiator or another warm place for about 6 hours.

6. At the end of the suggested time, carefully uncover your yogurt and tilt the container slightly. If it has a custard-like consistency, it's done. You can refrigerate it and let it chill before eating. If the yogurt is not thick enough, cover it again and leave it alone for another hour or so. Then repeat the test.

If you have trouble making yogurt there are a number of things that could have gone wrong:

- Perhaps the milk mixture was disturbed while incubating. Even a few tilts or knocks can cause the whey to separate from the curd. Instead of getting a thick and smooth yogurt, it may be watery and lumpy.

- Maybe your mixture was too hot or too cool. If the mixture gets too cool, the growth of the yogurt bacteria will be retarded. If it gets too hot, the bacteria may be killed off. Add more starter, incubate longer, and adjust temperature if either happens.

- Milk or starter that is not fresh will not work as well as when it is fresh. The older either is, the longer it will take to incubate and the more starter you should use. For best results, neither should be more than five days old.

- Yogurt gets thicker and tarter the longer it incubates, so if yours is either too thick or too tart, remember to reduce incubation time next time you make yogurt.

Bread

Another food that we'd suggest you try making at home is bread. As far as homemade bread is concerned, we can't answer Question #1 with an emphatic yes. Bread is by no means as easy to make at home as it is to buy. Bread making doesn't require any special equipment, but it takes time and effort and some skill. It should take you roughly 20 minutes to mix up a batch of bread dough and knead it the first time. Then you've got to let it rise, punch it down, put it in pans, let it rise at least once again. The rising can take between 1 and 4 hours generally (two rises for 1 to 2 hours each) and the baking about an hour for most breads. Of course, you're not working with the bread during the rising and cooking, but you've got to be around the kitchen. Kneading and mixing bread dough is a little strenuous, but usually quite satisfying. Lots of people find it therapeutic to let out frustrations and tensions by punching and squeezing dough during the kneading process. A little skill that comes through experience is necessary to knead the dough just right for just long enough and to know when the dough has risen enough and can be baked.

Question #2: We can answer this one a little more positively. You can buy bread for as little as 25 to 45¢ a pound loaf, but that's for white bread that tastes like nothing because there's nothing left of it after the millers and bakers get through with it. For real bread you pay more, quite a bit more. Honest-to-goodness whole grain bread (not the caramel-colored fake whole wheat bread) costs about 60¢ a pound loaf. Here's a breakdown on what it'd cost you to make a similar loaf at home:

Ingredient	Cost
8 cups stone-ground whole wheat flour	$ .80
1 package baker's yeast	.20
1/2 cup honey	.20
1/4 cup vegetable oil	.17
total	$1.37 for 3 1 1/2-pound loaves
each loaf	$ .45
each pound bread	about $ .30

Question #3: Yes, homemade bread is almost always more nutritious and more natural than the store's best breads. As you'll see a little later, you can add your own enrichers and leave out the artificial vitamins and minerals, flavorings, and colorings; you also don't have the calcium propionate or other preservatives that are in even most of the commercial "natural" breads. (*Warning:* because your own bread won't contain these preservatives, it'll get stale in just a few days, so refrigerate, or better yet, freeze it if it'll be around for a while.)

The How-To's Many liquids can be used for bread baking, including water left over from sprout making, water in which vegetables have been cooked, milk, or potato water. The latter can be made from a raw, diced potato with enough liquid added to make the amount needed for your recipe. Whiz the potato and water in a blender until smooth, and use in your bread. Milk used in bread recipes should be boiled first to kill off bacteria that may interfere with yeast activity. If you're reconstituting nonfat dry milk powder to use as liquid, it is helpful to heat it slightly to dissolve all the milk powder.

Some bread recipes (notably French or Italian breads) do not call for shortening or oil, but most recipes do require some oil. Use vegetable oil, not margarine or shortening. Some oils have strong tastes, and you might have to experiment to find your favorite, or the one that best complements your recipe. If you're using nonfat dry milk, be sure to use oil in your bread, or to use butter on the bread when you eat it. Your body needs some fat in order to use the fat-soluble nutrients in the milk.

Kneading stretches the gluten in yeasted breads. It should always be done on a firm, lightly floured surface. (Never use the same cutting board for kneading bread and cutting meat; bacteria from the meat may get into nicks and cuts on the board and contaminate your dough.) Keep adding more flour to the board to prevent the bread from sticking to it, but try to avoid kneading extra flour into the bread; this may result in a tough loaf. You can stop kneading when the dough is no longer sticky and is springy and dry-moist to the touch. You'll find that, with practice, you'll develop a rhythm and feel, and that kneading will become anything but the guesswork that it is in the beginning.

The bread should be set in a warm, dry place to rise. Dough was, in former times, allowed to rise in a specially made doughbox, but you can place a clean towel over an oiled mixing bowl. Allow room for the bread to rise. A good way to see if the dough has risen is to jab two fingers into it; if the holes remain in the dough, the loaves are ready to be cut and shaped.

If you're using a loaf pan and you want to see if your bread has baked enough, turn it upside down; if the loaf falls out readily and sounds hollow when tapped on the bottom, it's probably done. Don't be too discouraged if baking times vary from those given in a recipe. Different oven and climatic conditions cause these variations. The addition of certain ingredients to your bread may vary baking times, too. For example, soy flour is oil-rich and results in a thick, brown crust if the oven temperature is not lowered during baking. If you're using ¼ cup or more of soy flour in a recipe for three loaves, turn the oven temperature down 25°F. Experience is the best judge of baking time.

Try brushing the tops of your loaves with butter before you bake them. This results in a rich, soft crust. A mixture of egg white and water makes a good glaze, and is good for a hard-crusted bread. Whole milk gives a sweet, moist crust.

Wheatmeal Oatmeal Bread

1¾ cups milk, scalded
½ teaspoon honey
4 teaspoons dry yeast
2 cups oatmeal
1 tablespoon oil
2½ tablespoons honey
½ tablespoon salt
2½ cups whole wheat flour
½ to ¾ cup whole wheat flour (for kneading)

Cool ¼ cup hot milk and stir ½ teaspoon honey into it. Soften yeast in this milk and honey mixture. Stir remaining hot milk into the oatmeal and then add oil, honey, and salt. When this mixture is lukewarm, stir in the yeast mixture and then add the flour. It will be a stiff dough.

Cover bowl with a damp towel and put in a warm, draft-free place to rise. It will take about 2 hours. Punch down dough and knead for at least 5 minutes, using extra flour as required. Shape into a round loaf, lightly oil surface of loaf, and place on oiled cookie sheet. Allow to rise almost double (about 1 hour).

Place in a cold oven, heat to 325°F. and bake for 1 to 1¼ hours or until inserted toothpick comes out clean. Cool on wire rack.

Yield: 1 loaf

Clear-Out-the-Cupboard Bread

When bread-baking day arrives, go through your cupboards and bring out those little bits of flour, grains, and beans which have a way of accumulating over the weeks and months, then grind them in your blender and use them to replace the flour called for in bread recipes. You can use brown rice, cornmeal, oatmeal, and wheat in this way, as well as lentils, split peas, and baby limas. Any bean will do, and using the protein in beans in conjunction with that in wheat gives you a more complete form of protein.

You can grind dried beans, seeds, and grains in your blender if you work with ¼ cup at a time, sifting out the coarse particles each time to be reground with the next batch. We suggest a combination of ½ to ¾ cup of any one or a mixture of beans, ¼ to ½ cup of any one or a mixture of seeds, bran, or wheat germ. Then add a combination of grains for a total of 5 to 6 cups of the mixture.

At the Fitness House kitchen we used buckwheat groats and rye, along with brown rice, oatmeal, and wheat — we had 4 cups of grains in all. We used about ¾ cup of a mixture of sunflower and sesame seeds and wheat germ, and about ¾ cup of lentils and kidney beans combined. We added these grains, seeds, and beans to the milk and yeast mixture as outlined below, and stirred or kneaded the flour in — 4½ cups of whole wheat and 1 cup of rye flour. This made two rather small loaves, chewy in texture and with an unusually good flavor.

1 package dry yeast
⅓ cup warm water
1 teaspoon honey
1 quart milk

¼ cup oil
¼ cup honey or molasses
5 teaspoons salt
grain/bean/flour mixture (see above)

Soak 1 package dry yeast in ⅓ cup warm water to which 1 teaspoon honey has been added. Scald 1 quart milk, and add to it the oil, ¼ cup honey or molasses, and salt. When the milk mixture is lukewarm, combine it with the soaked yeast, and add the grain, bean, and seed mixture.

From here on you must "play it by ear." Stir some flour into your dough until it comes away from the sides of the bowl. Then scoop more flour onto your kneading surface, and knead in as much as the dough will take. To develop the gluten in the flour, knead for at least 3 to 5 minutes.

Let the dough rise once, punch down, and let rise again. Form into loaves, allow them to rise. Put them into a preheated 425°F. oven for 10 minutes; then turn the oven down to 350°F. and bake another 30 minutes or until done.
Yield: 2 small loaves

Sprouts

Sprouts are almost as simple to make at home as yogurt, and you almost have to grow your own if you want to have a steady, fresh supply because few stores sell them.

Question #1: Although you can get fancy with special sprouting equipment, all you really need is a strainer or glass jar with a piece of mesh or cheesecloth stretched and fastened over its mouth, and a container to catch the rinse water. You've got to have a reasonably warm place (70 to 75°F.) and take about 1 minute twice a day for 3 to 5 days to rinse the sprouts. No effort and no skill needed.

Question #2: It's hard to compare costs of homegrown sprouts with those you can buy because sprouts are hardly sold anywhere. You'll find them in a natural foods store maybe, and you can get canned mung bean sprouts (minus the bean) in most supermarkets. However, sprouts you grow at home will be cheaper than any you can find in a store. A pound bag of alfalfa seeds costs about $1.75, and from that you'll get about 64 cups of sprouts!

Question #3: Even homegrown garden vegetables can contain some insecticide brought in by the wind from a neighbor's garden, and chemical herbicides and fertilizers could have been applied to the soil before you planted there without your knowing it. Sprouts are the one vegetable that won't have any chemical spray residue on them for sure.

Compared to the cabbage you might ordinarily use in soups and salads (1.3 percent protein) and the lettuce usually starring in tossed salads (.9 percent protein), sprouted mung beans or soybeans used instead or additionally offer 4.3 percent and 13.1 percent protein, respectively. As an added health benefit, cooked soybean sprouts boast three times more fiber (2.5 percent) than cooked cabbage (.8 percent), and five times more fiber than raw lettuce (.5 percent). Alfalfa and lentil sprouts also outshine cabbage and lettuce in terms of protein and fiber.

On the vitamin score sheet, cabbage offers two or more times as much vitamin C as any of the popular sprouts — however, lettuce is a poorer source than any of the sprouts. However, both mung bean and soybean sprouts contain anywhere from three to eight times more of the major B complex vitamins than cabbage and lettuce. Alfalfa and lentil sprouts are also richer than cabbage and lettuce in the B vitamins.

Since sprouts can also be served as a buttered hot vegetable side dish or used as a casserole component, it's interesting to compare them with peas — a highly nutritious legume that shoppers have to buy canned or frozen for much of the year. Although cooked peas contain more vitamin C, niacin, and iron than cooked soybean sprouts, the sprouts are much richer in protein (13.1 percent versus 5.4 percent), calcium (81.7 mg per 100 grams versus 23 mg), and the important mineral zinc (2.1 mg per 100 grams versus .69 mg). Soybean sprouts also contain more fiber than peas.

Cooked lentil sprouts also compare well with peas, offering 8.8 percent protein (versus 5.4 percent for peas), one-third more iron, over twice as much zinc, and slightly more vitamin C.

The How-To's   Obtain any of the following seeds or beans which have not been treated with chemicals (many natural foods stores and mail-order seed houses carry untreated seeds for sprouting):

Mung beans
Soybeans
Lentils
Alfalfa
Wheat
Rye
Flax
Triticale
Sunflower
Radish
Watercress

Put about ¼ cup of seeds or beans in a quart jar filled with water, and soak them for 8 hours or overnight.

Then drain the soaked seeds, by pouring them in a strainer. Or cover the jar in which they are soaked with cheese-cloth or nylon netting which is secured by a rubber band around the neck of the bottle, and turn the jar upside down.

Then rinse the seeds and drain them again. If you're using a jar, leave the jar tilted top-side down so that any moisture will drain off. Put the jar or strainer in a dark place that gets neither too hot nor too cold, but stays at about room temperature.

At the end of the day, rinse the sprouts again in order to remove any fungus which may have started to grow.

Repeat this rinsing process twice a day for at least three days, until the sprouts are as long as desired. Mung, soy, and lentil sprouts are most palatable when the sprout is ½ to 1 inch in length; alfalfa, wheat, rye, radish, and watercress are best when the sprout is no longer than the seed.

Then refrigerate in a closed container. Sprouts keep well in a refrigerator eight to ten days. They may be frozen, but after being thawed they do not retain their crispness, so should be used for soup or in a hot dish instead of for salad.

Breakfast Cereals

Here we're talking about both hot and cold cereals. We found there are advantages to making your own mixed cold cereals and advantages to making whole grain hot cereals.

Question #1: A good blender or a home grain mill is necessary if you want to make your own cream of wheat, rice, or rye, but it's not necessary for many of the cold cereals. No other special equipment is needed.

The time involved depends on what kind of cereal you're making. The Swiss muesli-type cereal shouldn't take you very long to make at all. The cracked grain cereals are somewhat time-consuming because you have to roast and crack the grains yourself. Granola won't take much time to mix, but you'd better figure on about an hour and a half to roast the mixture. You can do anything else that you want for this hour and a half, as long as you can take a minute every once in a while to peek in the oven and make sure the cereal isn't getting too brown.

If you're using a hand grinder your arm will get a workout, but other than that, how much effort is there in cutting up some dried fruit and mixing grains and such together?

Question #2: Name-brand granolas cost about 90¢ a pound, and the one we made using the directions that follow (with 3 cups rolled oats, 1 cup chopped or slivered almonds, ½ cup wheat germ, ½ cup sesame seeds, 1 cup unsweetened coconut, 1 cup honey, ¼ cup oil, and 1 cup raisins) cost 69¢ a pound. Similar savings are usual when making your own hot or cold cereal. If you can get granola in a co-op it may make more sense just to buy it. But you've got to figure that the basic ingredients from which you can make your own are also cheaper at a co-op.

Question #3: The granolas you find on supermarket shelves are certainly a lot better nutritionally than the sugar-laden and artificially flavored and/or colored puffed corn, popped oats, and such that come in other cereal boxes. But while the new "natural" cereals don't have artificial colors or flavors, they do contain a lot of sweetening. Most have both sugar and honey, and sugar is often the second ingredient

listed on the box, which means that by weight it's the second
most plentiful ingredient in that box. Homemade granola
doesn't need to contain all that sweetening. In the granola we
made the honey accounted for only ¹/₁₂ the weight of the cereal,
and it was sweet enough for us.

The difference in quality between the homemade and
store-bought Swiss muesli and roasted and ground hot cereals
are not all that great. It is nice, though, to be able to adjust the
sweetening to suit your taste in your own Swiss muesli, and by
popping and grinding grains for hot cereals you can be sure
that only the whole grain is used.

The How-To's   Most natural foods stores offer a variety of
natural ingredients for concocting your own cereals. Among
the grains you might choose from are popular standbys like
rolled oats and wheat germ, plus rye, wheat, millet, and rice in
flakes and flours, as well as cornmeal and rolled bran. Your
own garden might offer sunflower, squash, and pumpkin seeds
to supplement the natural food store's sesame seeds and their
cashews, pecans, walnuts, almonds, hazelnuts, and peanuts.
You could add raisins, chopped dates and prunes, snipped figs
and apricots, or dried peaches, apples, and pears. You may find
that you prefer no other sweetening than that naturally
present in the fruits and grains, or you could try using honey,
molasses, maple syrup, or date sugar.

Cream of Wheat, Rice, or Rye

You can make your own cream of wheat, rice, or rye
cereals too. It's a simple process of "popping" the whole grains
in a dry frying pan over medium heat, and then grinding them
coarse or fine according to how crunchy or creamy your family
prefers its hot cereals. There's no need to cover the frying pan
as you do when popping corn; just shake gently to prevent
scorching until all the grains have browned and smell nutty.
After grinding either in a blender or small home grain mill,
you can toast the grains lightly again if you wish. Store the
cooled, ground grains in a tightly covered container in the refrigerator.

To prepare four servings, bring 4 cups of milk and 1 teaspoon salt to a boil, then stir in 1 cup of the ground grains.
Lower heat, cover the pan, and allow it to simmer until the

cereal is as thick as you like. You could add wheat germ, sesame or sunflower seeds, ground or chopped nuts, milk, butter, honey, molasses, or maple syrup, and dried or fresh fruits.

Crunchy Granola

For a crunchy granola-type cereal, start with three parts rolled oats, one part of another flaked grain or mixture of grains, one part nuts, one part seeds, and one part unsweetened, dry coconut shreds. You could boost its nutritional value with soy grits (about ½ part) or a little brewer's yeast or powdered milk. Combine ¼ to ½ part honey, ¼ part oil, a little water, and a little vanilla if you desire. Add to dry ingredients, stirring until well mixed. Pour the mixture into a large, shallow baking pan which has been lightly oiled, then toast in a low oven (250°F.) for 1 to 1½ hours, stirring every 10 to 15 minutes, or until mixture is dry and lightly browned and crisp. Remove cereal from the oven and allow it to cool. Add 1 to 2 parts raisins or other dried fruit. Store in a glass jar in the refrigerator or a crock in a cool place.

Swiss Muesli

For an untoasted Swiss-type cereal, start with 2 parts rolled oats or oat flakes. Now add 1 part wheat germ and 1 part of another flaked or rolled grain. Hazelnuts and almonds characterize the traditional cereal, but you can choose any combination of nuts and seeds which appeals to you and add 1 to 2 parts. If you like, also add 1 part (or more) raisins and 1 part of another dried fruit chopped into bite-sized pieces, or you can add fresh fruit at the table. It's up to you either to sweeten the mix before storing with date sugar, or plan on serving it with honey or maple syrup. Or simply rely on the sweetness of the fruit. Store your cereal in a covered container in the refrigerator. By adding skim milk powder (about ⅓ cup for each cup of cereal) you'll have a lightweight, but satisfying campsite breakfast that requires only the addition of water. At home, serve it with milk, yogurt, buttermilk, or fruit juice.

Crackers

Like bread, we can't come on with an unqualified "yes" for Question #1. No special equipment is needed, except maybe a blender if you want to grind seeds, nuts, or grains. You will need a rolling pin, though, and some cookie sheets. You don't need any particular skill, but a little patience is necessary, since you've got to roll the cracker dough very thin — about ⅛ inch thin. (Read on and you'll find a couple of things our Fitness House experimental kitchen has learned about rolling cracker dough.)  You've got to stick around the oven for the entire cooking time since the time in the oven depends upon how thick the crackers are, and they can burn very easily.

Question #2: Packaged crackers can cost anywhere from $.67 to $.91 a pound for the plain crackers to about $1.10 a pound for the fancier kinds, and $1.20 for imported rice and other exotic crackers. Sesame crackers run from about $.95 to $1.60 a pound in the supermarket. The sesame crisps that we made up from the recipe that follows cost us $.65 a pound.

Question #3: Store-bought crackers most often have refined white flour, sugar, and more salt than necessary in them. Many contain artificial coloring, flavoring, or both. The ones you make, of course, need not contain any of these ingredients. However, homemade crackers are often harder or crunchier and heavier than commercial kinds, and not everyone will like them as much, despite the fact that they're usually better for you.

The How-To's Before we give you the recipes for some of our favorite crackers, we'll share with you two suggestions from our kitchen staffers.

Rolling out the dough: Instead of rolling dough between sheets of wax paper and having to move it to a cookie sheet, try greasing the back of the cookie sheet and rolling the dough right on it with a rolling pin. Then the dough simply needs to be scored with a knife in squares or diamonds and then baked. We found we could roll our cracker dough right on top of the baking sheet, which is even better than using the bottom, but this depends on the size of your pans, whether they have sides or not, and on the length of your rolling pin. Our rolling pin is 11 inches long without the handles. Each handle is 3½ inches in length. This size works fine with our baking sheets, which are 14 x 16 inches. It also works fine with a smaller sheet which is 11¾ x 14½ inches.

The cookie sheets: Whole grains, and especially rye, really seem to adhere to oiled surfaces, a fact we had noted when oiling bread pans. Butter works better, but it takes a generous amount and butter is expensive. It is also a saturated fat and we should use it sparingly.

Stan and Floss Dworkin, authors of *The Good Goodies,* have a better solution. We tried it and highly recommend it. They use liquid lecithin for greasing all their pans for cakes, cookies, and crackers. Lecithin, the food supplement which many people take to help their bodies control cholesterol, is an emulsifier which is widely used in the baking and candy industry. It is also the basic ingredient of a commercial product which can be sprayed on surfaces to prevent food from sticking to them. It is cheaper, healthier, and more ecological to buy the lecithin without the propellant and to spread it on by hand.

There is a technique to this. Pour as small an amount as possible onto the baking sheet, and with one finger, daub it all over the surface. Then with that same hand, using fingers and palm, smear the lecithin over the whole pan. This requires really bearing down with your hand, but eventually the small amount of lecithin will lightly coat the whole surface and that is all it takes. We found with most of the crackers we made this "greasing" would be sufficient for two batches. The lecithin washes off the pan and your hands easily; in fact, it acts as a sort of skin softener, so rub into your hands what is left on them before washing with soap and water. You can buy liquid lecithin at any natural food store. It may seem expensive, but it will go a long way.

Sunflower Seed Crackers
(no-grain cracker)

1 cup sunflower seeds, freshly ground in blender (if not fresh,
    sunflower seed flour can become bitter and unpleasantly
    "hot" to the taste)
½ cup unsweetened coconut (dried)
¼ cup cold water
liquid lecithin for "greasing" the pan

Combine ingredients, and pat out dough on baking sheet
which has been lightly coated with liquid lecithin. Lay a sheet
of wax paper on top of the dough and roll out to the edges of the
pan, using a rolling pin. Don't roll it any thinner than ⅛ inch.
Score with a knife in squares or diamonds. Place pan in cold
oven, turn oven to 300°F., and bake for 15 to 20 minutes or
until lightly golden in color. Let cool for 5 minutes before removing crackers from pan.
Yield: approximately 2 dozen crackers

Sesame Crisps

1 cup short grain brown rice, cooked to the soft, mushy stage
salt to taste
3 tablespoons unhulled sesame seeds
liquid lecithin for "greasing" the pan

Preheat oven to 300°F.
Bring 1 cup raw short grain rice to a boil in 3 cups water.
Turn down to a simmer and let cook for 45 minutes. Drain, set
aside all but 1 cup for another use. Combine the 1 cup of mushy
rice with salt to taste and the sesame seeds. Mash with a potato
masher or fork. On a flat surface pat out rice mixture between
two sheets of wax paper the same size as your baking sheet.
Roll out as thin as possible with a rolling pin. Gently peel off
the top sheet of wax paper. Then turn bottom sheet of paper

(with the rice on it) upside down onto the baking sheet which has been coated with the lecithin. Gently peel off this paper, using a knife to loosen stubborn spots. Score with knife in desired shapes. Bake in preheated oven for 45 minutes or until golden in color. Let cool 5 minutes before removing crackers from pan.

Yield: approximately 2 dozen crackers

Cornmeal Cheese Crackers

1 cup cornmeal
1 cup whole wheat flour
¼ teaspoon salt
½ cup water
2 tablespoons oil
3 ounces sharp cheddar cheese

Preheat oven to 300°F.

Combine water, oil, and cheese in container of electric blender and blend until smooth before stirring in the dry ingredients.

Bake in preheated oven for 20 minutes. If desired, top with grated cheese and cumin seeds and toast under broiler to melt cheese before serving.

Yield: approximately 4 dozen crackers, each 2 inches square

Rye Crackers

½ cup lukewarm water
1 tablespoon dry yeast
1⅛ cups whole rye flour plus a bit more, if necessary for rolling
½ teaspoon salt
1 teaspoon caraway seeds
liquid lecithin for "greasing" the pan

Sprinkle yeast over surface of water. Set aside for 5 minutes. Combine flour and seasonings. Prepare baking sheet with liquid lecithin, coating entire surface lightly. When yeast is soft stir yeast mixture into dry ingredients, mixing until a cohesive ball is formed which is no longer sticky. Pat out dough on baking sheet in the shape of the pan, and then, using more rye flour if necessary, roll dough with a rolling pin out to the edges of the pan, to a thickness of ⅛ inch. Don't roll it any thinner than this, or it may be difficult to remove. Thicker, it won't be crisp. Score with a knife in squares or diamonds, cover, and set aside in a warm, draft-free place for 1 hour. Then place pan of crackers in cold oven, turn oven to 225°F., and bake for 15 minutes. Then raise heat to 300°F. and bake another 15 to 20 minutes until crackers are brown. Let cool 5 minutes before removing them from pan.
Yield: approximately 2 dozen crackers

Noodles

Although not terribly practical for everyone, noodle making can be fun and reasonably satisfying.

Question #1: Thinking about the answer to this one may disqualify noodles right away as one of your high priority make-at-home foods. They *are* tricky to make. Although the only equipment you'll need is a large space on which to roll out the dough, you do need lots of elbow grease and patience, and also some time — an hour or so, especially if you're a beginner.

Question #2: Based on our supermarket survey, packaged egg noodles cost from 49¢ to 79¢ a pound. Other pasta made without eggs run from 39¢ to about 50¢ a pound. The egg noodles made from the recipe below will cost you about 34¢ a pound. If made without the eggs, they should cost about 15¢ a pound.

Question #3: Homemade whole wheat noodles, like the ones you can make from the recipe that follows, are certainly more nutritious than the supermarket kinds which are only made with enriched white flour. We want to warn you, though, that the noodles you make, especially if you're new at this, might be thicker than the kind you buy. And whole wheat noodles are heavier than those made with white flour. They can get mushier than white flour noodles, so watch them as they cook and take them out of the boiling water as soon as they're tender.

The How-To's

Whole Wheat Noodles

about 2 cups whole wheat flour
2 teaspoons salt
about 6 tablespoons water (if you're making egg noodles, skip
　　the water and substitute 3 to 4 eggs)

　　Pour the 2 cups of flour on your clean work space and make a well in the middle. Add the salt and water or eggs into this well. Work the flour into the ingredients in the well by folding the flour over the wet ingredients until you have an even-textured ball of dough, which is in no way sticky. Add more flour, little by little, if necessary.

　　If you want to make spinach noodles, add at this point 4 to 8 tablespoons cooked spinach that has been well drained and chopped fine.

　　Pull a piece of the dough off — a hunk an inch or so in diameter will do nicely for the first trial. Start rolling in all directions. Turn the dough over frequently and keep plenty of flour on your work space, your rolling pin, and your hands. Thin is what you want — much thinner than pie crust or ravioli dough, if you've ever made that. If your dough was stiff enough, you should be able to roll that tiny piece you started with to the size of a large pizza. Remember that this dough has no shortening, so it's pretty tough stuff. Besides, a small hole or two won't matter.

　　When you've rolled the dough as thin as it'll go, roll a little more and you're ready to start cutting and shaping. For lasagna, cut the dough long and wide; for noodles, short and skinny. Use your imagination and have some fun. Circular and star-shaped noodles make for interesting soups. Fancy maca-

roni and rigatoni can be shaped around a straw or a small wooden spoon. The stiff dough will hold its shape surprisingly well. If you want to use the pasta right away you may, but be sure the water is boiling when you drop the noodles into the pot. Otherwise, dry them in a very low oven for two or three hours and store them in a canister until you need them.
Yield: about 1¼ pounds dried noodles

Convenience Foods

If you found advantages to making your own yogurt and bread and sprouts at home, you'll probably find that there are even more good reasons to skip the store's "convenience foods" (if you buy them in the first place) and make your own instant sauces, mixes, and dressings.

We're not going to give you the same breakdowns as we did earlier for the foods below because we're convinced that the commercial "convenience foods" cost a great deal more than you can make them for at home and usually in less than the time it'd take you to go to the store and buy them. Also, these foods are notorious for the additives they contain — additives that don't improve the quality of the products, but mask the second-rate and artificial ingredients that go into most of them. Some additives are used to add to  the shelf life of the foods, but you can keep the ones that would otherwise need preservatives in the refrigerator. (Many, by the way, don't need refrigeration *or* preservatives.)

Some Recipes for Homemade Convenience Foods

Pudding and Pie Filling

In earlier times, these were known as cornstarch puddings. But that isn't a particularly appealing name.

3½ cups instant nonfat dry milk
¾ cup sugar
¾ cup cornstarch

Combine ingredients and store in tightly covered container in cool dry place.

To make vanilla-flavored pudding: Stir the basic mix thoroughly and measure out 1 cup. Gradually add 2 cups of cold water and then bring mixture to boil, stirring over low heat. Mixture is boiling when it bubbles and plops. Add 1 teaspoon butter or margarine and ½ teaspoon vanilla. Stir until butter melts; pour into serving dishes and refrigerate.

For chocolate pudding: Combine mix and water as directed above. Stir in either 1 ounce of unsweetened chocolate or 4 tablespoons unsweetened cocoa and ½ teaspoon vanilla. Stir to mix well and pour into serving dishes. Refrigerate until set.

Yield: 4 half-cup servings

Biscuit and Pancake Mix

8 cups unsifted whole wheat flour
¼ cup plus 2 teaspoons baking powder
4 teaspoons salt
2 cups shortening
2 cups instant nonfat dry milk powder

Sift dry ingredients together twice. Cut in shortening and place in a covered jar. Store in refrigerator and mix as needed. It will keep for 1 to 2 months.

To make biscuits: Use about ⅓ to ½ cup milk to 1 cup of mix and bake 12 to 15 minutes at 375° to 400°F.

To make delicious pancakes: Beat 1 egg. Add 1 tablespoon honey and 1 cup water. Then beat in 1⅓ cups mix and fry on hot griddle.

Yield: about 48 biscuits or about 70 pancakes

Seasoned Coating Mix

2 cups whole wheat flour or 1 cup whole wheat flour and 1 cup
  whole wheat bread crumbs
2 tablespoons salt
1 tablespoon celery salt
1 tablespoon pepper
2 tablespoons dry mustard
4 tablespoons paprika
½ teaspoon thyme
½ teaspoon sweet basil
½ teaspoon oregano or marjoram

In large bowl, combine all seasonings with 1 cup of the
flour and mix well with hands or a spoon. Add last cup of flour
and blend thoroughly. When dredging meat for stew, Swiss
steak, cutlets, fish, etc., use equal amount of seasoned flour
and plain whole wheat flour, but for spicier dishes, use just this
mix.
Yield: about 3 cups

Barbecue Sauce

3 tablespoons vinegar
1 cup catsup
½ cup water
1 tablespoon honey
6 tablespoons chopped onion
1 bay leaf
½ teaspoon dry mustard

Combine ingredients in saucepan and simmer 5 minutes.
Remove bay leaf and store in refrigerator.
Yield: about 2 cups

Cornmeal Mix

4 cups flour
4 cups cornmeal
1½ cups nonfat dry milk
¼ cup baking powder
1 tablespoon salt
1½ cups shortening

Stir dry ingredients together until mixed. Cut in shortening until well blended. Place in a glass jar, tin can, or plastic container with a tight-fitting cover. Keep tightly closed in a cool place. Use the mix within a month.
Yield: 12 cups

To make cornbread: combine 4½ cups cornmeal mix, 2 eggs, beaten, and 1⅓ cups water, and stir just enough to moisten dry ingredients. Pour into greased pan about 8 inches square. Bake in hot oven (425°F.) about 25 minutes. Cut into serving-size pieces.
Yield: 12 pieces

To make cornmeal drop biscuits: add water (about ½ cup) to 2 cups of the cornmeal mix to make a soft dough. Drop dough by tablespoonfuls onto a greased baking sheet. Bake in hot oven (425°F.) about 12 minutes.
Yield: 12 medium-size biscuits

To make cornmeal muffins: Grease medium-size muffin pans. Combine 2¼ cups cornmeal mix, 1 egg, beaten, and ⅔ cup water and stir just enough to moisten dry ingredients. Fill muffin cup two-thirds full. Bake in hot oven (425°F.) 20 minutes.
Yield: 12 muffins

Instant Cocoa Mix

1 1-pound package instant nonfat dry milk powder (about 4 cups)
1 cup sugar
¾ cup cocoa
¼ teaspoon salt (optional)

Mix all ingredients together well or blend them in a blender. Store in a cool place in a tightly covered container.
Yield: 27 to 30 servings

Carob Drink Mix

2 cups carob powder
4 cups instant nonfat dry milk powder
8 tablespoons sugar or honey (if using honey, add ½ tablespoon
    to each individual drink before serving)

Mix the ingredients together well. You may want to blend them to get rid of all lumps and be sure the ingredients are well mixed. Then store in an airtight container in a cool place.

To make a drink, stir ½ cup mix into about ½ cup hot or cold water. (If using honey, add it at this time.)
Yield: 16 servings

"Instant" Soups

Very good soups can be made quickly from canned vegetables (either home-canned or store-bought) so long as you have a blender. Basically all you do is blend a 17-ounce can of any vegetable with about ½ cup of water, chicken or beef broth or bouillon, or tomato juice until the mixture is smooth. Then heat it up (unless you'd rather have it cold), season to taste, and serve. If you want creamed soup, replace the water or broth or juice with milk, or mix half milk, and half of another liquid.

Here are two recipes that serve as good examples of variations on the above:

Borscht

1 17-ounce can chopped beets
¼ of an onion, chopped
1 cup tomato juice
salt and pepper
yogurt (optional)

Put canned beets, chopped onion, and tomato juice in a blender and whiz until smooth. Heat in a saucepan to boiling, season to taste, and pour into bowls. Garnish each with a spoonful of yogurt and serve. This soup may also be served cold.
Yield: 2 servings

Cream of Asparagus Soup

1 17-ounce can asparagus bits
½ cup water, or chicken or beef broth
4 to 6 tablespoons heavy cream
salt and pepper to taste

Pour all of the canned asparagus, except for a few pieces, into a blender with the water or broth. Whiz until smooth. Place in a saucepan with the asparagus pieces and heat. Pour into bowls and add 2 tablespoons of cream to each bowl. Season and serve immediately.
Yield: 2 to 3 servings

Cooking Ahead

Many other "convenience foods" that take more preparation time, like soups, heavy sauces, and casseroles, can be made in large quantities and then canned or frozen for later use.

Of course, prepared ahead dishes are also great to use when you've just gotten home from work and are starving, or when there are unexpected mouths to feed for dinner.

Cooking ahead is mostly a matter of common sense, but there are some things to keep in mind:

- Not all recipes can be tripled or quadrupled exactly. You shouldn't have much problem with soups, stews, and such, but be careful when you're using lots of spices and working with thickening agents. If you want to prepare tricky foods in large quantities, experiment first or find a recipe that multiplies the ingredients for you.

- Store the food carefully. Use the same precautions you'd use when storing garden produce or meat you buy in quantity. Use airtight freezing containers or good canning lids and jars. Follow directions carefully.

- A casserole can be frozen in a stainless steel container or baking pan, or bread pan. When the food is frozen, it can be taken out of the pan by a quick dip in hot water. The frozen block of food can be wrapped in plastic and heavy aluminum foil and labeled. Stacking is especially easy if you've frozen the food in a bread pan because it comes out as a nice rectangular block. When ready to use the casserole, just unwrap and put in a pan to cook on the stove or in the oven. Precooked foods should be heated without thawing. If thawing is necessary to separate portions, it should be done in the refrigerator. Room temperature thawing for 2 to 3 hours may encourage spoilage in these foods.

- Label everything. Tuna fish casserole looks pretty much like eggplant parmesan when it's frozen in an opaque container, and it's hard to tell whether a home-canned soup is beef vegetable or beef barley. And don't forget the date, so that you can use things pretty much in the order in which they were frozen or canned.

Some Cook-Ahead Recipes

Middle Eastern Lamb

½ cup vegetable oil
4 ounces (1 stick) butter
10 pounds lamb (from leg), cut in 2-inch cubes
15 medium onions, peeled and thickly sliced
2 tablespoons flour
1½ teaspoons garlic powder
1 tablespoon cumin
2 teaspoons allspice
1 6-ounce can tomato paste
3 cups beef stock (homemade if possible)
salt and pepper to taste

Heat oil and butter and sauté meat until it browns. Remove meat, then add onions and cook over low heat for 5 minutes. Add flour and spices and cook 3 to 4 minutes longer. Stir in tomato paste and stock; blend until smooth; return meat to pot; season to taste with salt and pepper.

Cover pot and place in 350°F. oven. Cook for 1½ to 1¾ hours, until meat is tender. Refrigerate overnight. Next day, skim off fat, then freeze.
Yield: 20 servings

You can often save money by cooking for several meals at one time because you can take advantage of the cheaper price of larger quantities. Large tom turkeys are less expensive per pound than smaller hen turkeys and there's more meat per pound than bone, and many stores offer savings on "family packages" of chicken parts, stewing and chopped meat, and so forth. You can also take advantage of store specials by buying several pounds of a sale item at a time for a cooking-ahead project.

So much of the time in preparing food comes from assembling the ingredients and equipment, standing over the stove or oven, and cleaning up. Naturally if you're cooking enough for several meals at once you'll only be doing these things one time, and thereby cutting your time and work in half or more.

Another nice thing about cooking ahead is that you can cook when you really do have the time and are in the mood. Then cooking can be fun, and you can do things right, without looking for shortcuts that might mean grating less cheese than the casserole really calls for, or not mincing the onions but chopping them, or only simmering the soup for 3 hours when you *know* it really takes 4 hours to get all the flavor and gelatin out of the bones.

If you're the kind of person who enjoys sitting down to a dinner someone else cooked but doesn't have much of an appetite for one you just spent a couple of hours preparing, you should love cooking ahead. You can get something out of the freezer or canning jar, cook it up quickly and easily, and really enjoy eating it.

Beef Barley Soup

6 pounds short ribs of beef
4 tablespoons chicken or other fat
salt and pepper to taste
1 garlic clove, crushed
4 tablespoons parsley
4 quarts water
½ cup barley
2 cups scraped, cubed carrots
½ cup chopped onion
1 cup chopped celery
4 cups cooked or canned tomatoes

Remove meat from bones and brown meat in hot fat. Simmer meat, bones, salt and pepper, garlic, and parsley in water, covered, for 1 hour. Add barley; cook for 1 hour longer. Remove bones. Cool and skim off fat. Add vegetables and cook for 1 hour more. Other vegetables, meat or bones, leftover or fresh, may be added in this last hour.
Yield: about 4 quarts

Meat Loaf with Oatmeal

6 pounds lean ground beef (chuck or round)
1 cup wheat germ
1½ cups oatmeal
6 tablespoons chopped parsley
1½ teaspoons pepper
2 teaspoons salt
1½ cups chopped onion
¼ cup oil
6 eggs, lightly beaten
¾ cup nonfat dry milk powder
1½ cups water
1½ cups tomato juice

In a large mixing bowl, combine ground beef, wheat germ, oatmeal, chopped parsley, pepper, and salt; set aside. Sauté onion in oil until tender but not brown; add to meat mixture.

Beat eggs lightly. Combine skim milk powder and water with a wire whisk, and add to eggs. Blend together and add to meat mixture; then add tomato juice. Mix thoroughly.

Oil three 9 x 5 x 3 loaf pans. Turn meat mixture into pans, packing down well. Allow to rest 10 to 15 minutes in refrigerator. Run spatula around edge of meat loaf to loosen. Carefully turn out onto a cookie sheet, keeping original shape as much as possible. Freeze uncovered on the cookie sheet, and when frozen remove from sheet and wrap individually.

When ready to cook, place unthawed meat loaf on a lightly oiled shallow baking pan and brush the surface with oil. Place on middle rack of a 350°F. oven and bake for about 2 hours. Remove from oven and allow to rest 10 minutes.
Yield: 3 loaves that each make 6 servings

Lima Bean Casserole

2 pounds dried lima beans, washed and drained
1 teaspoon salt
6 medium onions, chopped (about 3 cups)

¾ cup vegetable oil
2 tablespoons flour
3 teaspoons salt
2 teaspoons paprika
1 teaspoon pepper

Place beans in large saucepan; add water to cover. Heat to boiling and boil 4 minutes. Remove from heat; cover and let stand 2 hours. Heat to boiling; reduce heat and cover. Simmer until beans are tender, about 1½ hours. (Add water if necessary.) Drain beans, reserving 1½ cups liquid. Mix beans and 1 teaspoon salt.

Cook and stir onions in oil over low heat until tender and light brown, about 25 minutes. Stir in flour, salt, paprika, and pepper. Gradually stir reserved bean liquid into onion mixture. Cook and stir until thick.

Choose two freezer-to-oven 1½-quart casserole dishes. In each, layer one-quarter of the beans, then spread each with one-quarter of the onion mixture. Repeat with remaining beans and onion mixture.

To cook, place unthawed in 375°F. oven and bake about 2 hours.

Yield: 2 casseroles that each make 8 servings

Zucchini Stuffed with Meat and Cheese

20 fresh, young zucchini, about 1¼ to 1½ inches in diameter
6 tablespoons vegetable oil
5 cups thinly sliced yellow onions
4 tablespoons chopped parsley
4 tablespoons tomato paste diluted with 1 cup water
6 tablespoons milk
2 slices whole wheat bread
1 pound lean beef, chopped
2 eggs
6 tablespoons freshly grated Parmesan cheese
2 teaspoons salt
pepper to taste

Clean zucchini, slice off ends, and cut into lengths of about 2½ inches. Hollow them out completely, removing the pulp* with a vegetable corer or peeler, being careful not to perforate the sides. The thinned-out wall of the zucchini should not be less than ¼-inch thick.

Put oil in a large covered skillet and slowly cook the sliced onions until tender and considerably wilted. Add the parsley, stirring two or three times. Then add the tomato paste diluted in water and cook slowly over low heat for about 15 minutes.

Warm the milk and mash the bread into it with a fork. Let cool.

In a mixing bowl put the chopped meat, eggs, grated cheese, and the bread mush. Mix thoroughly with your hands. Add the onion and tomato mixture, salt, and pepper to taste.

Stuff the mixture into the hollowed-out zucchini sections, making sure they are well stuffed but not pushing too hard, to avoid splitting the zucchini.

Pack the stuffed zucchini into meal-sized containers and freeze, or wrap each separately in freezer paper or double thickness aluminum foil.

To cook, place unthawed zucchini in a skillet and cook covered on low for about 1½ hours or until done (the bigger the zucchini, the longer the cooking time). Turn the zucchini from time to time. When done, they should be tender but not too soft.

If, when the zucchini is cooked, there is too much liquid in the skillet, uncover it and raise the heat to high; boil away the excess liquid for a minute or two, turning the zucchini once or twice. Taste for salt, and transfer the zucchini to a serving platter, allowing them to settle for a minute or two.
Yield: 10 to 12 servings

*Note: Although the zucchini pulp is not used in this recipe, don't throw it away. It can be used later to supplement a recipe such as zucchini puffs (page 363).

Beef Goulash

6 pounds boneless lean beef chuck or beef stew meat, cut in 1½-inch cubes
½ cup oil
8 onions, chopped

½ cup flour
salt
¼ cup paprika
1¼ teaspoons thyme
3 pounds tomatoes
water
32 ounces tomato sauce
8 bouillon cubes
5 garlic cloves, minced
bouquet garni (1 bay leaf, 1 stalk celery, few sprays parsley
    tied together)

Brown beef slowly in oil. Add onions and cook until onions
are tender. Blend flour, salt, paprika, and thyme into the onion
and meat.

Drain tomatoes, reserving liquid. Add water to liquid to
make 6 cups and add to meat. Add tomatoes to remaining ingredients; heat to boiling.

Reduce heat, cover, and simmer (do not boil) about 3 hours
or till meat is tender, stirring occasionally. Remove bouquet
garni, spoon into meal-sized containers, and freeze.
Yield: 24 servings

Turkey

Turkey is an excellent food to cook
ahead and freeze for later eating. Besides
being an inexpensive food that can be prepared in so many ways after it's roasted,
turkey meat is a good quality protein
source. Frances Moore Lappé points out
in *Diet for A Small Planet* that "turkey
apparently surpasses all other meat and
poultry in its ability to complement plant
protein. Experiments show that if you add
only one-fifth as much turkey to a meal of
wheat, peanuts, or black-eyed peas, the
protein quality will be the same as if the
entire meal had been beef." One hundred grams of turkey (3
medium-sized roasted slices) contain more grams of protein
than ½ pound of raw, lean porterhouse steak. In addition, that
100 grams of turkey add up to 200 calories, while the steak is
about 800 calories.

From a 13-pound bird, yielding approximately 6 pounds of cooked meat, it is quite possible to get from 20 to 24 servings, if you make such dishes as turkey croquettes, turkey chow mein, and of course turkey soup.

All these dishes call for cooked turkey meat, so pick a day when you'll be around the kitchen and begin by roasting your bird. Everybody has his or her own way to roast turkey and here's the way they do it at the Fitness House kitchen:

Wash the bird well inside and out. Tuck the wing tips underneath the bird (to enable the breast to brown and cook evenly). Salt inside and out if desired. Either stuff the bird, or put a celery stalk with leaves and an onion into the cavity. Cut these in halves or quarters so they will fit. They will add flavor to the meat and to the juices which you will use for sauce or gravy.

If your turkey is frozen when purchased, it is important to thaw it according to the printed instructions before removing its wrapper. Otherwise, the skin dries out badly. It is best to thaw it in the refrigerator, unless you have a cool place to leave it for the length of time needed (2 hours per pound in refrigerator and 1 hour per pound at room temperature). Turkey, chicken, or any kind of poultry is particularly susceptible to contamination if it is left too long at room temperature once it is thawed and also after it is cooked. This is especially true in warm weather. And you've probably heard that a turkey should not be stuffed the night before it is to be roasted. It is fine to make the stuffing then, but refrigerate it and the turkey separately, then fill the bird in the morning just before putting it into the oven. Slightly warm stuffing inside the turkey, even in a refrigerator, will not cool fast enough to keep harmful bacteria from developing.

Set the bird breast-side-up in a roasting pan. If your roasting pan has a lid, use it to cover the turkey during the roasting period up to the last 30 or 45 minutes, when it should be removed if you like your turkey to be golden brown. If the turkey is too big for your roaster, any large pan can be used, providing it is at least 3 inches deep. The bird should be covered, and although aluminum foil will work quite well for smaller turkeys, the best cover is an oiled cloth — a piece torn from a clean sheet is perfect. Saturate the cloth with rendered chicken or turkey fat or vegetable oil. This will keep the breast from overcooking and drying out over the necessary long cooking period. If you use foil, be sure to coat the breast well with fat before covering it. According to nutrition writer Adelle Davis, basting (spooning the juices in the pan over the turkey periodically) dries out the meat and increases evaporation by washing off the fat. If you have covered the bird with an oiled cloth, basting is not necessary.

The temperature should be low — 300°F. for a bird weighing 18 to 25 pounds and 325°F. for one which weighs less. For the larger bird allow 15 minutes per pound and for the smaller, 20 to 25 minutes per pound.

The perfectly cooked turkey will have a juicy breast which carves nicely into slices instead of falling apart into stringy shreds. The dark meat will literally fall off the legs. To achieve this, it takes care and close attention toward the end of the cooking period. Use a cooking or carving fork with wide-set, long tines and insert this into the thickest part of the breast. Juice should appear at the surface and be clear, not pink. If the breast is a bit too done, no juice will appear and the fork, when removed, will leave well-defined holes. The meat at the "knee" of the leg should yield when it is lightly pinched between thumb and forefinger. To be sure, you can insert the fork into the meat on the inside of the leg to test the color of the juice. If the breast seems to be done and the legs aren't, you can cut them off, remove the bird from the oven and wrap it in foil to keep it warm, leaving the legs to cook a bit longer.

To carve, first remove the legs, then the wings. Cut between the leg and the body, through the skin and down to the joint. Take hold of the leg and gently twist, to find the point where the knife can easily sever the leg from the hip joint. Take hold of the wing and pull it out away from the breast, cutting through the shoulder joint. Try to leave the breast intact. Then with the tip of the knife, cut down the center of the breast dividing it in half. Now, using the knife to loosen the meat from the bone, starting at the breast bone, cut down along the rib cage, and in this way remove each half of the breast in one piece. This can then be laid flat on the board and sliced straight down as you would a loaf of bread across the grain into lovely succulent slices. Some can be left unsliced and frozen for future sandwiches, cold meat platters, or salads. Remove the meat from the legs and cut it into chunks or slices. A surplus of dark meat can also be frozen for the future.

After the meal is over or a little later, remove skin and tough or dry bits, and reserve for soup. Keep juicy meat for turkey newburg or à la king and reserve any tougher pieces to be used in the soup or chopped up for croquettes. Be sure to remove all the meat from the back, breast bones, neck, wings, etc. There is a lot there if you look for it. Add more onion and celery tops to the bones and skin, cover with cold water, salt to taste, and bring slowly to a boil in a large covered pot. Turn heat down to simmer and cook for 2 to 3 hours. Vinegar may be added (2 tablespoons to a quart of water) to help dissolve the calcium out of the bones. Strain soup stock, remove any meat left on bones, then discard the bones. Pour stock into containers and store in refrigerator or freezer when cool. (Leave room for expansion in container if freezing.) In warm weather, it is important to get the stock into a refrigerator quickly, so it may be necessary to cool it by setting the container of stock in a sink of cold water, stirring it occasionally. In winter, if you have a cold room or enclosed back porch, you can safely set the hot stock there overnight to cool slowly, but you must remove the lid, covering the pot with a clean cloth if you want, but leaving it open to the air.

Here are some recipes which will help you make the most of your turkey for present or future eating. Turkey newburg — creamed turkey made elegant by adding egg yolks and sherry — can be made from thawed-out turkey meat that you roasted and froze at an earlier time or from just cooked meat. Turkey chow mein is a good dish for freezing and is economical because it stretches the roasted turkey meat. Turkey vegetable soup can either be made right after you roast the turkey and make the stock and then frozen, or it can be made from thawed-out frozen stock and turkey meat. Turkey croquettes are great for a cook-ahead and then freeze meal; a recipe appears on page 426.

Turkey Newburg

½ pound fresh mushrooms, thinly sliced
¼ cup oil or turkey fat
¼ cup oat or wheat flour
2 cups turkey stock (see above)
½ cup nonfat dry milk powder
2 tablespoons cornstarch
1 cup cold water

4 cups turkey meat (approximately 1¼ pounds)
salt to taste
2 egg yolks
¼ cup sherry (optional)

In heavy-bottom pot, sauté mushrooms in oil or turkey fat until tender. Stir in flour. Add turkey stock, stirring constantly; continue to simmer over low heat.

Meanwhile, combine skim milk powder, cornstarch, and cold water, using wire whisk. Stir into sauce and cook until cornstarch has lost its raw taste and sauce is thick (about 10 minutes). Add turkey. Salt to taste.

Beat egg yolks and add some of hot turkey mixture to egg yolks; then add egg yolk mixture to turkey, stirring all the time. Cook 1 minute longer. Add sherry, if desired. Serve with brown rice.

Yield: 6 to 8 servings

Turkey Chow Mein

⅓ cup peanut oil or other light vegetable oil
2 pounds sliced mushrooms
2 green peppers, cut into long thin strips
12 green onions with tops or 3 large onions
8 large ribs of celery or Chinese cabbage
8 cups cooked slivered turkey
2 8-ounce cans water chestnuts, drained
2 pounds mung bean sprouts (canned or home-sprouted)
1½ pounds snow peas or pea pods (optional)
8 cups turkey broth
½ cup soy sauce (preferably tamari)
½ cup cornstarch
2 cups toasted slivered almonds

Place a large skillet, preferably cast-iron, over medium-high heat, add oil, and heat until oil is hot. Then add mushrooms, green peppers, onions, and celery or Chinese cabbage, and stir-fry for about 5 minutes. Then add cooked turkey, water chestnuts, sprouts, and snow peas, and stir-fry for about 2 minutes.

In a saucepan, combine 6 cups of the turkey broth and soy sauce. Heat to boiling, lower heat, and simmer for 5 minutes. Blend the cornstarch with the remaining 2 cups of turkey broth, then add to the simmering broth and soy sauce. Cook, stirring gently, until thickened and clear. Add the thickened turkey broth to the turkey and vegetable mixture.

Unless you are serving this dish immediately, do not add the almonds, since they lose their crispness when they have been frozen.

To freeze, spoon the turkey chow mein into meal-sized freezer containers and freeze. To serve, thaw the carton enough so that the contents slip out. Put into a saucepan and warm over low heat until hot. Add the toasted almonds and serve immediately on hot brown rice. Be careful not to overcook because the vegetables will become mushy.

Yield: 24 servings

Turkey Vegetable Soup

8 cups turkey stock (see earlier in chapter)
2 cups skinned tomatoes (fresh or canned; if canned add liquid)
½ cup corn (preferably fresh)
¼ cup chopped onion
½ cup chopped celery
1 cup chopped cabbage
salt and pepper to taste
about 2 cups cooked chopped turkey

Combine all but the turkey meat and simmer uncovered for about ½ hour or until the vegetables are tender.

Then add turkey meat and cook another 5 to 10 minutes, until meat is warm.

Yield: 8 to 10 servings

Lamb Pinto Stew

4 pounds lamb shoulder, cut in cubes
½ cup flour
6 tablespoons oil
2 medium onions, sliced
2 cups stock or bouillon
2 teaspoons salt
1 teaspoon pepper
1 teaspoon basil
1 teaspoon thyme
3 cups pinto beans, cooked
24 ounces whole kernel corn
2 4-ounce jars pimentos, drained and chopped
2 medium green peppers, cut in strips

Coat lamb with flour. In large skillet brown meat well in hot oil. Remove lamb; add onion to skillet and cook until golden. Stir in remaining ingredients along with lamb. Turn into lightly greased casseroles and freeze.

To cook, bake in a 350°F. oven for about 2 hours for large casseroles and 1½ hours for smaller ones.
Yield: 16 servings

Gypsy Stew

4½ pounds boneless pork shoulder
2 teaspoons salt
1 teaspoon paprika
½ teaspoon pepper
½ garlic clove, minced
2 large onions, chopped
6 cups cooked chick-peas with their cooking liquid
3 medium cabbages

Cut pork into 1 inch by 1½-inch strips. Toss with the seasonings and put in a large skillet with the onion.

Sauté until onion is lightly browned, then add chick-peas and the liquid in which they were cooked. Spoon into freezer containers, leaving plenty of headspace on each. Then cut the cabbage into small wedges, place them on top of the meat mixture in the containers, and freeze.

To cook, put into a covered skillet or pan and cook over medium heat for about 1 hour or until meat is tender.
Yield: 14 to 18 servings

How to Use Leftovers Creatively

Leftovers can either be the remains of yesterday's meal or the beginning of today's — it just depends upon your attitude. When you come right down to it, they are no different from processed food (minus the additives, of course) because they've already been prepared and usually cooked. Because the hard work has already been done, leftovers shouldn't be a problem but an asset around which a future meal can be created.

Some cooks develop a sixth sense about leftovers, automatically incorporating them into the meals within a day or two of their first appearance. This is a good idea because although some food improves with age, as a rule leftovers don't.

There are a few basic things to keep in mind when working with leftovers. Don't recook a food that has been cooked once — or cook it as short a time as possible — and add fresh flavor to it in the form of sautéed onion and/or garlic. In our Fitness House experimental kitchen, soups and salads most often allow for inclusion of some remaining tidbits, often producing raves and even a request for the recipe (an embarrassing situation).

Another skill that is important to acquire when working

with these foods is the ability to know which foods can best be combined and which should be left separate. To explain, let us list some of the contents of our refrigerator on one particular day. Creamed turkey and mushrooms, sautéed chicken livers, canned corn, turkey broth, and some rice. After a little thought, the cook could see that here was a fine chicken soup in the making. Turkey and chicken livers were after all in the same "family"; mushrooms, corn, and rice were frequent ingredients of chicken soup; so why not combine them all? She chopped the turkey and livers a bit finer, added some freshly minced and sautéed onion, seasoned to taste, and there was the mainstay of lunch, simmering merrily on the stove.

Another day, one which was a bit too warm for soup, we had what you might call Salad Surprise, for lunch. You may laugh, but we used up all our leftovers and those who ate it loved that salad. Here is what went into it: cooked kidney beans, pickled zucchini, tiny pickled onions and tops, raw cucumber, cauliflower, tomato, celery, green pepper, radishes, carrot, cabbage, small cubes of cooked meat, lemon juice, mayonnaise, herbs, and seasonings.

If you're a "list" person, try making a list periodically of the contents of your refrigerator and freezer. This helps when you are pondering about menus for the next few days. A few foods don't lend themselves very well to second use — cabbage is one of these; it tends to get strong. Try to cook only enough cabbage for one meal. It could be added to a vegetable soup the next day, but after that, it is best thrown out. Other cooked vegetables, such as cauliflower, broccoli, asparagus, green beans, peas, corn, beets, carrots, turnips, are delicious marinated in an oil and vinegar dressing, and served on salad greens with a bit of mayonnaise. Cooked spinach can, with the addition of a little yogurt, become a nice filling for an omelet or a crêpe. Potatoes, once they have been cooked and are cold, require extra care in order to be incorporated into a dish. They do not always reheat very well. It helps to grate or "rice" them through a food mill so that you don't end up with lumps. Besides the obvious uses like hash-browned they also can be grated into soup to thicken it slightly. The other day on the spur of the moment, the cook cooked potato into sauerkraut, just to use it up. She hates to throw any food away, and we guess this is a requirement for a successful leftovers cook. Potatoes make a lovely light bread, of course, or rolls — even dumplings.

Chef Salad

Leftovers: cooked meat
cheese pieces
cooked beans

Suppose you have a small piece of a roast, chicken leg or some wings, and a hard piece of cheese left over, and also some odds and ends in the salad crisper — one carrot, the end of a cucumber, half a green pepper — and you want to use all of them up. Why not make a chef salad? Just about any meat or cheese can be used, provided it is trimmed and cut in slivers or small pieces, and even marinated beans or other vegetables can be included. You can toss everything together with a dressing or toss just the greens and arrange the meats, cheese, hard-boiled eggs, tomatoes, etc., over the top in a pattern.

½ head romaine lettuce
1 head iceberg lettuce
2 cups spinach leaves, broken into bite-sized pieces
4 radishes, sliced
1 cup cooked pinto or kidney beans, marinated in vinegar and oil dressing
2 cups cooked, slivered beef
1 cup cooked turkey or chicken, slivered
¼ pound Swiss cheese, slivered
1 medium-sized cucumber, thinly sliced
4 hard-boiled eggs, quartered
2 tomatoes, quartered
1 cup fresh sprouts (mung beans, lentil, alfalfa, wheat — any kind)
watercress for garnish

Wash romaine and iceberg lettuce and spinach, and crisp in refrigerator. Line salad bowl with lettuce leaves. Break remaining lettuce into bite-sized pieces, combine with radishes and beans, and put into salad bowl.

In wagon-wheel fashion, arrange beef, turkey or chicken, cheese, and cucumber over surface of salad. Decorate with quarters of eggs and tomatoes. Sprinkle sprouts over the top and tuck sprigs of watercress here and there to garnish. Serve accompanied with favorite dressing.

Yield: 6 to 8 servings

Prune-Bread Pudding

Leftovers: whole grain bread pieces

This dessert adds heartiness and protein to a light meal. Prunes make a nice change from the usual raisins in this recipe.

5 cups whole grain bread cubes
1 cup cooked prunes, pitted and chopped (raisins may be substituted)
2½ cups nonfat dry milk
6 cups water
2½ tablespoons honey
3 eggs

Preheat oven to 350°F.

Cut whole grain bread into cubes. Do not trim off crusts. Put bread and prunes into a 3-quart casserole.

Combine nonfat dry milk and water, using a wire whisk, and heat to the boiling point, stirring constantly to prevent scorching. Dissolve honey in hot milk mixture. In a bowl, beat eggs and gradually add hot milk mixture, stirring constantly.

Pour custard mixture over bread. Leave to soak for about 10 minutes. Set casserole in a pan of water and bake for 1 hour in preheated 350°F. oven. Cool before serving.

Yield: 6 to 8 servings

Chinese Fried Rice

Leftovers: cooked rice
             cooked peas
             cooked meat or fish

Fried rice is a light but filling dish — an excellent way to utilize cooked rice, small amounts of cooked meat or fish, and vegetables, both raw and cooked. The scrambled egg strips are a nice touch, added just before serving. Sprouts and soy sauce help to supply the authentic flavor and appearance of this popular Chinese dish. Sprouts are also very nutritious (see page 293).

2 to 3 tablespoons oil
2 eggs, slightly beaten
2 green onions and tops, thinly sliced
1 stalk celery, diced
1 small green pepper, diced
1 cup cooked peas or uncooked frozen
3 cups cooked brown rice
1 cup cooked meat, poultry, or fish, slivered
1 cup mung bean sprouts (other sprouts may be substituted)
salt to taste
tamari soy sauce to taste

In large skillet, heat ½ tablespoon oil and lightly scramble eggs, just until they are no longer liquid. Remove from pan and set aside.

Using remaining oil as needed, sauté onions and tops, celery, green pepper, and peas if using frozen ones, for just a minute or two. Add cooked rice, slivered meat, poultry, or fish, sautéing lightly and tossing together as you add each ingredient.

Cut scrambled eggs into small pieces and add along with the sprouts and peas if using cooked ones. Season to taste with salt and tamari soy sauce and continue to cook just long enough to heat through completely. Serve immediately.
Yield: 4 servings

Whole Grain Pasta Salad

Leftovers: cooked peas
cooked carrots
cooked kidney, garbanzo, or navy beans
cooked noodles, spaghetti, or macaroni
cheese ends

Here is a superior version of the picnic favorite — macaroni salad — using whole grain pasta instead of the more anemic white version. This is a good way to use the leftover spaghetti or noodles which are often thrown out in American homes for lack of imagination. If the pasta is whole grain, there's even more reason to find a use for it. Combining it with cheese and beans makes it a protein-salad, and the brewer's yeast is an extra nutritional bonus.

2 cups cooked whole grain noodles, spaghetti, or macaroni
1 cup grated cheddar cheese
½ cup cooked peas
½ cup cooked carrots, cubed
½ cup cooked kidney, navy, or garbanzo beans
¼ cup green pepper, diced
¼ cup celery, diced
2 tablespoons onion, minced
½ cup sprouts (mung bean, alfalfa, wheat, any kind)
1 teaspoon dry mustard
1 to 2 tablespoons brewer's yeast (optional)
1 tablespoon lemon juice
½ to ¾ cup mayonnaise
2 to 3 tablespoons catsup (optional)
3 or 4 leaves fresh basil snipped with kitchen shears or 2 teaspoons, dried
salt and pepper to taste
salad greens
2 tablespoons chopped parsley

If using noodles, spaghetti, or long macaroni, cut it into approximately 1-inch lengths.

Combine all ingredients except last two, adding as much mayonnaise as desired. Chill thoroughly and serve on salad greens, garnished with chopped parsley.
Yield: 6 to 8 servings

Cream of Chicken Soup

Leftovers: chicken gravy
chicken stock
cooked chicken
cooked rice or noodles

Making soup always enables you to use stocks and gravies which sometimes accumulate in the refrigerator. The chicken and/or rice isn't necessary if you prefer just a thin soup for a lighter meal.

¼ cup green onion and tops, sliced thin (other onion may be substituted)
1 tablespoon chicken fat or butter
½ cup nonfat dry milk
2 cups chicken stock
1 cup chicken gravy
1 cup cooked chicken, cubed (optional)
1½ cups cooked brown rice (optional — or noodles may be substituted)
chopped parsley for garnish

Using 1½-quart saucepan, sauté onion and tops in chicken fat or butter. Reconstitute nonfat dry milk with chicken stock, and combine with onions, gravy, chicken, and rice in saucepan. Bring to a boil, turn heat down, and simmer soup for 20 minutes or so. Add parsley before serving.
Yield: approximately 4 cups

Fish Chowder

Leftovers: cooked potatoes
cooked fish

You don't have to use shellfish for chowder, and tuna or salmon aren't the only fish to be made into salad or casseroles. Canned mackerel makes fine sandwiches and salad. Haddock, turbot, cod, or any poached or baked fish will do equally well for chowder, salad, or casseroles. Fish should make its appearance on your dinner table often, because it is so high in top quality protein and low in fat and calories.

1 medium-sized onion, minced
½ cup raw celery, diced
½ cup raw carrot, diced
3 tablespoons butter
2 cups cooked potatoes, peeled
1 cup fish or chicken stock
½ cup nonfat dry milk
1 cup water
1½ cups cooked fish, boned and broken into bite-sized pieces
1 bay leaf
¼ teaspoon kelp powder
salt and pepper to taste
1 to 2 tablespoons cider vinegar (optional)
chives or fresh coriander or fresh fennel, for garnish

Using a large saucepan, sauté onion, celery, and carrot in butter for a few minutes. Cube or grate potatoes and add to sautéed vegetables. Stir in stock and bring it to a boil. Reconstitute milk with water and add to the soup. Add fish, bay leaf, and kelp powder and simmer for 30 minutes or so. Season to taste with salt and pepper. Add vinegar if using it. Garnish with snipped chives, fresh coriander, or fennel before serving.
Yield: 4 servings

Lemon-Rice Pudding

Leftovers: cooked rice

This pudding is a heavy, nutritious dessert quite different from other rice puddings. It is almost a rice custard, and the lemon sauce is a nice accompaniment.

Pudding
1 cup nonfat dry milk
3 cups water
2 eggs, slightly beaten
¼ cup honey
1½ cups cooked brown rice
⅛ teaspoon salt
grated rind and juice of one average-sized lemon

Sauce
¼ cup lemon juice
¾ cup water
2 tablespoons honey
1 tablespoon cornstarch
1 tablespoon butter

Preheat oven to 325°F.
Reconstitute nonfat dry milk with water. Combine all ingredients of the pudding and pour into casserole. Bake in preheated oven until pudding is set, approximately 45 to 60 minutes. Test for doneness by inserting table knife into pudding. When custard is done, knife will be clean when removed.
To make sauce, combine lemon juice, water, and honey. Moisten cornstarch with a little of the liquid and then stir it into the mixture. Heat to the boiling point, stirring constantly. Blend in butter. Serve warm.
Yield: 4 to 6 servings

Avocado Half Stuffed with Chicken Rice Salad

Leftovers: cooked chicken
cooked rice

This is a luncheon dish which can be varied according to season or depending on what your larder has to offer. The salad can be made of turkey or fish instead of chicken, and bulgur, wild rice, or buckwheat kasha can substitute for the rice. Avocado halves set off the salad in a festive manner, but tomatoes can be used instead.

3 cups cooked chicken, cubed
1½ cups cooked brown rice
1½ cups celery, diced
2 green onions and tops, sliced thin
4 to 6 tablespoons lemon juice
1½ cups mayonnaise
salt and pepper to taste
3 medium-sized avocados
salad greens for garnish
paprika for garnish
snipped fresh basil for garnish

Combine cooked, cubed chicken with cooked rice, celery, onion, lemon juice, mayonnaise, and seasonings.

Cut avocados in half, remove pit, and peel. Arrange salad greens on individual plates and place an avocado half on each one. Fill with chicken salad. Garnish with paprika and snipped fresh basil before serving.
Yield: 6 servings

Meat or Fish–Potato Patties

Leftovers: cooked meat or fish
cooked potatoes

We came across the idea recently of making not just potato patties, but meat or fish *and* potato patties, so we tried it. Along with a salad and fruit it proved to be a very satisfying and tasty meal — and still another way to use up cooked potatoes.

¼ cup onion, minced
¼ cup carrot, grated
3 to 4 tablespoons butter
2 cups cooked and minced meat or flaked fish
2 cups cooked potatoes, peeled and grated
1 teaspoon thyme
1 tablespoon tamari soy sauce
salt and pepper to taste
4 to 6 tablespoons "sauce" (cream sauce, gravy, mayonnaise, or
    catsup)
¼ cup wheat germ

Sauté onion and carrot in some of the butter until tender. Combine meat or fish, potatoes, and seasonings. Add enough sauce to hold mixture together.

Form into patties. Dip them in wheat germ and sauté them in remainder of butter, until they are golden brown on both sides and heated through, about 5 to 10 minutes. Serve hot.

Yield: 4 servings

Cheesy Vegetable Casserole

Leftovers: cooked vegetables (cauliflower, celery, carrots, broccoli, peas, green beans, lima beans, corn, any of these may be used)
sharp cheddar cheese ends
whole grain bread ends and crumbs

A cheese sauce dresses up and binds together a variety of vegetables in this casserole. As well as being party fare to grace your buffet as accompaniment to a cold meat platter, this dish is quite capable of standing alone — the entrée for a family meal.

¾ cup nonfat dry milk
1½ cups water
3 tablespoons butter
3 tablespoons whole wheat flour
salt and white pepper to taste
¼ teaspoon paprika
¼ teaspoon dry mustard
1 cup grated sharp cheddar cheese
6 cups (approximately) cooked vegetables
dry whole grain bread crumbs for topping
butter

Preheat oven to 350°F.

Reconstitute nonfat dry milk with water. In saucepan, heat butter, stir in flour, and add milk gradually, stirring to prevent lumps. Cook until sauce is thick. Add seasonings, and then stir in cheese until it is melted.

Combine cooked vegetables in a casserole and pour cheese sauce over them. Sprinkle whole grain bread crumbs over the top and dot with butter. Bake in preheated oven for about 15 minutes or place 5 inches under broiler until top is brown.
Yield: 6 to 8 servings

Potato Soup

Leftovers: mashed potatoes

If the day is damp or cool, it is almost time for lunch, and yesterday's mashed potatoes are staring you in the face when you open the refrigerator door, don't despair. In 15 minutes your potato soup can be simmering on the stove while you put the finishing touches on the salad.

1 medium-sized onion, minced
1 tablespoon butter
2 cups cooked potatoes, peeled
1 cup meat or poultry broth
½ cup nonfat dry milk
1 cup water
salt and pepper to taste
dill weed for garnish
chopped parsley for garnish

Using a large saucepan, sauté onions in butter for a few minutes. If using a blender, combine cubed potatoes, broth, nonfat dry milk, water, and sautéed onions in blender and purée. Otherwise, cube or grate potatoes and add them to onions. Stir in broth and bring it to a boil. Reconstitute milk with water and add to soup.

Season to taste with salt and pepper. Simmer for 30 minutes or so. Garnish with dill and parsley just before serving.
Yield: 4 servings

Hard-Boiled Egg and Beet Salad

Leftovers: hard-boiled eggs
cooked beets

Beets and hard-boiled eggs do a lot for each other, especially if accented with dill in a mayonnaise dressing.

2 eggs, hard-boiled and chopped
4 cups cooked beets, diced
½ cup celery, minced
1 tablespoon green onion and tops, minced
1 tablespoon lemon juice
½ cup mayonnaise
½ teaspoon dill weed
salt and pepper to taste

Combine all ingredients. Serve on a bed of salad greens.
Yield: 6 servings

Chapter 9

Using Your
Food Supply
More Efficiently

Most Americans still believe that the only way to have a
protein-rich diet is to eat lots of "good red meat." This is a
myth, as so many recent nutrition books and articles and
cookbooks have explained. In terms of weight, eggs and milk,
fish and chicken all contain more protein than a piece of steak.

Another common American misconception is that all good
protein is derived from animal sources. The truth of the matter
is that there are many vegetable sources of first-rate protein.
Among these are whole grains, legumes, and nuts and seeds.
And one vegetable, the soybean, has so much high-quality protein that it rivals meat. In fact, soybeans offer a more
concentrated protein than either lamb or ham. Not only are
these grains, legumes, and seeds and nuts good sources of protein, they are also high in many vitamins, minerals, and one
valuable food element meats contain none of — fiber. (See
chapter 2 for a more complete discussion of food value.)

Most other countries eat a great deal more vegetable protein than we do and don't seem the worse for it. Grains provide
almost half of the world's dietary protein, and legumes rank
just behind grains in feeding the world's population. Almost
every foreign country features a grain or legume dish among
its national specialties (and we'll see some examples of this a
little later on).

337

By stocking up on a good variety of grains and legumes and learning to combine them creatively with other foods, especially those foods that maximize their usable proteins (see the discussion of complementary proteins on page 72), you'll be able to take care of your protein needs and experience some new flavors and textures. You'll also be able to save yourself some money because vegetable proteins are usually much cheaper per pound than animal proteins.

While you're probably familiar with many of the different kinds of grains and legumes, the following list will remind you of the ones you have to choose from and give you directions for cooking and ideas for serving.

Legumes

Black or Turtle Beans — Small, dark oval beans. Used primarily in soups popularized in South America.

Black-eyed Peas or Cow Beans — These oval beans are creamy white with a small black eye. Particularly popular in the South in "Hoppin' John."

Chick-Peas or Garbanzos — The nut-like flavor of these beans makes them a great favorite in the Mideast where they are puréed and seasoned with garlic and tahini for dipping, or shaped into balls and deep fried as the filling for a spicy sandwich known as falafel. Spanish cuisine favors them in a tomato sauce or seasoned with salt and pepper and served cold for snacking.

Fava Beans — These beans are sold both fresh and dried. They resemble lima beans in appearance and can be prepared in the same way. They are used in place of chick-peas to make Arabic falafel.

Kidney Beans — Deep red and shaped like a kidney. Best known for their use in chili.

Lentils — Unlike most other beans, they do not require presoaking and need only 45 minutes cooking. They are most famed as lentil soup but team up well with other vegetables, grains, or meat for a hearty casserole. In Egypt, the national dish, kushari, features lentils, rice, and macaroni heaped into a large bowl and topped with a thin, hot tomato sauce and crisply fried onions. Made with brown rice, this dish is an excellent source of protein.

Lima Beans — The flat, broad beans come in a variety of sizes. They are excellent in casseroles and rich soups and can be served alone as a vegetable.

Mung Beans — Small green beans, not found in the general marketplace, but available in most natural food stores. Used primarily for sprouting since they produce sweet crunchy sprouts that can be eaten raw or cooked. Mung beans can be used unsprouted in soups and stews, like all legumes.

Pink and Pinto Beans — Relatives of the kidney bean and used interchangeably with red and kidney beans.

Soybeans — The world's most valuable bean, offering all the essential amino acids needed by the body to synthesize protein. In addition they contain about twice as much calcium and thiamine as other beans. You can cook soybeans like any other bean, but see later for special cooking considerations. Don't expect soybeans to get really soft like other beans, because they are compositionally very different from the others.

Split Peas — Available in both green and yellow, these tiny beans have had their skins removed by mechanical processing. Cooking time is relatively short (45 minutes) and split peas do not require presoaking.

White Beans — This category includes marrow beans, Great Northern beans, navy beans, and pea beans. Although they vary in size, they are all mild in flavor. Encountered most often in soups and as Boston baked beans.

The How-To's

Cooking   Little work is involved in basic bean cookery — only time — and the same guidelines apply for cooking all beans:

1. Wash beans in cool water.

2. Place in large saucepan with three times their volume of water (3 cups water per 1 cup beans) and soak at least 8 hours; or bring beans and water to boil, cook 2 minutes, remove from heat, cover, and soak at least 1 hour. This soaking is necessary to replace water removed when beans were dried and reduces cooking time. Split peas and lentils are fairly quick cooking to begin with and require no soaking. Freezing the beans after soaking will make them more tender.

3. After soaking, drain off the soaking liquid, add fresh water, bring beans to a boil, reduce heat as low as possible, cover and cook gently until tender — about 2 hours (45 minutes for split peas and lentils). Be sure to cook soybeans for the full time because raw soybeans have an enzyme that inhibits protein utilization. Low heat helps prevent sticking and keeps beans from splitting.

You can also pressure cook all beans but split peas and lentils for 15 to 30 minutes at 15 pounds pressure instead of cooking them over low heat for 2 hours. To prevent frothing, add 1 to 2 teaspoons of vinegar to the cooking water.

4. A tablespoon of oil added during cooking keeps the foam down. Salt and acid ingredients such as tomatoes, lemon juice, vinegar, or wine slow down the softening process, so do not add these until beans are almost tender. Chopped onion, garlic, pepper, herbs, or meats can be cooked along with the beans for additional flavor.

5. Although often suggested in older cookbooks, never add baking soda to the bean pot. It destroys thiamin (vitamin B_1).

Remember to allow room for expansion when cooking beans. One cup dried beans will make two to three cups cooked beans, ready to serve as they are, or incorporated into savory soups, bean stews or loaves, spicy salads, or even bean puddings.

Because beans store well, you can save time for future meals by cooking up a large pot of beans and storing the extras in the refrigerator where they will keep at least one week. Frozen, beans can be kept four to six months.

Serving   There are so many ways to serve beans, peas, and lentils, you'll find it difficult to make a choice. In the most simple form they can be served as an accompaniment to your meal flavored with tomatoes, Italian seasonings, or chili powder, or lightly sweetened with molasses. Marinated in your favorite French dressing, they offer a cold salad side dish.

A wide variety of thick, savory bean soups can serve as a filling main course or appetizer. The more familiar ones include split pea soup, lentil soup, Italian minestrone, and South American black bean soup. Of course you can use any bean or combination of beans to create your own specialty. A marrow bone is often included in the soup pot to impart a deep flavor. For those who wish to exclude meat from the recipe, a similar "meaty" taste can be obtained by adding a tablespoon of brewer's yeast to the soup pot, also increasing the protein and B-vitamin content.

Bean Burgers

2 cups cooked beans (preferably red or pink variety), ground or
   puréed
⅔ cup ground sunflower seeds
¼ cup chopped onion
½ teaspoon chili powder
1 teaspoon salt
2 tablespoons oil
3 to 4 tablespoons catsup
about ½ cup wheat germ
8 thin slices cheddar or jack cheese (optional)

Preheat oven to 350°F.

Combine all ingredients except cheese, adding enough wheat germ so that the mixture will hold its shape. Form into 8 small patties.

Place on lightly oiled baking sheet and bake at 350°F. for 15 to 20 minutes. Or broil on each side about 5 minutes until lightly browned and crusty. If desired, place a slice of cheese on each burger and place under boiler heat to melt just before serving.

Yield: 4 servings

Spanish Style Chick-Peas

1 pound dried chick-peas
water to cover (about 6 cups)
5 tablespoons oil, divided
1 green pepper, chopped
1 sweet red pepper, chopped
1 chili pepper, chopped
1 large onion, chopped
1 large garlic clove, finely minced
4 large tomatoes, chopped
1 tablespoon chopped parsley
1 teaspoon salt
1 tablespoon brewer's yeast (optional)

Wash beans. Soak in water using either method outlined in the guidelines for basic bean cookery. Add 3 tablespoons oil to the soaked beans and cook gently over low heat until almost tender, about 2 hours.

Meanwhile prepare sauce by heating remaining 2 tablespoons oil in large skillet and sautéing the peppers, onion, and garlic until onion is tender. Add tomatoes, parsley, and seasonings and cook over low heat until tomatoes are pulpy, about 30 minutes.

Add beans to the sauce and continue cooking until tender.

Serve over a mixture of cooked grains, like brown rice and cracked wheat or buckwheat.

Yield: 6 to 8 servings

Beans, Barley, and Beef

1 cup dried lima beans
3 tablespoons oil
3 onions, chopped
4 potatoes, quartered
½ cup barley
3 pounds short ribs of beef
1 tablespoon salt
1 teaspoon pepper
1 teaspoon paprika
1 teaspoon unbleached flour
boiling water
2 carrots, cut in half

Wash the beans, soak 1 hour in warm water to cover, and drain. Heat oil in large heavy saucepan or Dutch oven. Add onions and sauté until golden. Add beans, potatoes, and barley, and stir. Place meat in center of pot. Combine seasonings and flour and sprinkle over meat and vegetables. Add boiling water to reach 1 inch above ingredients.

Cover and cook 5 hours over very low heat, or bake in a 300°F. oven 3½ to 4 hours. Halfway through cooking add the carrots.

Check the casserole occasionally to determine if more water is needed to keep vegetables from sticking. Barley absorbs a good deal of the liquid; if you don't want to concern yourself with adding more liquid, cook the barley partially before adding it to the pot.

Yield: 6 servings

Baked Soybeans

⅔ cup dried soybeans
water for soaking
4 cups fresh water (approximately)
½ garlic clove, crushed
½ cup chopped onion
1 cup chopped tomatoes with juice
1 cup cooked corn
1 green chili pepper, chopped
4 tablespoons wheat germ
1 teaspoon oregano
dash of Worcestershire sauce
1½ teaspoons salt (approximately)
½ cup grated sharp cheese

Soak and cook soybeans as directed on page 339, but add garlic and onion to the cooking water for flavor.

Take the beans out of the pot, and wash, dry, and butter it well. Put the beans back in, add the rest of the ingredients except the cheese, and stir them together. Cover the pot and simmer for about 1 hour. It should cook down to a fairly thick consistency without being completely dry. If it gets too dry add a little tomato juice. Sprinkle with grated cheese 5 or 10 minutes before you remove the beans from the heat. (This dish can also be baked in a buttered casserole in the Dutch oven.)

Yield: 4 servings

Grains

Barley — "Naked barley" is much better for you than the "pearl barley" that has the bran removed.

Buckwheat — It's not a grain, but it is eaten in the same way and has a similar food value. In the United States buckwheat is usually ground into flour, but buckwheat groats (unhulled, whole buckwheat, also called kasha) can be cooked much like rice.

Bulgur — This is essentially wheat that has been parboiled so that it can be cooked and served like buckwheat or rice.

Millet — These seeds vary greatly in size, shape, and color, but those commonly available in this country are tiny, shiny, white or cream-colored ovals. When cooked, millet is chewy, yet tender and good for puddings.

Rice — Stick with natural brown rice, not the white or parboiled rice that's so popular in this country. Brown rice contains the bran, which is the part of the grain richest in vitamins and minerals.

The How-To's

Cooking When grains are cooked, they absorb liquid and swell; uncooked bulgur, rice, and buckwheat triple in volume, while millet and barley increase to four times their original amount. Plan on serving ½ cup cooked grain per person for breakfast or as an accompaniment to the meal, and 1 cup cooked grain for main-dish servings.

The same basic cooking method can be applied to all the cereal grains:

1. Rinse raw grain in cold water and drain well. This will help remove both surface contamination and excess starch, as well as start the swelling process.

2. Bring to a boil cooking liquid equal to twice the volume of the uncooked bulgur, buckwheat, or rice, and three times the volume of the uncooked millet or barley. Meat or vegetable stock, juice, milk, or water may be used. The more flavorful the cooking liquid, the more flavorful the cooked grain will be.

3. Add boiling liquid to the grain in a pot just large enough to accommodate the increase in volume after cooking. Stir once.

4. Allow the liquid to return to boiling, then turn heat down to the lowest possible setting, cover and cook grains slowly until all liquid is absorbed. This will take anywhere from 30 to 45 minutes. Millet, bulgur, and buckwheat cook

rather quickly, while rice and barley may require additional time.

To determine if the grain is cooked, use the bite test: well-cooked grain will be chewy, but not tough or hard. If not quite done, add a little more water, cover, and continue cooking.

If you'd like a creamier product, for porridge or pudding, do not heat the cooking liquid initially, but combine it first with the uncooked grain, then bring the mixture to a boil. Cover and continue as above.

The addition of salt slows the cooking, so it is best to wait until the grain is tender, then season. Many people prefer using soy sauce instead of salt. Allow ¼ to ½ teaspoon of salt or about 1 teaspoon of soy sauce per cup of cooking liquid used.

Too much stirring makes the grain gummy, so stir only as suggested.

Cooked grain can be held in a covered pot off the heat until needed. This will keep it hot and allow further drying.

Cooked grain has a delicious nutty flavor, but for an even nuttier taste, try the sautéing technique: Place the rinsed grain in a pot and stir over low heat until dry. Then add enough oil to just coat each kernel, about 1 to 2 tablespoons per cup, and continue to cook and stir until dry and golden. For added savor sauté a chopped onion along with the grain. When the grain takes color (and the onion is limp) add the boiling liquid and continue as above.

Serving There's a place for grain dishes in every course of the meal from soup to dessert. Grain prepared according to the basic cooking instructions can be served as an accompaniment to meat or fish or used as a base for vegetables or stew. The cooked grain can be seasoned with honey, dried fruit, herbs, or cheese for a breakfast or dinner porridge. Cook the grains in a pot of soup for a rich chowder. Knead leftover grains into dough for a very special bread.

Cereal grains open the door to creativity in your kitchen. To get you started you'll enjoy trying some of these exciting ways of introducing cereal grains to your table.

Kasha Knishes

Inspired by Jewish cuisine, these whole grain burgers can be served as an entrée, allotting two per person; as the vegetable course; or for an intriguing hors d'oeuvre or snack. To prepare snack-size knishes, use 2 tablespoons of the mixture for each; in this case your yield will increase to 32 miniature buckwheat balls.

3 medium potatoes, about 1 pound
water
1 cup buckwheat groats
3 tablespoons safflower oil, divided
2 onions, chopped
2 eggs, divided
1½ teaspoons salt
¼ teaspoon pepper
½ to ¾ cup wheat germ

Quarter unpeeled potatoes and cook in boiling water until tender, about 20 minutes. Press through sieve or food mill. Wash buckwheat in cold water and drain well. Cook over low heat until dry. Add 2 tablespoons oil and continue cooking until buckwheat is dry and lightly browned.

Pour in 2 cups boiling water, cover, reduce heat, and cook until all liquid is absorbed, about 30 minutes. Sauté the onions in remaining 1 tablespoon oil until golden.

Combine sieved potatoes, cooked buckwheat, onion, 1 egg, salt, and pepper; form into 8 balls, using ½ cup of the mixture for each. Beat remaining egg. Roll each ball in wheat germ, dip in beaten egg, then coat again with wheat germ.

Bake on greased baking sheet in 350°F. oven until golden, about 25 minutes. Extras can be cooled, wrapped in foil or freezer paper, and frozen.

Yield: 8 kasha knishes or 32 small buckwheat balls

Lentil and Barley Bake

Try this casserole for a high-protein meatless main dish.

1 cup lentils
6 tablespoons barley
3½ cups water
1 onion, chopped
2 carrots, diced
½ teaspoon salt
1 bay leaf

Sauce: 3 tablespoons molasses
  2 tablespoons cider vinegar
  ⅓ cup reserved cooking liquid
  1 garlic clove, crushed
  1 teaspoon dry mustard powder
  ½ teaspoon salt
Topping: 1 egg
  6 tablespoons cornmeal
  ½ teaspoon salt

Wash lentils and barley in cold water and drain well. Combine lentils, barley, water, onion, carrots, salt, and bay leaf in large saucepan. Bring to boil, cover, reduce heat, and let simmer 45 minutes. Strain, reserving ⅓ cup of the liquid, and transfer cooked grain and vegetables to a 1¾-quart casserole.

Prepare sauce by combining molasses, vinegar, reserved cooking liquid, garlic, dry mustard powder, and salt. Pour over vegetables in casserole. Mix remaining ingredients together for topping and spread over vegetables.

Bake in 350°F. oven until liquid is absorbed and topping browns lightly, about 20 minutes.

Yield: 4 to 6 servings.

Stuffed Summer Squash

Here is a vegetable-grain combination designed to enliven any meal. Vary it on occasion with a topping of freshly grated Parmesan cheese.

4 medium zucchini (about 1 pound)
1 tablespoon peanut oil
1 onion, chopped
¾ pound tomatoes, chopped
1 teaspoon honey
1½ teaspoons salt
¼ teaspoon pepper sauce
½ cup brown rice
2 tablespoons chopped parsley
½ teaspoon cinnamon

Trim off stem end and slice each zucchini in half lengthwise. Scoop out pulp, leaving shell intact. Heat oil in large skillet, add zucchini pulp, onion, and tomatoes. Cook until vegetables are soft and liquid begins to separate out, about 5 minutes. Add honey, salt, and pepper sauce.

Wash rice in cold water, drain well, and combine with chopped parsley and cinnamon.

Place zucchini shells, skin side down, in shallow baking dish. Fill cavity with rice mixture. Pour vegetable mélange over all, cover, and bake in 350°F. oven 45 minutes. Remove cover and continue to bake until liquid is almost completely absorbed and rice is tender, 30 to 40 minutes longer.

Yield: 4 servings

Sweet Millet Pilaf

Millet is especially fine in puddings and other dessert dishes.

½ cup millet
juice of 2 oranges
water
¼ teaspoon salt
¼ cup chopped nuts (walnuts, almonds, peanuts, or a combination)
¼ cup raisins
2 tablespoons honey
juice and grated rind of 1 orange
1 tablespoon safflower oil
8 pitted dates
8 whole almonds

Wash millet in cold water and drain well. Add water to orange juice to equal 1½ cups liquid and combine with millet and salt in saucepan. Bring to boil, cover, reduce heat, and cook until grain is tender, about 30 minutes.

Chop together nuts and raisins. Beat in honey, orange juice, grated rind, and oil. When millet is cooked, toss with raisin-nut mixture.

Pile onto dessert dishes and garnish each serving with 2 dates stuffed with the whole almonds. Serve warm or at room temperature.
Yield: 4 half-cup servings

Simple Bulgur

2 tablespoons oil
1 cup bulgur
1 tablespoon chopped onion
2 cups chicken broth or water
½ teaspoon salt
dash pepper

Put the oil in a skillet; add bulgur and onion. Stir and cook until golden. Add broth and seasonings. Cover and bring to a boil; reduce heat; simmer 15 or 20 minutes, without stirring.
Yield: 6 half-cup servings

A Dozen No-Meat Meals

As we mentioned earlier, good alternatives to meat protein include grains, legumes, eggs, and several dairy products. Each is good alone, but is actually more valuable when two or more are combined for protein complementarity. (Again, see page 72.)

The meals that follow make use of a variety of these protein alternatives, but use no meat, fish, or poultry. We've given you ideas for complete meals rather than just individual dishes to show how to complement flavor, texture, and food value of one dish with all the others in that meal. In these menus desserts and side dishes as well as the entrées provide the necessary nutrients. There is a recipe for each dish that is marked with an asterisk (*).

Look the recipes over and try as

many as you like. We hope you'll be pleased enough with them to turn to other cookbooks and your own imagination for other meatless meals.

Meal #1

*Supreme Sauce D'Oeufs
Steamed Brown Rice
Salad with Herbs
Sliced Chilled Watermelon

*(Dishes with asterisk have recipes following.)

Supreme Sauce D'Oeufs

6 eggs, hard-cooked
¾ pound green beans (1 10-ounce package frozen)
1⅓ cups skim milk powder
4 tablespoons safflower oil
4 tablespoons whole wheat flour
1 tablespoon chopped fresh chives
1 teaspoon dried basil
½ teaspoon salt

Hard-cook and peel eggs.

Cook beans which have been cut into 1-inch pieces, in an inch of boiling water until just tender. Drain beans and save cooking water. Add the bean cooking water to the skim milk powder. Now add water to make 1 quart of skim milk.

Put oil in skillet and slowly add flour to make a paste. On medium heat, add the skim milk slowly to the flour-oil mixture until the entire quart is added. Keep stirring the mixture until it is slightly thickened. Add chives, basil, and salt.

Pour the sauce over the beans and eggs in a casserole dish. The dish can be covered and heated briefly in the oven or kept till serving time.

Yield: 8 servings

Meal #2

*Baked Spinach and Macaroni
*Israeli Carrot Salad
Whole Wheat Bread
* Assorted Fruit with Honey-Lime Dressing

Baked Spinach and Macaroni

3 10-ounce packages frozen chopped spinach, cooked and drained
1½ cups milk
6 eggs, beaten
2 teaspoons salt
¼ teaspoon pepper
1 tablespoon grated onion
1 tablespoon vinegar
3 tablespoons butter, melted
5 ounces whole wheat macaroni (or spaghetti), cooked and drained
3 eggs, slightly beaten
salt and pepper
2 tablespoons butter

Cook and drain spinach. Combine next 7 ingredients. Stir in spinach. Spoon into 3-quart ring mold.

Combine macaroni or spaghetti, beaten eggs, salt, and pepper. Mix until blended and spoon over spinach mixture. Dot with butter. Set mold in baking pan. Pour boiling water to depth of 1 inch into baking pan. Bake at 350°F. for 1¼ to 1½ hours until spinach is set and macaroni is brown.
Yield: 14 to 16 servings

Israeli Carrot Salad

1 pound carrots
½ cup orange juice
2 tablespoons sesame seeds
½ cup raisins
2 oranges, peeled and sectioned

Cut carrots into 1-inch pieces. Grate a few at a time with orange juice in blender. Put mixture in a bowl. Garnish with sesame seeds, raisins, and orange sections. Chill.
Yield: 4 servings

Assorted Fruit with Honey-Lime Dressing

2 medium nectarines
1 small honeydew melon
½ pint blueberries
⅓ cup honey
3 tablespoons lime juice
mint leaves for garnish

Cut nectarines into wedges; cut honeydew into bite-size chunks. In medium bowl, combine all ingredients except mint leaves. Cover and refrigerate 1 hour until well blended. Dish out into individual portions and garnish with mint sprigs.
Yield: 6 servings

Meal #3

*Creamy Avocado and Zucchini Salad
*Bulgur with Corn, Carrots, and Seasonings
Whole Wheat Muffins
*Strawberry Yogurt Sherbet

Creamy Avocado and Zucchini Salad

¼ cup plain yogurt
2 tablespoons mayonnaise
½ teaspoon salt
⅛ teaspoon basil
⅛ teaspoon oregano
1 small garlic clove, minced

1 medium avocado, cut into bite-size pieces
1 pound zucchini, thinly sliced (approximately 3 small zucchini)
romaine leaves

In large bowl, combine yogurt, mayonnaise, salt, basil, oregano, and minced garlic. Gently stir in avocado and zucchini until well mixed. Spoon mixture onto romaine-lined platter. Chill until ready to serve.
Yield: 8 servings

Bulgur with Corn, Carrots, and Seasonings

2 tablespoons salad oil
1 egg
2 cups bulgur
5 cups water
2 cups cooked corn or 1 10-ounce package frozen corn
2 carrots cut into 2-inch lengths and into sticks
½ teaspoon marjoram
3 tablespoons chopped fresh parsley

Heat oil in pan. Beat egg and add bulgur, combining them completely. Add to oil and heat mixture until dry.
Boil water. Stir in corn, carrots, marjoram, parsley, and bulgur-egg mixture. Turn heat to low, cover, and simmer until all water is absorbed and carrots are tender (approximately 10 minutes).
Yield: 8 servings

Strawberry Yogurt Sherbet

1 pint frozen strawberries in light honey-water syrup*
1 envelope unflavored gelatin
1½ cups yogurt

At least 4 hours before serving, drain ½ cup strawberry syrup into small saucepan. Sprinkle gelatin evenly over syrup; cook over low heat, stirring constantly, until gelatin is dissolved.

In large bowl, stir gelatin mixture, strawberries and remaining syrup, and yogurt until well combined. Cover bowl and freeze mixture until partially frozen, about 1½ hours.

With mixer at medium speed, beat mixture until smooth but still frozen, scraping bowl with rubber spatula. Cover and freeze 2 hours longer or until firm. (If firm, let sherbet stand at room temperature about 10 minutes for easier serving.)
Yield: 6 servings

*Note: Strawberries were frozen with a syrup of 1½ cups of water to ½ cup of honey and 8 teaspoons of lemon juice. Cook sauce a few minutes to combine ingredients.

Meal #4

*Vegetarian Nut Patties
Steamed Snow Peas with Bamboo Shoots and Soy Sauce
*Vegetable Salad Medley
Whole Wheat Bread
Blueberries and Skim Milk

Vegetarian Nut Patties

1 cup soft bread crumbs
1 tablespoon butter
1 cup cooked rice
2 teaspoons sage
½ teaspoon paprika
¾ cup chopped cashews
¾ cup chopped walnuts
2 eggs, beaten
½ teaspoon salt
¼ teaspoon celery seed
1 teaspoon minced onion
¼ cup oil

Combine all ingredients, except oil, thoroughly. Shape as patties and sauté until golden brown in the oil.
Yield: 6 to 8 servings

Vegetable Salad Medley

2 large tomatoes, sliced
1 medium onion, thinly sliced
1 large green pepper, cut in rings
1 medium cucumber, thinly sliced
salt
3 tablespoons cider vinegar
1 tablespoon salad oil
1 teaspoon paprika
½ teaspoon dry mustard
½ teaspoon celery seed

In shallow dish, arrange vegetables in single layers, sprinkling each layer lightly with salt. In a cup, stir remaining ingredients until well combined; pour over vegetables. Cover and refrigerate several hours or overnight.
Yield: 4 servings

Meal #5

*Baked Vegetable Omelette
*Chilled Marinated Celery
Whole Wheat Bread
*Plum Betty

Baked Vegetable Omelette

1 zucchini, thinly sliced
1 carrot, grated
½ small onion, grated
1 potato, grated
dash salt
1 cup whole wheat bread crumbs
2 eggs, beaten
¼ cup alfalfa sprouts

Preheat oven to 350°F.

Combine all ingredients, except alfalfa sprouts, in bowl, mixing well. Oil a 1½-quart casserole and pour mixture into casserole. Bake for about 20 minutes, or until eggs have set. Top with alfalfa sprouts before serving.
Yield: 4 servings

Chilled Marinated Celery

1 bunch celery
¼ cup safflower oil
¼ cup sliced pimentos
2 tablespoons wine vinegar
½ teaspoon salt
1 tablespoon sesame seeds

Trim celery and cut into 4-inch lengths; cut each length into 4 slices lengthwise. Boil 1 inch of water in a skillet. Add celery and return water to boiling. Reduce heat and cover. Simmer 15 minutes.

Combine remaining ingredients except sesame seeds in a baking pan. Drain celery and place celery in baking dish. Baste celery with marinade. Cover baking dish and refrigerate until chilled. Before serving, place celery on a leafy green and sprinkle sesame seeds over celery.
Yield: 6 servings

Plum Betty

4 cups plums, pitted
6 tablespoons water
4 to 6 tablespoons honey to taste
1 tablespoon lemon juice
4 cups whole grain bread, cubed (7 or 8 slices)
¼ cup butter
¼ teaspoon nutmeg
⅜ teaspoon cinnamon
2 tablespoons honey
whipped cream for garnish

Preheat oven to 350°F.
Combine plums & water and simmer until fruit is tender. Stir in honey and lemon juice.
Sauté bread cubes in butter, sprinkling spices over bread as it browns. Drizzle 2 tablespoons honey over bread cubes and stir to coat evenly. Put one-third of bread cubes in a buttered casserole. Spread half of cooked plums over layer of bread, then another layer of bread, then the remainder of the plums and finally the top layer of bread.
Bake in preheated oven for 20 to 30 minutes, until plums are boiling and top is brown. Serve warm with whipped cream.
Yield: 4 to 6 servings

Meal #6

*Baked Broccoli and Cheese Timbale
*Buckwheat Pilaf
Fresh Vegetable Salad
*Macédoine of Fruit

Baked Broccoli and Cheese Timbale

1 10-ounce package frozen chopped broccoli
¾ cup nonfat dry milk powder
¾ cup shredded Swiss cheese
2 eggs
2 tablespoons lemon juice
2 tablespoons butter, melted
⅛ teaspoon pepper
½ teaspoon dry mustard
1¼ cups hot water

Cook broccoli according to package directions and drain. Beat remaining ingredients until combined. Place broccoli in a 1½-quart casserole. Pour cheese-milk mixture over broccoli.
Set casserole in shallow pan on oven rack; add hot water to measure 1 inch around casserole. Bake at 350°F. for 40 to 45 minutes or until knife inserted in center comes out clean and top is browned.
Yield: 6 servings

Buckwheat Pilaf

1½ cups buckwheat groats (be sure to buy hulled groats)
1 egg, beaten
1¼ cups water
1¼ cups tomato juice
1 small onion, chopped
½ green pepper, chopped
3 tablespoons oil
1 pound fresh mushrooms or 1 8-ounce can, drained
salt to taste
⅓ cup cheddar cheese, grated

Put buckwheat groats into skillet or heavy-bottom sauce-pan. Stir in a beaten egg and cook over medium heat, stir-ring until grains separate (just a minute or two). Gradually add water and tomato juice, stirring constantly. Cover and cook over low heat for about 15 minutes, or until the liquid is absorbed.

Meanwhile, in another skillet, sauté onion and green pepper in oil until onion is golden brown.

When the groats are cooked, combine them with the sautéed vegetables. Salt to taste. Place pilaf in oven-proof serving dish, garnish with grated cheese, and place under the broiler or in the oven. Melt the cheese until it bubbles and browns slightly before serving.
Yield: 6 to 8 servings

Macédoine of Fruit

¼ cup raisins
white grape juice
4 dried figs, chopped
1 red apple, diced
1 orange, peeled and sliced
1 pear, diced
1 banana, sliced
flaked coconut
sunflower seeds

Soak the raisins overnight in white grape juice. Combine all fruits and raisins in grape juice. Top with flaked coconut and sunflower seeds.
Yield: 6 to 8 servings

Meal #7

*Savory Onion Tart
Green Beans with Sautéed Sunflower Seeds
Scalloped Tomatoes
Whole Grain Bread
*Puréed Fruit in Season

Savory Onion Tart

1½ cups dry whole grain bread crumbs
4 tablespoons oil
4 tablespoons butter, melted
1 pound onions (approximately 3 cups), peeled and sliced thin
2 tablespoons oil
1 tablespoon butter
3 eggs
1 cup cottage cheese (not the dry kind)
2 tablespoons lemon juice
1 teaspoon oregano*
1 teaspoon basil
½ teaspoon salt
¼ teaspoon paprika
dash of freshly ground black pepper

Preheat oven to 400°F.
In a bowl, combine crumbs, oil, and melted butter. Press crumbs into lightly oiled 9-inch pie plate. Bring up sides to form an even edge.
Sauté onions in oil and butter until they are somewhat transparent but not brown. Set aside to cool while mixing remaining ingredients.
Put eggs, cottage cheese, lemon juice, herbs, and seasonings into blender container and blend until mixture is smooth.

Combine mixture with sautéed onions and pour into prepared pie shell.

Bake in preheated oven for 10 minutes. Lower heat to 300°F. and bake for 10 minutes longer or until filling is set. Serve piping hot.

Yield: 8 servings

*Herbs or seasonings such as dill, parsley, caraway, or celery seeds, may be substituted.

Puréed Fruit in Season

2 cups water
1 pint strawberries or other berry in season
2 slices lemon
1 cinnamon stick
potato starch
2 tablespoons honey

Combine the water, strawberries, lemon slices, and cinnamon stick in a saucepan. Bring the sauce to a boil, lower the heat, and simmer for about ½ hour. Remove the cinnamon stick and the lemon. Purée the mixture in the blender or a food mill.

For every 2 cups of purée, add 1½ teaspoons of potato starch. Add the potato starch to a small amount of purée and dissolve completely before combining with remaining mixture. Add the honey to the purée and stir with a wire whisk. Bring the purée to a boil, stirring constantly. Remove from heat and pour into serving bowl and chill. This purée can be dished into individual serving dishes as well. This dessert can be poured over cakes or yogurt.

Yield: 4 to 6 servings

Meal #8

*Tomato, Eggplant, and Potato Stew
*Rice Casserole
*Cheese and Lima Bean Salad
Whole Wheat Bread
*Raspberry Yogurt

Tomato, Eggplant, and Potato Stew

2 tablespoons oil
2 medium onions, sliced
1 medium eggplant, cubed
5 medium potatoes, cubed
1 28-ounce can tomatoes
2 teaspoons salt
¼ teaspoon pepper

In hot oil, cook onions until golden. Add remaining ingredients; simmer, covered, 20 minutes or until vegetables are tender.
Yield: 8 servings

Rice Casserole

2¼ cups water
1 cup brown rice
1 teaspoon salt
bay leaf
20 fresh mushrooms, sliced
2 onions, chopped
2 garlic cloves, mashed
2 tablespoons oil
pinch thyme
salt and pepper to taste

Boil water. Add rice and salt and turn temperature to low. Add bay leaf, cover pot, and simmer until all the water is absorbed, about 30 minutes.

Sauté mushrooms, onion, and garlic in oil until soft. Toss together with rice and seasonings in casserole. Can be reheated.
Yield: 4 servings

Cheese and Lima Bean Salad

1 10-ounce package frozen lima beans, cooked and drained
1 8-ounce package cheddar cheese, diced
1 cup chopped celery
10 to 12 radishes, thinly sliced (1 cup)
1 small onion, chopped
¼ cup mayonnaise
2 tablespoons yogurt
½ teaspoon salt
dash pepper
lettuce leaves

In medium bowl, stir all ingredients except lettuce until well combined. Serve on lettuce.
Yield: 4 servings

Raspberry Yogurt

1 pint raspberries, cleaned and sliced
1 cup yogurt
2 tablespoons honey

Combine above ingredients.
Yield: 6 servings

Meal #9

*Zucchini Puffs
*Marinated Vegetables
Fresh Spinach with Oil and Vinegar Dressing
*Walnut Apple Dessert

Zucchini Puffs

½ cup shredded cheddar cheese
2 cups shredded zucchini
3 tablespoons grated onion
½ cup whole wheat bread crumbs
½ teaspoon salt
¼ teaspoon basil
¼ teaspoon parsley
2 eggs
3½ tablespoons whole wheat flour
¼ cup safflower oil

Combine all ingredients except safflower oil. Stir with a fork until well blended.

In a 12-cup muffin pan, spoon 1 teaspoon of safflower oil into each cup. Heat the pan for a few minutes in the oven. Carefully spoon the batter evenly into the muffin cups. Bake at 375°F. for 20 minutes or until golden brown.

Yield: 12 puffs

Marinated Vegetables

1½ pounds of zucchini
18 large cherry tomatoes
½ pound small mushrooms
½ cup oil
3 tablespoons wine vinegar
¼ teaspoon dried marjoram
¼ teaspoon basil
1 tablespoon parsley
½ teaspoon salt

Cut zucchini into ½-inch slices. Combine all ingredients in a small bowl and let marinate for about 4 hours in the refrigerator.

These can be eaten raw or the dressing can be drained off the vegetables. Heat the salad dressing and then add vegetables and quickly stir-fry the vegetables about 10 minutes or until they are just tender crisp.
Yield: 6 servings

Walnut Apple Dessert

⅓ cup butter
2 cups soft whole wheat bread crumbs
4 large apples, sliced
¼ cup honey
½ teaspoon cinnamon
¼ teaspoon nutmeg
½ cup walnuts
1 tablespoon lemon juice
¼ cup water

Melt butter; toss with crumbs. In 1½-quart baking dish, arrange half the apples; sprinkle with half the honey and spices, half the walnuts, half the crumbs.

Top with remaining apples. Mix lemon juice with water; drizzle over the top. Sprinkle with remaining ingredients. Cover and bake at 350°F. for 30 minutes. Uncover and bake 30 minutes longer till apples are tender and top is crusty and brown.
Yield: 6 to 8 servings

Meal #10

*Barley and Lentil Kasha
*Zucchini and Scalloped Tomatoes
*Peach Soufflé

Barley and Lentil Kasha

1 cup dry lentils
water for soaking and cooking lentils
½ cup pearled barley
2 cups vegetable stock
1 pound fresh mushrooms, sliced, or 1 8-ounce can, drained
4 to 6 green onions and tops or 2 medium-sized yellow onions
4 tablespoons oil
4 tablespoons butter
½ to ¾ cup tomato juice
½ teaspoon marjoram
½ teaspoon oregano
½ teaspoon basil
salt and pepper to taste
chopped parsley for garnish

Soak lentils for 30 minutes. Drain water off. Add fresh water until it is 1 inch above lentils. Bring to a boil, turn heat down, and simmer over medium heat for 30 minutes or until soft. Add drained lentils to cooked barley.

Wash and slice fresh mushrooms or drain canned ones. Reserve juice to add later with tomato juice. Sauté onions and mushrooms in oil and butter for about 5 minutes. Set aside some mushrooms for garnish. Add lentil-barley mixture, sautéing lightly. Add tomato juice, herbs, salt, and pepper to taste. Garnish with chopped parsley and mushrooms before serving.
Yield: 6 servings

Zucchini and Scalloped Tomatoes

1 small onion, diced
1 green pepper, diced
1 stalk celery, cubed (about ½ cup)
2 tablespoons salad oil
2 cups tomatoes or tomato juice
1 large zucchini, sliced
½ cup grated cheddar cheese

Sauté onion, green pepper, and celery in oil until golden and wilted. Add tomatoes and zucchini and simmer until the zucchini is tender.

Pour mixture into a quart casserole and top with the cheese. Place in the oven and bake at 350°F. until cheese is melted.

Yield: 4 servings

Peach Soufflé

¼ cup butter
5 tablespoons whole grain flour (rye or wheat)
½ cup orange juice
2 tablespoons lemon juice
2 cups peach purée (unsweetened)
¼ cup honey
4 egg yolks
½ teaspoon nutmeg
12 egg whites
peach sauce or vanilla sauce as accompaniment (see recipe in this book)

Preheat oven to 400°F.

In saucepan, melt butter, add flour, and cook 1 minute or so. Then add orange and lemon juice, stirring until smooth. Add peach purée and honey, stirring to blend.

Remove from heat and combine with egg yolks, by blending a little of the hot mixture into the egg yolks first, and then stirring this gradually back into the hot mixture. Blend in nutmeg.

Beat egg whites until stiff. Fold carefully into hot mixture and turn into ungreased souffle dish. Bake in preheated oven 10 minutes. Turn heat down to 375°F. and continue to bake for 15 to 20 minutes or until puffed up and golden on top. Serve immediately. Serve peach sauce or vanilla sauce separately.

Yield: 4 to 6 servings

Meal #11

*Soyballs and Whole Wheat Spaghetti
*Fresh Spinach Salad
*Blueberry Custard Pie

Soyballs

3 cups cooked soybeans
9 tablespoons safflower oil
1½ onions, chopped
1½ cups peanuts
1½ carrots
3 eggs, well beaten
¾ cup whole grain bread crumbs
1½ tablespoons tamari soy sauce
1½ garlic cloves

Soak and cook soybeans the day before.

Heat about 2 to 4 tablespoons safflower oil in a skillet. Add onions and sauté until golden. Put soybeans, peanuts, and carrots through meat grinder. Add onions, eggs, bread crumbs, and soy sauce to the ground mixture. Shape into balls. Mince garlic and heat remaining oil in skillet. Add garlic and stir until garlic is lightly browned. Add the balls and sauté until the balls are nicely browned.

Yield: 36 balls

Whole Wheat Spaghetti

1½ pounds whole wheat spaghetti
½ cup butter
2 cups grated Parmesan cheese
2 cups finely chopped parsley

Cook spaghetti until tender and drain in a colander. Turn out into large serving bowl and toss with butter, Parmesan cheese, and parsley.
Yield: 12 servings

Fresh Spinach Salad

1 pound fresh spinach, torn into pieces
3 oranges, sectioned
⅔ cup safflower oil
⅓ cup orange juice
1 tablespoon honey
1 tablespoon vinegar
¼ teaspoon salt
¼ teaspoon dry mustard

Wash the spinach and place in bowl. Add oranges. Combine remaining ingredients and pour over salad.
Yield: 6 to 8 servings

Blueberry Custard Pie

1 9-inch pie crust
2 cups fresh blueberries or 1 pound frozen blueberries (unsweetened)
6 tablespoons honey
¼ teaspoon cinnamon
pinch nutmeg
3 eggs
1 cup yogurt
1 tablespoon arrowroot or cornstarch (omit if using fresh blueberries)

Preheat oven to 400°F.

If using fresh blueberries, combine them with the honey, seasoning, eggs, and yogurt.

If using frozen blueberries, heat them with the honey for a few minutes, stirring constantly, just to thaw them. Do not cook them. Drain well. You should have 2 cups berries and 1 cup juice, approximately. Combine berries with seasonings, eggs, and yogurt. Dissolve arrowroot or cornstarch in blueberry juice and add to berry mixture.

Pour blueberry mixture into unbaked pie crust. Bake for 10 minutes in preheated oven. Turn down oven to 325°F. and bake for 25 minutes longer or until filling is set. Serve warm or cold.

Yield: 1 9-inch pie

Meal #12

*Creamy Vegetable Soup
*Oatmeal and Nut Roast
Steamed Green Beans
*Yogurt Banana Dessert

Creamy Vegetable Soup

1 small onion, sliced
½ green pepper, slivered
2 tablespoons oil
½ cup shredded carrot (1 carrot)
3 cups corn
2 cups water
2 tablespoons flour
1½ teaspoons salt
2 cups milk

Cook onion and pepper in oil until golden. Add rest of ingredients except milk. Cook until vegetables are tender. Add milk slowly and heat until milk is warm. Do not boil.

Yield: 8 servings

Oatmeal and Nut Roast

1½ cups cooked oatmeal
2 eggs, beaten
½ cup walnuts, chopped
½ cup cashews, chopped
2 tablespoons safflower oil
⅓ cup powdered nonfat dry milk
¼ cup grated onion
2 teaspoons concentrated yeast extract
⅔ cup cottage cheese
½ teaspoon salt
½ teaspoon sage

Mix all ingredients together. Place in well-buttered loaf pan. Bake at 375°F. for 45 minutes.
Yield: 8 servings

Yogurt Banana Dessert

(no sugar or honey added)

1 cup shredded, unsweetened coconut (fresh or dried)
3 to 4 tablespoons butter
⅛ to ¼ teaspoon cinnamon to taste
⅛ teaspoon nutmeg to taste
4 small bananas, sliced ½-inch thick
1 cup yogurt

Over low heat, sauté ¾ cup coconut in half the amount of butter, stirring constantly. Reserve remaining coconut. Add spices to taste, while sautéing the coconut, then stir in banana, using more butter if needed, and continue to sauté just until banana is cooked and coconut is light brown. Be careful not to burn it.

Add yogurt, stirring it in gradually. Remove from heat and pour into individual dessert dishes. Chill completely.

Toast remaining ¼ cup coconut in a low oven for 5 to 10 minutes or until it is light brown. Watch it carefully. Sprinkle some over each dessert before serving.
Yield: 4 servings

Ethnic Cooking—
Often a Matter of Making Do

Lots of places around the world have made a real art of eating low off the hog because they've had to do it for centuries. It takes a creative and resourceful cook to make bland bean and grain dishes aromatic and flavorful, find a multitude of ways to use only the fruits and vegetables in season, and use every bit of meat or fish so as not to waste any of the expensive food. Probably the best and most wholesome traditional dishes of the world have come out of making do with what was available.

We've chosen four of the cuisines that have mastered the art of combining cheaper cuts of meat and less expensive vegetable proteins with rich sauces, relishes, and spices to create exciting dishes that appeal to the nose, the eyes, and the taste buds. Researching and writing about the cooking of Japan, India, the Middle East, and Mexico was fascinating, and we hope you'll find the exotic quality of these cuisines attractive enough to make you want to try some of the recipes we've included.

Japanese Cooking

Formal Japanese cuisine is considered an artistic form of expression equivalent to flower arranging. A beautifully presented dish is intended to be food for the soul as well as the body. The Japanese take delight in form, flavor, texture, and color, and most ingredients are prepared so that each retains its own uniqueness. A whole fish may be cleaned and carved into bite-sized pieces and then artistically arranged to resemble the live fish. A bowl of clear soup may have floating in it a carrot cut to resemble a maple leaf or a radish shaped like a flower bud. Each food is cut to a certain shape and size and either served alone, to be mixed at

the table with any of many sauces, broths, and pickles, or cooked seconds before serving with a few other foods or subtle sauces.

In the countryside of Japan the cooking is less formal, but there is still the same respect for each food's own characteristics. Here too the foods are cooked only a few minutes — just long enough to soften them slightly, never causing them to lose their color, flavor, or much of their food value.

Japanese cooking is a good example of an efficient, natural cuisine. Foods are steamed, braised, boiled, or grilled. Little oil is used; even soups are oil- and fat-free. Vegetable oils (especially unrefined sesame, which has a pleasant nutty flavor) are used more for seasoning than they are for cooking as such. Only a few drops are used to season any one dish. Frying, sautéing, and the use of animal fats are not traditionally Japanese, although many cooks have now adopted them.

Japanese foods are built around rice just as ours are built around meat. Poultry and pork are sometimes used, beef much less, and when meat is used it is as one ingredient among several vegetables. This is not only a good way to save money, it's important for people who must watch their cholesterol intake. Yet Japanese people do not lack protein, due to the extensive use of fish, eggs, and tofu (soybean curd).

Fish supplies high quality protein — in most fish, the quality is superior even to that of meat. Four ounces of fish can supply 40 to 50 percent of the needed daily protein requirement. It is especially high in lysine — the amino acid which is limited in rice. This explains why rice and fish together provide an adequate staple diet for the people of Japan.

Tofu (soybean curd), a staple food which is eaten at every meal in some form, is made from soybean milk and among plant proteins ranks very high in quality — above all other legumes and grains except rice. It is also very low in calories. The soybeans are soaked, ground, or put into an electric blender and chopped, then cooked, and the milk is strained off. To make tofu, a precipitating agent is added to the soy milk. Lemon juice may be used, though some prefer either magnesium sulfate or calcium sulfate, which causes the milk to separate into curds (tofu) and whey. Tofu can be purchased fresh at Oriental food markets, or it is sometimes available canned and in powdered form. It can be made in your own home. For directions and where to get a tofu press, see *The Book of Tofu* in the list at the end of the book.

Another soy food which is indispensable to Japanese cooking is "miso," a fermented soybean paste. This is considered an essential flavoring and thickener for soups, sauces, and marinades. There are two basic types of miso — shiro or white, which is light beige in color and milder in flavor, and aka or red, which is dark brown and stronger in flavor. The type of miso varies with the length of time the soybeans are fermented and the type of grain added to act as catalyst for the fermentation. Rice bran malt makes a lighter miso, and wheat bran malt is used to make the darker kind. Misoshi, a hearty soup with full-bodied flavor, is the national breakfast beverage, looked upon in Japan as we look upon coffee.

There are as many as 21 edible varieties of seaweed used in Japanese cooking. Seaweed supplies a major portion of calcium in the Japanese diet as well as appreciable amounts of iron, iodine, potassium, magnesium, phosphorus, vitamins A, B_2, and niacin. Four of the most popular varieties are hijiki, kombu, nori, and wakame.

Hijiki is a small, spindle-shaped seaweed which contains 57 percent more calcium by weight than dry milk, and is rich in iron. One tablespoon of cooked hijiki contains the same amount of calcium as a glass of milk. Hijiki is sautéed with vegetables, or added to cooked soybeans, soups, or salads.

Kombu, also called kelp, is especially rich in iodine, vitamin B_2, and calcium. Dashi, the delicate fish stock which is the basis for most of the soups and many of the vegetable and meat dishes, is made from kombu and dried bonito flakes. There are six main species of kombu used for food in Japan, each one being appropriate for a certain kind of dish. One type is added to simmering vegetables, another to salads, one is used as an hors d'oeuvre — even a kind of chewing gum and a chewy candy are made from a species of kombu.

Nori, also called dried purple laver, is usually sold in the form of purplish-black, paper-thin sheets. Nori contains an abundant supply of protein, and vitamins A, B_2, B_{12}, D, and niacin. Each individual sheet of nori is toasted by holding it above a hot burner until it turns a sort of brownish-green color and becomes rather brittle. Then it is crumbled or slivered for a garnish with chilled tofu, buckwheat noodles, or in soups and rice dishes. Nori is an essential ingredient in maki-zushi, one of the many variations of sushi. Basically a vinegared rice to which is added various seasonings or sauces, braised vegetables, fish, or sometimes an omelet cut into fine strips, sushi is the Japanese national dish. In maki-zushi, the rice is spread on a toasted sheet of nori and rolled into a cylinder with a hot radish or another tasty filling in the center. Then the cylinder is cut into one-inch thick slices. These are served as appetizers and as a sort of Japanese "sandwich."

Wakame contains 50 percent more calcium than dry milk and is rich in protein and niacin. In Japan, it is very popular as an ingredient in miso soups and is often added to simmered vegetables. Considered to have the best flavor and texture, it is usually sold fresh in Japan. It is simply cut into short lengths and served as it is, or if it is added to soups, it is only cooked one minute. It is well suited to Western-style dishes too, such as salads or sandwiches. Dried wakame can be soaked and used in the same way as the fresh.

The large amount of calcium in these different varieties of seaweed, together with the fact that seaweeds comprise 20 percent of the Japanese diet, explains why the Japanese get along so well without dairy products. Seaweed is as much a part of their daily food as is milk or cheese a part of ours.

Breakfast in Japan might consist of miso shiru (soybean paste soup), a bowl of rice topped with a raw egg, two or three thin sheets of nori, and a dish of pickles. For lunch, there might be chawan mushi (steamed custard) and a clear soup with some kind of sushi (vinegared rice dish, garnished with nori), while the evening meal would almost certainly include at least one fish entrée, perhaps a teriyaki, as well as a chicken and vegetable simmered dish and steamed rice. If the weather is cool a soup would probably be served, but it might be served toward the end of the meal as is the custom at formal occasions. Salads or relishes as we know them are not a part of Japanese cuisine, but their aemono and sunomono can be considered salads in the sense that they are usually either a mixture of vegetables, fish, or poultry tossed with dressings and sauces, or vegetables alone or with fish in vinegared dressings. They are served as side dishes.

The Japanese use sesame seeds liberally as a seasoning. Whether they are added to fish or vegetables, whether in sushi or in a dressing for tofu, they are always lightly toasted in a dry skillet before being added. Often they are ground with mortar and pestle (or in a blender) to release their full flavor. One interesting fact about sesame seeds is that, unhulled, they are exceptionally high in calcium and proportionately low in phosphorus — a fact that sets them apart from all other seeds.

Most people take in ample phosphorus if they eat any meat, cheese, whole grains, or nuts, but do not find it quite so easy to eat enough calcium-rich foods. Sesame oil too is used to some extent, giving a distinctive flavor to a sauce or dressing.

As we explained earlier (see page 293), eating fresh bean sprouts is a pleasant way to increase your intake of vitamins. There are not as many Japanese recipes which call for fresh bean sprouts as one would expect, but of course sprouts can be added to almost any of the traditional dishes. Soups, braised vegetables, pickles, sukiyaki, and sushi all will be enhanced nutritionally, and if not entirely authentic, they will be delicious, and who knows — they could be an improvement on the original.

In the recipes that follow, sugar and MSG (monosodium glutamate) have been omitted because they're really unnecessary and not very good for you. Tamari soy sauce is called for because it does not contain MSG, and brown rice is used instead of the more traditional polished white rice. If rice vinegar is not available, white distilled vinegar may be substituted. If dried bonito flakes are difficult to obtain, dried anchovies may be used. Wherever possible, even if ingredients must be ordered by mail, it is worth the extra trouble to get the true Japanese products, because they do impart a particularly authentic (and delicious) flavor. Canned bamboo shoots and water chestnuts are interchangeable and widely available. But in many recipes there simply are no substitutions for tofu, seaweed, or miso. Sometimes Chinese or Japanese restaurants will sell these items. Fresh tofu will keep well for a week in the refrigerator if it is kept submerged in cold water and the water is changed every day. Miso will keep indefinitely in the refrigerator. Fresh gingerroot is being sold now in some supermarkets. It does not keep well refrigerated but can be frozen very easily. Just freeze without peeling, then take out as much as you need for a recipe and peel, grate, or chop. Powdered dry ginger can't be substituted in every case because the volatile oil present in the fresh ginger has largely disappeared in the dry, and the fresh and dry gingers impart quite different tastes.

Unhulled sesame seeds can be bought in natural foods stores and are much less expensive than those little jars of sesame seeds in the supermarket spice racks. For sesame oil which has not been refined and which retains its full flavor, it may be necessary to visit an Oriental foods store.

Daikon, the Japanese radish, and hakusai, the curly sort of Japanese cabbage, can be bought also at an Oriental foods store, or often the cabbage, called "celery cabbage," is available in supermarkets. White turnips can be substituted for daikon.

Our Japanese Menu
Miso Shiru
Maki-Zushi
Japanese Cabbage with Hijiki
Bean Sprouts, Spinach, and Cucumber with
Sesame Dressing
"Japanese" Rice
Fish Teriyaki
Chawan Mushi

Miso Shiru
(soybean paste soup)

¼ pound raw shrimp (optional)
5 cups dashi I (see below)
1 cup miso shiru (white)
1 square of tofu (fresh bean curd) about 3 inches square
4 scallions including tops, sliced thin

If using shrimp, shell, devein, and cut into bite-sized pieces.

Bring shrimp to a boil in dashi and simmer 5 minutes. Add miso to soup by pushing it through a strainer with the back of a spoon over the soup, dipping the strainer briefly into the liquid until the miso is all blended in. Keep soup warm but do not boil.

Cut tofu into ¾-inch cubes. Serve each bowl individually, adding tofu and scallions just before serving.

Yield: approximately 6 cups

Dashi I

5 1-inch pieces kombu seaweed
5 cups water
1 cup dried fish (dried bonito flakes), or substitute dried anchovies
2 teaspoons tamari soy sauce

Rinse kombu well, place in water, and bring to a boil. Remove kombu and reserve. While broth is still boiling, add dried bonito flakes. Remove from heat and let stand for about 3 minutes. Strain the broth, reserve bonito, and add tamari soy sauce to the broth.
Yield: 5 cups

Dashi II

⅓ cup dried fish (dried bonito flakes), or substitute dried anchovies
3 cups water
reserved kombu and dried fish from dashi I

Combine all ingredients, bring to a boil, remove from heat, and strain.
Yield: 3 cups

Note: For miso shiru (soybean paste soup), use dashi I.
 For Japanese cabbage with hijiki and chawan mushi, use dashi II.

Maki-Zushi

(sushi wrapped in seaweed — a simplified version)

2 cups cooked rice (very well cooked and sticky)
¼ cup rice vinegar or white distilled vinegar
3 Chinese mushrooms or 6 large white mushrooms
dashi II
4 ounces fish (sea trout, bluefish, bass, mackerel, turbot, etc).
¼ cup bamboo shoots, cut into fine strips
½ cup carrots, cut into fine strips
4 sheets nori (paper-thin seaweed)
4 tablespoons tamari soy sauce
4 tablespoons water

Toss rice gently, while it is still hot, with vinegar. Cool to room temperature. Soak mushrooms in hot water to cover, until they are soft. Drain, squeeze water out, and reserve water. Cut out and discard stems; cut tops into strips. Add dashi to mushroom water to make 1 cup liquid, then simmer fish in this until tender (about 10 to 15 minutes). Lift fish out and set aside to cool. When cool, skin and bone fish.

Using the same liquid the fish cooked in, simmer mushrooms, bamboo shoots, and carrots until tender. Drain. Add vegetables and flaked fish to rice, tossing all ingredients together lightly.

Toast nori, by holding one sheet at a time above a burner on high heat, waving it back and forth until it has turned a dark green-brown color and has become more rigid. Combine tamari soy sauce and water and spread some over one side of the sheet of nori. Spoon the rice mixture down the center of the sheet of nori. Wrap the nori around it, pulling over and tucking under first one side then the other, to make a cylinder about 1½ inches thick. Cut this cylinder into slices about 1 inch thick and serve at room temperature.

Yield: 4 cylinders of 4 or 5 slices each; approximately 4 servings

Japanese Cabbage with Hijiki

1 pound hakusai (Japanese cabbage or celery cabbage)
1 cup dashi II
½ cup hijiki, soaked in cold water for 20 minutes
1 onion, minced
1 tablespoon sesame oil
1 tablespoon tamari soy sauce

Cut cabbage crosswise into thin slices. Combine with dashi and bring to a boil, simmering until cabbage is tender but still firm to the bite.

Drain hijiki, reserving soaking water for another use, and cut into bite-sized pieces. Sauté onion lightly in sesame oil, add tamari soy sauce and hijiki, and simmer for 5 minutes.

Toss cabbage and onion-hijiki mixture lightly together and serve.

Yield: 4 to 6 servings

Bean Sprouts, Spinach, and Cucumber with Sesame Dressing

½ pound fresh spinach
1 medium-sized cucumber
¼ cup sesame seeds (unhulled)
1 tablespoon tamari soy sauce
1 tablespoon rice vinegar or white distilled vinegar
1 cup fresh mung bean sprouts

Clean spinach and cook it, covered, over medium heat for about 3 minutes with just the amount of water which clings to the leaves after washing it. Chop coarsely.

Peel and seed cucumber, if necessary, and cut into julienne (thin) strips.

Toast sesame seeds in a dry skillet for 1 or 2 minutes, watching them carefully and shaking the pan from time to time so they do not burn. Grind toasted seeds with a mortar and pestle or just "bruise" them with a rolling pin, then mix them with tamari soy sauce and vinegar.

Combine bean sprouts, spinach, and cucumbers and toss lightly in sesame seed dressing.

Yield: 6 to 8 servings

"Japanese" Rice

1 cup brown rice (short grain)
2 cups water

Combine rice and water in a pot with a tight-fitting lid. Bring to a boil, then turn down heat and simmer for 15 minutes. Increase heat to high again and cook for 1 minute. Remove from heat and let stand, covered, for 15 minutes. Do not remove cover or stir during this whole process. Serve rice as soon as possible after it is done.

Yield: approximately 3 cups

Fish Teriyaki

⅔ cup tamari soy sauce
2 tablespoons grated fresh gingerroot or 2½ teaspoons powdered ginger
2 tablespoons honey
¼ cup lemon juice
⅔ cup cold water
1 small garlic clove, minced
¼ cup dry sherry (optional)
2 pounds turbot or any mild-flavored fish

Combine all ingredients except fish. Pour over fish and marinate for at least 5 hours. Broil fish until tender, brushing teriyaki sauce over it several times during the broiling.

Yield: 4 to 6 servings

Chawan Mushi

(steamed custard)

3 eggs, beaten
2 cups dashi II
1 teaspoon salt
1 tablespoon tamari soy sauce
1 raw chicken breast (from 5-pound chicken), cut into thin slices
¼ cup cooked, clean shrimp, diced
3 water chestnuts (canned), diced
1 tablespoon sherry (optional)

In a bowl, mix eggs, dashi, salt, and half of the tamari soy sauce. In another bowl, combine chicken, shrimp, water chestnuts, sherry if you're using it, and the rest of the tamari soy sauce. Divide chicken mixture equally in 6 custard cups. Pour egg mixture into cups filling each almost to the top.

Cover each cup with foil, place on a rack in large pot over boiling water which is about 1½ inches deep. Cover pot first with a tea towel, then loosely with the pot lid. Steam over medium heat for 12 to 15 minutes. Test for doneness by inserting a toothpick. When custard is set, the hole made by the toothpick remains. Do not overcook or custard will separate. Serve warm, not hot.
Yield: 6 servings.

Indian Cooking

In India, spicing food has reached a point of near perfection, and it is this custom perhaps more than any other which distinguishes the cooking of India from that of almost every other country. The test of culinary excellence in India is the nature of the spice mixture or "masala" and the skill with which it is used in the cooking of any particular dish. Rarely are any two masalas exactly the same — a fact that may come as a surprise to us in the West who think of Indian food as curry which is made by  adding curry powder to a cream sauce along with meat, eggs, or vegetables. No Indian cook would ever use a prepared curry powder. Each food or combination of foods, be it fish, meat, or vegetables, calls for an appropriate masala, and the blend of the spices reflects the ingenuity, imagination, and individuality of the cook. Also a spice loses its freshness once it is ground, and most Indian cooks grind the spices needed for the day every morning.

Spices are more than just a seasoning, and Sanskrit writings which are 3,000 years old stress the importance of spices for their preservative and medicinal value. Pepper and chilies were recommended for treating digestive ailments; ginger was thought to cure liver complaints and to counteract flatulence. Turmeric apparently was made into a paste and applied to the skin to stop itching or to clear up skin diseases. Cardamom is served today in modern India at the end of a meal along with cloves and the betel nut and its leaf to freshen the breath and help the digestion. In the Sanskrit treatise, cardamom was described as a remedy for halitosis, nausea, headaches, fevers, colds, piles, and eye diseases. Coriander was recommended for constipation, insomnia, and childbearing. Many of these ideas persist today, and ginger is still added to lentils or peas when they are cooked in order to counteract flatulence. Refrigerators even today are a rarity in India and the preservative function of spice is of obvious importance.

The word "curry" refers to the combination of seasonings with which a food is cooked. These seasonings or masalas can be dry or wet. Wet masalas use fresh or green foods and spices — like chilies, coriander, onions, garlic, or coconut — and these are ground with dry spices and a liquid, which can be water, lime juice, or even coconut milk. These wet masalas are popular in the south of India, where they accompany the plain boiled rice which is served at every meal. The dry masala is a mixture of dry spices which is usually made ahead and stored in an airtight container for up to six months. This dry or garam masala never takes the place of the freshly ground dry spices which are used in every dish. The garam masala is added along with the other spices, as one of the recipe ingredients. The way a masala is used is as important as its ingredients. Spices must never taste raw; they must be mellowed by just the right amount of cooking. You should not be able to taste any one spice more than any other. The masala must provide a subtle flavor which enhances the food rather than dominating it.

There is no such thing as a "typical Indian meal." India,

sometimes called a subcontinent, is made up of many diverse cultures, languages, religions, and climates, and this diversity is reflected in the variety of dishes encountered in the different regions.

The foods in northern India are richer and more elaborate and bear some resemblance to the foods of the Middle East. The influence of the Moghuls from Persia who invaded northern India in the sixteenth century can be seen in the grilled meat kabobs and pulaus (pilafs). Homemade wheat breads, similar to Arab flat bread, are a staple in the north, and ghee (clarified, cooked-down butter) is used for cooking instead of the sesame or coconut oil used in the south. The people in the north drink hot spiced tea sweetened with honey during the cold winters, but the southern Indians favor freshly roasted and ground coffee with sugar and milk.

Lamb is the favored meat in the north, but chicken and duck are also eaten. Seafood of all kinds is a staple in the coastal regions; beef is almost never eaten because the cow is sacred to the Hindu. However, cattle are used for work in the fields and their milk and milk products such as yogurt, buttermilk, cheese, and ghee are a valued part of the Indian diet.

The people who live in the south are also mostly vegetarian. Rice is the main staple and it is eaten at every meal and sometimes in several different forms. It may be steamed, boiled, fried, ground into flour for pancakes, or pressed or puffed for a sweet snack. There is a wide variety of rices to choose from — long grain which is best for pulaus, round grain for sweets, rice that is polished, parboiled, partly husked, etc.

Vegetarian cookery relies heavily on lentils, dried beans, and peas. Dal, the Hindi name for all members of the legume family, also refers to a sauce made from lentil or pea puree, seasoned with spices, onion, or garlic. It is eaten along with the rice or bread and at least one kind of lentil. Dal is a part of every meal. The Indian people have long known the value of combining grains with legumes for superior protein quality, and the cuisine of south India reflects some ingenious examples of this.

A favorite at breakfast is the idli — a steamed rice and lentil cupcake which is leavened by slightly fermenting the lentils. As it is described, the flavor would seem to resemble that of our sourdough. The rice is soaked, then drained, dried, and ground. The lentils are soaked, then ground before being mixed with the rice and left overnight to rise. Sometimes this same basic dough is spiced and thinned to make a batter, then baked and served as a pancake or folded and filled as we do crêpes.

A meatless diet need never be a monotonous one, as anyone who has eaten Indian food knows. In fact quite the opposite is true. It is our usual meal of meat and potatoes which seems dull and unimaginative by contrast. With centuries of experience behind them, the Indian people are masters at creating a vegetarian cuisine rich in variety of taste, texture, and color from their abundance of vegetables and fruits unknown to us.

In a typical well-to-do Hindu home, a simple meal will consist of six to eight dishes all served simultaneously; a curry of two or three vegetables, a lentil dal or dried bean curry, a chutney, a rayta (yogurt mixed with a fruit, vegetable, herb, or sometimes coconut), a bread, plain boiled rice, and fruit. To this may be added another vegetable dish, such as a pakora (a fritter made by dipping pieces of a vegetable like eggplant or cauliflower in chick-pea and rice flour, then deep frying it), or koftas (deep-fried vegetable balls made of mashed potatoes, mashed fresh peas, and chick-pea flour) or a samosa (a wheat pastry turnover filled with vegetables). Another rice dish may be served also, and in this one the rice might be flavored with coconut, yogurt, lime juice, or other fruits, nuts, vegetables, and spices.

A chutney is a sort of relish which is made fresh daily — usually from fruit and spices, though it can be made from a vegetable. Some chutneys are sweet, some sweet-sour, some are very hot. A salad or pickle sometimes takes the place of the chutney. The rayta not only helps to cool the mouth during the meal but it also helps to digest rich, spicy food after the meal. Raytas are made of raw or cooked eggplant, potatoes, cucumber, spinach, and even bananas, but the base is aways yogurt, a nutritious food in itself (see page 285).

The Indian bread which is most familiar to the Westerner is the chapati. This is an unyeasted flat bread made of whole wheat flour. If made properly, it puffs up rather like a balloon. Whether or not this happens depends on how well and long the dough is kneaded and whether the technique of baking is correctly imitated in the Western kitchen. Patience and persistence are rewarded with a great sense of achievement — and an authentic chapati. The bread is baked on an ungreased skillet. The puri is basically the same bread only it is deep fried in hot oil. Most of the breads in Indian cuisine are a variation of this basic recipe.

Here is a simple vegetarian menu, offering a choice of curry, rayta, and chutney.

Our Indian Menu

Broccoli, Bean, and Coconut Curry
or Cauliflower, Potato, and Pea Curry
Yogurt with Mint and Cucumber or Eggplant with Yogurt
Rice
Chick-Pea and Lentil Dal
Chapatis
Tomato, Onion, and Radish Relish or
Mango Chutney or Date Chutney

Garam Masala

(roasted ground spice mixture)

4 3-inch pieces cinnamon sticks
¾ cup cardamom pods
3 tablespoons whole cloves
6 tablespoons whole cumin seeds
3 tablespoons whole coriander seeds
3 tablespoons whole black peppercorns

Preheat oven to 200°F.

Spread out spices on cookie sheet in one layer and roast for 20 minutes in a preheated oven. Shake pan after every 5 minutes to keep them from browning. Cool. Break open cardamom pods, remove seeds, discard pods. Crush cinnamon sticks with a rolling pin.

Put all spices into container* of electric blender and "grind" until spices are powdered. Stop blender every 30 seconds or so to stir spice mixture, then "grind" again, until you have a uniformly ground mixture. Store in an airtight jar. **Yield:** approximately 1 cup

*A pint canning jar with a standard-size mouth will fit perfectly into most blender bases. For fine grinding, it is best to use a smaller container on the blender. Just put the spices in the jar, place the blade, rubber, and screw bottom of blender container onto the jar as you would a lid. Turn jar upside down, place in blender base, proceed with "grinding."

Broccoli, Bean, and Coconut Curry

2 cups fresh coconut or 1 cup dried coconut
1 cup water (if using dried coconut, use 2 cups water)
½ teaspoon mustard seed
2-inch piece gingerroot, chopped, or 2 teaspoons powdered ginger
2 garlic cloves, minced
¼ cup oil
1 medium-sized onion, chopped
2 tablespoons coriander (ground)
½ teaspoon turmeric
¼ cup water — plus a bit more if needed
2 green peppers, chopped coarsely
½ pound green beans, cut in 1-inch lengths
1 stalk broccoli, cut in 1-inch lengths
6 scallions, sliced thin
2 teaspoons salt
1 fresh hot green chili, seeded and chopped (optional)

Combine coconut and water in container of electric blender and blend to a purée.

In a heavy-bottom pan, sauté mustard seed, ginger, and garlic in oil for about 30 seconds.

Add onion and cook 5 minutes or until lightly browned, stirring to prevent burning.

Add coriander, turmeric, and water and mix in well. Stir in the vegetables, coating them evenly with the spice mixture. Add the coconut purée, salt, and hot chilies, if using them, and blend well.

Cover pan and simmer until vegetables are tender but still firm — about 10 to 15 minutes. Add a bit more water throughout the cooking if it is needed.
Yield: 4 to 6 servings

Cauliflower, Potato, and Pea Curry

1 medium-sized onion, chopped
2 tablespoons oil
¼ teaspoon black pepper
2 teaspoons coriander, ground
1 teaspoon turmeric
1 teaspoon garam masala
¾ teaspoon cumin, ground
1 medium-sized head cauliflower, broken into flowerlets
2 medium-sized potatoes, peeled and cubed
¾ cup water
1 bay leaf
1 10-ounce package frozen peas
salt to taste

Sauté onions in oil with spices for about 5 minutes, then stir in cauliflower and potatoes. Add water and bay leaf, cover pot with lid, turn down heat, and steam for 15 minutes or until vegetables are just tender. Add peas and salt to taste. Cook about 5 more minutes. Be careful not to overcook. Keep warm on low burner until serving time.
Yield: 8 to 10 servings

Yogurt with Mint and Cucumber

1 medium-sized cucumber, peeled, seeded, and finely chopped
¼ cup fresh mint leaves, finely chopped, or 4 teaspoons dried
    mint leaves, crushed
¼ cup onions, finely chopped
1 teaspoon fresh hot chili, finely chopped
½ teaspoon salt
1 cup yogurt

Combine all ingredients except yogurt. When they are thoroughly mixed, stir in the yogurt. Cover and refrigerate for at least an hour before serving.
Yield: 4 to 6 servings

Eggplant with Yogurt

1 eggplant (approximately 1 pound)
2 medium-sized onions, chopped
2 garlic cloves, minced
1½ tablespoons oil
1 teaspoon fresh gingerroot, grated, or ½ teaspoon powdered ginger
¾ teaspoon cumin, ground
¾ teaspoon coriander, ground
1 cup yogurt
salt to taste
1 tablespoon parsley, chopped

Preheat oven to 350°F.

Wash eggplant, prick skin over whole surface with a fork. Place on pan in preheated oven and bake about 50 minutes, until tender but firm. Strip off skin and chop into cubes about ½ inch square.

Using medium heat, sauté onion and garlic in oil with ginger, cumin, and coriander, adding the eggplant after about 5 minutes. Turn down heat, cover pan, and let steam for 10 minutes or so, stirring occasionally. Stir in yogurt, salt to taste, garnish with chopped parsley, and serve.
Yield: 4 to 6 servings

Chick-Pea and Lentil Dal

½ pound chick-peas
½ pound red lentils
2 medium-sized onions, chopped
¼ cup oil

3 to 4 teaspoons fresh gingerroot, grated, or 1 to 2 teaspoons
  powdered ginger
¼ to ½ teaspoon cayenne pepper
2 teaspoons garam masala
2 teaspoons cumin, ground
1 teaspoon turmeric
salt to taste
3 tablespoons lemon juice
parsley, chopped, for garnish

Soak chick-peas overnight in water to cover. Discard
water. Bring chick-peas, covered, to a boil in fresh water, turn
heat down to low, and simmer for 30 minutes. Again discard
water. Bring them to a boil again in fresh water, turn heat
down, and simmer 1½ hours or until tender. (The discarding of
the soaking and first cooking waters helps to remove
flatulence-causing carbohydrates from the chick-peas.)

Cook lentils in boiling water, covered, until tender (about
1 hour).

Sauté onions in oil with spices for about 5 minutes, then
stir in drained, cooked chick-peas and lentils. Season with salt
to taste and lemon juice. Add some of the final cooking water
from chick-peas if it is needed. Garnish with parsley before
serving.

Yield: 8 to 10 servings

Chapatis

3½ cups (approximately) whole wheat bread flour (not pastry
  flour)
½ teaspoon salt
3 tablespoons oil
1⅓ cups water

Combine flour and salt, leaving a little of the flour for
kneading. Combine oil and water and stir into the flour mixture, until it becomes impossible to mix with a spoon. A bit
more or less water may be added to make a soft pliable dough
which forms itself into one mass.

Turn out onto floured board and knead for at least 5 minutes, using more flour as needed, to develop the gluten in the flour. Form dough into a ball, lightly coat surface with oil, cover, and leave at room temperature for 1 hour.

Divide the dough into 20 equal pieces, by rolling it into a long cylinder and cutting it in half, then in quarters, then each quarter into 5 pieces. Flatten each piece with the palm of your hand, and using a rolling pin, roll each chapati to about 6 inches in diameter and ⅛-inch thick. They can be stacked with wax paper between them, and covered with a damp towel to prevent them from drying out if they are made far ahead of baking time.

Heat a dry (ungreased) cast-iron skillet to medium heat, place chapati in center of pan for about 30 seconds, then turn it and leave it another 30 seconds. Lift chapati out and place it on a long-handled skimmer*; hold it about 3 inches above a burner which is turned to the highest heat, until it begins to puff up like a balloon. When the puffing stops, turn chapati over and let it puff on that side. Wait a few seconds until puffing has stopped and the chapati has cooked through, then serve immediately, or keep warm between cloth towels in a low oven. Chapatis should be served as soon as possible after being baked and should not be allowed to get cool before serving.
Yield: 20 chapatis

*Note: If a long-handled skimmer is not available, a wire cake rack can be substituted, held with pot holders or preferably by hooking a long-handled kitchen fork into one end of the rack. The skimmer, or rack, must be of wire or woven steel which is very open, exposing most of the surface of the chapati to the heat.

Tomato, Onion, and Radish Relish

1½ cups tomatoes, finely chopped
¼ cup green pepper, finely chopped
3 tablespoons radishes, finely chopped
¼ cup onions, finely chopped
½ teaspoon salt
2 teaspoons lemon juice
paprika to taste

Combine all ingredients and serve.
Yield: 6 to 8 servings

Mango Chutney

2 cups cider vinegar
½ cup lime juice
5 tablespoons honey
4 large ripe mangoes, peeled and sliced
¾ cup dried currants
½ cup raisins
½ cup onion, minced
1 cup green pepper, chopped
⅔ cup almonds, chopped
3-inch piece gingerroot (fresh or dry), peeled and cut fine
1 tablespoon crushed mustard seed
2 teaspoons salt
2 tablespoons fresh hot pepper, minced, or 1 ground dried chili
    pepper

Combine all ingredients. Bring to a boil, then turn heat down and simmer for 30 minutes. Drain off juice and boil it down to half of its volume. Add it to chutney and ladle into hot, sterilized jars.
Yield: 3 pint jars

Date Chutney

½ pound pitted dates, sliced (1½ cups)
1 cup water — plus a bit more if needed for blending
½ teaspoon salt
3 tablespoons lemon juice
½ cup fresh coconut, cut into thin slices, or ¼ cup dried coconut
2 tablespoons gingerroot, chopped, or 2 teaspoons powdered
    ginger
black pepper, freshly ground — 1 or 2 grindings to taste

Combine all ingredients in container of electric blender and blend to a purée. Add a bit more water if necessary. Store in refrigerator.
Yield: approximately 2 cups

How to Buy and Prepare a Fresh Coconut Before purchasing a coconut, shake it to make sure it is full of liquid. If not, or if "eyes" are moldy or wet, the coconut may be too old or spoiled. To open the coconut puncture two of the three eyes with an ice pick. You may need to hammer the icepick into them. Drain all the liquid (coconut milk) into a container. Either refrigerate or freeze the milk for future use.

Bake empty coconut in oven which has been preheated to 400°F. for 15 minutes. Remove from oven and place it on a board. While it is still hot, split the coconut by giving it a sharp blow with a hammer. The outer shell should fall away from the meat. It may be necessary to pry out some of the meat with a knife. The meat can be frozen for future use or grated right away and stored in the refrigerator. Peel off the dark skin with a knife or potato peeler, and grate on hand grater, one piece at a time.

Middle Eastern Cooking

Middle Eastern food perhaps holds more fascination for Westerners than any other food. Whether this is because of Arabic names like baba ghannooj and hummus bi tahina or because of the antiquity of this area of the world, there is a mystique surrounding these cultures which many Americans find irresistible.

It is a fact that agriculture actually began here. In a hilly region known as Kurdistan, which reaches into Turkey, Iran, and Iraq, as early as 6800 B.C., man learned to cultivate plants and domesticate animals — wild sheep to be specific. Wheat still grows wild in Kurdistan and is gathered by today's peasant in much the same way as it was then. In light of this, it is only natural that wheat should still be a basic staple throughout this area of the world.

Much of this wheat is ground into flour for bread, for in this part of the world bread is truly the "staff of life." In parts of Egypt, the adult peasant eats three pounds of bread every day. In most homes, bread is baked fresh daily, and if it is not homemade, it is bought fresh and warm at least once a day. There are of course many varieties of bread in these countries, but one which particularly catches the imagination is the disc-like Arab bread sometimes called pita. It is traditionally made of white flour, but our version is made completely of whole wheat flour. When it is baked in a very hot oven it puffs up, developing a large "pocket" which subsides slightly upon cooling, but remains large enough to allow for a filling when the bread is broken in half. This could be called the Arab "sandwich"; in many ways it is a delicious improvement on ours when filled with piquant avocado or eggplant dip.

Not all of the wheat is ground into flour. A lot of it is made into burghul. Grains of wheat are boiled until they burst open, then they are dried (often in the sun) and coarsely ground. Burghul is served daily in soups, as stuffing for fish or vegetables, as an appetizer (tabbouleh), or in the form of a pilaf instead of rice.

We are fortunate to be able to obtain bulgur, as we call it, now in America. In this country bulgur is made by first soaking it and then cooking it under pressure at 250°F. for 1½ minutes. It is then dried and coarsely ground. This precooking process does not affect the nutritional value of the wheat any more than would the longer cooking of the wheat grain which would otherwise be necessary. Bulgur is a form of wheat that is convenient to use because it requires only a few minutes to soak and cook, and it is a good alternative to potatoes or rice. Having been partially cooked, bulgur is resistant to insects and can be more safely stored than wheat flour, another reason for its being a staple in hot climates like that of the Middle East.

A Greek variation of burghul is called trahana and combines bulgouri, as it is called by the Greeks, with sheep or goat milk, cooking and drying these foods together so as to preserve both for winter meals when milk is not available. Those Greek peasants may not know about amino acids or protein complementarity, but they do know from experience that wheat and milk eaten together provide a nourishing diet which can replace meat. Trahana is used as a main dish seasoned with onions and tomatoes, as a stuffing for peppers and tomatoes, and in soups much the same way that meat is used.

Lamb, the basic meat in all these Middle Eastern countries, was being roasted over live coals on the spit or the skewer before the birth of agriculture. And to these people, "shish kebab" is nothing new or unusual, as it is to many of us. The words come from the Turkish words "sis," meaning sword or skewer, and "kebab," meaning roasted meat. If you eat this dish where it originated it may include bits of heart, spleen, liver, and other innards secured to the skewer by means of elaborately braided sheep entrails. These people know the extra nutritional bonus that comes from eating organ meats with their wealth of iron, vitamin A, riboflavin, and niacin. Another traditional lamb dish is called "kibbi" in Lebanon and Syria, "kobba" in Jordan, and "kubba" in Iraq, though essentially it is made in the same way in all these countries. Raw lamb is pounded to a paste, then onion, salt, pepper, and burghul are pounded into the meat each in turn. It may be served raw, or formed into meatballs or large patties and fried or broiled; it may be layered in a casserole with a layer of spiced lamb between. At festive occasions, there may be several different dishes of kibbi on the table at the same time.

Seafood and chicken are eaten and enjoyed, but to a lesser extent than lamb. As would be expected, fish and shellfish of all kinds are available in the countries surrounding the Mediterranean, though for Orthodox Jew and Muslim alike, shellfish and of course pork are forbidden. Octopus is considered a delicacy in Greece, as is broiled eel. Whole fish are often stuffed and baked whole, and the ingredients used in the stuffing reflect the cuisine of each particular culture.

The original baked fish in the menu below was stuffed with a walnut and pomegranate seed mixture. Adapting it for use in America, we substituted a fresh tomato for the pomegranate seeds and added some bulgur to it. The garlic sauce which is poured over the fish before serving is a frequent addition to the meal in all of the Arab states. Its basic ingredient is tahini or sesame seed paste.

In the dip, hummus bi tahina, it is combined with puréed chick-peas; in baba ghannooj, with eggplant purée. It may accompany a vegetable such as cauliflower. Used in such quantity and so frequently, sesame seed paste becomes a valuable source of calcium in these countries where dairy products are scarce. Sesame seeds combined with chick-peas provide a high quality protein due to the complementary amino acid makeup of seeds and legumes.

Lentils and fava beans are important in the diet of these peoples too, and for many peasants breakfast may consist of boiled beans topped with lemon juice and olive oil. Chick-peas are roasted and eaten as we eat peanuts. Felafel, a popular snack sold by street vendors, and sometimes called the "Israeli hot dog," consists of chick-peas mixed with burghul and seasonings which are rolled into balls and deep fried. Or there is chick-pea salad and the eggplant dish musakka'a, which in the Arab states is made using chick-peas instead of meat. An Iranian stew is a savory mixture of tomato, onion, and turmeric with chick-peas as the main ingredient. For a special occasion, lamb will be added.

It is said of the Syrian or Turk that he can boast of knowing 1,000 recipes for eggplant — it can be stuffed, sliced, mashed, stewed, and chopped; it can be dressed with yogurt as a relish or salad. Eggplant is a most versatile vegetable and perhaps the most popular in these lands. However, many vegetables are grown and relished in these countries — all those we enjoy as well as some which are less popular here such as okra. Grapevine leaves are used widely in much the same way as we use cabbage leaves; they can be filled with rice stuffing, though in Greece currants and dill or mint might be added and not necessarily meat. Another interesting difference in Middle Eastern food is in the lemon juice which flavors the stock in which the stuffed vine leaves are simmered. Lemon is used often in soups and with vegetables as a flavoring, just as mint too is uniquely used in entrée and vegetable dishes. The recipes for green beans à la Grecque and celery in egg-lemon sauce are examples of this. Vegetables like tomatoes, peppers, and zucchini are also stuffed with rice and meat mixtures. This is a good way to stretch the meat and increase the intake of vegetables and whole grains. We've included a recipe below for stuffed zucchini to better illustrate vegetables stuffed Middle Eastern style. Dandelion greens, freshly dug in spring, are as prized in Greece as they are in the Pennsylvania Dutch country; there they are served with lemon juice and olive oil.

Olives grow in many shapes, sizes, and colors throughout this area and are an ever-present accessory to meals. Olive oil is the "butter" of the Middle East and imparts a meat-like flavor to the food. Because olive oil is only partially unsaturated, we suggest using half olive and half safflower oil in these recipes. In this way, your food will still have the authentic distinctive taste, but without the unnecessary saturated fat.

Dried fruits, rich in calcium, iron, and potassium, are grown in abundance in the Middle East. Three-quarters of the world's supply of dates comes from Iraq, and Turkish figs are some of the best to be had. Iran is renowned for her delicious dried apricots which are so high in vitamin A. Pomegranates and quinces, cherries, kumquats, and of course a wide variety of melons are native to the area. With fruits such as these, there is no need for prepared desserts, and the famed sweets like halva and baklava are reserved for festive occasions.

The Persians were making yogurt from the milk of goats, sheep, camels, and water buffaloes earlier than the third century. According to Dorothy Parker in *The Wonderful World Of Yogurt,* "For millennia, Mongolians, Arabs and other Middle Eastern peoples have been souring the milk of various milk-producing mammals, and for millenia the people of these regions have been notable for life spans far beyond the world average . . . Today in the West it is Bulgaria that is chiefly associated with yogurt and for very good reason: It has long been one of that country's principal foods and is considered responsible for the people's unusual record of health and longevity. . . . About 180 times as many Bulgars as Americans survive past the century mark . . . Bulgarians don't become bald, their hair does not turn gray, and many continue to beget offspring at amazing ages." Some Bulgarians eat as much as six pounds of yogurt a day.

Ms. Parker continues: "Yogurt is a busy and versatile aid to digestion . . . it breaks down casein, dissolves calcium, and contains, manufactures and renders accessible the whole group of B vitamins so important to health and long life. It has a higher percentage of vitamins A and D than does the milk from which it was made and it is higher in protein and lower in fat than that same milk . . . The beneficial bacteria in yogurt make it a natural antibiotic; its natural enemies are the harmful bacteria of the large intestine. It can also counteract the bad effects some people experience from the use of manufactured antibiotics."

In these Middle Eastern countries, yogurt is made from whole milk, using a culture saved from the previous batch, and many a cook who has left this homeland to live in new country has taken his or her prized yogurt starter along. Yogurt is eaten at any and all times of day in this part of the world, as a snack between meals, as soup, relish, side dish, or one ingredient of a stew, or in a rich dessert cake. In Turkey, yogurt is diluted with water, salted, and drunk as a refreshing beverage; in Iran the yogurt whey is used in this way. Called laban in Jordan, mast in Iran, yaourti in Greece, and yoghurt in Turkey, yogurt is without doubt the most nourishing food to come to us from the Arab world, and for this we owe them a great debt of thanks.

These Middle Eastern recipes do not really comprise a typical meal — rather they are examples of the different kinds of dishes you might be served if you visited in these countries.

Baba ghannooj and hummus bi tahina may be served as appetizers with Arab bread, as a dip, or as a filling for the "pocket" in the bread.

Our Middle Eastern Menu

Cucumber Yogurt Soup
Arab Bread
Baba Ghannooj
Hummus bi Tahina
Baked Fish with Walnut-Bulgur Stuffing and
Garlic-Sesame Sauce
Zucchini Stuffed with Rice and Lamb
Celery in Egg-Lemon Sauce
Green Beans à la Grecque

Cucumber Yogurt Soup

2 cucumbers, chopped or grated (about 4 cups)
1 to 2 garlic cloves, minced — to taste
2 cups yogurt
2 teaspoons lemon juice
1 teaspoon olive oil
2 teaspoons fresh mint, chopped, or 1 teaspoon dried mint
½ teaspoon dill weed
1 teaspoon salt
4 to 6 ice cubes
fresh mint leaves for garnish

Peel and chop or grate the cucumber, removing any large seeds. Combine cucumber, garlic, yogurt, lemon juice, oil, and seasonings and chill. Before serving, put 1 ice cube into each soup bowl and garnish with mint leaves.
Yield: 4 to 6 servings

Arab Bread

¼ teaspoon honey
2 tablespoons lukewarm water
2 teaspoons dry yeast
3⅓ cups whole wheat flour (approximately)
1 teaspoon salt
1¼ cups lukewarm water
2 tablespoons oil (olive or other if preferred)
¼ cup cornmeal

Add honey to lukewarm water and sprinkle yeast over surface. Set aside for 2 or 3 minutes, then stir to dissolve yeast completely. Set aside again for 5 minutes until mixture is "working."

Combine 3 cups of flour and the salt in a bowl. Combine lukewarm water with oil, add to yeast mixture, and pour into center of flour, stirring until dough forms one mass and leaves the sides of the bowl. Turn dough out onto lightly floured board and knead for 8 to 10 minutes, using approximately ⅓ cup flour in the kneading process.

Lightly oil surface of dough, cover, and leave in a warm draft-free place for 45 minutes to an hour, or until dough has doubled. Punch down dough, form into 4 balls about 2½ inches in diameter. Cover and let them "rest" for 30 minutes. Roll out each ball to a diameter of 8 inches, with a thickness of ⅛ inch. Sprinkle cornmeal on baking sheet wherever breads are to be placed, and lay them 2 inches apart on the baking sheets. Cover and let "rest" 30 minutes.

Preheat oven to 500°F. Bake breads 4 minutes on lowest rack of an electric oven (if you have a gas oven, bake the breads 4 to 5 minutes on the floor of the oven), then bake them 3 to 4 minutes on the rack about 3 inches above the lowest rack (or floor of oven). Breads should puff up about 2 inches while on the lower shelf, and after being moved up, they will turn brown and cook through, remaining puffed. If not serving them immediately, wrap cooked breads in foil and set aside until serving time. When unwrapped, these breads will have fallen somewhat, but the pocket will remain in each one. They may be broken apart and eaten with butter, or broken in half and

each half filled with mixtures such as chick-pea spread, avo-cado dip, or finely cut salad and alfalfa sprouts, with a hot sauce.
Yield: 4 8-inch breads

Baba Ghannooj

(eggplant-sesame purée)

1 eggplant (approximately 1 pound)
¼ cup lemon juice
1 garlic clove, minced
2 tablespoons tahini (sesame seed paste)
½ teaspoon salt
1 small onion, chopped
2 tablespoons parsley, chopped fine

Preheat oven to 350°F.
Wash eggplant, prick skin over whole surface with a fork. Place on pan in preheated oven and bake about 1 hour, until tender enough to mash.
Strip off skin and mash the pulp to a purée. Combine egg-plant, lemon juice, garlic, tahini, and salt. Mound the purée in a bowl and garnish with chopped onion and parsley.
Yield: approximately 2 cups

Hummus bi Tahina

2 cups cooked chick-peas
½ to 1 cup bean broth or water
2 garlic cloves
6 to 8 tablespoons lemon juice to taste
1 teaspoon salt
½ cup tahini (sesame seed paste)

Combine cooked chick-peas, bean broth or water, garlic, lemon juice, salt, and tahini in container of electric blender and blend to a smooth purée. Thin to desired consistency with more bean broth or water.
Yield: approximately 3 cups

Baked Fish with Walnut-Bulgur
Stuffing and Garlic-Sesame Sauce

1 cup bulgur
water to cover
1 medium-sized onion, minced
2 medium-sized green peppers, chopped
1 cup walnuts, chopped
2 tablespoons olive oil
2 tablespoons safflower oil
1 fresh tomato, cut carefully into ½-inch pieces
salt and pepper to taste
1 teaspoon oregano
2 pounds whole fish (bass, bluefish, mackerel, etc.)
sliced lemons for garnish
chopped parsley for garnish

Preheat oven to 350°F.
Put bulgur to soak in water to cover for 5 minutes or so.
Drain and reserve excess water for soup (so as not to waste B
vitamins). Sauté onion, peppers, and walnuts in oils for a few
minutes. Add drained bulgur, tomato, and seasonings, stirring
to combine.
Stuff fish, cover with foil, and bake in preheated oven for
20 to 30 minutes, until fish is tender. Serve "glazed" with
garlic-sesame sauce, topped with lemon slices and parsley.
Yield: 4 to 6 servings

Garlic-Sesame Sauce

½ cup tahini (sesame seed paste)
2 garlic cloves
½ teaspoon salt
3 to 4 tablespoons lemon juice to taste
1 to 1½ cups water (thin to desired consistency)

Put tahini in blender container. Add garlic, salt, lemon
juice, and water and blend to a smooth purée. Serve warm or
cold, but if heating it, be careful to use low heat and stir
constantly to prevent lumping and scorching.

Zucchini Stuffed with Rice and Lamb

4 large zucchini (approximately 4 pounds)
2 medium-sized onions, diced
¼ cup oil
1 pound ground raw lamb
1 cup cooked brown rice
1 teaspoon salt
freshly ground black pepper to taste
½ teaspoon mace
½ cup parsley, chopped
2 tablespoons fresh mint, chopped
2½ cups (approximately) canned tomatoes
1 tablespoon cornstarch
1 tablespoon water

Halve zucchini, scoop out center using an apple corer, taking care not to split them. Leave shell ½-inch thick. Dice zucchini taken from the center.

Sauté onions in oil until soft. Add lamb and sauté it until it is no longer pink. Add diced zucchini and let it cook 1 to 2 minutes. Then add rice and seasonings. Remove from heat and stir in parsley and mint. Stuff zucchini halves with mixture.

Place tomatoes and juice in the bottom of a heavy skillet, lay stuffed zucchini halves on top, cover skillet, and cook over medium heat for 10 to 15 minutes or until the zucchini shells are tender but not too soft to hold the filling.

Lift out the zucchini halves and keep them warm. Dissolve cornstarch in water, add to tomato and juices in the skillet, and cook over low heat until thickened. Serve this sauce with the zucchini.
Yield: 6 servings

Celery in Egg-Lemon Sauce

1 small onion, minced
1 pound celery (about ½ bunch), cut into 1-inch lengths
1½ tablespoons olive oil
1½ tablespoons safflower oil
2 cups chicken stock
3 tablespoons lemon juice
1 egg yolk
salt and pepper to taste

Sauté onion and celery in oils for a few minutes. Add chicken stock, turn down the heat, and cover. Cook until celery is just tender but still firm. Combine lemon juice with egg yolk, and stir a little of the broth from the celery into this mixture, then return this gradually to the celery. Season to taste. Remove from heat and set aside, covered, for about 5 minutes before serving.

Yield: 4 to 6 servings

Green Beans à la Grecque

1 small onion, minced
1 garlic clove, minced
1 tablespoon olive oil
1 tablespoon safflower oil
1 pound fresh green beans, cut into 2-inch lengths
1 cup tomatoes (canned), drained
salt and pepper to taste
2 tablespoons parsley, chopped
1 teaspoon fresh mint, chopped, or ½ teaspoon dried mint

Sauté onion and garlic in oils for a minute or so, then add the beans. Mash the tomatoes, and add them with the seasoning and herbs. Turn down the heat, cover, and cook until the beans are just tender, but still firm. Serve hot.

Yield: 6 servings

Mexican Cooking

Ground whole corn and dry beans of many varieties are the two foods most used in Mexican cooking, but other basic ingredients also include rice, wheat, cheese, avocados, some meat and poultry, onions, and tomatoes — along with many other fresh garden vegetables. Special mention must be made of that unique food, the chili pepper. Thought to be only a seasoning agent by most Americans, it is actually much more than that in Mexico, where many different kinds are eaten in great quantity.

Chilies are available in different degrees of strength, from slightly hotter than lettuce to those so hot they virtually glow in the dark. And according to a research specialist at New Mexico State University, there is no difference in nutritional levels between the very mild and strong varieties. Information from the U.S. Department of Agriculture shows that one ounce (2 to 3 tablespoons) of ground dried chili can contain as much as 20,000 units of vitamin A. (That's equal to about nine pounds of raw asparagus.) Fresh pods of the chili have even higher levels of A, as well as an appreciable amount of vitamin C.

The chili pepper is a member of the nightshade family like potatoes and tomatoes. It was used in folk medicine as a remedy for inflamed kidneys, diarrhea, chills, heart pains, internal tumors, and many other ailments. Work done at the Max Planck Institute for Nutritional Physiology in Germany (reported in *New Scientist,* 1967) has shown that certain aromatic substances such as chili can promote the circulation of blood through vessels of the skin, and the increased blood flow in tissue of congested areas may account for their beneficial effects on sinus and head-cold headaches. In this country Dr. Lora M. Shields of New Mexico Highlands University in 1964 reported to the American Association for the Advancement of Science that chili may help rid the body of enough fats to lower the consumer's blood fat level and to reduce his or her chances of heart attack. This may explain why in a small area of the Southwest, where a record yearly crop of 55,000 tons of chili peppers is produced, the people have the lowest death rate from heart disease and cancer of any comparable area in the United States.

While the chili pepper is still green it can be prepared in many ways. Peppers can be stuffed with cheese, used as the main item in casserole-type dishes, or just stewed with a small amount of meat and beans — the original version of chile con carne. The red chili has an additional quality which was also reported by New Mexico State University of Las Cruces: it acts as an antioxidant and retards the oxidation of meat and fats, and thus serves very well as a natural preservative.

For those of us who are not yet accustomed to eating hot chilies, but want to acquire the taste, it is good to know that honey is a food used in many Mexican restaurants to help newcomers extinguish the fire in the mouth sometimes resulting from eating hot Mexican food.

When Mexican housewives go to market to buy their week's supply of "frijoles" (beans), they have a wide variety to choose from: red, pink, black, speckled, and tan. Many families grow their own, and if you should visit there in the autumn you would see the flat Mexican rooftops piled with the bean vines, drying in the sun. A large pot of beans is kept simmering at the back of the stove in the kitchen, and the freshly cooked beans in it are served into soup plates along with their broth, sometimes topped with chopped onion and green chili peppers. Once the newly cooked beans have been served this way the remaining ones are usually "fried" to be served at the next meal or next day. "Fried" beans are a wet and creamy mixture of mashed and whole beans, with some of the broth and seasonings added. The remaining beans may also be made into refritos or refried beans. These beans are mashed and fried in oil, sometimes with onions and seasonings, until they are dry and crispy. Refritos are usually served with tacos. They also sometimes accompany scrambled eggs for breakfast and are essential in tostadas.

All beans have an appreciable amount of the B vitamins, calcium, phosphorus, magnesium, and iron, along with valuable protein. They're good food for weight-watchers and penny-watchers, and they need no refrigeration for long storage. We would be wise to learn all we can from the Mexicans about their ways with beans.

A cornmeal tortilla, served with refried beans and garnished with cheese, is a good example of protein complementarity. Combining a grain with a legume and a dairy product adds up to a well-balanced amino acid pattern, comparable to meat in protein quality.

Probably the taco, tostada, and quesadilla would not be served in the same meal, but the recipes that follow will give you an idea of the many different ways a tortilla can be used. Traditionally, the tortilla is made only of finely ground corn which has been soaked in lime water. In this country many tortilla fanciers use a commercially processed product called "masa harina." We prefer using whole grains in an additive-free formula, so have taken the liberty of using half whole wheat flour and half cornmeal and adding eggs to produce a pliable and easy-to-make tortilla. This recipe may be used in any of the above recipes. In the tacos de gallina it is rolled after being filled; in the tostadas it is deep fried; and in the quesadilla it is folded over like a turnover, after being stuffed

with cheese. It can also be used in another tortilla-based dish
— the enchilada — which is made by dipping a tortilla in
sauce, frying it lightly, filling and rolling it, and finally covering it with sauce.

The recipe for eggless tortillas is our adaptation of the
Mexican "flour tortilla." It cannot be rolled but is very good
eaten as it is, or as the beef taco with which most Americans
have become familiar. In this, the tortilla is made into a kind of
shell and filled with a ground beef mixture, topped with shredded lettuce and cheese. This requires deep frying the tortilla
and lifting both sides with tongs, holding them in a U shape
until the shell has become crisp and will hold its shape.

Before we leave the subject of tortillas, we want to un-
derline the fact that a tortilla can only be as good as the cornmeal from which it is made. The best cornmeal is that made
from whole corn which has not been degerminated. This can be
bought in a natural foods store. If you must buy it elsewhere,
try to get cornmeal which is bolted, or water-ground, as this
will probably be a superior grade — better than the ordinary
kind available in most stores.

There are two types of soups served in Mexico. One is a
liquid, the other is dry. This recipe for dry rice soup is similar
to one for a pilaf, but these dry soups can also be made using
vermicelli or tortillas, cut into strips and fried, and combined
with sauce, cheese, etc., served in a casserole. A festive meal
always begins with a liquid soup, followed by a dry one. An ordinary meal usually includes just the liquid soup (most are
similar to ours), but because of the unique idea of a dry soup,
we are including it in our menu instead. And also because by
adding rice to the meal of beans and cornmeal, we increase the
protein quality.

The Mexicans are far from being vegetarians, but they are
wise and thrifty in the way they often serve their meats —
stretched with rice, sauce, and beans, or in a tortilla filling. In
this way they capitalize on the flavor of the meat, but a little
goes a long way.

There is one aspect of Mexican cooking which we think
could be improved upon. In most of the recipes, the tortilla is
fried at least once, sometimes twice, before being served, and
this method of cooking seems to be the one most used in all of
the traditional cuisine. One reason for this may be that most of
the cooking is done on top of, not inside, the stove. We have
substituted warming in the oven wherever possible instead of

the second frying, and we have suggested using as little oil as possible where frying is necessary.

Avocados are native to Mexico and, along with the tomato and chili pepper, date back to the Aztec civilization, so it is only natural to include an avocado salad in this Mexican meal. Botanically speaking, the avocado is a fruit and a unique one because it contains more fat than any other fruit except the olive. However, the fat is largely of the unsaturated kind which includes linoleic acid — the important essential fatty acid which helps to control cholesterol. As well as being high in the beneficial minerals magnesium and potassium, avocados are also considered weight-watcher food. They add appreciably to your caloric intake, but they also slow digestion and reduce your appetite.

It is best to buy avocados when they are firm and leave them at room temperature for five to seven days to ripen slowly. When ripe, they are slightly soft all over, and the skin can be easily stripped away, leaving the green outer flesh intact. This will turn brown when exposed to the air, so it is best to coat the exposed flesh with lemon juice if preparing it ahead of serving time.

Our Mexican Menu

Sopa Seca de Arroz
Tacos de Gallina
Tostadas
Quesadilla
Eggless Tortillas
Frijoles Refritos
Ensalada de Aguacate

Sopa Seca de Arroz

(dry rice soup)

1 small onion, chopped
1 garlic clove, minced
2 tablespoons oil
1 cup brown rice (uncooked)
¼ cup tomato purée
3 cups chicken stock or water
1 pound sausage, cooked and cut into slices
salt and pepper to taste

Sauté onion and garlic in oil for a few minutes until onion is tender. Stir in rice. Add tomato purée, chicken stock or water, and sausage. Cover, bring to a boil, then turn heat down and simmer for 30 to 40 minutes, until rice is cooked and liquid is absorbed. Do not stir during cooking. Season to taste and serve.

Yield: 6 servings

Tacos de Gallina

(rolled tortillas with chicken)

2 cups cooked, shredded chicken
¼ cup gravy or cream sauce
8 tortillas (6 inches in diameter and ⅛ inch thick)
½ cup grated cheese
2 cups hot chili sauce (see recipe below)

Moisten chicken with gravy or sauce and spread approximately 3 tablespoons of this mixture on each tortilla. Roll and secure with a toothpick.

Fry filled tortillas on both sides, in skillet (using as little oil as possible) or warm them in the oven until crisp.

Place 1 or 2 tacos on a serving plate, sprinkle with grated cheese, pour hot chili sauce over them, and serve.

Yield: 4 to 6 servings

Hot Chili Sauce

1 small onion, minced
1 tablespoon oil
2 cups tomato purée or drained, canned tomatoes
1½ tablespoons vinegar
1 teaspoon oregano
salt to taste
hot chili peppers, minced — to taste or if not available, substitute chili powder and cayenne — to taste

Sauté onion in oil for a few minutes. Stir in all remaining ingredients. If using canned tomatoes, mash them to a pulp. Cover and simmer for 15 minutes over low heat. Serve hot or cold with tacos and tostadas.

Yield: approximately 2 cups

Tostadas
(crisp fried tortillas)

oil
8 tortillas
4 cups refried beans
1 cup grated cheese
1 cup lettuce, finely shredded
1½ cups hot chili sauce (see recipe)

Heat oil in a cast-iron skillet. It should be approximately 1-inch deep. Fry tortillas one at a time in the hot oil, turning them, if necessary, to get them crisp and golden on both sides. Remove from skillet and drain off excess oil between paper towels. Keep them warm in a low oven.

To serve, heap ½ cup refried beans on each fried tortilla, sprinkle with 2 tablespoons grated cheese, and then shredded lettuce. Pour about 3 tablespoons hot chili sauce over each and serve.
Yield: 4 to 6 servings

Quesadilla
(tortillas stuffed with cheese)

1 cup grated cheese
8 tortillas (6 inches in diameter and ⅛ inch thick) — see recipe below

Put about 2 tablespoons grated cheese on each tortilla, fold it over like a turnover, secure with toothpicks, and cook in a hot, ungreased, cast-iron skillet, turning it often until cheese has melted. Serve immediately with refried beans.
Yield: 4 to 6 servings

Tortillas

1 cup whole wheat flour
1 cup cornmeal, as finely ground as possible
½ teaspoon salt
4 eggs, beaten
2 tablespoons oil
1½ to 2 cups water

Combine flour, cornmeal, and salt in a bowl. Combine beaten eggs with oil and 1½ cups water and pour gradually into dry ingredients, to prevent lumping. Thin to desired consistency, using more water if necessary. The amount of water will vary according to the coarseness of the cornmeal.

Dip a paper towel in a little oil, and wipe out a cast-iron skillet which is about 8 to 10 inches in diameter. Turn burner to medium heat and preheat the skillet. Pour about ¼-cup batter into skillet and tilt or rotate pan, swirling the batter around evenly to make a "pancake" about 6 inches across and ⅛ inch thick. Leave it a few minutes until it is brown underneath, then turn the tortilla over and leave a very short time to brown on the other side. Do not leave it too long, or it may become too stiff to roll or fold. Keep tortillas warm until use by stacking them with a cloth towel between and over them, in a low oven.

Yield: approximately 24 tortillas

Eggless Tortillas

½ cup whole wheat flour — plus a few more tablespoons for kneading
½ cup cornmeal
¼ teaspoon salt
1½ tablespoons oil
5 tablespoons water

Mix flour, cornmeal, and salt. Combine oil and water and add gradually, stirring it in until the dough forms a ball. Knead the dough, using as little more flour as possible, for at least 5 minutes.

Make dough into 6 small balls about the size of an egg, and leave them, covered, at room temperature for 15 minutes. Roll each ball out with a rolling pin until it is as thin as possible. Cook in hot, ungreased cast-iron skillet for about 2 minutes on the first side, then 1 minute more on the other side.

These may be eaten as they are, as we eat bread with the meal, or may be deep fried and formed into a taco shell for beef tacos. They cannot be rolled, as they will break. These tortillas should be served as soon as possible after they are made.

Yield: 6 tortillas

Frijoles Refritos

(refried beans)

2 cups (approximately ¾ pound) beans (black, pinto, or kidney)
water to cover
salt to taste (added during last half hour of cooking)
¼ to ½ cup oil
2 onions, chopped
2 garlic cloves, minced (optional)
¾ cup tomato purée (optional)
cayenne to taste

Soak beans in water to cover overnight. Discard water. Bring beans to a boil in fresh lukewarm water. (The warm water prevents the skins from toughening.) Turn down heat and simmer beans for 30 minutes. Discard this water. Bring beans to boil in fresh lukewarm water, turn down heat and simmer them until they begin to break open and are tender (1 to 1½ hours). Salt during last half hour of cooking. The discarding of the soaking and first cooking waters helps to remove flatulence-causing carbohydrates from the beans. Be sure to cook beans the last time in enough water so they will not cook dry and so that there will be enough broth left to be used if needed.

Using as little oil as possible, sauté onion and garlic, if using it, then add some drained beans, mashing them well and stirring them around as they cook. They may be seasoned with tomato purée and cayenne, if desired. Cook them until they are dry and crispy, but be careful that they do not burn.

Yield: 6 to 8 servings

Ensalada de Aguacate

(avocado salad)

1 avocado
salad greens
lemon juice to taste
salt and pepper to taste

Shortly before serving, cut avocado in half lengthwise, and remove seed and peel. Cut each half crosswise into ½-inch

thick slices, and arrange on individual plates of salad greens. Sprinkle lemon juice over avocado and season to taste.
Yield: 4 to 6 servings

Other Ethnic Dishes: Regional U.S. and Foreign

Although we singled out Japan, India, the Middle East, and Mexico, we don't by any means want to imply that these are the only parts of the world that can teach us things about good food preparation and management. Every part of the world — including the United States — has its own ethnic cooking that grew out of a need to make the most of what's available. Each country and region of each country can boast of traditional dishes that are cheap and easy to make, beautiful to look at, delightful to smell and taste — simply good food.

Think of this country and what traditional foods it has to offer. In New England it's fish chowders and baked beans; in much of the South, black-eyed peas with ham hocks, neckbones, or potlicker to add flavor, and cornbread with cracklings; in Louisiana, red beans and rice; and in the Southwest, beans again, as in chili or with tortillas.

Here are some recipes from parts of this country and parts of the world that we think are good examples of making do. Of course this is a small sample of good ethnic dishes, and the list of recommended cookbooks that are at the end of this chapter will introduce you to many more.

Boston Baked Beans

4 cups dried beans (preferably Great Northern)
1 teaspoon salt
2 medium-sized onions, peeled
4 cloves
½ cup molasses
¼ cup honey or brown sugar
2 teaspoons dry mustard
1 teaspoon black pepper
2 cups water
¼ pound salt pork

Wash the beans well, put them in a large bowl, cover them well with water, and let them soak 8 hours or overnight. Then drain off the soaking water, put them in a pot with new water to cover, add salt, and simmer them slowly for about ½ hour or until tender. Drain the beans again.

Preheat the oven to 250°F. Grease a casserole dish or a 4-quart bean pot. Stick each onion with 2 cloves and place them in the bottom of the bean pot or casserole. Pour the beans on top and pour over them the sauce you've made by mixing together the molasses, honey or sugar, mustard, pepper, and water. Add the salt pork and push it beneath the surface of the beans.

Cover your bean pot or casserole and bake for 5 to 6 hours.
Yield: 6 to 8 servings

New England Fish Chowder

3 to 4 pounds of cod head (gills removed)
2- to 3-inch cube of salt pork
2 cups onions, thinly sliced
6 to 7 potatoes, sliced or cubed
1 quart milk
salt and freshly ground pepper
2 tablespoons butter

Reserve any nice pieces of flesh and put aside with the heads. Cover the bones and trimmings with water and cook for 40 minutes.

Meanwhile, cut the salt pork into small cubes and sizzle lightly in a soup pot. When they start to get nicely crisp, add the onions and fry lightly.

Strain the fish broth into the pot and add the fish heads, making sure they are well covered. When it simmers again, add the potatoes. A bit later, add the fish chunks and simmer until all is tender. Scald the milk and add to the chowder. Salt and pepper to taste — remember the salt pork. Put the butter on top and allow to melt.

Certain New England traditions insist that the onions and pork be strained out, and some maintain that it must be thickened with crumbled crackers.
Yield: 6 to 8 servings

Charleston Okra Soup

2 cups black-eyed peas
1 large beef bone (with plenty of meat)
2½ quarts water
1 cup chopped celery
2 cups chopped green pepper
2½ pounds fresh okra or 4 10-ounce packages, frozen
2 medium onions, chopped
2 teaspoons salt
½ teaspoon pepper
2 bay leaves
8 large, fresh tomatoes or 2 cans tomatoes (#2½ or 28-ounce can)

Soak black-eyed peas in water to cover overnight.
Cook meat bone in water slowly for 1½ hours. Skim top of soup. Add remaining ingredients, including drained black-eyed peas, and cook until the peas are tender, approximately 2 hours.
Yield: 12 servings

Southwestern Black Bean Soup

2 cups black beans
2 quarts water
1 medium beef bone, meaty
2 tablespoons chopped onion
4 tablespoons cooking oil
2 ribs celery, chopped
2 teaspoons salt
½ teaspoon pepper
¼ teaspoon dry mustard
2 tablespoons whole wheat flour
3 tablespoons sherry (optional)

Soak beans overnight. Drain. Add to water and beef bone.
Sauté onion in 2 tablespoons oil. Add onion and celery to

beans and simmer 3 to 4 hours in covered heavy pot until beans are soft. Put through fine strainer for a smooth soup.

Reheat to boiling and add salt, pepper, mustard, 2 tablespoons oil, and flour. Add sherry when ready to serve.
Yield: 8 to 10 servings

Corn Bread

4 teaspoons dry yeast
½ cup warm skim milk
2 tablespoons honey
1 teaspoons frozen concentrated orange juice
½ teaspoon salt
4 tablespoons vegetable oil
½ cup whole wheat flour
½ cup cornmeal
1 large egg
1 cup whole wheat flour

Preheat oven to 350°F.

In a bowl dissolve the yeast in the milk. Add honey, concentrated orange juice, salt, oil, whole wheat flour, and cornmeal. Beat for 1 minute. Add egg and remaining whole wheat flour. Beat 1 minute.

Spoon mixture into well-oiled loaf pan (3¾ x 7½ x 2-inch pan). Allow to rise to the top of the pan. Put in preheated oven and bake for 40 to 50 minutes until a rich golden color. Cool in pan and remove carefully.
Yield: 1 loaf

Note: To make corn bread with cracklings, substitute melted bacon drippings for the vegetable oil. Oil the pan by placing a tablespoon of bacon fat in the pan and then place the pan in a hot oven until the fat melts and starts to sizzle. Then pour in batter and return to the oven to bake.

Chili Con Carne

2 cups kidney beans, cooked
2 pounds ground beef
1 onion, chopped
1 cup celery, chopped

½ cup green pepper, chopped
1 garlic clove, minced
2 tablespoons oil
3 cups tomatoes, fresh or canned
2 teaspoons cumin, ground
2 teaspoons chili powder
1 teaspoon salt

The day before you cook and serve this dish, soak and cook the kidney beans. Do this by soaking the beans in water and removing the ones that float. After soaking for 2 hours, the beans can be drained and frozen.

In the morning of the next day, remove beans from freezer and add water to cover in large pot. Cook until tender, at least 1 hour. Then drain the beans, reserving the liquid.

In heavy skillet, brown ground beef, onion, celery, green pepper, and garlic in oil. Stir in tomatoes, add seasonings and the cooked beans. Simmer slowly for 30 minutes, adding as much of the liquid drained from the beans as you wish.
Yield: 6 to 8 servings

Southern Black-Eyed Peas and Ham Hocks

2 pounds smoked ham hocks, a meaty ham bone, or pieces of
    slab bacon with the rind on
2 cups (1 pound) dried black-eyed peas
1 cup coarsely chopped onions
1 cup chopped celery
1 fresh hot red chili, about 3 inches long, washed, stemmed,
    seeded if desired, and coarsely chopped
freshly ground black pepper

Place the ham in a heavy large pot and add enough water to cover the meat by at least 1 inch. Bring to a boil over high heat, reduce the heat to low, and simmer partially covered for 2 hours, or until the ham is tender.

Wash the black-eyed peas well under cold running water. Add the peas, onions, celery, chili, and a few grindings of black pepper to the pot, mix well, and bring to a boil over high heat. Reduce the heat to low and simmer partially covered for 1 to 1½ hours, or until the peas are tender. Check the pot from time to time and add more boiling water if necessary. When the peas are fully cooked, they should have absorbed almost all of the pan liquid.

Taste for seasoning and serve at once.

Yield: 6 to 8 servings

Louisiana Red Beans and Rice

6 cups water
1 pound dried small red beans or red kidney beans
4 tablespoons butter or vegetable oil
1½ cups finely chopped onions
1 teaspoon finely chopped garlic
2 pounds smoked ham hocks or meaty ham bone
½ teaspoon freshly ground black pepper
6 to 8 cups freshly cooked, long-grain brown rice

In a large saucepan, bring the water to a boil. Drop in the beans and boil briskly, uncovered, for 2 minutes. Then turn off the heat and let the beans soak for 1 hour. Drain the beans in a sieve set over a large bowl; measure the soaking liquid and, if necessary, add more water to make 4 cups. Set the beans and liquid aside.

Melt the butter or oil in a heavy large casserole set over moderate heat. When hot, sauté the onions and the garlic for about 5 minutes, until translucent.

Stir in the beans and their liquid, the ham and pepper. Bring the mixture to a boil over high heat, reduce the heat to low, and simmer partially covered for about 3 hours, or until the beans seem dry. Then add up to 1 cup more water, a few tablespoonfuls at a time. During the last 30 minutes or so of cooking, stir frequently and mash some of the beans against the sides of the pan to form a thick sauce for the remaining beans.

Take out the ham and remove the meat. Dice it and return it to the pot. Season the beans and serve over rice.

Yield: 4 to 6 servings

Chilean Cranberries with Squash and Corn

3 cups fresh cranberries, shelled or dried navy beans that have
  been soaked overnight
5 cups water
¼ cup olive oil
1½ cups chopped onions
½ teaspoon minced garlic
6 medium tomatoes, peeled and chopped
1½ teaspoons basil
1 teaspoon oregano
black pepper to taste
1 pound of any winter squash, peeled, cleaned, and cut into 1-
  inch cubes
½ cup fresh corn
1 teaspoon salt

Rinse the beans well, and then simmer them on top of the stove with the 5 cups of water.

In a heavy skillet, heat the oil and sauté the onions and garlic until the onions are transparent. Then stir in the tomatoes and the seasonings and cook on high, stirring constantly to evaporate most of the water. When the tomato mixture has become thick, add it and the squash to the simmering beans. Cover and cook on low heat for about 2 hours or until the beans are tender. Then stir in the corn and simmer another 5 minutes. Season and serve.

Yield: 6 servings

Russian Cabbage Soup

1 pound flank or shin beef
3 pounds beef bones
8 cups water
1 head cabbage (3 to 4 pounds), shredded
1 large onion, diced
3 tablespoons butter
4 29-ounce cans tomatoes
5 pitted prunes
¼ cup raisins
1 tablespoon salt
3 tablespoons lemon juice
2 tablespoons honey

Boil the meat and bones in the water for 30 minutes. Skim off the top.

Sauté the cabbage and onion in the butter for 3 minutes. Add the tomatoes and cook until the cabbage is limp. Add the cabbage-tomato mixture to the stock.

Add the remaining ingredients. Bring the soup to a boil and then simmer for 1½ hours or until the meat is tender. Remove the meat from the pot, slice into cubes, and return to the pot. Heat and serve.

Yield: 16 to 18 servings

Russian Black Bread

4 tablespoons butter
¼ cup molasses or sorghum syrup
2 cups lukewarm water
3 tablespoons dry yeast
¼ cup coffee
2 cups rye flour
2 cups toasted whole wheat crumbs
½ cup bran flakes
¼ cup carob powder
½ teaspoon fennel seeds, crushed
2 tablespoons caraway seeds
1 tablespoon salt
¼ teaspoon ginger
2 to 3 cups whole wheat flour
cornmeal
Glaze:
1 egg yoke
1 teaspoon coffee

Melt the butter and combine it with the molasses. Let the mixture cool to lukewarm.

Put the water in a bowl. Sprinkle the yeast over the water. When the yeast is dissolved, add the coffee and the butter-molasses mixture.

Mix the rye flour, crumbs, bran, carob, fennel seeds, caraway seeds, salt, and ginger. Add the yeast mixture to the flour mixture. This should be sticky. Gradually add the whole wheat flour until the dough is solid and manageable but moist.

Turn the dough out onto a lightly floured board. Knead until smooth and firm. Add more whole wheat flour as necessary. Form the dough into a ball and put it in an oiled bowl. Turn the ball so that the top will be coated with oil. Cover the bowl with a clean towel and let rise in a warm, draft-free place. This should take about an hour. When the dough is double in bulk, punch down the dough. Cut it in half.

Knead each half on a lightly floured board just long enough to make the dough firm enough to mold into nice round shapes. Sprinkle cornmeal on the bottom of a cookie sheet. Place the rounds on the cookie sheet, and with a knife, slash a cross in the center of each round. Cover with a lightly moistened towel and let rise for ½ hour or until double in bulk.

Preheat oven to 375°F. Bake the bread for 30 minutes and then brush tops with the glaze. Continue baking for 10 minutes more and then test to see if the bread is done. Tap it with your knuckle and if it has a nice hollow sound, it is done. Let the bread cool on a rack before cutting.

Yield: 2 loaves

Italian Minestrone

¼ cup safflower oil
1 garlic clove, minced
1 cup chopped onion
1 cup chopped celery
1 6-ounce can tomato paste
2½ quarts beef stock
1 cup chopped cabbage
1 10-ounce package frozen peas and carrots or 1 cup peas and 1 cup diced fresh carrots
2 teaspoons salt
¼ teaspoon pepper
½ teaspoon rosemary leaves
2 cups cooked kidney beans
1 cup whole wheat macaroni
grated Parmesan cheese

Heat oil and sauté garlic, onion, and celery for 5 minutes. Stir in tomato paste and next 7 ingredients. Bring to a boil,

cover, and simmer slowly 1 hour. Add macaroni and cook 15 minutes longer. Garnish with Parmesan cheese.
Yield: 6 to 8 generous servings

Welsh Rabbit or Rarebit

2 cups (½ pound) grated cheddar cheese
1 tablespoon flour (preferably whole wheat)
¼ cup beer
1 tablespoon butter
1 teaspoon Worcestershire sauce
¼ teaspoon dry mustard
pinch cayenne pepper
1 egg
4 slices homemade bread (white bread is traditional, but we prefer whole wheat)

Combine cheese, flour, beer, butter, Worcestershire sauce, mustard, and cayenne pepper in a saucepan and cook over moderate heat. Stir constantly until the cheese has melted completely and the mixture is smooth.

Beat the egg in a separate bowl. Take the cheese mixture off the heat and stir the egg into it.

Place the slices of bread in an oven-proof dish, and pour the cheese sauce over it. Place under the broiler for a minute or two to brown the cheese slightly, and serve at once.
Yield: 2 to 4 servings

Spanish Chicken with Rice

2 tablespoons butter
2 tablespoons olive oil
4-pound roasting chicken, cut into serving pieces
salt and pepper to taste
1 onion, chopped
1 garlic clove, minced
1 green pepper, chopped
1½ cups rice (white is probably traditional, but we prefer brown)
large pinch saffron
3 cups hot chicken stock

In a large casserole dish, heat butter and oil and brown the chicken. Season with salt and pepper and remove from casserole.

Sauté onion, garlic, and pepper in the remaining fat in the casserole dish, and cook until onion is transparent. Add the rice and cook, stirring until the grains are well coated. Then add the saffron and blend into the rice mixture. Cover the rice with the chicken pieces and pour the chicken stock over the chicken.

Bake, uncovered in a 350°F. oven for about 1 hour or until the chicken is tender and the liquid is absorbed.

Yield: 6 servings

Mediterranean Ratatouille

2 medium-sized onions, peeled and sliced
1 garlic clove, minced
5 tablespoons olive oil
2 small zucchini (one-pound size), washed and thinly sliced
2 small eggplants (about one pound each), peeled and cubed
2 medium-sized green peppers, washed, stem and seeds removed, cut into 1-inch strips
5 medium-sized tomatoes, peeled and quartered, or 2 cups canned tomatoes, coarsely chopped
2 tablespoons freshly snipped basil or ½ to 1 teaspoon dried basil leaves
2 tablespoons freshly snipped parsley
1 teaspoon salt
1 teaspoon kelp powder
¼ teaspoon freshly ground pepper

Using a large, heavy skillet, sauté onions and garlic in 2 tablespoons olive oil for 5 minutes.

Add zucchini, eggplant, and green pepper to skillet, adding more oil as needed. Stir gently, but thoroughly. Sauté mixture for 10 minutes. Stir in the fresh or canned tomatoes, basil, parsley, salt, kelp, and pepper. Reduce heat, cover skillet tightly, and continue to simmer for 15 minutes longer. Serve immediately.

Yield: 8 to 10 servings

Hungarian Split Pea Soup

1 pound split peas
½ pound beef or ox tail
1 tablespoon safflower oil
½ green pepper, finely chopped
1 onion, finely chopped
1 clove garlic, minced
1 large can tomatoes
1 tablespoon paprika
½ tablespoon caraway seeds
salt to taste
3 quarts beef stock
2 cups cubed potatoes

Lightly sauté meat, onion, green pepper, and garlic in oil. Add crushed tomatoes, seasonings and stock, and split peas. Bring to boil. Reduce heat and allow to simmer 2 hours or until split peas are tender.

Remove beef or bones and cut meat into bite-sized portions. Return meat to soup. Add potato cubes a short time before serving so that they retain their shape and texture.
Yield: 20 servings

Inexpensive Dinners

To balance things out somewhat we include these recipes for inexpensive dinners. These dishes do use vegetable and dairy proteins and a few ideas from regional American and foreign cuisines. For the most part, however, they are examples of how to make the most of less expensive kinds and cuts of meats and conventional, but modestly priced raw ingredients, many of which you may already grow and store yourself.

There are a number of basic principles you can use in order to save money as well as nutrients in most of your meals. For example, meat can be extended by using bread or cracker crumbs, potatoes, or other vegetables. The meats and the vegetables you use may be the less expensive ones without sacrificing nutrients. Most of the vegetables in these recipes are the dark green, red, or yellow ones which are actually richest in vitamins and minerals. Fruits should be the ones which are in season, for it is then when they are plentiful and the cheapest, as well as most flavorful. Nonfat dry milk, reconstituted with water, instead of whole milk is used in these recipes; this cuts the cost of the milk in half.

All but two of the main dishes suggested here (the orange-glazed chicken and quick hamburger bake) can be made from leftover meat or fish. There is not one "convenience food" included in these easy recipes — each dish is made from "scratch" — thus you are paying for the basic food, not the brand name, not the packaging, and not the processing. Having some idea about menus, using a shopping list, and buying the store brands rather than the name brands, as well as buying the largest size for your use, all help to save money.

Menu #1

*Beef and kidney pie
Parslied carrots and turnips
Green salad — romaine lettuce, escarole,
or spinach with vinegar and oil dressing
*Plum or cherry soup
Yogurt

Combining beef kidney with beef stew and topping it with a flaky crust makes a highly nutritious and festive meal. The British have always loved their steak and kidney pie. We Americans would do well to learn how to use kidneys. They are less expensive than most meats, rich in vitamin B_{12}, and delicious, if not overcooked. They need only be sautéed lightly until the pink disappears. If cooked with care, they remain tender and have a mild flavor.

Beef and Kidney Pie

1 recipe for flaky pastry
2 pounds beef for stewing
2 medium-sized onions, chopped
3 to 4 tablespoons oil
water to cover beef
1 pound potatoes, peeled and cubed
1 beef kidney
¼ cup rye or whole wheat flour
1 cup water
salt to taste
½ teaspoon ginger
½ teaspoon allspice
¼ cup sauterne wine (optional)

Preheat oven to 400°F.

Make pastry dough (see next recipe) and set aside.

In a Dutch oven, brown beef and onions in some of the oil. Add water to cover and cook with lid until beef is tender (approximately 1 to 2 hours). Add potatoes for last half hour of cooking.

Wash and cut fatty center out of kidney, snipping it into small pieces about ½-inch square (a kitchen scissors is handy for this). Drain on paper towels. Lightly sauté kidney in more of the oil, just until it is no longer pink. Add to the cooked beef and potatoes.

Dissolve flour in water a little at a time and stir into stew. Simmer until thickened. Stir in salt, ginger, allspice, and sauterne, and turn into casserole.

Roll out flaky pastry dough ¼-inch thick between sheets of plastic. Place oven-proof egg cup or custard cup upside down in center of casserole to hold up pastry. Wet rim of casserole and lay pastry on top, pressing it down over the rim all around to seal it. With a knife, slit the pastry in several places to allow steam to escape.

Bake in preheated oven for 30 minutes, turn heat down to 350°F., and continue to bake 30 minutes longer, or until crust is brown.

Yield: 8 servings

Flaky Pastry

1 cup whole wheat pastry flour
1 cup rice flour
½ teaspoon salt
4 tablespoons butter
2 tablespoons oil
2 tablespoons ice water

Preheat oven to 400°F.

Sprinkle a 9-inch pie pan lightly with flour. Combine flours and salt in a bowl and cut butter in with knives or a grater. Add oil gradually, working it in with fingertips, then add the ice water, mixing it in. Knead dough briefly to blend water in evenly.

Press dough into prepared pie pan or roll out between well-floured sheets of plastic and place in pie pan, making a high fluted edge around the rim. If baking crust without a filling, prick it all over well with a fork.

Bake in preheated oven for 10 to 12 minutes.

Yield: 1 9-inch pie crust, or if rolled thin, 1 crust and a lattice top

Plum or Cherry Soup

2 cups plums, pitted and cut into eighths, or 2 cups cherries, pitted
¼ cup honey
½ teaspoon cinnamon
¼ lemon, seeded and sliced very thin (omit if using sour cherries)
2½ cups water
1 tablespoon tapioca granules
1 egg, beaten

In a medium-sized saucepan, combine plums or cherries, honey, cinnamon, lemon, and 2 cups water, and simmer, covered, for 15 minutes or until plums are soft.

In another medium-sized saucepan, combine tapioca and ½ cup water, bringing it to a boil and stirring it frequently until tapioca is transparent. Add this to the plum mixture and bring it to a boil, stirring occasionally.

Remove from heat and add a little of the hot soup to the beaten egg, stirring to blend. Stir this back into the soup, let it cool, and serve warm or cold.

Yield: 1 quart

Menu #2

*Turkey croquettes with sauce
Peas
Cole slaw
*Strawberry-applesauce

This meal, except for the peas, can all be prepared ahead of time. The turkey croquettes can be made when you have leftover turkey on hand and frozen for future use. On the day of serving, just thaw and sauté them and make the sauce. The dessert is simple to make but different from the usual applesauce because of the added fruit.

Turkey Croquettes

1 small onion, finely chopped
1 stalk celery, finely chopped (approximately ⅓ cup)
3 tablespoons butter or turkey fat
1 cup turkey stock
2½ cups (12 ounces) cooked turkey, cut into very small pieces
¼ cup whole wheat or rye flour
1 tablespoon cornstarch
2 tablespoons water
salt and pepper to taste
dash cayenne
¼ teaspoon nutmeg
1 teaspoon dried basil
2 egg yolks, beaten
6 tablespoons soft whole grain bread crumbs
1 tablespoon vinegar or lemon juice
dry whole grain crumbs (for breading)
butter or oil

Sauté onion and celery in 1 tablespoon butter or turkey fat. Add ½ cup turkey stock, cover, and simmer for 10 minutes. Add to cooked turkey and set aside.

In a large pan, over low heat, melt 2 tablespoons butter or turkey fat, add flour slowly and blend. Stir in ½ cup turkey broth, dissolve cornstarch in water, and add to mixture. Cook until thick. Add seasonings, turkey mixture, and egg yolks. Continue to cook over low heat for another minute or so, stirring constantly. Remove from heat. Stir in soft bread crumbs and vinegar or lemon juice.

Chill mixture thoroughly (at least 2 hours). Shape into 10 oblong croquettes, roll each in dry bread crumbs, and sauté in butter or oil until golden brown on all sides. Serve hot with turkey croquette sauce (see next recipe).
Yield: 5 servings

Turkey Croquette Sauce

2 tablespoons butter
1½ teaspoons oil
3 tablespoons whole wheat flour
1 cup turkey broth
2 teaspoons cornstarch
⅓ cup milk or water

Heat butter and oil in saucepan. Stir in flour slowly. Add broth gradually, stirring to prevent lumps. Dissolve cornstarch in milk or water, then add gradually, stirring constantly until sauce is thickened. Season to taste.
Yield: approximately 1½ cups

Strawberry-Applesauce

1 cup strawberry juice (cherry or another sweet fruit juice may be substituted)
½ cup honey
2 quarts tart apple slices
1½ cups fresh or frozen strawberries (cherries or another sweet fruit may be substituted)

In a large pan, combine strawberry juice, honey, and apple slices. Simmer together until apples are tender. Add strawberries, cool, and serve warm or cold.
Yield: 6 to 8 servings

Menu #3

*Broccoli-fish bake
Boiled potatoes
Pickled beets
Celery sticks
*Blueberry flummery

Fish should be included in every week's menus because it is such a good form of protein. Broccoli and mild-flavored fish go well together. They complement each other in taste and color. The cheese sauce enhances both, making for a moist and appetizing casserole. Blueberry flummery is apparently a dessert devised by the New England colonists to utilize their bread when it was a bit dry but too good to throw away. It didn't take them long to discover how good it was after it had soaked up all that wild blueberry juice.

Broccoli-Fish Bake

1½ pounds fresh or frozen fish (turbot, haddock, cod)
2 10-ounce packages frozen broccoli or 1½ pounds fresh broccoli
2 tablespoons butter
4 tablespoons whole wheat flour
3 tablespoons instant nonfat dry milk
1¾ cups water
¾ cup grated cheddar cheese
1 teaspoon tamari soy sauce

Preheat oven to 350°F.
Place fish with a little water in a baking pan. Cover with foil. Bake in preheated oven for 20 minutes or until fish is tender. Steam broccoli until tender.

In a small saucepan melt butter and slowly stir in flour. Dissolve instant nonfat dry milk in water and add slowly, stirring to prevent lumping. Add cheese and stir until it has melted. Season with tamari soy sauce.

Lay cooked fish in bottom of a casserole, top it with the cooked broccoli, and pour sauce over both. Place casserole under a broiler, if desired, for 5 minutes before serving to brown surface slightly.

Yield: 6 servings

Blueberry Flummery

2 cups blueberries, fresh or frozen
¼ cup honey
½ teaspoon lemon rind
1 tablespoon lemon juice
½ teaspoon nutmeg
4 slices (soft or hard) whole grain bread, cubed
¼ cup butter, melted
whipped cream as accompaniment

Preheat oven to 350°F.

Combine berries, honey, lemon rind and juice, and nutmeg. Simmer over low heat for 10 minutes, stirring constantly until it makes its own juice.

Line a buttered casserole with half of the bread cubes. Drizzle half of the butter over the bread and spoon half of the cooked berries over this. Then make another layer with the rest of the bread cubes, drizzle remaining butter over it, and spoon remaining berries over the top.

Bake in preheated oven for 20 minutes. Serve warm with whipped cream.

Yield: 4 servings

Menu #4

*Pork liver loaf
Zucchini and tomatoes
Green salad — romaine lettuce and endive
with vinegar and oil dressing
*Date oatmeal bar

Pork liver is not usually bought by homemakers because it tends to have a stronger flavor than beef or calf liver. However, it is used commercially in making liverwurst. This recipe is a valuable one because it includes herbs, spices, and flavorful crumbs which mask any strong liver taste which some people find objectionable. Pork must always be well cooked because of the danger of trichinosis. There is no chance of the pork being undercooked in this recipe because in it the liver is cooked twice. The first time it is sautéed, then after being ground and combined with the other ingredients it is cooked again for almost an hour.

Zucchini and tomatoes go so well together and are particularly good with this loaf, filling the need for a sauce.

The date oatmeal bar is more than a cookie; it is a satisfying dessert.

Pork Liver Loaf

2½ tablespoons oil
1 tablespoon butter
1 medium-sized onion, chopped
1 pound pork liver, skinned and cut into strips
1⅔ cups whole grain bread or cracker crumbs
½ teaspoon dill weed
⅛ teaspoon pepper
1 tablespoon parsley, chopped
1⅓ cups beef broth
2 eggs, slightly beaten

Preheat oven to 350°F.

In oil and butter, sauté onion and then the liver until it is well-cooked.

Combine crumbs, seasonings, and broth. Grind cooked onions and liver in a meat grinder, using the fine attachments. Combine liver and crumb mixture, add eggs, and mix well.

Pack into a loaf pan (4 x 8 x 2½ inches) and bake for 50 to 60 minutes in preheated oven until loaf is set. Serve hot or cold, sliced thin, or dip cold slices in whole wheat flour and sauté in oil.

Yield: 5 servings

Date Oatmeal Bar

3 cups oatmeal
⅓ cup rice flour
¼ cup whole wheat or oat flour
½ teaspoon salt
½ teaspoon cinnamon
¼ cup butter
1 egg, beaten
2 tablespoons oil
¼ cup honey
½ cup water
1 cup dates, pitted
1 cup water

Preheat oven to 350°F.

In a large bowl, combine oatmeal, flours, salt, and cinnamon. Grate butter into oatmeal mixture and work it in with your hands.

Combine beaten egg, oil, honey, and water and stir into oatmeal mixture to make a soft dough. Pat half the dough into a buttered, 9-inch-square pan, pressing it down to make a solid layer.

Heat dates in water just long enough to soften them, and purée in an electric blender. Spread purée over the layer of oatmeal dough. Pat remaining oatmeal dough evenly over the date filling and bake in preheated oven for 35 minutes or until top is golden brown. Cool on rack before serving.

Yield: 16 squares

Menu #5

*Orange-glazed chicken
Butternut squash
7-minute cabbage
*Concord grape pie or peach pie

Orange, lemon, and lime juices add an exotic touch to the traditional roast chicken in this menu. Be careful to cook the chicken slowly on very low heat to avoid possible scorching due to the natural sugar in the orange juice.

When butternut squash is in season, it makes a perfect accompaniment for chicken. Just peel, cube, and steam it over a little water until it is tender. Then it can be served as is or mashed up with a potato masher. Out of season, frozen winter squash is available in many stores and may be substituted.

Concord grapes make a wonderful pie, but if it's not grape season, you can use fresh or frozen peaches instead.

Orange-Glazed Chicken

1½ cups orange juice, fresh or frozen
½ lemon, juiced
1 lime, juiced (lemon may be substituted)
1 medium-sized onion, sliced
2 tablespoons prepared mustard
1 large garlic clove, minced
2 to 4 tablespoons oil
3 to 4-pound roasting chicken
cornstarch (allow 2 teaspoons per cup marinade)
cold water (double the amount of cornstarch)

In a medium-sized bowl, combine orange, lemon, and lime juices, onion, mustard, and garlic. Using the oil, brown chicken on all sides in a Dutch oven on top of the stove. Pour orange sauce over the chicken, cover pot, and turn heat down to a low simmer. Cook for 1 to 1½ hours or until chicken is done.

Thicken broth in pot, if desired, by dissolving cornstarch in cold water and stirring it into the boiling broth. Cook until thickened. Carve the chicken, pour some of the gravy over it, and serve the remainder separately.

Yield: 4 to 6 servings

Concord Grape Pie

1 unbaked 9-inch pie crust and pastry for lattice top (1 recipe
    flaky pastry — see page 425)
4 cups grapes, stemmed and washed (about 2 pounds before
    preparation)
6 tablespoons honey
grated rind from 1 lemon
1½ tablespoons lemon juice
3 tablespoons quick-cooking tapioca
1 tablespoon butter

Preheat oven to 400°F.

Slip grape pulp out of skins. Bring pulp to a boil, turn heat down, and simmer for 5 minutes or until seeds are loose from pulp. Put pulp through colander and/or strainer to remove seeds.

Combine puréed pulp and skins and stir in honey, lemon rind, juice, and tapioca. Turn into pie shell. Cut butter into small bits and distribute evenly over surface of filling.

Roll out remaining pastry into an oblong shape. Cut it into strips ½-inch wide. Lay the strips across the filling, parallel to each other about an inch apart. Turn pie slightly and instead of laying the top layer of strips perpendicular or at right angles to the bottom layer of strips, lay them diagonally, or on the slant. This gives the impression of a woven lattice, without actually weaving one. Lay a strip of pastry all around the edge of the pie pan, covering the ends of the strips. Pinch pastry all around to make an attractive edge.

Bake in preheated oven for 15 minutes. Turn heat down to 350°F. and bake 30 minutes longer or until filling is boiling and tapioca is cooked. Cool on a rack. Serve warm or cold.
Yield: 1 9-inch pie

Peach Pie

1 unbaked 9-inch pie crust and pastry for lattice top (1 recipe
   flaky pastry — see page 425)
2 tablespoons tapioca granules
½ cup honey
1 tablespoon lemon juice
2 tablespoons cornstarch
¼ teaspoon cinnamon
⅛ teaspoon salt
5 cups sliced, peeled peaches (4 to 5 medium-sized)
1½ tablespoons butter

Preheat oven to 400°F.

Sprinkle 1 tablespoon tapioca over the bottom of the pie crust.

In a large bowl, combine honey, lemon juice, cornstarch, tapioca, cinnamon, and salt. Gently mix in peaches and pile into pie crust. Cut butter into bits and distribute evenly over the peaches.

Roll out remaining pastry into an oblong shape. Cut it into strips ½-inch wide and lay the strips across the peaches, parallel to each other about an inch apart. Turn pie slightly and instead of laying the top layer of strips perpendicular or at right angles to the bottom layer of strips, lay them diagonally, or on the slant. This gives the appearance of a woven lattice without actually weaving one. Lay a strip of pastry all around the edge of the pie pan, covering the ends of the strips. Pinch pastry all around to make an attractive edge.

Bake in preheated oven 15 minutes. Turn oven down to 350°F. and bake for 30 to 40 minutes longer until filling is boiling and peaches are tender. Cool on a rack. Serve warm or cold. **Yield:** 1 9-inch pie

Menu #6

*Lamb-stuffed acorn squash
Raw vegetable salad — grated turnips, cabbage, sliced green pepper, and radishes with Russian dressing
*Baked custard

Acorn squash is a marvelous vegetable — its shape, texture, and flavor are distinctive. The "stuffing," which requires very little meat, resembles Middle Eastern cuisine in its combination of rice, lamb, and spice. For this reason, this is a fine entrée to serve to guests, as well as an economical dish and a handy one for using leftovers.

Serving baked custard for dessert adds to the protein content of the meal.

Lamb-Stuffed Acorn Squash

2 acorn squash (large size)
2 medium onions, chopped
1 garlic clove, minced
3 tablespoons oil or butter
3 cups cooked, cubed lamb (beef or poultry may be substituted)
1 cup cooked brown rice
1 cup fresh or frozen peas
½ teaspoon allspice
salt and pepper to taste

½ to ¾ cup meat stock
2 tablespoons wheat germ

Cut each acorn squash into 3 wedges lengthwise and remove seeds. Cook squash by steaming pieces skin side down in about 1 inch of water in a covered pot for 20 minutes or so. When squash is tender, lift out and place in oven dish. Keep warm in low oven.

Sauté onions and garlic in oil or butter until tender. Add meat, rice, peas, seasonings, and enough stock to moisten mixture. Continue to sauté, stirring, until mixture is heated through. Pile into squash wedges, top with wheat germ, and serve.

Yield: 6 servings

Baked Custard

2 eggs
½ cup nonfat dry milk powder
⅛ teaspoon salt
2 cups warm water
2 tablespoons honey
1 teaspoon pure vanilla extract

Preheat oven to 350°F.

Beat eggs until frothy. Mix skim milk powder and salt and make a paste of them by adding some of the water gradually. Dissolve honey in rest of warm water and gradually add this to the dry paste, stirring until it is smooth. Stir in beaten eggs and mix thoroughly. Add vanilla.

Pour into ungreased casserole. Set casserole into a pan with warm water and place in oven. (This is to insure slow cooking so that the custard won't overcook and separate.) Bake for 30 to 45 minutes or until knife inserted in custard comes out clean.

Blender method: Simply put all ingredients into blender and blend until thoroughly mixed. Then bake according to directions given above.

Yield: 4 servings

Menu #7

*Quick hamburger bake
Tossed salad — spinach, lettuce, and grated carrot
with yogurt dressing
*Fruit gelatin

This is another good do-it-ahead meal — a big help for the working cook because the main dish and the dessert can be assembled and refrigerated before you leave in the morning. The casserole can be put into the oven when you return home and be served within 60 to 75 minutes.

A fruit gelatin made with apple juice may be sweet enough with no honey added — a boon to those who want to avoid sugar or any concentrated sweetening. Any fruit juices or fruits may be included as long as the ratio of gelatin to liquid is approximately 1 envelope (1 tablespoon) to 2½ cups juice.

Quick Hamburger Bake

1½ pounds ground chuck
3 tablespoons minced onion
2 teaspoons salt
¼ teaspoon freshly ground pepper
4 medium-sized potatoes
3 cups canned tomatoes, sieved
2 tablespoons chopped parsley
½ teaspoon dried basil, crumbled, or 1 tablespoon fresh chopped basil
½ teaspoon soy sauce
¼ teaspoon cayenne powder
3 tablespoons wheat germ
3 tablespoons grated Parmesan cheese

Preheat oven to 350°F.

Combine ground chuck, minced onion, 1 teaspoon salt, and pepper in medium-sized bowl and mix together. Spread the mixture evenly over the bottom and on the sides of an oiled, 2-quart baking dish. Set aside.

Scrub and pare potatoes. Slice the potatoes very thin and layer them on top of the ground meat mixture. Combine and mix together the sieved tomatoes, chopped parsley, basil, soy sauce, cayenne, and 1 teaspoon salt. Pour over potato-meat mixture. Cover and place in a preheated oven on middle rack. Bake for 1 hour.

Mix wheat germ and cheese. Uncover casserole and sprinkle mixture over the top. Continue to bake 15 minutes longer or until potatoes are tender when pierced with a fork. Remove from oven and serve immediately.

Yield: 6 servings

Fruit Gelatin

1 envelope unflavored gelatin
1 cup cold water
3 tablespoons honey
1¼ cups unsweetened apple juice
1 cup unsweetened, canned pineapple chunks, drained
2 medium-sized oranges, peeled and separated into segments
1 banana, sliced
1 apple, cored and sliced, or 1 cup seeded grapes, cut in half

Soften gelatin in cold water. In small saucepan, warm gelatin mixture and honey just enough to dissolve gelatin and soften honey. Add apple juice and cool until almost set.

Add pineapple chunks, orange segments, sliced banana, apple or grapes, and chill until set.

Yield: 4 to 6 servings

Recommended Reading

Gardening

Abraham, George and Katy. *Organic Gardening Under Glass: Fruits, Vegetables, and Ornamentals in the Greenhouse.* Emmaus, PA: Rodale Press, 1975.

Foster, Catharine Osgood. *Terrific Tomatoes.* Emmaus, PA: Rodale Press, 1975.

Foster, Catharine Osgood. *The Organic Gardener.* New York: Knopf, 1975.

Hylton, William H. *The Rodale Herb Book: How to Use, Grow, and Buy Nature's Miracle Plants.* Emmaus, PA: Rodale Press, 1974.

Jeavons, John. *How to Grow More Vegetables Than You Ever Thought Possible on Less Land Than You Can Imagine.* Palo Alto, CA: Ecology Action of the Mid Peninsula, 1974.

Johns, Glenn. *Best Ideas for Organic Vegetable Growing.* Emmaus, PA: Rodale Press, 1975.

Logsdon, Gene. *The Gardener's Guide to Better Soil.* Emmaus, PA: Rodale Press, 1975.

Logsdon, Gene. *Successful Berry Growing.* Emmaus, PA: Rodale Press, 1974.

Newcomb, Duane. *The Postage Stamp Garden Book: How to Grow All the Food You Can Eat in Very Little Space.* Los Angeles, CA: J. P. Tarcher, 1975.

Olkowski, Helga and William. *The City People's Book of Raising Food.* Emmaus, PA: Rodale Press, 1975.

Philbrick, Helen and John. *The Bug Book: Harmless Insect Controls.* Charlotte, VT: Garden Way Publishing, 1974.

Riotte, Louise. *Planetary Planting: A Guide to Organic Gardening by the Signs of the Zodiac.* New York: Simon and Schuster, 1975.

Rodale, J. I. *Encyclopedia of Organic Gardening.* Emmaus, PA: Rodale Press, 1974.

Rodale, Robert. *The Basic Book of Organic Gardening.* New York: Ballantine, 1971.

Stout, Ruth. *Gardening Without Work*. Old Greenwich, CT: Devin-Adair, 1974.

Vivian, John. *The Manual of Practical Homesteading*. Emmaus, PA: Rodale Press, 1975.

Yepsen, Roger. *Organic Plant Protection*. Emmaus, PA: Rodale Press, 1974.

Yepsen, Roger. *Trees for the Yard, Orchard,and Woodlot*. Emmaus, PA: Rodale Press, 1976.

Livestock

Baïracli-Levy, Juliette de. *Herbal Handbook for Farm and Stable*. Emmaus, PA: Rodale Press, 1976.

Belanger, Jerome D. *The Homesteader's Handbook to Raising Small Livestock*. Emmaus, PA: Rodale Press, 1974.

Bennett, Robert. *Raising Rabbits the Modern Way*. Charlotte, VT: Garden Way Publishing, 1975.

Luttmann, Rick and Gail. *Chickens in Your Backyard*. Emmaus, PA: Rodale Press, 1976.

Morse, Roger A. *The Complete Guide to Beekeeping*. New York: E. P. Dutton Co., 1972.

Root, A. I. *The ABC and XYZ of Bee Culture*. Medina, OH: A. I. Root Co., 1974.

Spaulding, C. E. *A Veterinary Guide for Animal Owners*. Emmaus, PA: Rodale Press, 1976.

Food Preservation

Ball Corporation. *Ball Blue Book: Easy Guide to Tasty, Thrifty Canning and Freezing*. Muncie, IN: Ball Corp., 1972.

Batchelor, Walter D. *Gateway to Survival Is Storage*. Salt Lake City, UT: Hawkes Publishing Co., 1974.

Bradley, Hassell, and Sundberg, Carole. *Keeping Food Safe: The Complete Guide to Safeguarding Your Family's Health While Handling, Preparing, Preserving, Freezing and Storing Food at Home*. Garden City, NY: Doubleday & Co., 1975.

Hériteau, Jacqueline. *The How To Grow and Can It Book of Vegetables, Fruits and Herbs*. New York: Hawthorn Books, 1976.

Hertzberg, R., Vaughan, B., and Greene, J. *Putting Food By*. Brattleboro, VT: The Stephen Greene Press, 1973.

Levinson, Leonard Louis. *The Complete Book of Pickles and Relishes*. New York: Hawthorn Books, 1965.

Meyer, Hazel. *The Complete Book of Home Freezing*. New York: J. B. Lippincott Co., 1970.

Stoner, Carol. *Stocking Up: How to Preserve the Foods You Grow Naturally*. Emmaus, PA: Rodale Press, 1973.

U.S. Department of Agriculture. *Complete Guide to Home Canning, Preserving and Freezing*. New York: Dover Publications Inc., 1973.

Zabriskie, Bob R. *Family Storage Plan*. Salt Lake City, UT: Bookcraft Inc., 1966.

Cooking

Albright, Nancy. *The Rodale Cookbook*. Emmaus, PA: Rodale Press, 1973.

Beard, James, Glaser, Milton, and Wolf, Burton. *The Cooks' Catalogue*. New York: Harper and Row, 1975.

Brown, Edward Espe. *The Tassajara Bread Book*. Berkeley, CA: Shambhala Publications, 1971.

Buck, Pearl. *Pearl S. Buck's Oriental Cookbook*. New York: Simon and Schuster, 1972.

Burrows, Lois M., and Myers, Laura G. *Too Many Tomatoes, Squash, Beans and Other Good Things: A Cookbook for When Your Garden Explodes*. New York: Harper and Row, 1976.

Dutt, Monica. *The Art of Indian Cooking*. New York: Bantam Books, 1972.

Dworkin, Stan and Floss. *The Good Goodies: Recipes for Natural Snacks 'N' Sweets*. Emmaus, PA: Rodale Press, 1974.

Evans, Travers M., and Greene, David. *The Meat Book: A Consumers Guide to Selecting, Buying, Cutting, Storing, Freezing and Carving the Various Cuts*. New York: Charles Scribner's Sons, 1973.

Ewald, Ellen Buchman. *Recipes For a Small Planet*. New York: Ballantine Books, 1973.

Ford, Marjorie, Hillyard, Susan, and Koock, Mary. *The Deaf Smith Country Cookbook.* New York: MacMillan Publishing Co., 1973.

Goldbeck, Nikki and David. *The Supermarket Handbook: Access to Whole Foods.* New York: Harper and Row, 1973.

Gupta, Pranati Sen. *The Art of Indian Cuisine.* New York: Hawthorn Books, 1974.

Hettleman, Richard. *Yoga Natural Foods Cookbook.* New York: Bantam Books, 1970.

Hogrogian, Rachel. *The Armenian Cookbook.* New York: Atheneum Publishers, 1971.

Hunter, Beatrice Trum. *Consumer Beware: Your Food and What's Been Done to It.* New York: Simon and Schuster, 1971.

Hunter, Beatrice Trum. *The Natural Foods Primer.* New York: Simon and Schuster, 1972.

Kennedy, Diana. *The Tortilla Book.* New York: Harper and Row, 1975.

Keys, Ancel and Margaret. *How to Eat Well and Stay Well the Mediterranean Way.* Garden City, NY: Doubleday and Company, 1975.

Kinderlehrer, Jane. *Confessions of A Sneaky Organic Cook.* Emmaus, PA: Rodale Press, 1971.

Lappé, Frances Moore. *Diet for a Small Planet.* New York: Ballantine Books, 1971.

McCracker, Mary Lou. *The Deep South Natural Foods Cookbook.* Harrisburg, PA: Stackpole Books, 1975.

Nakamura, Julia V. *Japanese Recipes for the American Cook.* Hicksville, NY: Exposition Press, 1975.

Parker, Dorothy. *The Wonderful World of Yogurt.* New York: Hawthorn Books, 1972.

Ramazani, Nesta. *Persian Cooking.* New York: Quadrangle, 1974.

Roden, Claudia. *A Book of Middle Eastern Food.* New York: Vintage Books, 1974.

Rombauer, Irma, and Becker, Marion. *Joy of Cooking.* New York: The Bobbs-Merrill Co., 1975.

Spira, Ruth Rodale. *Naturally Chinese.* Emmaus, PA: Rodale Press, 1974.

Showalter, Mary Emma. *Mennonite Community Cookbook.* Scottsdale, PA: Herald Press, 1957.

Shurtleff, Bill, and Aoyagi, Akiko. *The Book of Tofu.* Berkeley, CA: Bookpeople, 1975.

Thomas, Anna. *The Vegetarian Epicure.* New York: Vintage Books, 1972.

Zelayeta, Elena. *Elena's Famous Mexican and Spanish Recipes.* Englewood Cliffs, NJ: Prentice-Hall, 1962.

Index